OTHERS OF MY KIND

UNIVERSITY OF CALGARY
Press

OTHERS OF MY KIND

Transatlantic Transgender Histories

by Alex Bakker,
Rainer Herrn,
Michael Thomas Taylor,
and Annette F. Timm

University of Calgary Press
2500 University Drive NW
Calgary, Alberta
Canada T2N 1N4
press.ucalgary.ca

LIBRARY AND ARCHIVES CANADA CATALOGUING IN PUBLICATION

Title: Others of my kind : transatlantic transgender histories / by Alex Bakker, Rainer Herrn,
  Michael Thomas Taylor, and Annette F. Timm.
Names: Bakker, Alex, 1968- author. | Herrn, Rainer, 1957- author. | Taylor, Michael Thomas, 1977-
  author. | Timm, Annette F., author.
Description: Includes bibliographical references and index.
Identifiers: Canadiana (print) 20200306022 | Canadiana (ebook) 20200306073 | ISBN 9781773851211
  (softcover) | ISBN 9781773851228 (open access PDF) | ISBN 9781773851235 (PDF) | ISBN
  9781773851242 (EPUB) | ISBN 9781773851259 (Kindle)
Subjects: LCSH: Transgender people—North America—History—20th century. | LCSH: Transgender
  people—Europe—History—20th century. | LCSH: Sexual minority community—North America—
  History—20th century. | LCSH: Sexual minority community—Europe—History—20th century. | LCSH:
  Transgender people—Medical care—North America—History—20th century. | LCSH: Transgender
  people—Medical care—Europe—History—20th century.
Classification: LCC HQ77.9 .B35 2020 | DDC 306.76/80904—dc23

The University of Calgary Press acknowledges the support of the Government of Alberta through the Alberta Media Fund for our publications. We acknowledge the financial support of the Government of Canada. We acknowledge the financial support of the Canada Council for the Arts for our publishing program.

This book has been published with the support of the University of Calgary's Faculty of Arts.

Printed and bound in Canada by Friesens
♻ This book is printed on 70lb Sterling Premium Matte

Copyediting by Kathryn Simpson

Cover image: Harry Benjamin, *The Transsexual Phenomenon*, 1966, photograph section. University of Victoria Libraries, Transgender Archives collection. Harry Benjamin, *The Transsexual Phenomenon*. New York: Ace Publishing Corp, 1966. Special Collections call number RC560 C4B46 1966.

Cover design, page design, and typesetting by Melina Cusano

Contents

Galleries

Michael Thomas Taylor and Rainer Herrn

Foreword

Aaron Devor

As this book goes to press, the two most widely used medical diagnostic manuals in the world take differing approaches to the pathologization of gender diversity. The American Psychiatric Association's *Diagnostic and Statistical Manual of Mental Disorders* (DSM-5) (2013) includes "gender dysphoria" as a mental illness, whereas the United Nations' World Health Organization's *International Statistical Classification of Diseases and Related Health Problems* (ICD-11) (2019) lists "gender incongruence of adolescence or adulthood" as a "sexual health condition," rather than as a pathology, thereby opening a door to providing health care rather than treating disease.

Clearly, while the medical community generally agrees that medical interventions should be provided to those who need them, they are divided on the question of what constitutes "need." Those who might request such services are not always in agreement about what level of access is appropriate. Should treatment be provided on demand, by informed consent alone? Should physicians screen patients? Are psychiatric assessments needed? What we learn in this book is that these questions have been with us for more than a century.

The authors of this book have become colleagues and friends as a result of our shared commitment to understanding how trans and other gender diverse people have actively contributed to medical discourse about gender diversity. I have been an eager supporter as they developed their ideas and created effective vehicles for getting them out to the public. As the world's first Chair in Transgender Studies, I am pleased and honoured that they approached me to write this foreword.

I first met Rainer Herrn, Michael Thomas Taylor, and Annette Timm in March 2016 when they came to talk about this work at one of the "Moving Trans History Forward" conferences that I host in Victoria, British Columbia. By June 2016 the *TransTrans* exhibit discussed in this book was opened for public display at the Nickle Galleries at the University of Calgary, in conjunction with the annual Congress for the Humanities and Social Sciences. At Annette Timm's invitation, I provided some context for the show by giving an archivist's talk about the Transgender Archives that I founded at the University of Victoria, and by participating in a curator's roundtable.

Later that month I met Alex Bakker in Amsterdam at the twenty-fourth Scientific Symposium of the World Professional Association for Transgender Health (WPATH) for which I serve as the official historian, an author of their *Standards of Care* since 1999, and the coordinator since 2014 of multiple translations of the WPATH *Standards of Care* (eighteen at last count). At those meetings, Alex appeared on the program directly after the official opening by Her Majesty Queen Máxima of the Netherlands and spoke movingly about "Transgender Holland: Sixty Years of Culture and Care."

This book, which grew out of those talks, considers and illuminates the complex relationships that trans and gender-diverse people have always had with medical service providers. Over the past several years, and extending into the foreseeable future, trans and other people who contribute to gender diversity have been leading a movement to depathologize gender transitioning. Those who promote this approach argue that so long as being gender diverse remains defined as a mental illness, as it is in many parts of the world, trans and other

people who contribute to gender diversity will continue to be treated as incapable of making their own informed medical decisions and will suffer from high levels of discrimination and violence. Ironically, despite supposed mental incapacities gender-diverse people find that they most often have to educate medical professionals about how to provide them with proper medical care.

However, many contemporary people argue that a medical diagnosis of some sort is in the best interests of those who wish to engage medical professionals in their gender transitions. After all, medical providers generally swear an oath to do no harm, most of them like to get paid for their work, and no one wants to get sued. Furthermore, people often fail to understand that many gender-diverse people have legitimate needs for medical interventions. Having an officially recognized medical diagnosis on the books helps more people to understand that being gender diverse is a real part of natural human variation, and this better understanding helps to decrease stigmatization and violence. A diagnosis also guides medical service providers in how to care for trans and other people who contribute to gender diversity, to do so with little fear of malpractice litigation, and to get paid for bona fide medical services.

Others of My Kind: Transatlantic Transgender Histories gives us a richly illustrated window into how these kinds of questions were handled by gender-diverse people and by medical professionals from the end of the nineteenth century until the 1960s; from the time of Magnus Hirschfeld, who oversaw some of the first attempts at transsexual transitions in the Western world, to that of Harry Benjamin, who wrote the first book on transsexualism and oversaw some of the first medical transitions in the United States. In this book, we learn new information about how the medical knowledge gained about gender diversity in early twentieth-century Germany traveled from gender-diverse people to medical professionals, and across the Atlantic to the United States.

Virtually unknown until this book, are the names and contributions of those gender-diverse people who taught the pioneering giants of trans medicine. What we learn in *Others of My Kind* is that there is nothing new about gender-diverse people educating their doctors. Magnus Hirschfeld, Alfred Kinsey, Harry Benjamin, and many of the other great pioneers of trans medicine were taught by gender-diverse people – people who knew that they were not delusional and who were eager to have their gender identities recognized by doctors, and by a diagnosis. Christine Jorgensen and Roberta Cowell are names known to many people. Less well known are Otto Spengler, Carla Erskine, Louise Lawrence, Lotte Hahm, Willy Pape, John O., Baron Hermann von Teschenberg – all of whom taught the fathers of trans medicine about gender diversity.

Each of the authors in this book gives us a different take on how trans and other people who contribute to gender diversity interacted with the most sympathetic medical men of their day. Each chapter is generously illustrated with rare historical photographs. Rainer Herrn introduces for the first time in English the earliest

known magazine for transvestites, *Das 3. Geschlecht* (The 3rd sex). (Herrn previously published a facsimile of the entire German publication run.)

Annette Timm recounts how Otto Spengler befriended Bernard Talmey, who wrote about transvestite social networks in a 1914 article in the *New York Medical Journal*. Timm also elucidates how Alfred Kinsey and Harry Benjamin built a friendship and a knowledge base about gender variance, and about how Carla Erskine and Louise Lawrence, who thought of themselves as "doing missionary work for our cause" (p. 103), befriended and assisted Kinsey and Benjamin as they learned about genders beyond women and men.

Alex Bakker recounts stories about Dutch trans pioneers of the 1950s and 1960s that he learned from archival research and oral histories he conducted. Bakker explains the harsh realities of life during this period for gender-diverse people. He recounts that there was one doctor in the Netherlands who would do the desired surgeries at a time when none would do so in the United States. When, not long after the Christine Jorgensen story spread around the globe, Denmark closed its borders to foreigners seeking "the operation," Harry Benjamin arranged for some of his patients to travel to the Netherlands where castration was still possible for well-screened candidates. Later, many Dutch trans women and a few Dutch trans men journeyed to Casablanca, where Dr. Georges Burou famously operated on up to a thousand trans patients.

Michael Thomas Taylor then immerses us in the visual rhetoric of representation of gender diversity starting at the end of the nineteenth century and moving through the first half of the twentieth century. He analyses the use of photography by Hirschfeld, Benjamin, and others to produce "before" and "after," clothed and nude, pictures that together, and only together, illustrated that an individual was transvestite. In a final chapter, reflecting the shared curation of the four contributors, he also relates how the *TransTrans* team grappled with how to tell the story they wished to tell in the *TransTrans* exhibit with maximum respect for the long-dead people depicted in photographs of fifty and a hundred years ago. This chapter tells the story of the thinking that went into how the 2016 *TransTrans* art installation show at the University of Calgary and in Berlin was fashioned

This is an important book. Most people who think at all about the relationships between medical communities and gender-diverse people assume that, until very recently, trans and other people who contribute to gender diversity have been passive and grateful consumers of medical expertise. This work shines a light on the many ways that gender-diverse people have been very proactive about bringing their

needs to the attention of medical experts for more than 100 years. In the late nineteenth and early twentieth centuries, to have a gender identity other than what your sex dictated that it should be was to be entirely delusional. To have a medical condition was something else entirely. With proper medical documentation, one could go out in public dressed in accordance with one's gender identity, and sometimes even receive treatment to effect physical transition. A few brave gender-diverse people on both sides of the Atlantic made it their project to enlist medical professionals to create diagnoses so that they could be seen as real and be provided with treatment. This could only happen when they were willing to take the risk to trust the few doctors who were curious and willing to learn.

Aaron Devor, PhD, FSSS, FSTLHE
Founder and Inaugural Chair in
    Transgender Studies
Founder and Academic Director,
    Transgender Archives
Founder and Host, Moving Trans History
    Forward conferences
Professor, Sociology Department
University of Victoria, Canada

Acknowledgements

This was a complex project that required the help and guidance of many people. We would first like to thank the people who made our first exhibition – *TransTrans* in Calgary in June 2016 – possible. The early archival research was funded by the Social Sciences and Humanities Research Council of Canada, and the Faculty of Arts at the University of Calgary provided funds to mount the exhibit through a program for interdisciplinary symposia that took place at the 2016 Canadian Congress of the Humanities and Social Sciences. Reed College in Portland, Oregon, also supported some of the research for the exhibition. We would particularly like to thank Nancy Janovicek, who was Annette Timm's partner in applying for the symposium funding and in organizing the "Spaces of Gender and Sexual Security" workshop, of which *TransTrans* was a component. The director and associate directors of the Kinsey Institute's Library and Special Collections, Liana Zhou and Shawn Wilson, were incredibly helpful and supportive, and we were particularly grateful that they trusted us to display rare objects from their collection in our exhibition in Calgary. We are also very lucky to have had the unfailing support of the curators of the Nickle Galleries at the University of Calgary, Christine Sowiak and Michele Hardy. They were there from the very early brainstorming stages of our exhibition, and Michele Hardy expertly shepherded us through various technical challenges to get things mounted. John Hails and Doug McColl did a fabulous job of mounting the exhibit, and Marla Halsted offered critical moral support to Annette in the midst of a jungle of wires and failing computer equipment. We were also thrilled that Melanie Kloetzel was willing to draw on her own research and her collaboration with the Scottish playwright Rose Ruane, to choreograph a fabulous dance performance, "Big Head/Small Neck," for the vernissage. An image of her kloetzel&co dancers appears in this book. Thanks too to Shawn Bracket and Amy Herr for helping with the filming of the video *Carla's Couch* and to all those individuals, particularly Annette's colleagues and students in the Department of History, who were willing to be part of this project by taking a seat on that couch. We thank Veronica Reeves for being willing to turn Annette's amateur filming into a much more polished final video. Special thanks to Amelia Marie Newbert and her colleagues, who made it possible for us to go shopping for furniture in Theatre Calgary's props storage facility and who also provided set-design expertise. We are particularly grateful to the wonderfully supportive members of our advisory committee from the local community: James Demers, Tonya Callaghan, Mason Jenkins, Amelia Marie Newbert, Anne Drew Potter, and Mina Harker. Aaron Devor, Chair in Transgender Studies at the University of Victoria, kindly agreed to write our forward and provided critical advice at key moments. We were able to present our research to precisely the right audience at his "Moving Trans History" conference in Victoria, B.C., and he also led a post-opening round table in the exhibition space, which was enormously helpful in allowing us to think through some of the issues we have explored in this book.

We were delighted to be able to slightly rethink and remount the exhibition at the Schwules Museum (Gay Museum) in Berlin between 7 November 2019 and 2 March 2020. We are very grateful to the museum's director, Birgit Bosold, and to the director of their archive, Peter Rehberg, for their initial enthusiasm, their conceptual and institutional support, and their efforts to secure generous financial support from the Berlin Senate. The exhibition production in Berlin was expertly managed by Justus Heitzelmann, Mayan Printz, and Tomka Weiß. Maya Guttman was responsible for the beautiful technical installation, and we would also like to thank Kristine Schmidt for help with archival sources housed at the Schwules Museum and Daniel Sander for the press and publicity work that helped bring in a large audience. We thank the Kinsey Institute and the Transgender Archives of Victoria, B.C. for allowing us to reproduce archival images.

A new aspect of the collaboration in Berlin was our work with the filmmakers Sabrina Rücker and Brian Andrew Hose. Their film *Carlas Wohnzimmer* was produced in close collaboration with the curators and, as Nora Eckert wonderfully details in her contribution to this book, it captures the spirit of our intention to evoke the atmosphere of supportive intimacy that we first intuited from the images we had found of trans women sitting in a 1950s living room. There is nothing like film to bridge the gaps of time, and Sabrina and Brian's excellent ideas about how to confront present-day trans people with an uncomfortable yet still familiar past helped make the exhibition relevant to a Berlin audience. Thanks too, to Athanasios Karanikolas for recommending these extremely promising artists to us, to the Met Film School Berlin for donating studio space, and to all of the interviewees in the film, who donated their time and shared their emotions with us and our audience.

Neither of the two incarnations of *TransTrans* would have been possible without the amazing design work of Andreas Puskeiler, who has followed us through all the stages of this project and who was single-handedly responsible for the professional aesthetic of the various incarnations of our exhibitions. We know that this was a labour of love, and we thank him for his patience and resilience. We are also thankful for having wonderful images of the exhibitions themselves to work with, provided by Andreas Puskeiler and by the professional photography services of Dave Brown in Calgary and Paul Sleev in Berlin.

Each of us also incurred some personal debts in the process of conducting our research. Rainer would like to express his thanks to Carolin Pommert for editing images from *Das 3. Geschlecht*, Katharina Sykora for help in understanding the visual practices of the magazine, Wolfram Setz for the courage to publish a facsimile edition in print, Egmont Fassbinder for makeing rare issues of the magazine available, and the employees of the Magnus-Hirschfeld-Gesellschaft for their support. Alex is very grateful to his interview subjects: Aaïcha Bergamin, Colette Berends, and Jeanne Lessenich (who have since passed away), Henk Asscheman, Margreet Groot, Joris Hage, Jos Megens, Jill Pattiradjawane, and Ms. B. He is also grateful to Walter van Emde Boas, for providing access to his father's personal files, and to Hilde Bakker for translating the original manuscript of his chapter. Annette would like to thank Katie Sutton for reading a draft of her chapter and Jill Suzanne Smith for the invitation to deliver a keynote talk about Alfred Kinsey at Bowdoin College, an occasion that provided the first draft for chapter 3 of this book. The other participants at that symposium, which celebrated the hundredth anniversary of Kinsey's graduation from Bowdoin, also provided very helpful feedback. Thanks to Donna Drucker, David Hecht, Dagmar Herzog, Michael Pettit, Marilyn Reizbaum, Lisa Sigel, Whitney Strub, Robert Deam Tobin, and Liana Zhou. Michael would like to thank Florian Sedlmeier, who not only made extraordinary personal efforts to help him obtain some much-needed research materials on a very short timeline but has been an unfailing friend and intellectual interlocutor throughout the entire span of this project. We are all particularly grateful to anonymous reviewer A, who provided excellent feedback and was particularly expert in helping us to rethink the sections on photography and visual imagery in this book.

And finally, we would like to express our gratitude to the University of Calgary Press, particularly Brian Scrivener and Helen Hajnoczky. Brian was enthusiastic from the start and continues to support the book's afterlife, and both of them have helped us think through the various design challenges that such an image-rich book presents. Melina Cusano created the gorgeous design and was patient with the various challenges of image numbering and placement. The press also found us an excellent copy editor in Kat Simpson, who truly went beyond the call in contributing to the discussion of various ethical and word-choice conundrums and who did her work under the most trying of circumstances. Books like this are very expensive to produce, and we are therefore happy that university presses in Canada are still willing to support such work.

1

Introduction

Annette F. Timm, Michael Thomas Taylor, Alex Bakker, and Rainer Herrn

The stories this book tells follow the guiding premise of transgender studies by turning traditional medical-scientific history on its head.[1] We draw on the pioneering efforts of scholars like Susan Stryker, Aaron Devor, and Ardel Haefele-Thomas to insist upon treating trans individuals themselves, rather than the scientists and doctors who studied them, as the primary agents of change in the story of how various societies have come to accept that the gender one is assigned at birth should not be considered definitive or unchangeable.[2] In exploring a network of individuals who profoundly shaped transgender identities between the turn of the twentieth century and the 1950s, the book documents the driving role that trans individuals played in shaping transgender histories. It reconstructs connections that unfolded across the Atlantic, and it tells the story of how trans individuals created photographs and other images and sent them to magazines or doctors for publication, creating communities and making visible these individuals' identities in public and private.

As a history of sexuality, the very categories and terms of identity of the stories we tell – primarily "transvestite" and "transsexual" – were coined by doctors and scientists, and it was such men (and they were virtually all men) who developed and controlled access to the evolving medical treatments

The era that is the focus of this book can be regarded as a kind of birthplace of modern trans identity.

desired by many (but not all) of the trans individuals who approached them.[3] As with other histories of sexual identities, those who adopted these labels appropriated and transformed – and later rejected – them, meaning that the terminology of the past is often uncomfortable for trans people today. The last chapter of this book discusses these etymological and taxonomical conundrums, and we recommend that anyone concerned about these issues read that chapter before proceeding. Here we will simply state that we approach this subject as historians who believe that historical understanding cannot be achieved without revealing the language, categorizations, and even misunderstandings of the past and that doing so is not a repetition but an explanation for ways of thinking that we might today find misguided or disrespectful. The stories we have reconstructed have implications for transgender history and for histories of sexuality that go beyond this interplay of agency and authority.[4] They offer direct evidence for how trans individuals influenced and participated in developing medical concepts and treatments and in fostering supportive communities for those seeking affirmation of their gender identities. Our aim is to follow the example of the pioneers of trans history by moving away from a vertical history of discovery by experts to a horizontal history in which trans individuals often create their own experts and instrumentalize them as mouthpieces for self-articulation – precisely because this path of medicine or science was the only path available to them.

We tell this story primarily through investigations of historical images. This focus arises partly from the origins of our joint research project, which began not as a search for material for a scholarly monograph but for a historical exhibition. *TransTrans: Transgender Histories Between Germany and the United States, 1882–1966* was staged at the Nickle Galleries at the University of Calgary in May and June 2016, and it was restaged and reconfigured for a European audience at the Schwules Museum (Gay Museum) of Berlin as *TransTrans: Transatlantic Transgender Histories* between 7 November 2019 and 2 March 2020.[5] Focusing on images makes logical sense when one is presenting history to the public in a museum/gallery setting. But there is a deeper justification for this practice, which is the crucial role that images play in any representation of one's own sexual subjectivity and particularly in the objectification of transgender individuals. This is a historical fact but also one that remains omnipresent in our own world today. For this reason, we have supplemented the book chapters with a series of image galleries.

Concretely, our project began as we attempted to trace a connection between the most prominent figures in this history, Magnus Hirschfeld, the innovative early twentieth-century sexologist, gay rights activist, and founder of Berlin's Institute for Sexual Science (in 1919), and one of his former mentees, the endocrinologist Harry Benjamin, who emigrated to the United States, collaborated with Alfred Kinsey, and wrote the first scientific investigation of what he called "transsexualism" in 1966.[6]

Exploring this relationship also brought to light a connection between seminal moments in twentieth-century histories of sexuality, and between Europe and the United States, that had been lost to public memory. But what we found in the archives was much more compelling and thought-provoking: not only photographs that vividly illustrated these life stories and offer a poignant window into private moments of self-creation, self-presentation, and self-disclosure, but also ethical questions for us about how to tell these stories. The questions concern historical method and our own curatorial practice, but most importantly, they touch upon our ethical quandaries and our feelings of responsibility for how we might look at, reconstruct, and witness the very personal stories that the archival traces document.

For it was images of individuals that first allowed us to reconstruct disparate parts of these histories and that drew us to the interplay of actors across the Atlantic, not to mention the structures of authority and community between the participants in these exchanges. It was in moments of archival work when images came to light that we stopped to admire and wonder about what we were witnessing. In browsing through the many images in published sources, we began to ask deeper questions about the life stories they often accompanied or were meant to illustrate. The images spoke to us in a way that the life stories, which most often had been reframed as clinical case studies, could not. And the images often give us so much incidental information about the time, situation, and context of these moments that is simply

lost when texts written by trans individuals about themselves are published by other authors.

The images often resist or disrupt the aim to generalize that characterizes most medical-scientific literature. At the same time, we are very conscious of the problem that the images can also pander to and feed voyeuristic and sensationalist impulses and intentions – both for those who published them and for us as we look at them today. These issues are especially acute when it comes to trans history – for which so much archival evidence is fragmentary or of a problematic nature (criminal, medical, ephemeral, not personally identifiable). The images we found reflect the fact that the archival record of trans histories is neither objective nor simply incomplete, but that it actively reflects "silences and exclusions," as K. J. Rawson has written about the significance of the archive for transgender history.[7] Conversely, as Rawson also points out, many transgender individuals do not want traces of their lives before their transition preserved: "Transgender people who transition their gender presentation may feel betrayed by the archive's stubborn and insistent refusal to forget."[8]

All of this is complicated by the fact that we bring our own identities into the process of describing the identities of trans people. The ethical questions that this process involves make it necessary to introduce ourselves. Rainer Herrn works at the Berlin research hospital Charité as a historian of medicine on the history of psychiatry and sexology and carries out research on the history of gender, sex, and sexuality as a member of the

Magnus-Hirschfeld-Gesellschaft. With a number of other gay men from East Germany, he played an instrumental part in assembling an archive of Hirschfeld's work, as well as other documents of sexology from before the Second World War. His current research focuses on the first Institute for Sexual Science in Berlin (1919–33). Herrn has been researching trans history for the last twenty-five years, along with the histories of other sexual and gender minorities. He is interested in the history of relationships between these groups and how it shapes present-day politics. This resulted in the first general history of transgender people in the German-speaking world, *Schnittmuster des Geschlechts: Transvestitismus und Transsexualität in der frühen Sexualwissenschaft* (loose translation: Patterns of gender: transvestism and transsexuality in early sexual science), which was published in 2005 and served as our starting point for the *TransTrans* project.[9] Michael Thomas Taylor worked for ten years as a professor in Canada and the United States, likewise focussing on questions of sexuality, including work on the history of marriage; he identifies as cis male, gay, queer, and as a radical faerie. Having mostly left academia, Taylor is particularly interested in communicating knowledge to communities beyond the university. Annette Timm is a historian of modern German and European history with a focus on the history of gender and sexuality. As a white, cisgender, and straight woman, she comes to this subject with a deep sense of respect for those with less privilege, both in the past and in the present. She also offers an intense

engagement with historiographical debates about representation and the perspective of temporal and geographical breadth that she has gained from her editorship of the *Journal of the History of Sexuality*. The ethical question most central to her contributions to this book is the dilemma of how to represent the identities of those who have lived in the past – always a foreign country no matter what our present-day identifications might be – without imposing our own, inevitably ephemeral, categorizations upon them. A fourth collaborator joins us for this phase of the project, Alex Bakker. Bakker is a Dutch historian and writer who also works as a researcher for documentaries and exhibitions. In 2014, he published an autobiographical novel about his transgender background, *Mijn valse verleden* (published in English in 2019 as *My Untrue Past*).[10] He is committed to investigating the lives of trans pioneers – lives that risk being forgotten – and as an interviewer he makes frequent use of oral history. (As a reflection of the collaborative nature of this project, we will now switch to using first names in speaking about ourselves or referencing each other's work.)

Despite the commitment of the original three curators to sensitively portraying the experiences of all the historical subjects we investigate in our quite varied historical work, we believe that being joined by a trans co-curator was essential to the success of the Berlin iteration of *TransTrans*. As we note in the chapter of this book describing our exhibitions, we also drew from feedback given to us by community members – from people who identify as trans, genderqueer, or gender nonconforming – at various points of the curatorial process in order to ensure that we remained as sensitive as possible to the dilemmas of terminology and the particularly painful aspects of these histories for those still struggling with prejudices against trans people today.

And yet uncovering any history creates unique traumas that no attention to present-day sensitivities or cleansing/modernization of terminology can preclude. What Ardel Haefele-Thomas announces in *Introduction to Transgender Studies* could also be said of this book: "By the time you have this book in your possession … the language will most likely have changed again." We believe that sensitive readings of the fact that human categorizations have changed over time also have the power to point towards individual emancipation, because they indicate that if things have changed once, they can change again. In the foreword to Haefele-Thomas's text, Susan Stryker encourages students to immerse themselves in the history of gender systems they find objectionable. She asks them "to reflect on how best to acknowledge that human cultures throughout time and around the world have concocted a great many gender systems" and to avoid "assuming that all that diversity can be squeezed into the three little syllables of 'transgender,' or that everybody who has ever lived a life at odds with currently dominant forms of Eurocentric gender categorization can properly be referenced by that perpetually fraught pronoun, *we*."[12] We take inspiration from this perspective.

To show concretely how these reflections come to bear on our project,

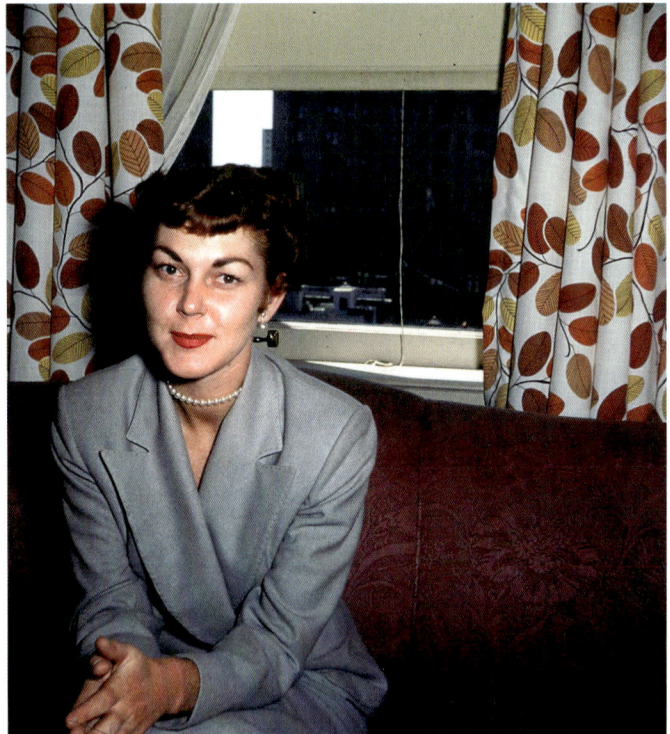

FIGURE 1.1: First slide Annette Timm found in the Harry Benjamin files, Kinsey Institute Library and Archives, Harry Benjamin Collection (hereafter KILSC-HB), Box 17. Copyright © 2017, The Trustees of Indiana University on behalf of the Kinsey Institute. All rights reserved.

allow us to tell a brief story, the first of several that we will use to introduce this book. While working with Michael in the archives of the Kinsey Institute Library and Special Collections in Bloomington, Annette came across a colour slide, mixed in with Harry Benjamin's personal vacation photos from Knott's Berry Farm, California, and Banff, Alberta, that immediately grabbed her attention.

Beginning in the 1950s, Benjamin was almost single-handedly responsible for introducing the diagnosis and treatment of what he was then referring to as "transsexualism" to the United States, and he became widely known and influential after he published his book *The Transsexual Phenomenon* in 1966. We therefore immediately assumed that the beautiful woman in figure 1.1 might have been one of Benjamin's trans patients. As it turned out, this image (which we have taken from the original stereoscopic slide) was just one of many in the boxes of Benjamin's personal effects housed at the Kinsey Institute. The assumption was slowly confirmed, as Annette found more and more images of this and other women sitting on the same couch in front of the same curtain with individuals who seemed to be their family members.

After a great deal of digging and following leads, Annette was able find the names and stories of the women on that couch. Letters between Benjamin and his trans patients revealed that a woman whom we are giving the pseudonym Carla Erskine was the photographer behind this image and other slides in Benjamin's collection. She had scraped together her very meagre funds to mail the slides to Benjamin in batches between 1953 and 1955. The essays that follow will engage in more detail with Erskine's history and with the history of how trans people very often photographed themselves for the purposes of advancing scientific knowledge. Erskine's slides were taken during gatherings of trans women in the San Francisco apartment of Louise Lawrence, a research assistant for Alfred Kinsey and self-described "permanent transvestite." As Joanne Meyerwitz, a pioneer of American trans history notes, Lawrence was "a one-woman social hub" for gender nonconformists in the San

Francisco Bay area.[13] Hers is a story that has been frequently told, but we were interested in tracking the stories of those more private individuals who sought refuge on Lawrence's couch and whose complex interpersonal relationships represent a key point of knowledge transmission. Following Lawrence's example, Carla was eager to provide information to Kinsey that might, as she put it to Benjamin, "be of help to others of my kind."[14] Those words inspired the title of this book and led us to search for more examples of how personal networks amongst trans individuals and between them and their doctors helped build knowledge and understanding.

This book and our exhibition *TransTrans* originated in such questions. As we looked at this material, we found many stories like Erskine's hiding in plain sight within medical and scientific publications. When Michael and Annette visited the Kinsey Institute they were already well acquainted with Rainer Herrn's research on the very first generation of trans people who had contacted medical researchers for help: people like John O. and Otto Spengler, both born in Germany in the late nineteenth century and of whom more will be said below.[15] We were thus predisposed to see Erskine and her friends' relationship to Kinsey and Benjamin through these eyes: with attention to how self-made images of trans people played a role in the creation of medical knowledge, to how those images became public, and to how the personal, private side of these stories has often remained hidden. We are not the first historians to note that uncovering such intimate glimpses of the lives of marginalized individuals is central to the discovery of how sexual knowledge is transmitted through private networks. Referring to a cache of intimate photos held at the Art Gallery of Ontario that depict cross-dressers in a compound in New York called Casa Susanna in the 1950s and 60s, Elspeth Brown notes the importance of "the relationship of image making to the formation of queer, trans and cross-dressing communities from the 1950s to today."[16] Unlike the Casa Susanna photos, though, we discovered that some of the intimate photos we had found in the boxes of Benjamin's effects did not remain private but were reproduced, anonymously, in his scientific studies. Our focus, then, was on the gaps that we saw between how these photographs were made and how they were used, between the events they appear to record and what those events meant in context – the context of their own time and the context of what they might mean for us today. This also meant telling the story of the photographs themselves. We asked how they were published, shared, and archived, and what these uses mean for the stories they hold.

Aside from the discovery of Benjamin's slides, this project had other moments of serendipity. It was only along a circuitous route of luck and misfortune that Rainer Herrn was able to acquire all five issues of *Das 3. Geschlecht* (The 3rd sex) – the world's first magazine for people who called themselves transvestites, which published in Germany between 1930 and 1932, and of which only one copy of a single issue exists in any public library in the world. In 2005, a Berlin antiquarian bookshop called

Ars Amandi sent him a gift of a full copy via post, but the package was lost or stolen from his mailbox, forcing him to start the search again from scratch. In his 2005 book on transvestites, Rainer had pointed out the rarity of the publication, which drove prices significantly higher.[17] After finally managing to obtain issues one through four, he located a copy of issue five with a Munich dealer, but it sold so quickly and at such a prohibitive price that he could not obtain it. Fortunately, however, the dealer agreed to give him a scan first.

Another moment of discovery explains Alex Bakker's contribution to our project. During his research for his book *Transgender in Nederland: een buitengewone geschiedenis* (Transgender in the Netherlands: an extraordinary history), Alex came upon another historical fact that had disappeared into oblivion.[18] In the middle of the 1950s, the Netherlands was one of the few places in the world where trans people could obtain gender-affirming surgery.[19] There were various different surgical techniques employed at this time, and access was restricted; only a happy few could afford surgery, which remained a far-off dream for members of oppressed minorities, such as the poor and colonized. But it did mark the early beginnings of a long and rich history of transgender care in the Netherlands. Since the operations were carried out in secrecy, Alex only found one or two textual sources referring to them, which left him with more questions than answers.[20] When he found, in Benjamin's files in the Kinsey Archive, the letters of five American trans women who corresponded extensively with Harry Benjamin about

Carla Erskine's Slides

The stereoscopic slides that Annette and Michael found in the personal effects of Harry Benjamin, kept in the Kinsey Archive in Bloomington, Indiana, contained this image of Carla Erskine: Here is the slide itself:

Like Benjamin's other private snapshots, by itself this slide does not tell us much. The style and pattern of the fabrics used for the dress and the curtain give a sense of when the photograph was taken. The curtains in particular helped Annette and Michael connect the various photos as being located in the same room. Looking at the woman, we might remark on her comportment and the beautiful dress, which communicates a certain grace and dignity. It mattered to us as historians and curators, too, that this object was neither a photo nor a glossy image, but rather a slide: something less accessible but actually even more luminous – a window into another world. This particular slide is doubled because it is stereoscopic and meant

left FIGURE 1.2: Carla Erskine on Louise Lawrence's couch, San Francisco, California, circa 1953, KILSC-HB 17. Copyright © 2017, The Trustees of Indiana University on behalf of the Kinsey Institute. All rights reserved.

FIGURE 1.3: Carla Erskine on Louise Lawrence's couch, detail, KILSC-HB 17. Copyright © 2017, The Trustees of Indiana University on behalf of the Kinsey Institute. All rights reserved.

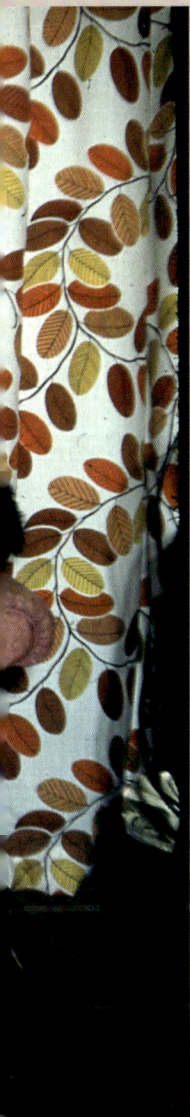

FIGURE 1.4: Stereoscopic slide viewer in Harry Benjamin's personal effects, KILSC, HB 17. Copyright © 2017, The Trustees of Indiana University on behalf of the Kinsey Institute. All rights reserved.

to be viewed in a viewfinder, which gives an illusion of three-dimensional depth and perhaps also, as some scholars have suggested, transforms the act of viewing into something especially individual, personal, and private – even voyeuristic.[1] "Seen in this contraption," Sandra Phillips writes, "the stereo created the impression of a privileged view – that the scene was enacted for the viewer's eyes only."

As an object and image, this slide was arresting. But what we as historians needed to understand it was more context – context for when and why it was taken, and for how it ended up in Benjamin's papers and personal effects and in Kinsey's archive. Other objects in this collection included patient records, correspondence, photographs, and personal items such as works of art made by patients. Viewing them reminded us of how intimate and private these histories were and demonstrated how easily these traces of Benjamin's personal connections with these people could get lost in perspectives that focus on clinical histories. And this mattered especially in this context, since many of the images we found – like that of Carla Erskine shown here – also had one thing in common: they were used as illustrations in Benjamin's 1966 book, *The Transsexual Phenomenon*.

Michael Thomas Taylor and Rainer Herrn   9

their stay in Amsterdam, it gave him goose bumps. Now he could finally put names to anonymous figures, identify addresses of unknown locations, and in general reconstruct and interpret this unique episode in transgender history, which – as you will read – offers some surprising twists.

These moments underscore once again that the story we are telling here is neither linear nor traceable to a moment of origin or birth, whether with us as researchers or in the lives we discuss. We also want to be careful to distinguish our own excitement and wonder in finding windows into these private lives from the stories themselves. These feelings reflect our own passion and commitment, but they also come from seeing something that – in many cases – was not meant to be public. We are aware of the voyeuristic connotations of these discoveries, and we know that our decisions about reproducing what we describe below as "difficult photographs" might make some of our readers uncomfortable. At the same time, these images are evidence of the fragility and marginalized nature of much of this history – especially since, or precisely because, it unfolded in very tight personal networks over nearly a century and in locations that were far apart from each other.

What we are doing here is not entirely new. Without hoping to do justice to the richness of the existing scholarly literature on trans history, we would like to briefly acknowledge pioneering works that have inspired us and on which we draw in the pages to follow. The biggest influence on three of us was the work of one of our collaborators: Rainer Herrn. It was Michael's

reading of Rainer's 2005 book *Schnittmuster des Geschlechts* that began this collaboration, and all of us have drawn inspiration from this book and Rainer's other publications for our curation and for all we have written here. Michael's review of *Schnittmuster* emphasizes that its contribution rests in a nuanced analysis of the emerging discipline of sexology that stresses the "relationship between politics and sexual science" and that details how "the medical paradigm dominating both case studies and autobiographical accounts gave [transgender] individuals new voices and a nascent sense of community [while also] … repeatedly prov[ing] inadequate to the reality of their lives."[21] We summarize many of Rainer's findings in the essays to follow in the hopes of demonstrating aspects of this history that have been missed or misinterpreted in English-language summaries of German sexology and trans history.

Despite the fact that the German story has not been as well understood as many of the broader narratives about trans history have made it appear, we have also benefitted enormously from the work of historians of the United States and other places. Of particular note here is the pioneering work of Joanne Meyerowitz, Susan Stryker, Genny Beemyn, Susan Rankin, Leslie Feinberg, Deborah Rudacille, and, most recently, Julian Gill-Peterson, all of whose work has influenced our perspectives.[22] Meyerowitz, Stryker, and Beemyn have been particularly influential and pathbreaking in laying out the overarching structure of trans history in the United States, while Rankin, Feinberg, and Rudacille give voices to individual transgender people,

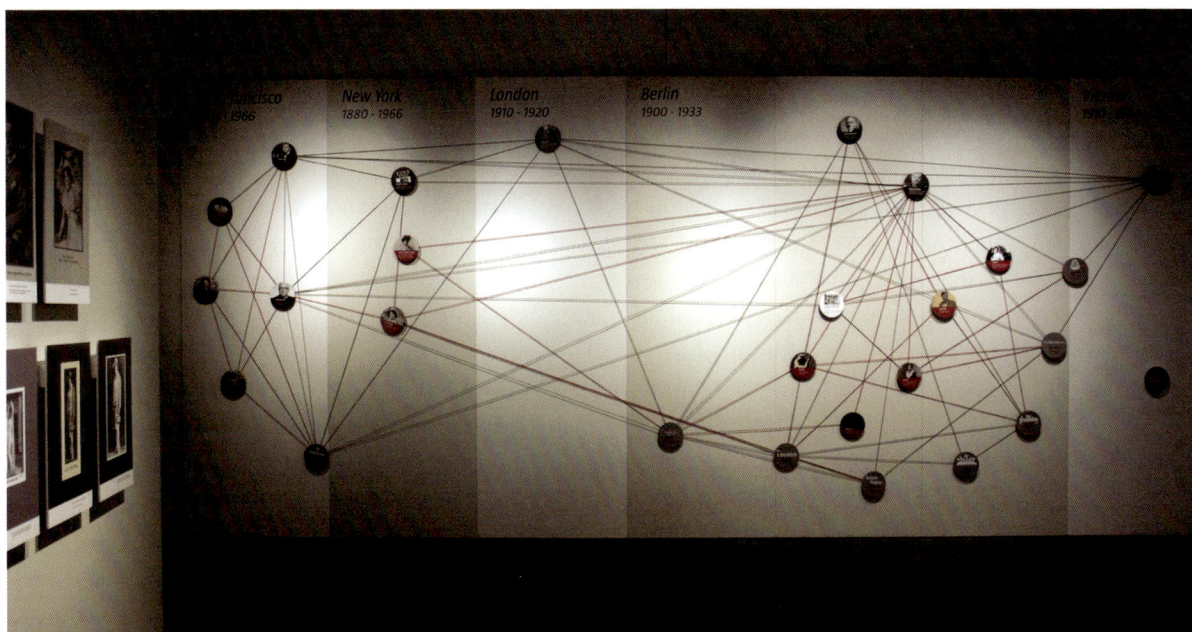

FIGURE 1.5: Network Wall in the *TransTrans* exhibition, Calgary, Alberta, 27 May–10 June 2016. Copyright © 2017, The Trustees of Indiana University on behalf of the Kinsey Institute. All rights reserved.

some of whom are only now recognized as such. But there is still often a gap between scholarship that focuses on memoir or autobiography (such as that of Feinberg or Julia Serano, Sandy Stone, and others) and more traditionally historical accounts like Meyerowitz's *How Sex Changed*, which follows professional historical standards of anonymization and relies on individual stories as illustrative examples within a more broadly thematic structure.[23] We seek to combine these trends in trans history by giving individual people a clear voice (tracking their stories across various levels of anonymization and historiographical analysis) while still remaining resolutely focused on historical contextualization.

Following the iconic intervention of Sandy Stone, whose fierce rebuttal of transphobia in "The Empire Strikes Back: A Posttranssexual Manifesto" empowered a generation of scholars to engage in new interdisciplinary investigations of trans lives,[24] a vibrant field of transgender studies now exists, and we have drawn on the work of many nonhistorians to guide us through the conundrums of presenting a contemporary audience with the taxonomical, ethical, and political intricacies of the historical record (and silences) of trans history.[25] A key difference between this book and most other treatments is our time frame. Transgender studies can be decidedly presentist or focused on only the most recent past. Here we draw attention to the less well understood histories of the immediate post-First World War and post-Second World War periods, and we focus particularly on the transatlantic connections between medical researchers but also more importantly between trans subjects themselves. Despite these differences, past historical and transgender studies scholarship has guided not only our writing here, but less transparently our collaborative curatorial work.

Preparing for the first iteration of *TransTrans*, and the second version in Berlin, we were most inspired by scholarly work that highlights the complicated personal, international, and intimate interconnections between medical researchers and networks of trans people. In both exhibitions, we attempted to visualize these personal interactions as a network wall spreading across two continents. (See figures 1.5, 1.13, and 6.6.)

The wall depicted the key people, institutions, and publications in our network of stories. While the geographic and temporal organization – San Francisco (1904–66), New York (1880–1966), London (1910–20), Berlin (1900–33), Vienna (1910–44), as well as (in the Berlin exhibition) Copenhagen (1951–55), Amsterdam (1954–55), and Casablanca (1956–76) – refer to the interventions of medical scientists or to massive political ruptures like the destruction of the discipline of sexology by the National Socialists, the intersecting red nodes and red lines depict transgender individuals themselves. In San Francisco, several of these transgender individuals were grouped around Harry Benjamin, who spent his summers in the city (sometimes joined by Alfred Kinsey): Christine Jorgensen, who became a celebrity when she returned to the United States in 1952 after undergoing a series of gender affirmation surgeries in Denmark; Louise Lawrence; and Carla Erskine. Benjamin of course also belongs in New York, where his practice was located – and in Germany, where he grew up and where he continued to visit Hirschfeld in the 1920s. In New York, we also find Bernard S. Talmey, like Benjamin a German immigrant to the United States, a doctor who published the first American article about transvestites in 1914. Both Talmey and Benjamin knew another trans individual from New York, who was described in Talmey's 1914 article as his "first patient"; we now know that this was Otto Spengler. New York was also where we placed another individual who moved between Germany, New York, and San Francisco: a German immigrant to the United States, described in the medical literature as John O. and known at least privately to some in San Francisco as Jenny, whose letters to Magnus Hirschfeld were published in 1910 in *Die Transvestiten* (The transvestites), a word that he applied to people we would today call transgender, and the etymology of which is described in more detail in the concluding chapter). In Germany, we placed Magnus Hirschfeld and a number of transgender individuals whom the exhibition highlighted, and who also appear in this book. Important institutions and publications included Hirschfeld's and Benjamin's books, Hirschfeld's Institute for Sexual Science, and several magazines published in Germany in the 1920s and early 1930s by the gay activist and publisher Friedrich Radszuweit. These were aimed at gay men, at lesbians, and – with *Das 3. Geschlecht* (The 3rd sex), the first magazine of its kind in the world – at transvestites. In Vienna, we find Eugen Steinach – an endocrinologist whose work was crucial for the entire history we discuss here and which was well received by the German public. And in Amsterdam, Copenhagen, and Casablanca, we find the trans women and doctors who form the focus of Alex's chapter.

First patient.

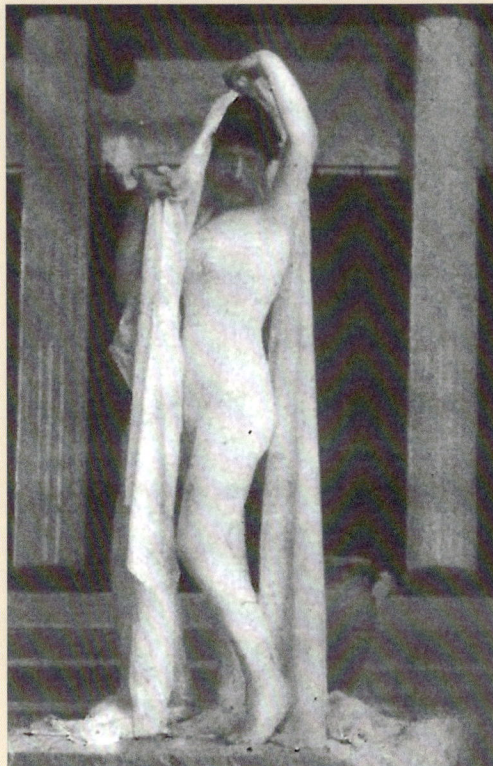

FIGURE 1.6. AND 1.7. Images of Otto Spengler, reproduced in B. S. Talmey, "Transvestism: A Contribution to the Study of the Psychology of Sex," *New York Medical Journal* 99, no. January to June (1914): 362–68.

Images of Otto Spengler

Reconstructing the circuitous routes of knowledge transmission that are the focus of *TransTrans* involved delving into the archives, but also doing genealogical research and careful readings of how trans lives were represented in both popular and medical publications. The case of German-American immigrant Otto Spengler is instructive. Spengler was first described, without being named, in a 1914 article by Bernard S. Talmey in the *New York Medical Journal*.[1]

Talmey's article presents this "First patient" as appearing in the guise of the Prussian "Queen Louise" (b. 1776, d. 1820). In the second, as we read in the caption, this patient appears "in imitation of a celebrated painting." Here, we can recognize artistic conventions of femininity and the importance of popular figures to individual expressions of gender identity.

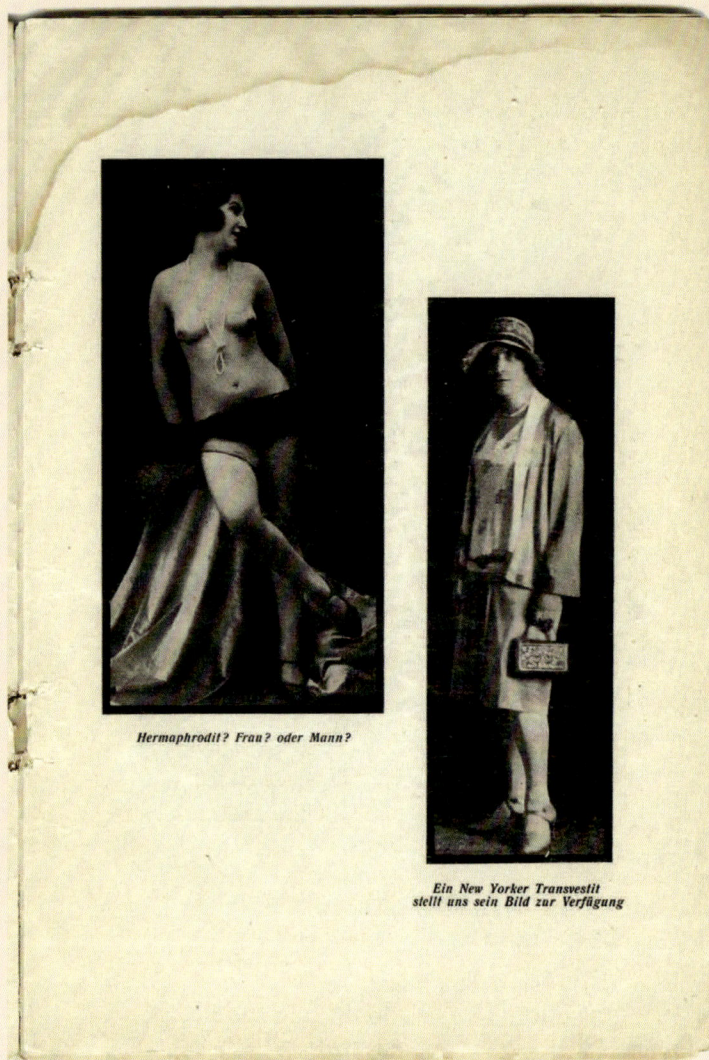

Hermaphrodit? Frau? oder Mann?

Ein New Yorker Transvestit
stellt uns sein Bild zur Verfügung

FIGURE 1.8: IImage of Otto Spengler (right) in *Das 3. Geschlecht* 3 (1931): 17.

Two other images in this article, which also describes four other transvestites, are photographs of Otto Spengler. Talmey knew Spengler personally, and Spengler's desire for hormonal treatment and Spengler's knowledge of German and Austrian scientific research led him to seek out another German-American in New York, Harry Benjamin. Recovering Spengler's story, in other words, requires paying attention to the tight personal networks established in the German emigrant community in New York. We found other traces of Spengler's life in the letters between Harry Benjamin and Alfred Kinsey and in the anonymized biographical account published much later in George W. Henry's 1948 medical text *Sex Variants: A Study of Homosexual Patterns*.[2] Intriguingly, images of Spengler with no further biographical detail also appear twice in *Das 3. Geschlecht* (The third sex), a German magazine aimed at transvestites. To the left is reproduced one of those two images as it appears in the magazine.

This image of the "New York transvestite" is juxtaposed with what clearly appears to be a female body with exposed breasts. The nudity suggests the playfulness of a variety performer and, in being placed next to the "New York transvestite," perhaps

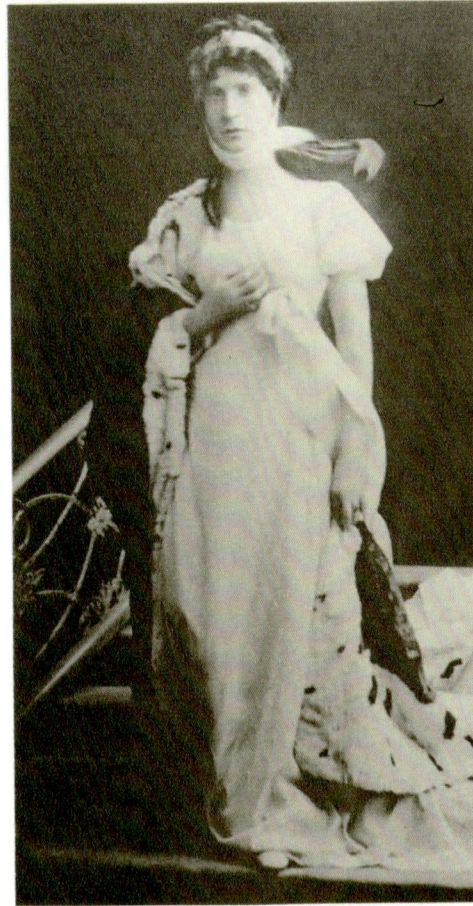

also hints that something similar might be hiding beneath the proper exterior of this subject's outfit and demeanour. Spengler must have sent this image to the magazine. The magazine published many calls asking for its readers to submit images and texts, and it is unlikely that the publisher received images from other sources. This image of Spengler is thus a first hint of how photographs that trans individuals took of themselves circulated in both medical and popular contexts, and of how the meaning of such images was framed and determined by the way in which they were published. It is also a sign of the courage and strength Spengler displayed in providing this photo for publication, even though it mentions no name. Harry Benjamin donated a print of this same photograph to Alfred Kinsey where it was catalogued in 1948 under the heading of "transvestite" without any further identifying information or history.

We found yet another print of Spengler in Kinsey's archive, again posing in the ermine robes of a queen, further evidence of the fact that Benjamin was the source for most of Kinsey's information about trans individuals.

Like the image of Spengler posing in imitation of a painting that was published in 1914, this photograph, too, copies a famous painting: Gustav Richter's 1879 portrait of Queen Luise. The marriage of Luise to Friedrich Wilhelm III in 1793 was a popular sensation, widely represented in public sources and immortalized as a marriage for love when the queen unexpectedly died in her husband's arms in 1810. She was the source of widespread popular adoration in the late nineteenth century, and Spengler's decision to pose in imitation of this painting reflects a widespread practice. Another example is this postcard, sent in 1908 (figure 1.11).

Our exhibitions retraced the paths that images of Spengler took across these contexts and continents. In both exhibitions, Spengler was a node in our network wall (figure 1.12). In our exhibition in Calgary, Spengler's was one of four trans stories opening the exhibition. And in our exhibition in Berlin, all of these images came together in a cluster (figure 1.14).

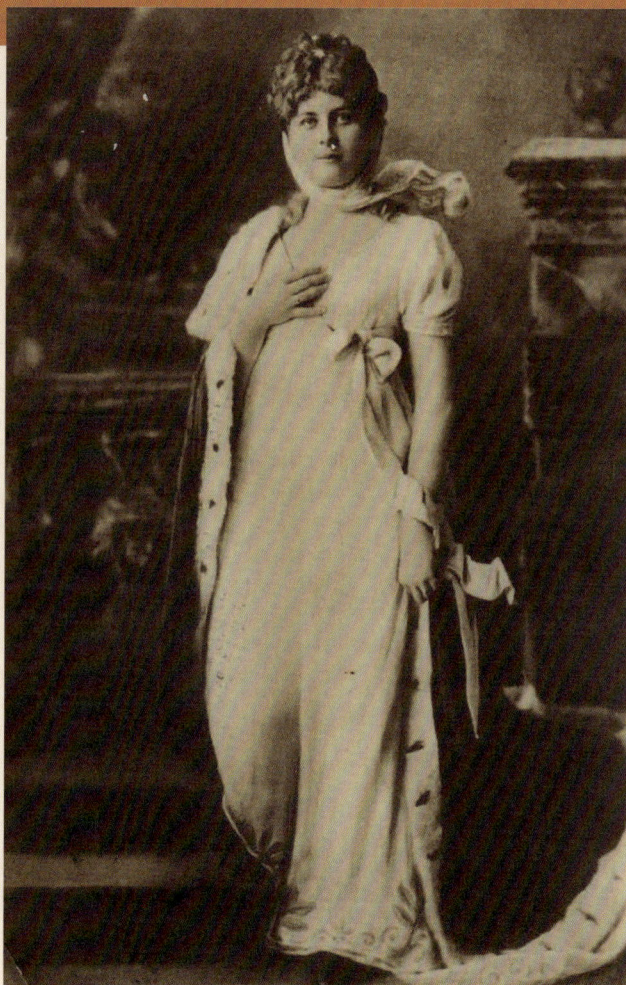

FIGURE 1.11: Queen Luise, postcard, early twentieth century

FIGURE 1.12: Otto Spengler on Network Wall, at *TransTrans* exhibition, Calgary 2016.

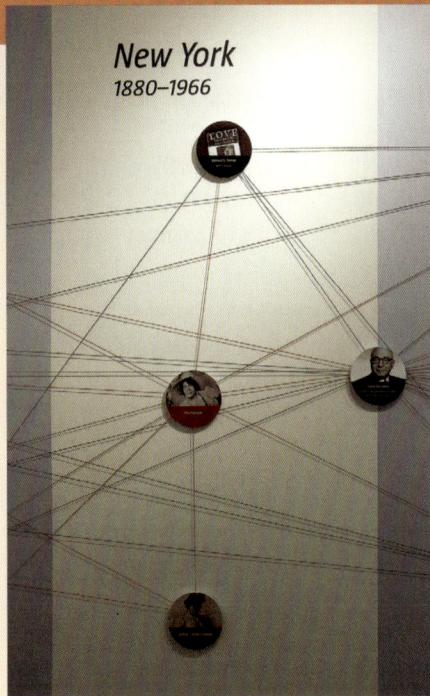

FIGURE 1.13: Otto Spengler on Network Wall, at *TransTrans* exhibition, Berlin, 2019.

FIGURE 1.14: Cluster devoted to images of Otto Spengler in Berlin. Photo credit: Paul Sleev.

FIGURE 1.15: Clusters devoted to Otto Spengler and to Gender Play, *TransTrans*, Berlin 2019. Photo credit: Paul Sleev.

This book will tell these stories in more detail. For the moment, we will simply state that it was often the trans individuals themselves who connected the experts or publishers, usually behind the scenes. It was trans individuals who approached experts and publishers to ask that their stories be told, their images be shown, or that the doctors change or modify their categories to better describe trans individuals' experiences and self-understandings. We have attempted to mirror this cooperative networking in our own work, remaining in constant discussion with each other and translating individually arrived-at scholarly analyses into a larger narrative. We seek to provide not a seamless narrative but rather an indication of the complex threads that tied trans individuals and their medical collaborators together across the Atlantic.

For this book, and for the exhibition in Berlin, we expand our view to return, as it were, from the United States to Europe and specifically to the Netherlands, where some of Harry Benjamin's patients were among the individuals able to obtain gender-affirming surgeries in the 1950s – an option that was officially closed down by authorities in the 1960s. The Netherlands is a crucial site for our history because it was unique in offering access to this kind of care and pioneering new treatment models. Yet such treatments remained difficult to access unless one had both the will and the resources to travel outside traditional medical networks.

In telling these stories, we were continually aware of yet another ethical dilemma of this history: the problem of revealing the life stories of those who did not want to be famous in any way. One of the challenges of writing trans history is the ethical necessity to protect the privacy of individuals whose material well-being and physical safety depend upon successfully passing undetected within intolerant communities. This is almost as true today as it ever was, but for the first individuals to medically transition passing was existential (in the sense of being necessary for survival), and tracking these stories involves particular research challenges for historians. Although significant publicity and even fame followed some early twentieth-century cases of surgical transition (Lili Elbe in Germany, Christine Jorgensen in the United States, and Roberta Cowell in England, to name just a few),[26] the vast majority of individuals seeking medical help in the early and mid-twentieth century had to contend with public disavowal, police repression, and the likelihood that any discovery of their previous life histories would make it impossible for them to earn a living. It is also important not to fall into the trap of arguing about what the *first* case of surgical transition was – a pronouncement that makes for good publicity (as was the case with the filmic representation of Elbe in the 2015 film *The Danish Girl*),[27] but which ignores the historical reality that doctors who performed the earliest surgeries (such as the Berlin surgeon Richard Mühsam, who operated on Rudolf Richter [Dora or Dorchen] and Toni Ebel in 1920) had to fear prosecution for purposely damaging healthy tissue and were thus not likely to publicize their procedures.[28] Talking about the "first case" also denies agency to earlier trans people, some of whom lived in parts of the world where these histories remain taboo and who might have performed (or had performed upon them) various kinds of surgical interventions. What kind of surgery counts as surgery; are we speaking only of clinically sterile contexts common to Western medicine?[29] Even as we focus on European and American people who did find access to care, we must remain aware that this covers only a small percentage of trans people in the world and that it fails to acknowledge those trans people who managed to live without medical intervention or discovery.[30] We leave the story of their lives for others to tell.

It is important to remember that most trans people lived very private lives and left few or very scattered archival traces. We purposely chose to focus on people who did not seek fame but who nonetheless made a significant impact through their determination to educate medical authorities or to form supportive communities. This often meant reconstructing threads of relationships that are not immediately apparent in the anonymized images in publications catering to the interests of trans individuals or in the papers of the doctors who treated them. One of our goals in this book is to follow some of these threads of connection across the Atlantic in order to upset standard biomedical narratives regarding how knowledge about sexuality is transmitted.

The work also involves finding the names and life stories of individuals who might not have wanted to be found. As we will try to demonstrate through careful naming practices and explicit links

between the four chapters of this book, many of the individuals in Europe and North America who wanted to transition from the 1910s to the 1960s knew each other or knew of each other. They either sought each other out (as was the case with several people whom Otto Spengler found and corresponded with) or they were put in touch by doctors. These communities were sometimes quite intimate, as was the case in 1950s San Francisco, where many transitioning individuals sought out and found a sympathetic ear in the living room of Louise Lawrence. Trans women in particular shared information about sympathetic doctors, surgical techniques, and the new challenges of fashion, hair styling, and makeup. It is no accident that, in the same way that Spengler appears in both the American and the German story we tell here, other people pop up both in 1950s San Francisco and then in Amsterdam, and later in Casablanca.

The era that is the focus of this book can be regarded as a crucial moment in the history of modern trans identities. New medical possibilities for hormonal and surgical transitions that arose in the 1920s and 1930s and became more commonly practiced in the fifties gave some trans people a concrete goal: to obtain this medical care. This was particularly true after December 1952, when former American soldier Christine Jorgensen returned to the United States after having surgery in Denmark, an event that immediately unleashed massive media interest. Jorgensen's fame made it clear to people all over the world that the promise of physical transition did exist.[31] Many transgender people had not even known how to understand their own feelings and thought they were crazy. The Jorgensen case changed – or at least it added a new dimension to – the concept of transgender identity, making completed transition the focus of public attention and perhaps overshadowing the existing diversity among trans people.

The relationship between medical authorities and trans people in the 1950s can be described as one of dependency but also as what one might call benevolent paternalism. With all due respect to the patients themselves, it would be inaccurate to ignore the fact that they were still dependent upon medical practitioners, and their ability to obtain the care they sought was always limited by their subjection to expert opinion. Despite this obvious disparity of power, the relationships formed between these patients and their doctors were often unusually intimate. That the medical decisions made were particularly personal is demonstrated by the fact that, as Alex explains in his chapter, very personal evaluations were made about an individual's ability to "pass" before permission to undergo surgery was granted. Nonetheless, the transfer of knowledge was mutually beneficial. The transgender individuals needed the medical professionals, and the doctors needed to develop their expertise based on the input they received from their patients, including the life stories collected in psycho-therapeutic sessions, medical tests, and oral or written testimonies of trans experiences. For surgeons this mutual transfer of knowledge was less important: they generally relied on the diagnoses

that psychiatrists had already made. In some cases, as Alex will detail, they simply did what trans people asked them to do. This was true of Dr. Georges Burou, who perfected surgical techniques in the 1950s that helped between 800 and 1,000 trans women who found their way to his clinic in Casablanca.[32]

But psychiatrists and sexologists, like Harry Benjamin, who wanted to play a role in constructing scientific knowledge about trans identity and in providing care, felt the need to thoroughly examine their patients and lay out screening protocols. The emphasis on screening tended to focus on the goal of what was then called sexual reassignment surgery (SRS) and is today generally known as gender-affirming surgery. The prospect of performing life-altering surgery on bodies that the medical science of the day decreed to be healthy and not in need of intervention made many doctors anxious, since they feared that they could be held liable for doing harm. For this reason, they placed high value on the potential to "pass": the thought was that people who were allowed to go through surgery should later be able to live convincingly in the desired sex role, anonymously disappearing into society.

It must be acknowledged that becoming invisible in society was the personal wish of most post-operative trans people of this period. And yet this very invisibility also made it possible for members of the broader society to avoid discussing the actual sexual diversity in their midst. The trans people, mostly trans women, who were not able or did not want to live invisibly, could only reside on the fringes of society, often finding their communities or their livelihoods in the realms of adult entertainment and night life.[33] As long as one's identification did not match one's gender identity or gender expression, these individuals were subject to arrest in countries, including the United States, Germany, and the Netherlands, where cross-dressing could be prosecuted under various laws against "masquerading," hiding one's identity, or "the excitement of public nuisance" (*Erregung öffentlichen Ärgernisses*).[34]

Such harsh judgements about individuals who were simply trying to live private lives and thus could not avoid being seen in public makes the careful and historically contextualized use of terminology all the more critical. In deference to this difficult social and legal situation, and as the final chapter will outline more theoretically, we generally use the names and pronouns that the individuals themselves chose to use or were forced to use at the time. We use gender-neutral pronouns (they/their) only when we have no information about the individual's public presentation while simply avoiding pronouns altogether in cases, like that of Otto Spengler, where we know that the person was forced to carry on living a public persona in a gender they might have entirely rejected if this had been a socially and legally viable option for them.

Anonymization presents another challenge.[35] Remaining very sensitive to the desires for privacy of our trans subjects, we have chosen not to use the full names of anyone about whom we know that they did not want any publicity or fame. In some cases, this was a very difficult decision.

On the one hand, we want to accord these individuals their rightful place in history, granting them their full identities and describing the role they played in the advancement of knowledge. This goal, however, is much more complicated in cases where the individual lives described do not involve fame or activism.[36] The most difficult decision involved Annette's work on the life of Carla Erskine, who had consistently told Benjamin that she wished to remain a private person. For this reason, and in order to follow the wishes of the Kinsey Institute, we have chosen to fully anonymize her and the friends who were part of her story. But doing so also reflects the larger issues we have been discussing here. Benjamin's files contain a consent form signed by Erskine for the use of her images in his book that explicitly notes: "It is understood that my identity will not be revealed and that proper procedures are followed to ensure my anonymity."[37] This desire to contribute to science while maintaining individual anonymity creates dilemmas for us as researchers. On the one hand, it is possible to discover Erskine's identity from other sources (in online documents and blogs), meaning it is not a secret. But even when the curtains of anonymity might be easily parted, we have chosen to fully name only individuals who were already famous in their day or who have already been frequently mentioned in historical texts. We admit some discomfort about how anonymization works to minimize the agency of the others. Too often historians have, perhaps unwittingly, repeated the gesture of turning these fully realized individuals into medical specimens or case studies. For this reason, Annette made a very concerted, yet ultimately fruitless effort to find Erskine's living relatives or close friends, who might have been able to give permission to drop the anonymization. Despite this failure, we have nonetheless tried to avoid the kind of verbal dismemberment that can result when one life story gets scattered across a historical text. We have tried to present these individuals as individuals rather than as medical case studies.

One aspect of the story about trans identities in the period we investigate that certainly comes up a bit short in our narrative is the lives of trans men. As Annette will explain in her chapter, this has something to do with the prejudices of the scientists whose files we relied on (most of whom simply assumed that individuals labelled male at birth were much more predisposed to transsexuality than those labelled female), but it also has something to do with the fact that trans men were much more successful at passing without medical intervention than trans women. We also discuss this issue in an image gallery devoted specifically to trans men. As Emily Skidmore's research on trans men in the United States reveals, there are countless stories of trans men having been discovered only be accident after living almost their entire public adult lives as men.[38] Aaron Devor and Nicholas Matte have explained that it was only after 1964, when Reed Erickson, a very wealthy trans man, began overseeing millions of dollars of philanthropic spending to finance research into transsexual medicine that any significant attention was paid to the medical concerns of trans men.[39]

Finally, a word about intersectionality. As a discipline, transgender studies has been particularly attuned to the intersectional implications of gender identity. For the histories we tell, this is most relevant because of the fact that all of our figures are white. This is the historical reality with which we are dealing in the era before the 1960s. When we focus on trans men and women from this period who had access to treatment and were in contact with doctors and/or researchers, and who we can identify by name, we simply find very few examples of transgender people of colour. As George Chauncey notes in his forthcoming sequel to *Gay New York*,[40] many trans people of colour, particularly but not exclusively Latinx, could be seen on the streets of New York before the 1960s.[41] But the word "streets" is apropos, because that is where they were; they did not have the material or social capital to appear in doctors' offices. Choosing to focus on the life of Carla Erskine and on the American women who travelled to the Netherlands for surgery in the 1950s means that we end our story right before the story of how trans people of colour also accessed medical treatment begins. As with the story of anonymous trans men, this story is urgently in need of telling, but it is not our focus here.

These choices should not be read as an argument that trans people did not exist before the 1950s, simply that they appear in different contexts and tracking their story would involve different methodologies than the ones we deploy in this book. Magnus Hirschfeld included two people of colour on his "Wall of Sexual Transitions," a grid of photographs of sexual types that he used to educate the public about sexual diversity. Two of the individuals depicted on the wall were men with breasts – so-called *Gynäkomasten* (sufferers of gynomastia) and two were *Onnagata* (cross-dressing male actors from Japanese Kabuki theatre).[42] These individuals are never named, however, and serve only to underline Hirschfeld's claims about universal sexual variety. It is impossible to know who these people were, and they appear on the wall as anthropological specimens, completely detached from the kinds of personal relationships with the researchers that we are investigating. The anonymity and absence of people of colour is evidence of wider social judgements about race that informed ideals of feminine beauty and masculinity and determined who had financial and social access to medical treatment – who was socially visible or invisible and on what terms.

As far as we have been able to determine, the first person of colour to have accessed gender affirming surgery in Europe or North America was Delisa Newton in the United States,[43] but her surgical transition likely occurred around 1964, later than the focus of the American accounts we explore.[44] Of course, the reason why black people do not appear in Kinsey and Benjamin's documents in the 1950s is itself instructive. As Newton pointed out in her *Sepia* magazine article in 1966: "Because I am a Negro it took me twice as long to get my sex change operation as it would have a white person. Because I am a Negro many doctors showed me little sympathy and understanding. 'You people are too emotional for such an ordeal,' one doctor

told me. But finding medical attention wasn't the only problem complicated by the color of my skin. Even with my college and nursing education, I couldn't get a good, steady job to raise money for the operation."[45]

Newton's experience seems to have been typical, and as Hilary Malatino puts it, this compromised access to medical treatment for people of colour "manifests most often as archival absence. Trans and intersex folks of color are conspicuously missing from the medical archives of sexology."[46] It is therefore clear that the fact that medical intervention seems to have been confined to white people up until the mid-1960s had much to do with the intersection of race and class in America and elsewhere, a fact that was exacerbated by the even more condescending and sensationalized treatment that trans people of colour received in the popular press.[47] We have circumstantial evidence that some trans women of colour travelled to Casablanca for surgery in the 1970s, but this is a subject that awaits future research and will likely involve significant challenges, given the extreme marginalization of racialized trans people.[48] In short, tracking the stories of trans people of colour would require different sources (fewer medical papers, and more personal reminiscences and oral interviews) and a different geographic and/ or temporal focus than the ones we have chosen.

Most trans pioneers of the 1950s as described in this book were independent, able to travel freely, and pay for months of leave, travel, accommodation, and medical costs, though some, such as

Erskine, did so on the slimmest of budgets and in circumstances so precarious as to problematize the word "privileged." Nevertheless, we acknowledge that Carla and others like her had access to the social circles and social capital of a white resident of California, advantages from which trans people of colour in the United States of the 1950s and '60s were excluded.

Similarly, Hirschfeld's work with trans individuals in Germany was focused on white Europeans living in Berlin, even though some of his work on behalf of socially disadvantaged or marginalized individuals explicitly crossed lines of class. Hirschfeld was specifically interested in formulating universal theories of variance in gender and sexuality across cultural contexts, and he carried this out using the anthropological methods of his day (methods that were themselves evolving and highly contested). Yet as Heike Bauer has recently elaborated, the homosexual rights politics at the centre of Hirschfeld's work was also haunted by racism, colonial brutality, and gender violence.[49] Hirschfeld's strategy of appealing to human rights to argue for minority sexual rights also fell prey to the dangers of framing nonbinary genders within heterosexual and cisgendered norms. Bauer even argues for a "straight turn" in Hirschfeld's work (setting in with his world tour between 1930 and 1932) – which she sees continued by Alfred Kinsey – by which she means that Hirschfeld turned away from speaking up for the rights of queer individuals to focus instead on heterosexuality and marital love.[50] Most of the individuals whose stories we can reconstruct aspired to living within

the prevailing standards of white, Western, middle-class heterosexual comportment.[51] This was, in fact, often a prerequisite for access to treatment.

None of this means that race was absent in trans history. As scholars in postcolonial studies have shown, anthropological discourse has been conditioned and shaped by colonialist concepts, social structures, and relations of power. Transgender histories, too, point to the impact of Western colonialism on existing nonbinary conceptions of gender.[52] Our analyses of various images will show that Benjamin also relied on colonialist concepts of race in making some of his arguments. Most pertinently, the entire medical field on which these histories unfold developed out of eugenic discourse from the first decades of the twentieth century, discourses that were almost invariably tainted with racialized logics. The development of hormone treatments also involved projects of "rejuvenation" that promised eternally young, virile, fertile bodies that could be useful in various larger biopolitical contexts.[53]

Susan Stryker elaborates race as the biopolitical category defining life as worth living, meaning it underlies all other biological identity categories.[54] Our focus on white trans individuals must be read with this definition in mind, because the biopolitical structures of the mid-twentieth century in both Europe and North America were inextricable from the racialized political systems within which they developed. But we do not focus our analysis on the implications that these stories of white trans individuals have for wider histories of race. That is an analysis and history that is crucial to the overarching global history of transgender people but one that we leave for others to tell.[55] Our analyses of images will point, however, to instances where they reflect racist colonialist discourses – for example, Orientalist fantasies of artists or "natural" peoples.

Similarly, the stories we tell took place before the emergence of second-wave feminism. This book raises questions of how emerging transsexual identities – which represented highly normative notions of femininity and masculinity as well as challenges to existing gender norms – might have conditioned histories of feminism(s). A virulent backlash against the growing visibility of "transsexualism" (to use a historical term that offends many trans people today but that was widely used in the post-Second World War period) erupted in medical contexts in the 1970s and led to the closing of many clinics. This backlash was anchored in extremely static, binary conceptions of gender, some of which informed and continue to inform some strands of feminism. It is our hope that this book might lay the groundwork for discrediting hostile, transphobic feminist responses to transgender histories while providing fuel to more affirmative feminist arguments for accepting trans people's self-definition.[56]

At the same time, we are also highly aware of the power dynamics inherent in the photos we discuss and exhibit – and to the possibility that our work may reproduce scenes of forced exposure, voyeurism, or objectification. There is a large body of literature focusing on the history of how photography has been used to racialize, medicalize, or criminalize bodies, constituting what Alan Sekula called a "shadow archive" in opposition to the democratizing impulse of bourgeois portraiture.[57] Michael's essay engages with that history to situate the photographic practices of Hirschfeld and Benjamin, and this concept also conditions the more popular practices Rainer discusses. Katie Sutton has provided the most direct, comprehensive analysis of how photographs of trans identity drove what she calls "sexology's photographic turn."[58] Situating these images within a history of photography and queer history and theory, Sutton explicitly calls for further research in terms that resonate deeply with how we see our own work. She interrogates these "photographs of gender-atypical individuals in the sexological archive" in order to ask how historical investigation "might … emphasize or recover the traces of subjectivity that these medicalized images work to erase." Like Sutton, we believe that the "representational violence" of the "objectifying gaze" of both the original creators of these "overtly medicalized images" and the present-day viewer/reader must be counterbalanced by paying attention to "the representational practices of individuals who were starting to claim a trans and, specifically, a transvestite identity for themselves."[59]

We also draw from work that explicitly attends to the ethics of viewing what Susie Linfield calls "difficult photographs": photographs of "violence and suffering," of the Holocaust, of war, of racial violence.[60]

Linfield, Dora Apel, and Shawn Michele Smith, among others, call for more attention to the practice of historical witnessing. As Linfield writes: "photographs excel, more than any other form of either art or journalism, in offering an immediate, viscerally emotional connection to the world," which we must take as "a starting point of discovery: by connecting these photographs to the world outside their frames, they begin to live and breathe more fully. So do we."[61]

Providing this context is one of the main aims of our book, and as readers will note, this necessitates various temporal and analytical transitions. We begin with Rainer's investigation of how trans individuals shared their most intimate photographs, this time less in service to scientific research than to community building and peer support. He investigates the visual practices in the interwar Berlin magazine *Das 3. Geschlecht* and examines the complications of retracing the decision-making process of a commercially oriented publisher who reprinted private images with the stated purpose of providing self-empowerment and self-reassurance to an audience of readers presumed to themselves be transvestites. Two essays then shift the focus from the specifically visual to the experiences of trans individuals themselves and their role in the production of knowledge. Annette's contribution builds the historical bridge from Germany to the United States, tracing the lines of knowledge transfer from Magnus Hirschfeld to Harry Benjamin and then to Alfred Kinsey through a story that focuses on trans individuals themselves. The chapter is a

reflection on how historians can and should tell these stories – on how necessary it is to remember and celebrate how extremely marginalized individuals created their own life histories and contributed to the acceleration of medical knowledge. We see a similar process occurring after trans people's hopes for surgery in the U.S. were blocked by American laws in the 1950s and 1960s, forcing them to look to Europe for experts who could help them.

Alex's essay performs the vital service of continuing the story that in our first *TransTrans* exhibition in Calgary we had capped with the publication of Harry Benjamin's 1966 book *The Transsexual Phenomenon*.[62] Alex describes how the Netherlands became the new refuge for trans individuals after the path to Denmark, which banned surgery on foreigners as a response to the Jorgensen case, was blocked. Describing the social situation for trans people in the Netherlands in the 1950s and 1960s, Alex then follows these individuals as they take advantage of a new possibility for medical treatment: a trip to Burou's clinic in Casablanca. Quite unlike the other cases we have described, Burou focused almost exclusively on his surgical technique, a technique that other doctors eventually recognized as considerably ahead of its time. He trusted trans surgery seekers to make their own decisions and was untroubled by the fears that had shut down the surgical option in other countries. In 1966, the Dutch medical commission closed the loopholes that had made surgery in that country possible, stating that doctors should stay clear of these severely disturbed patients.

Michael's chapter then examines the (medical) visual rhetorics of the images on which our research is based, emphasizing how the context and intentions of the image's production mostly diverge from the ways in which they were used. He explores how this tension shaped the histories we are telling, focusing on the medical/scientific categories that Hirschfeld and Benjamin bring to these images – the shift from "cross-dressing" to "transvestite" to "transsexual" – and on the complex interplay this tension reflects between these assertions of authority and the moments of self-fashioning captured in the photographs. In a separate chapter, Michael then takes up our strategies as curators. Having described the exhibitions, we then turn to an intervention from one of the trans people who was central to their success: Nora Eckert. Eckert uses her participation in a video installation in the Berlin version of *TransTrans* as a jumping off point for a reflection on the transformations of trans identity that she has experienced in her lifetime. We conclude with a summary of how transgender terminology might be historicized.

As a whole, these chapters aim to shift the historical discussion about this history into realms both larger and smaller than previous accounts have emphasized. We seek to highlight the role of intimate relationships between the individuals themselves and between trans patients and their doctors while emphasizing the central importance of repeated flows of knowledge across the Atlantic. Although American media culture sensationalized and trivialized the fates of people like Jorgensen

with headlines like "Ex-GI becomes blond beauty,"[63] it also provided a vital service by revealing to trans individuals across the world that they were not, in fact, utterly alone. Personal and scientific knowledge networks then produced other refuges for these people, opening up services in the Netherlands under the auspices of a psychiatrist, Frederik Hartsuiker in Haarlem, whose expertise involved the castration of sex offenders. This last point is yet another demonstration of both some of the uncomfortable truths of this history and the intrepidness of trans individuals themselves, who encouraged a wide range of physicians and specialists to take up their cause.

In other words, these histories were never confined to one national context or scientific discipline. In each national setting, the reactions to the wishes of trans people met with a unique cultural response. While the progressive contributions of Weimar German sexological research were literally burned to the ground in the Nazi book-burning frenzies that followed Hitler's appointment as chancellor in January 1933, the knowledge produced had a very long reach, stretching across Europe and to North America.

GALLERY NOTES: Carla Erskine's Slides

1   Sandra S. Phillips in *Exposed: Voyeurism, Surveillance, and the Camera Since 1870*, ed. Sandra S. Phillips (New Haven: Yale University Press, 2010), 13.

GALLERY NOTES: Images of Otto Spengler

1   B. S. Talmey, "Transvestism: A Contribution to the Study of the Psychology of Sex," *New York Medical Journal* 99 (January to June 1914): 362–8.

2   George W. Henry, "Rudolf von H." in *Sex Variants: A Study of Homosexual Patterns* (New York and London: P. B. Hoeber, 1948), 487–98.

NOTES TO CHAPTER 1

1   The seminal issue of *Transgender Studies Quarterly (TSQ)*, for instance, defines the premise of transgender studies as transgender agency: "Perhaps most importantly, the field encompasses the possibility that transgender people (self-identified or designated as such by others) can be subjects of knowledge as well as objects of knowledge. That is, they can articulate critical knowledge from embodied positions that would otherwise be rendered pathological, marginal, invisible, or unintelligible within dominant and normative organizations of power/knowledge." Stryker and Currah, "Introduction," in "Postposttranssexual: Key Concepts for a Twenty- First-Century Transgender Studies," *TSQ: Transgender Studies Quarterly* 5, no. 1 (1 Feb 2018): 1–18, 9.

2   Susan Stryker's *Transgender History* (Berkeley, CA: Distributed by Publishers Group West, 2008) was a pivotal intervention that remains seminal. Sociologist Aaron Devor's work demonstrates both how far the discipline has come within academia and its central connection to a community of trans elders and pathbreakers. Ardel Haefele-Thomas's excellent new textbook promises to help establish transgender studies as an important teaching field on more university campuses. Ardel

Haefele-Thomas, *Introduction to Transgender Studies* (New York: Harrington Park Press, 2019). Other pathbreaking scholars will be mentioned in the pages to follow.

3   Katie Sutton has recently elaborated on scientific approaches to this subject in a book that was published too late to be entirely integrated into our account here. See Katie Sutton, *Sex between Body and Mind: Psychoanalysis and Sexology in the German-Speaking World, 1890s–1930s* (Ann Arbor: University of Michigan Press, 2019), especially the chapter "The Case of the Transvestite: Expert Knowledge, Subjects, and Trans Identity Politics," 173–201.

4   For an example of a history that focuses on the emergence of sexual science (sexology) while also demonstrating the importance of confession and life stories to the formulation of medical categorization, see Harry Oosterhuis, *Stepchildren of Nature: Krafft-Ebing, Psychiatry and the Making of Sexual Identity* (Chicago: University of Chicago Press, 2000).

5   *TransTrans: Transgender Histories between Germany and the United States, 1882–1966*, curated by Rainer Herrn, Michael Thomas Taylor, and Annette F. Timm in co-operation with the Nickle Galleries, University of Calgary; the Magnus-Hirschfeld-Gesellschaft in Berlin; the Institute for History and Ethics in Medicine of the Charité Clinic, Berlin; and the Kinsey Institute for Research in Sex, Gender, and Reproduction in Bloomington, Indiana. *TransTrans* was originally shown at the Nickle Galleries from 27 May to 10 June 2016 and was produced in co-operation with curator Michele Hardy and the support of Christine Sowiak. In Berlin, the exhibition was shown from 7 November 2019 to 2 March 2020. We especially thank Andreas Puskeiler, who designed significant sections of the shows in Calgary and Berlin. We would also like to thank Birgit Bosold, director of the Schwules Museum, and Peter Rehberg, director of the museum's archive, for their support and guidance in Berlin.

6   Harry Benjamin, *The Transsexual Phenomenon: A Scientific Report on Transsexualism and Sex*

Conversion in the Human Male and Female (New York: The Julian Press, 1966).

7   K. J. Rawson, "Archive," *TSQ: Transgender Studies Quarterly* 1, nos 1–2 (2014): 24–6.

8   "Archive," in *TSQ* 1, nos 1–2 (2014): 25.

9   Rainer Herrn, *Schnittmuster des Geschlechts: Transvestitismus und Transsexualität in der frühen Sexualwissenschaft* (Giessen: Psychosozial-Verlag, 2005).

10   Alex Bakker, *Mijn valse verleden* (Amsterdam: Nieuw Amsterdam, 2014); Alex Bakker, *My Untrue Past: The Coming of Age of a Trans Man* (Victoria, BC: Castle Carrington Publishing, 2019).

11   Haefele-Thomas, *Introduction to Transgender Studies*, xxx.

12   Susan Stryker, "Forward," in ibid., xxvii.

13   Joanne Meyerowitz, *How Sex Changed: A History of Transsexuality in the United States* (Cambridge and London: Harvard University Press, 2002), 185, and 154–5.

14   Letter from Carla Erskine to Harry Benjamin, 5 Oct 1953, Kinsey Institute Library & Special Collections, Harry Benjamin Collection (hereafter KILSC-HB), Box 4, Ser. II C.

15   Herrn, *Schnittmuster des Geschlechts*.

16   The photos were exhibited in 2016 as part of the exhibition *Outsiders: American Photography and Film, 1950s–1980*. See "Casa Susanna: On Photography and the Play of Gender," Art Gallery of Ontario, accessed 12 June 2019, https://ago.ca/events/casa-susannaphotography- and-play-gender. They were first published by Michael Hurst and Robert Swope as *Casa Susanna* (New York: PowerHouse Books, 2005).

17   Herrn, *Schnittmuster des Geschlechts*, 151. Herrn has since published a facsimile edition of all five issues: Rainer Herrn, *Das 3. Geschlecht: Reprint der 1930–1932 erschienen Zeitschrift für Transvestiten* (Hamburg: Männerschwarm Verlag, 2016).

18   Alex Bakker, *Transgender in Nederland: Een buitengewone geschiedenis* (Amsterdam: Boom Uitgevers, 2018).

19   Harry Benjamin tried to track as many of these surgeries as possible in the years leading up to the publication of his book (Benjamin, *The Transsexual Phenomenon*). The handwritten tables in his notes for this book include mention of four surgeries performed in Mexico between 1955 and 1960, three by Dr. Daniel Lopez Ferrer, and one (in 1960) by a Dr. Calderon. Benjamin lists six surgeries in the Netherlands in the mid-1950s (Drs. Koch and Nauta) but does not seem to track them after that. See KILSC-HB 28. One more surgery by Dr. Ferrer (Debbie Mayne in the mid-1950s) is mentioned in Meyerowitz, *How Sex Changed*, 147.

20   C. van Emde Boas, "De behandeling van transseksisten in Nederland 1953–1973: Een les van 20 jaar attitudeschommelingen," *Medisch Contact* 29 (1974).

21   Taylor, "Review of Schnittmuster," 314. This praise for the book was echoed by Vivian Namaste. See Viviane K. Namaste, review of *Schnittmuster des Geschlechts: Transvestitismus und Transsexualität in der frühen Sexualwissenschaft* by Rainer Herrn, *Journal of the History of Sexuality* 16, no. 2 (2007): 326–8.

22   To name only their most important publications for our purposes: Joanne Meyerowitz, *How Sex Changed: A History of Transsexuality in the United States* (Cambridge and London: Harvard University Press, 2002); Susan Stryker, *Transgender History* (Berkeley, CA: Seal Press, 2008); Genny Beemyn, "US History," in *Trans Bodies, Trans Selves: A Resource for the Transgender Community*, ed. Laura Erickson-Schroth (Oxford University Press, 2014), 501–36; Genny Beemyn and Susan Rankin, *The Lives of Transgender People* (New York: Columbia University Press, 2011); Deborah Rudacille, *The Riddle of Gender: Science, Activism, and Transgender Rights* (New York: Pantheon Books, 2005); and Leslie Feinberg, *Transgender Warriors: Making History from Joan of Arc to Rupaul* (Boston: Beacon Press, 1996). We received a copy of Julian Gill-Peterson, *Histories of the Transgender Child* (Minneapolis: University of Minnesota Press, 2018) too late to integrate all of its important insights here.

23   Leslie Feinberg, *Trans Liberation: Beyond Pink or Blue* (Boston: Beacon Press, 1998); Julia Serano, *Whipping Girl: A Transsexual Woman on Sexism and the Scapegoating of*

Femininity (Emeryville, CA: Seal Press, 2007); and Sandy Stone, "The Empire Strikes Back: A Posttranssexual Manifesto," *Camera Obscura: Feminism, Culture, and Media Studies* 10, no. 2 (1 May 1992): 150–76. See also: Pat Califia, *Sex Changes: The Politics of Transgenderism* (San Francisco: Cleis Press, 1997); Mario Martino, *Emergence: A Transsexual Autobiography* (New York: Crown Publishers, 1977); Dierdre N. McCloskey, *Crossing: A Memoir* (Chicago: University of Chicago Press, 2000); Livia Prüll, *Trans* im Glück – Geschlechtsangleichung als Chance: Autobiographie, Medizingeschichte, Medizinethik* (Göttingen: Vandenhoeck and Ruprecht, 2016); Mark Rees, *Dear Sir or Madam: The Autobiography of a Female-to-Male Transsexual* (London: New York, 1996); Renee Richards, *Second Serve* (New York: Stein and Day Pub, 1992); and Donna Rose, *Wrapped in Blue: A Journey of Discovery* (Round Rock, TX: Living Legacy Press, 2003).

24 Stone, "The Empire Strikes Back."

25 Again, we are limiting this list to the works that have been most influential for this book: Persson Perry Baumgartinger, *Trans Studies: Historische, begriffliche und aktivistische Aspekte* (Vienna: Zaglossus, 2017); Aaron Devor, *FTM: Female-to-Male Transsexuals in Society* (Bloomington: Indiana University Press, 2016); Richard Ekins, "Science, Politics and Clinical Intervention: Harry Benjamin, Transsexualism and the Problem of Heteronormativity," *Sexualities* 8, no. 3 (2005): 306–28; Viviane Namaste, *Sex Change, Social Change: Reflections on Identity, Institutions and Imperialism* (Toronto: Women's Press, 2011); Arlene Stein, *Unbound: Transgender Men and the Remaking of Identity* (New York: Pantheon Books, 2018); Amy L. Stone and Jaime Cantrell, eds, *Out of the Closet, into the Archives: Researching Sexual Histories* (Albany, NY: SUNY Press, 2015); Nicholas M. Teich, *Transgender 101: A Simple Guide to a Complex Issue* (New York: Columbia University Press, 2012); David Valentine, *Imagining Transgender: An Ethnography of a Category* (Durham: Duke University Press, 2007).

26 Much has been written about all three figures. For overviews, see: Rainer Herrn and Annette F. Timm, "Lili Elbe," in *Global Encyclopedia of Lesbian, Gay, Bisexual and Transgender (LGBTQ) History*, vol. 3 (Farmington Hills, MI: Charles Scribner & Sons, 2019), 500–502, which discusses why what is usually taken as her memoir (Niels Hoyer, ed., *Man into Woman: The First Sex Change: A Portrait of Lili Elbe: The True and Remarkable Transformation of the Painter Einar Wegener*, trans. James Stenning [London: Blue Boat Books, 2004]) needs to be read more circumspectly. See also: Richard F. Docter, *Becoming a Woman: A Biography of Christine Jorgensen* (New York: Routledge, 2007); and Roberta Cowell, *Roberta Cowell's Story* (New York: British Book Centre, 1954).

27 Tom Hooper, *The Danish Girl*, 2015.

28 Rainer Herrn and Michael Thomas Taylor, "Transvestites/Transsexuals," in *Global Encyclopedia of Lesbian, Gay, Bisexual and Transgender (LGBTQ) History*, vol. 3 (Farmington Hills, MI: Charles Scribner & Sons, 2019), 1640–44.

29 Given the much more multicultural atmosphere of German and Dutch cities today, it is not surprising that scholars who focus on the present have much more to say about colonial and racist contexts for trans lives. See Jin Haritaworn, *Queer Lovers and Hateful Others: Regenerating Violent Times and Places* (London: Pluto Press, 2015).

30 Non-European contexts for trans identity would raise very different questions than those we are able to address here, such as the relationship between trans identity and such cultural practices as eunuchism. See for example, Howard Chiang, *After Eunuchs: Science, Medicine, and the Transformation of Sex in Modern China* (New York: Columbia University Press, 2018); and Veronika Fuechtner, Douglas E. Haynes, and Ryan M. Jones, eds., *A Global History of Sexual Science, 1880–1960* (Oakland, CA: University of California Press, 2018).

31 Docter provides a detailed account of the media furor around Jorgensen's transition and describes her later fame. Docter, *Becoming a Woman*.

32 As far as we know, Burou did not keep careful records. This is an estimate derived from personal communications, detailed in J. Joris Hage, Refaat B. Karim, and Donald R. Sr. Laub, "On the Origin of Pedicled Skin Inversion

Vaginoplasty: Life and Work of Dr. Georges Burou of Casablanca," *Annals of Plastic Surgery* 59, no. 6 (2007): 723–9, esp. 725.

33   For examples of trans individuals who made their careers in entertainment, see: Herrn, *Schnittmuster des Geschlechts*, 76–7; Stryker, *Transgender History*, 23, 29, and 77; Katie Sutton, "'We Too Deserve a Place in the Sun': The Politics of Transvestite Identity in Weimar Germany," *German Studies Review* 35, no. 2 (2012): 335–54; and Alex Bakker's chapter in this book.

34   For a history of early measures in the United States, see Clare Sears, *Arresting Dress: Cross-Dressing, Law, and Fascination in Nineteenth-Century San Francisco* (Durham, NC: Duke University Press, 2014).

35   In a discussion of Casa Susanna photos, for instance, Ms. Bob Davis writes: "The use of aliases is evidence of the early community's relationship to the larger culture, a relationship based on fear of discovery and a need for secrecy. Though we can never be sure of an individual's motivation, it seems logical that within their community transgender people use names that accurately reflect their gender identities, rather than names assigned at birth. However, the use of multiple surnames means that some early community members were not out in their daily lives, a decision that archivists and researchers must respect" (626). See Bob Davis, "Using Archives to Identify the Trans* Women of Casa Susanna," *TSQ* 2, no. 4 (2015): 621–34, here 626.

36   For convincing evidence that trans activism has played a decisive role in the production of academic knowledge, see the various contributions to Dan Irving and Rupert Raj, eds *Trans Activism in Canada: A Reader* (Toronto: Brown Bear Press, 2014). 37 See the release form signed by Carla Erskine on 24 February 1964 in KILSC-HB, Box 25-1, Permissions (1964).

38   Emily Skidmore, *True Sex: The Lives of Trans Men at the Turn of the Twentieth Century* (New York: New York University Press, 2017).

39   See Aaron H. Devor and Nicholas Matte, "One Inc. and Reed Erickson: The Uneasy Collaboration of Gay and Trans Activism, 1964–2003," *GLQ: A Journal of Lesbian and Gay Studies* 10, no. 2 (2004): 179–209; Aaron Devor and Nicholas Matte, "Building a Better World for Transpeople: Reed Erickson and the Erickson Educational Foundation," *International Journal of Transgenderism* 10, no. 1 (2007): 47–68. The Erickson Educational Foundation made most of Harry Benjamin's later work possible, but as Abram Lewis argues, recognition of Erickson's contribution came late in part because of his drug use and his interest in New Age spirituality. Abram J. Lewis, "'I Am 64 and Paul McCartney Doesn't Care': The Haunting of the Transgender Archive and the Challenges of Queer History," *Radical History Review* 120 (2014): 13–34.

40   George Chauncey, *Gay New York: Gender, Urban Culture, and the Making of the Gay Male World, 1890–1940* (New York: Basic Books, 1994).

41   As told to Annette Timm by George Chauncey, Calgary, 23 Aug 2019.

42   Alex Bakker's interview partners and the *Paris Match* article that he cites in his essay did mention a few trans people of colour, but we simply have very little information about these individuals and there is no mention of them in the medical records we have relied on for this book. See Bakker's essay for allusions to his interviewees and V. Merlin, "L'homme qui change le sex," *Paris Match* (1974): 37–9.

43   Meyerowitz, *How Sex Changed*, 86 and 199–200. See also Emily Skidmore, "Constructing the 'Good Transsexual': Christine Jorgensen, Whiteness, and Heteronormativity in the Midtwentieth- Century Press," *Feminist Studies* 37, no. 2 (2011): 270–300, esp. 270.

44   As with other areas of trans history, it is often trans people themselves who are doing the most intrepid digging. See the discussion in the blog: Monica Roberts, "TransGriot: Who Was the First African-American Transwoman?," TransGriot (blog), 26 May 2009, accessed 28 June 2019, https://transgriot.blogspot.com/2009/05/who-was-first-african-american.html. For a pioneering study of black trans history, see C. Riley Snorton, *Black on Both Sides: A Racial History of Trans Identity* (Minneapolis: University of Minnesota Press, 2017).

45 Quoted from Delisa Newton, "From Man to Woman," Sepia (May 1966): 66 in Skidmore, "Constructing the 'Good Transsexual,'" 292.

46 Hilary Malatino, *Queer Embodiment: Monstrosity, Medical Violence, and Intersex Experience* (Lincoln: University of Nebraska Press, 2019), 119.

47 Skidmore contrasts stories about Newton and two other women of colour, Marta Olmos Ramiro and Laverne Peterson, in African American publications like *Sepia* and *Ebony* with the ridicule they endured in print in the mainstream tabloid press, particularly the *National Insider*, where they were regularly derided as not "authentic" transsexuals. She contrasts this with the relatively respectful treatment of Christine Jorgensen, Charlotte McLeod, and Tamara Rees. See Skidmore, "Constructing the 'Good Transsexual,'" esp. 271.

48 As Treva Ellison, Kai M. Green, Matt Richardson, and C. Riley Snorton have argued, exploring black trans histories involves an excavation of "repressed genealogies." We have not undertaken such an exploration here, not least because the stories we tell emerge primarily from the kind of archives (of the medical establishment) from which black subjects were generally excluded. Treva Ellison et al., "We Got Issues: Toward a Black Trans*/ Studies," *TSQ: Transgender Studies Quarterly* 4, no. 2 (2017): 162–9.

49 Heike Bauer, *The Hirschfeld Archives: Violence, Death, and Modern Queer Culture* (Philadelphia: Temple University Press, 2017).

50 Bauer suggests this was "direct response to the perilousness of [Hirschfeld's] political exile," rather than being motivated by shame or secrecy. Bauer, *Hirschfeld Archives*, 105.

51 For transvestites in Germany, see especially Katie Sutton, "'We Too Deserve a Place in the Sun': The Politics of Transvestite Identity in Weimar Germany," *German Studies Review* 35, no. 2 (2012): 335–54.

52 See for instance, Charlie McNabb, *Nonbinary Gender Identities: History, Culture, Resources* (Lanham, MD: Rowman & Littlefield, 2018). There is also a growing interest in colonial legacies within disciplines focusing on the present social and political position of trans people in Western societies, and much of it is framed in rather ahistorical terms. See for example, Jin Haritaworn, *Queer Lovers and Hateful Others.*

53 See especially Michaela Lindinger, *Sonderlinge, Aussenseiter, Femmes fatales: Das "andere" Wien um 1900* (Vienna: Amalthea, 2015). Lindinger notes that Benjamin was the only doctor among those she discusses who specialized in the rejuvenation of women (148); "Im Zentrum stand die '(Wieder-)Herstellung der Weiblichkeit an sich'" (the re-establishment of femininity stood at the center), 148. A fuller account of this earlier history can also be found in Heiko Stoff, *Ewige Jugend: Konzepte der Verjüngung vom späten 19. Jahrhundert bis ins Dritte Reich* (Cologne: Böhlau, 2004). Stoff focuses primarily on the history of masculinities, though he has some discussion of how neuroses related to masculine identity could be conditioned by ideas about femininity. More general overviews can be found in: Chandak Sengoopta, "The Modern Ovary: Constructions, Meanings, Uses," *History of Science* 38, no. 4 (2000): 425–88; and Chandak Sengoopta, *The Most Secret Quintessence of Life: Sex, Glands, and Hormones, 1850–1950* (Chicago: University of Chicago Press, 2006).

54 Susan Stryker, "Biopolitics," *TSQ: Transgender Studies Quarterly* 1, nos 1–2 (2014): 38–42.

55 For an important contribution to these efforts, focused on the nineteenth century, see C. Riley Snorton, *Black on Both Sides.*

56 In what Stryker describes as "the mother lode of transphobic feminist rhetoric, tropes, and discourse," Janice Raymond provided a blueprint for arguments about trans exclusion that continue to be repeated today. See Janice G. Raymond, *The Transsexual Empire* (Boston: Beacon Press, 1979). Recent popular media attention has created a new wave of public acrimony, too extensive to detail here, between feminists on either side of this debate. For an excellent overview see Sophie Lewis, "How British Feminism Became Anti-Trans," *New York Times*, 8 Feb 2019, sec. Opinion, https:// www.nytimes.com/2019/02/07/opinion/ terf-trans-women-britain.html. See also Jack Halberstam, "Trans* Feminisms," in *Trans*: A Quick and Quirky Account of Gender Variability* (Oakland: University of California

Press, 2018), 107–28. Halberstam asks about the "constellations of alliance and opposition" that emerge "when the male-female binary crumbles" (108); the book points, instead, to modes of embodiment and identity that move away from "idealized notions of discrete bodies laying claim to well-established categories of male and female" to offer "a different language for embodiment that draws from humananimal relations, uncertain experiences of embodiment, and haphazard, profuse, and viral models of embodiment" (127).

57   Allan Sekula, "The Body and the Archive," *October* 39 (Winter 1986): 3–64.

58   Katie Sutton, "Sexology's Photographic Turn: Visualizing Trans Identity in Interwar Germany," *Journal of the History of Sexuality* 27, no. 3 (Sept 2018): 442–79.

59   Sutton, "Sexology's Photographic Turn," 470.

60   Susie Linfield, *The Cruel Radiance: Photography and Political Violence* (Chicago and London: University of Chicago Press, 2010); Dora Apel and Shawn Michelle Smith, *Lynching Photographs* (Berkeley: University of California Press, 2007).

61   Linfield, *Cruel Radiance*; Apel and Smith, *Lynching Photographs.*

62   Benjamin, *The Transsexual Phenomenon.*

63   "Ex-GI Becomes Blond Beauty," *New York Daily News*, 1 Dec 1952.

2

Das 3. Geschlecht (The 3rd sex): Illustration Practices in the First Magazine for Transvestites

Rainer Herrn
Translated by Michael Thomas Taylor and Annette F. Timm

Many studies have appeared recently on the history of gender and sexual minorities, yet insufficient attention has been paid to the significance of images.[1] Among German historians of sexuality, specifically, only very few use images to add life to stories about important individuals, events, and documents. These scholars less frequently focus on historical practices of illustration themselves. This is hardly surprising, given that there are few images at all of marginalized minorities from the early twentieth century; with very few exceptions publications that focused on these individuals were sparsely or not at all illustrated.[2] In comparison to textual sources about these communities, we have very little analysis of visual documentation of their history.

An exception can be found in *Das 3. Geschlecht*,[3] a magazine aimed at "transvestites" in Germany.[4] Illustrations were central to the goals of this publication, which therefore offers us an incomparably rich source of images to work with. A visual analysis of this publication reveals that images often marked

"I cut out the pictures from the last issue and now always carry them with me."

a point of intersection between self-perception and the perception of the self by others, even when this intersection was not explicitly articulated.

This essay will begin by examining the context in which this magazine emerged and its role in expressing the nascent self-formation and self-expression of transvestites. My focus will be on the particular role that visuality played for cross-dressers of this period, as a constitutive element of a strategy of visual self-empowerment and self-reassurance. The crucial question in this context is how images were used to negotiate norms about how transvestites should appear. Taking up this question, the second part of the essay turns to the private use of images, and the third part discusses the influence that editors of *Das 3. Geschlecht* had on shaping images of transvestites. Looking synthetically at these different practices, the final two sections then ask about the photographs' visual language and the specific effects of how they were placed or collaged on the pages of the publication.

As part of a process of negotiation between cross-dressers and sexologists that began around 1900, Magnus Hirschfeld suggested in 1910 that cross-dressers should no longer be categorized as homosexuals, as had been the prevailing practice. Rather, he suggested that they be viewed as a "sexual" minority of their own, for which he coined the term "transvestite."[5] In line with criticism of the existing practice of understanding cross-dressing as a symptom of homosexuality, Hirschfeld first conceived of transvestitism as a heterosexual phenomenon existing for both

sexes.[6] Although there had been previous reports of isolated cases of the formation of network-like, private contacts between groups of cross-dressers, it was only in the Weimar period that transvestites began to more frequently form organizations and articulate their own identities as a unique subculture. These developments led to the publication of books and magazines.

For imperial Germany, there is but scant evidence of social infrastructure for cross-dressers. In one passage of his book, Hirschfeld writes about tensions between different sexual groups; according to Hirschfeld groups formed around sexual orientations and this had prompted the "transvestites" to split off from homosexuals as early as the turn of the century.[7] Hirschfeld notes that heterosexual transvestites (by which he meant cross-dressers whose love objects remained heterosexual with reference to the sex assigned at birth) "are not seldom extremely careful to avoid associating with homosexual transvestites; for example, they are incredibly keen to exclude them from transvestite organizations. Conversely, homosexual transvestites have not the least bit of understanding for heterosexual men who live in female clothing; homosexuals consider these men to be people who have gotten stuck in their development or they don't really believe that the heterosexual men are attracted to the other sex."[8] Reflecting on the impact of his own work in 1924, Hirschfeld noted that "the heterosexual transvestites hardly know each other; some of them have come together to form a group only since my book [*The Transvestites*, 1910], and they are now even occasionally united together into a little organization with the telling name of 'Two Souls.'"[9] In the same year, Lothar Goldmann reported that it was only with "political revolution and progressive research," meaning with the founding of the Weimar Republic, that many "transvestites" dared go public, having been strengthened in their confidence.[10] He reminds us that not long before the First World War a "women's club that was meeting in total secrecy [which also included transvestites] was broken up by the police."[11]

This repressive approach no longer existed in the same form in 1920s Germany. Goldman nevertheless concludes that "even though an enormous number of dance halls and localities [entertainment venues]" for homosexuals opened up "in all areas of Berlin, especially after the war … there were hardly any comparable places for transvestites."[12] For heterosexual transvestites, this at first left only private circles in which they had already been socially engaged, since, as Goldmann continues, in agreement with Hirschfeld: "The heterosexual transvestite with an inclination for normal women usually avoids homosexual circles."[13] Goldmann compares a private party to a so-called "costume ball," for which a venue was specifically rented: "Similar official events may proceed with just as much fun. But they naturally lose the discreet character of a private, closed circle. Even celebrations organized on such a scale often have participants of both sexes numbering many hundreds of people. Just recently, such an amusement took place in the Philharmonie in Berlin."[14]

Several other magazine projects for members of gender and sexual minorities provide evidence for an emerging liberalization at the beginning of the Weimar period. Beginning in 1924, the publishing house owned by the homosexual publisher and activist Friedrich Radszuweit published a supplement to the lesbian magazine *Die Freundin* (The girlfriend) devoted to "transvestites."[15] Between 1930 and 1932, Radzuweit's company published the first transvestite magazine in the world to be offered for sale: *Das 3. Geschlecht*. There is not a single library that considered it important to save this magazine. The failure to preserve these historical traces is evidence that the public viewed transvestite inclinations as bizarre and ridiculous whims, as stigmatizing descriptions about which marginalized transvestites repeatedly complained.[16]

The Role of Imagery and the Power of Images

One thing in particular characterizes the magazine *Das 3. Geschlecht*: Friedrich Radszuweit conceived it as an illustrated magazine, and he took care to emphasize its unusually rich visual content from the moment it was first announced. For instance, he advertises the first issue with the note: "Illustrated with twenty images," and for the fifth issue, "Illustrated with 30 images" (see figure 2.1). Only in one other magazine published at this time – a homosexual magazine also produced by Radszuweit's press – *Die Insel: Magazin der Einsamen* (The island: magazine for lonely

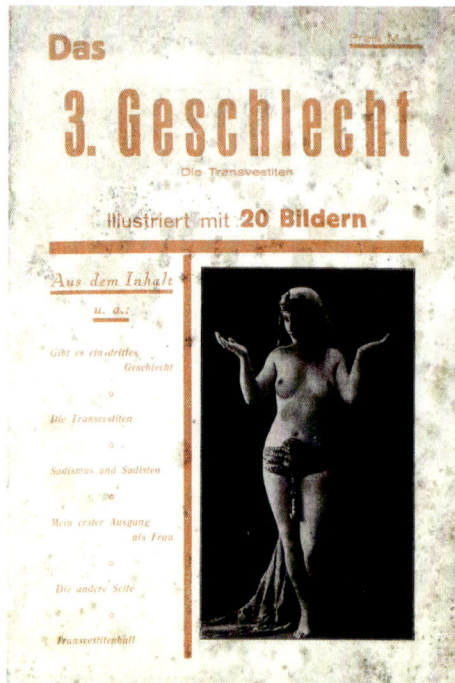

FIGURE 2.1 and 2.2: Cover of the first and last issue of *Das 3. Geschlecht*, issues 1 and 5.

souls) – was so much significance afforded to illustrations.

Die Insel's visual ethos depended primarily on photos of young, lightly clothed or naked men in chaste poses. While *Das 3. Geschlecht* sought to use images as a means to allow readers to identify with those depicted, *Die Insel* aimed to pique the erotic interest of male readers. And yet *Das 3. Geschlecht* also contained photos of scantily clad men and women, particularly on its cover pages, which were almost always decorated with extremely attractive women. This was likely not only an attempt to address the erotic desires of both heterosexual male and homosexual female transvestites, but perhaps also an effort to attract a wider

heterosexual readership, an audience that was less interested in transvestitism and much more interested in pictures of naked women.

The dominance of photography in the magazine prompts us to ask about photography's importance for transvestites. Already in his monograph *Die Transvestiten*, Hirschfeld had promised to produce an illustrated volume if it became clear that there was interest and if readers sent him photos. Hirschfeld must have received the material he needed. An illustrated volume containing only fifty-four images (likely because of the high printing costs) appeared soon thereafter, and additional volumes would soon follow.[17] The Radszuweit press also solicited photos from the reading public in this way, though its editor's aims were different from Hirschfeld's. Radszuweit was not primarily interested in providing visual evidence for scientific theories, or if so, only to the extent that science helped to popularize and stabilize a new form of identity. Rather, he was interested in establishing a medium for transvestites to construct their own identities and to organize themselves into groups. Imagery was central to both of these goals.

According to Hirschfeld, transvestitism consists in the desire to stage oneself in the clothing of the "other" sex, in a performative act in private or public, with or without an audience. Photography provided transvestites with a visual medium that made it possible to credibly represent a successful gender transgression. It allowed transvestites to record, and retrospectively confirm, ephemeral moments of the successful staging of an identity within the "other" sex. No other visual medium was considered to be so convincing in terms of its power to illustrate and reproduce reality. The often-elaborate preparations that go into getting ready for the camera are to be understood as acts with the power to engender identity, and they are occasionally also erotically charged acts of transvestitism, which Hirschfeld then mistakenly generalized in 1918: "The inclination to be photographed in clothing appropriate to their own unique character [*Eigenart*] is extraordinarily widespread among transvestites. They evidently find that strong feelings of desire often radiate toward them from a photograph reflecting their second or true self."[18]

Transvestites were also faced with the challenge of making their existence visible to themselves and to the world. Photography was able to do this. These visual practices can be understood as a strategy of "visual self-empowerment," although the photos in the magazine also enter into a dialogue with the texts.[19] Whereas the authors of the popular-scientific text contributions to *Das 3. Geschlecht* were usually identified with both their first and last names, the corresponding statements from transvestites are authored only with chosen names or pseudonyms. Most photos in the first issues are printed without names, even though the captions indicate that many of them depict transvestites who performed in public, people we would refer to as travesty artists, and whose faces are clearly recognizable. Artist names are given only in a few exceptions, such as in the photo of Voo-Doo, a dancer and cabaret artist whose real name was Willy Pape (discussed in more detail in the image gallery in this chapter and in Michael's essay).[20]

These portraits and still photographs, some of which were prepared in the style of artists' postcards, can be considered professional, even though the published sources of the time made no distinction between travesty and transvestitism. Travesty performances, which were very popular around the turn of the century, included men performing in women's clothing and women performing in men's clothing, and they ranged from grotesque stagings of gender irony to song numbers, performances of artistic whistling, and perfect stagings of Salomé's "Dance of the Seven Veils." Such forms of theatricalization played with the audience's gender awareness and drew from the tension between the body, the voice, movement, and clothing, which these performances perfected to a form of art. The performers worked with techniques of covering and uncovering, allusion and illusion, and they presupposed complicity in this gender play between the audience and those presenting themselves to be seen. Both scholarly and popular interpreters understood travesty acts as proof of transvestite desire. They were viewed as professionally perfect realizations of a drive-like inclination, as if the stage appearance were not thinkable without the "drive to cross-dress" upon which it was based.[21] One article in *Das 3. Geschlecht* described how circuses, cabaret, and the theatre were depicting "Men as Women – Women as Men"; it noted that these travesty artists' "desire to wear the clothing of the other sex must [certainly] be attributable to transvestitism."[22]

Emphasizing the role of stage performance is important because the photos in the first issues of *Das 3. Geschlecht* primarily depict performing artists. Illustrations in the first two issues are captioned, for instance; "Young artist makes a successful guest appearance as a woman and a man," or "Male artist who had great success as a female impersonator on the top stages at home and abroad."[23] In contrast, in depictions of female-to-male transvestites the camera focuses less on glamorous figures and more on nonartistic professions that were clearly masculine in their connotations, such as a ship's captain, a gentleman at a reception desk, or a sportsman (see figure 2.3).

We cannot really know, however, whether the captions reflect true facts or are fabrications from the editors. Perhaps it was decided to avoid naming the persons in the images because these individuals did not want to be given the label of "transvestite" in the only magazine that was aimed at transvestites? And perhaps what mattered for the illustrations was less the concrete persons being represented and more the positive and exemplary character of what they respectively represented: successful transvestites in various life situations, who appeared to have succeeded in having a career in their desired sex. The photographs constitute diverse class typologies of space (of freedom) and profession, which display the various ways in which these individuals might live out their passion and illustrate their fantasies of wish fulfilment.

Although it is hardly possible to make a clear distinction between "professional" photos and those that I will call "private" in what follows, this division nevertheless appears useful. For, as I have already mentioned, the editors of *Das 3. Geschlecht* frequently encouraged readers to send in suitable photographs for publication. We read in the second volume, for instance: "Here, the editors ask all transvestites to support the publisher by sending in texts, images, etc."[24] By presenting itself as the mouthpiece for transvestites, the magazine motivated its readers to cooperate by implying that they would be furthering their own interests.[25]

Readers apparently were happy to oblige, as the spectrum of private image and text contributions suggests: "Even if it's not literary, I would like to contribute

FIGURE 2.3: Female transvestites in male professions: "Female transvestite who works in a fashionable Berlin dance spot at a reception." "Female transvestite" and "Female transvestite as a sportsman." *Das 3. Geschlecht* 1 (1930): 5, 9, and 13.

something to the further success and declare my willingness to give you several images for publication – albeit only in *The 3rd Sex*."[26] The limitation to the permission points to the high level of identification that the reader feels with the magazine but also to the not unjustified concern that Radszuweit might be tempted to use the images in the homosexual magazines that he published.

Although the magazine made no explicit distinction between professional and private images, we can note a decrease in the number of photos that appear likely to have been taken by professional photographers and an increase in those that appear to have been sent in by readers. In issue one, only four photos out of twenty can be categorized as originating from a private context (see figure 2.7). By issue

two, the editors were able to print photo montages of private images, pointing to an increased number of private submissions. By issue five, the magazine can advertise itself by declaring the inclusion of "thirty completely new, not yet published images of male and female transvestites."[27] This emphasis points to the fact that the majority of photos printed in the earlier issues had already been published elsewhere, which a comparison with the *Die Insel* and the special supplement addressed to transvestites in *Die Freundin* confirms. The increasing publication of private photos met the taste of readers and reflected the growing need for self-images. For example, one reader expressed their opinion about issue two: "The images are again excellent and, as I see it, even better than in the first issue. *The 3rd Sex* has recognized

Lotte Hahm

Depictions of Lotte Hahm, a well-known out lesbian, political activist, and owner of several lesbian bars in Berlin during the 1920s, reflect shifting categories of identity. For example, Hahm appears in two photographs from the transvestite magazine *Das 3. Geschlecht*. In the first, she is unnamed but clearly recognizable, holding up a card advertising another magazine, *Die Freundin*, that was aimed primarily at lesbians (figure 2.4). In the second, she is identified by name and labelled a "female transvestite" (figure 2.5).

As an example of how these styles, and the gender play they represent, were popularized, consider two additional images from *Das 3. Geschlecht* (figures 2.5 and 2.6).

Lotte Hahm's visibility across categories of gender and sexuality reflects the shifting, imprecise boundaries between different groups and identities in this period. More pointedly, her identity as a woman – suggested by the fact that she appears in a magazine aimed at lesbians – reflects the gendered difference in these categories. Just as women who dressed as men were more socially accepted than men who dressed as women, it could often seem easier and less threatening to apply more fluid conceptions of gender or sexuality to women than to men. This was not the case, however, after the Nazis came to power. In 1933 Hahm was denounced by the father of her girlfriend for seducing a minor and sentenced to prison. In 1935, she was transferred to a concentration camp for women and released no earlier than 1938. She continued her activism after the Second World War and died in 1958.[1]

FIGURE 2.4: Lotte Hahm in *Das 3. Geschlecht*, 1930. "'Hooray !!! The Girlfriend is here again !!!.' 'The Girlfriend' is the up-to-date magazine for women who love women as well as for transvestites. Price 20 cents, available everywhere."

Dieser weibliche Transvestit ist „Lotte Hahm",
Leiterin der Transvestiten, Abteilung
des Damenklub „Violetta"

FIGURE 2.5: Lotte Hahm in *Das 3. Geschlecht*, 1930.
"This female transvestite is 'Lotte Hahm,' director of the
transvestite section of the women's club 'Violetta'"

FIGURE 2.6: "Elegant female transvestite living entirely as a
man" and "Woman as man," *Das 3. Geschlecht*, 1930.

Eleganter weiblicher Transvestit völlig als Mann lebend

Die Frau als Mann

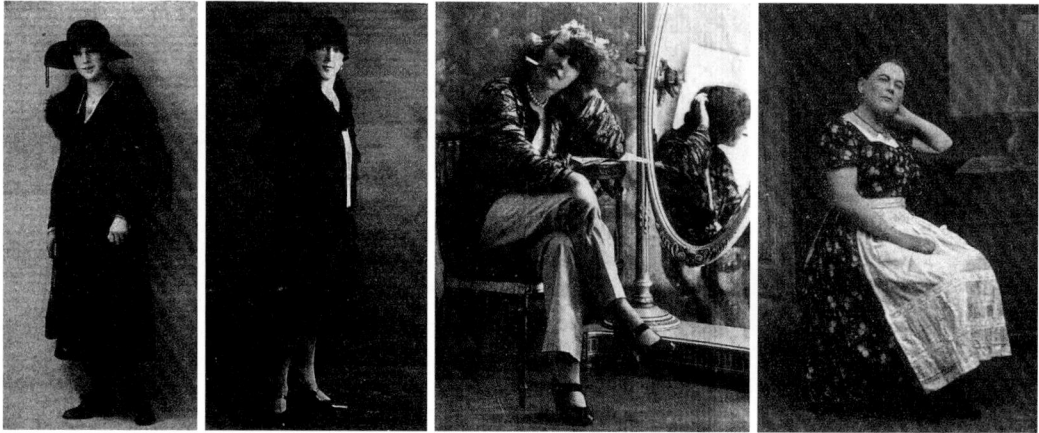

FIGURE 2.7: Four private photos from issue 1: "Male transvestite who goes out inconspicuously in public as a woman," "Male transvestite living as a woman," "Female transvestite hindered by her social position from living in public as a man," and "Male transvestite who attracts attention as a woman because of his body's shape and thus lives as a woman." *Das 3. Geschlecht* 1 (1930): 13, 17, and 31.

that transvestites do not only wear the clothing of the other sex as artists, [and] the images of transvestites from daily life are refreshing. Transvestites in their domestic clothing as they are trying to approach their feminine ideal."[28] Such direct reactions to the illustration practices of the magazine were only common from male transvestites: female transvestites, meaning women who preferred to wear men's clothing, were far less likely to write in. The share of images and texts representing them successively decrease, even though the magazine was conceived to equally appeal to both male and female transvestites.

As I have demonstrated, Hirschfeld and Goldmann provided evidence that even at the beginning of transvestite self-organization, before the First World War, there were fundamental differences between the heterosexual and homosexual factions of male transvestites that would prove impossible to overcome. (Such tensions

did not exist among groups of female transvestites.) Although working out these tensions could have made it possible to join forces, homosexual and heterosexual male transvestites in the Weimar period actively cultivated strife, as is vividly apparent from numerous statements in the letters and texts published in *Das 3. Geschlecht*.

In extant documents, we find no voices of heterosexual female transvestites. For this reason, we cannot say if there were any such tensions amongst female transvestites at all.[29] It is apparent from letters sent in by readers that homosexual male and female transvestites more strongly gravitated toward homosexual subcultures and publications – from which heterosexual male transvestites attempted to keep a strict distance. Or to put it another way, for homosexual male and female transvestites, sexual preference ranked higher in sociability than clothing preference. Consequently, the number of their image and text contributions sank, which is why *Das 3. Geschlecht* increasingly represented only the heterosexual male fraction of transvestites.

Visual Practices

The significance of the illustrations for these readers is also evident in how they used the images. For some readers, the photos developed a life of their own, as the following letter from a transvestite demonstrates: "I cut out the pictures from the last issue and now always carry them with me. The photos of the two Parisian women and the other two transvestites living as women are especially beautiful" (see figure 2.8).[30] Perhaps these photos also provided the "transvestite from the provinces," as this letter writer described themselves, as a comfort in times during which they were prevented from wearing the women's clothing that they loved in their professional life or at home. Or perhaps they represented a memory of past time spent in a big city or in Paris? In any case, this person wanted to be able to consider the cut-out photos in quiet seclusion. Perhaps the physical contact with the photos also gave them a pleasant, possibly erotic feeling, so to speak as a replacement for the articles of clothing they were forced to forgo, or because they were physically close to this person's ideal of beauty.

Evidently, the knowledge of the constant physical availability of these cut-out photos has the effect here of self-affirmation and self-reinforcement, which made it easier to cope with everyday life.

FIGURE 2.8: "Parisian male transvestites living as women." *Das 3. Geschlecht* 1 (1930): 13.

Another transvestite writes that they had "long collected essays from newspapers and magazines and photos from illustrated newsletters and magazines that are somehow related to our cause [*Sache*], transvestitism."[31] They believed this photo album to be a private archive, a "collection of great documentary value," and had organized it into three categories:

"nice little pictures," "women in pants," and "men in dresses."³² This practice of collecting and ordering images can be viewed as equivalent to how private photos of close or distant relatives are collected. This comparison allows us to argue that the collector's album of published photos was actually the creation of an equally imaginary yet illustrious circle of kinship, which perhaps gave them a certain sense of belonging and that helped them to achieve personal affirmation.

Editing and Captioning the Images

But individual appropriation is not the only way to view the images in *Das 3. Geschlecht*. We must also determine how the photos were staged and thus charged with specific meaning through their size and placement and how they were edited and captioned, for the publishers edited both the written contributions and the private images that readers sent to them. Many of them were cropped along the silhouette of the body. Sometimes this meant that the ends of the feet, parts of the head or its covering, dress sleeves or hems, elbows, or hands were cut off. This was especially true for photographs that were assembled into visual collages, as was central to the practice of photocollage in the 1920s. In these cases, the editors usually completely disregarded the original arrangements or overall staging of the photos, concentrating instead on details connected with these persons' bodies. This makes the photos seem decontextualized and deframed. The only thing that remains visible is the staging of their clothing and fashion accessories, their bodily comportment, gestures, hairstyles, and facial expressions (see figure 2.9).

Because of the way the photo on the left in the collage in figure 2.9 was cut, the overall staging of what is likely a cleaning woman can only be guessed at because of the headscarf tied round this person's head. This contrasts with the black stockings and pumps worn by the same person in the image on the right, where we see a person dressed to go out, wearing a Basque cap, in front of the same background. In the same way, the middle photograph in the triptych depicts another transvestite as a modern woman with a bob haircut (*neue Frau*) and gives us no sense of the surroundings. Only the corner of a bright tablecloth that protrudes into the left of the image, together with the resulting shadow, suggest the situation in which the image was made. The caption to the collage and the single photo next to it reads: "four male transvestites who know how to dress inconspicuously."

Just a few pages later, another triptych presents photographs of the same person in three different scenes (see figure 2.10).

On the left, the person appears in a relaxed pose, smiling into the camera, sitting in a summer house dress with legs resting on the handle of a basket – although the poor quality of the reproduction makes it impossible to tell if they are wearing a head covering or not. The image creates a strong contrast between the large dark shoes and the knee-high white stockings and between the bright dress against a shabby brick wall. In the middle of the triptych, we see a person standing in a somewhat formal pose with a serious face

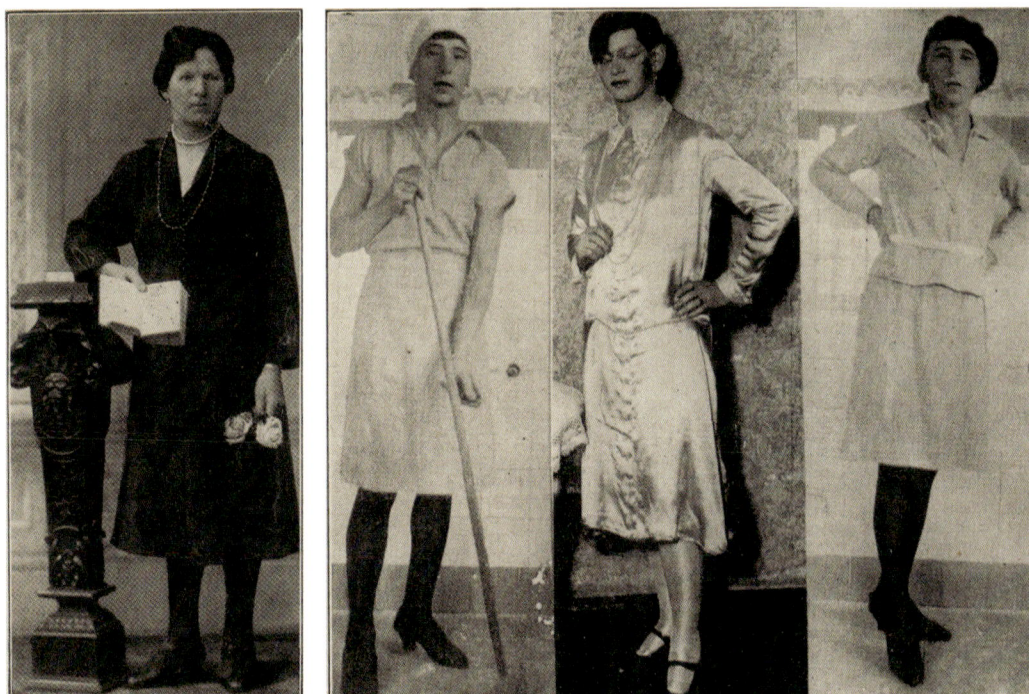

FIGURE 2.9: "4 male transvestites who know how to dress inconspicuously." *Das 3. Geschlecht* 2 (1930): 24.

and dressed up to go out; they are carrying a handbag and wearing a hat (from which the top edge has been cut off), a necklace, and elegant white strap shoes. The neutral background, which creates a spartan effect, does not reveal any details at all, nor does the next photo. The far right of the triptych displays a smaller, asymmetrically cropped photo of the same person (with the same hat), this time equipped for a walk in bad weather wearing a rain jacket (out from under which a checkered skirt peeks) and with an umbrella in their arm. The editors comment upon this collage by captioning it, without any further justification: "Male transvestites as they actually should not dress."

In contrast to these criticized scenes, the photo directly adjacent is captioned: "A well-dressed male transvestite." If the missing feet are any indication, this photo is also likely to have been cropped from a larger photo. Because of the broad posture and the comparatively large area of space the photo opens up, however, it is possible to recognize more details of the arrangement, which is quite conventional. This photo was even considered worthy of being reproduced as a positive example, in a significantly larger size, dominating an entire page opposite the collage. What stands out are the bourgeois attributes in the decor and clothing, even though this person does not really appear any more convincing in

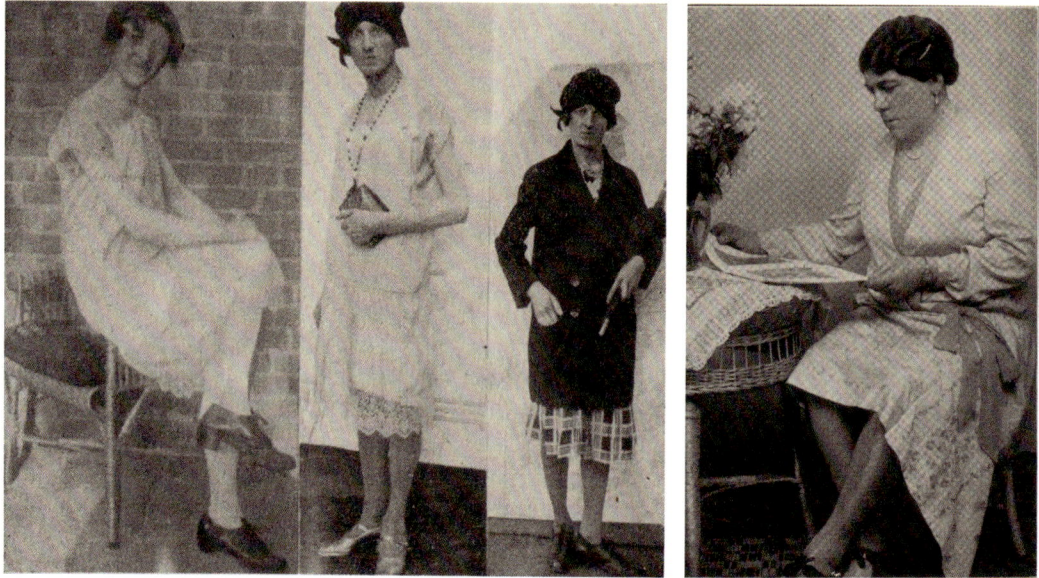

FIGURE 2.10: "Male transvestites as they actually shouldn't dress," and "A well-dressed male transvestite," from *Das 3. Geschlecht* 2 (1930): 31.

their staging of femininity than the one in the adjacent collage. For this reason, the difference between the photographs judged to have been "successful" or "not successful" appears to lie less in the question of whether the subjects were able to convincingly stage their femininity and more in the embodiment of different social styles of clothing. It is difficult, for instance, to see how the performance of femininity succeeds any better in the photograph of a male transvestite whom the editors describe as "well-dressed" on the right. The important difference between what is endorsed in *Das 3. Geschlecht* and what is criticized seems to have been determined on the basis of the different social milieus that the clothing choices represent. Bourgeois respectability was given preference over the plain clothing style of the "simple woman."

The judgemental commentary accompanying both photo collages makes clear the risks that individuals faced when they sent in their private photos. On the one hand, in contrast to the authors of the text contributions, these individuals could not hide behind pseudonyms. Their faces are clearly identifiable, even if they are not named or did not want to be named. In this sense, we can speak of the paradox of an anonymized outing. Sending in the photos was especially bold inasmuch as the individuals they depicted put themselves at the mercy of the editors and, in the case of publication, of readers.

The publication of private photos in *Das 3. Geschlecht* represented a form of going public in which an invisible interlocutor passed judgement on the success of the staging and performance. The editors expressed their judgements in commentaries that steer the readers' opinion. The extent to which those who sent in the photos consented to these appraisals and whether or not they aligned with those of readers remains unknown. But the negative judgements implicit in captions describing supposedly unsuccessful stagings certainly must have been problematic for these individuals, who must have hoped that the editors would provide positive affirmations of their presentation. The work that went into staging the photo shooting, the courage of presenting oneself to the photographer (an act that we might view as an open confession), and the decision to send in the photos for publication – none of these things were rewarded. Even worse, the person who submitted them was exposed and unprotected; their visible face opened them up to ridicule. This must have been humiliating. Hence the publication of these images must have been less likely to produce visual self-affirmation and more likely to fuel self-doubt (see figures 2.9 and 2.10).

Overall, the editorial captions appear less oriented toward judging whether these individuals really had succeeded in staging themselves more or less successfully as members of the sex they wished to present. Rather, the point seems to have been to judge whether the individuals depicted were "conspicuous" or "inconspicuous" in their self-presentation – whether they appeared "serious" or "fashionable" or simply "plain" and "ordinary." This differentiating evaluation is also prominent in the text contributions. Successful displays of bourgeois respectability, aesthetic balance, and professional success played a decisive

part in these judgements and were what produced a positive evaluation. In this regard, the image captions originated from a certain culturally and socially normative perspective. They served to sharpen the awareness of fashion in transvestite readers, to educate their taste, and to increase their stylistic confidence. That this was an area of specific concern amongst readers is clear in their letters to the editor: How should a "decent" transvestite dress and behave? This and similar questions were at the centre of debates published in *Das 3. Geschlecht*. In this regard, the image captions are representative of the broader discussions around self-image that were taking place between transvestites. We must also consider that the editors likely consisted of only homosexual men and women from the lower middle-classes, meaning members of a petit-bourgeois milieu,[33] who applied their own set of values in choosing, editing, and evaluating the images. Although cooperation with transvestites is mentioned many times, we have no evidence that any transvestites actually cooperated directly with the editors. In this sense, the published commentary mainly reflected the views of a certain social milieu.

Regardless of the discrepancy between the composition and interests of the editors, on the one hand, and the readers, on the other, looking at the self-images we find in *Das 3. Geschlecht*, we can postulate a difference between the texts and the photos that were submitted. Whereas the text contributions almost all speak about successful passing – the convincing performance in public as members of the opposite sex – the images illustrate how

FIGURE 2.11: "Male transvestite who goes out inconspicuously in public," "Inconspicuous male transvestites at home and on the street," and "Male transvestite on the street." *Das 3. Geschlecht* 1 (1930): 13; 3 (1931): 24; and 5 (1932): 31.

precarious this staging could be (see figure 2.11).

In comparison to today, there was a much more intense focus on maintaining norms of dress amongst the general population but particularly for authorities charged with keeping order, such as the police. Persons who stood out for wearing clothing of the opposite sex in public were generally charged with causing a public nuisance or with gross mischief. For this reason, Magnus Hirschfeld persuaded the police to issue so-called "transvestite passes," a practice that began in 1909 and then became widespread in the Weimar Republic. Issued on the basis of an expert diagnosis of transvestitism, this document was intended to protect transvestites from arrest.[34] We can therefore assume that the stories readers told the magazine about their direct experiences with appearing inconspicuous in public corresponded more

to fantasy than to reality, especially since only a very few of the published photos they had submitted appeared to have been taken in public. Sometimes photos described as street scenes turn out, upon closer inspection, to have been produced in a studio.[35]

The fact that passing appears to have been rare is highlighted in the letter of a person who calls themself "Transvestite Grete M.," according to whom "a vanishingly small number appear truly decent and inconspicuous." Grete warns that whoever is "in the fortunate situation of being able to live and present according to their true nature should significantly limit their appearance in public … unless they belong to the few able to appear as they are trying to be."[36]

In contrast to the frequently proclaimed need for unlimited visibility in public and for like-minded transvestites to join together, the illustration practice of *Das 3. Geschlecht* is actually evidence for the extreme social isolation of transvestites in this era. There is no photographic evidence of common activities or social gatherings, whether in public or in private, an impression that is reinforced in the editorial cropping and arrangement of images. We see the transvestites primarily as isolated individuals who stick out. From the texts it is clear that they lived out their passion within the protection of their own homes, in the company of close friends and closed private circles and occasionally with their wives. This self-limitation of heterosexual male transvestites to private spaces corresponds to the prevailing confinement of women to the domestic sphere during this period, and it is consistent with the magazine's general message that "true" transvestites should carry out female occupations in the household.

There is only one photo in the magazine, of two "male transvestites" wearing modern clothing and standing in a relaxed pose, that presents an urban scene on a public street. It is captioned "Parisian male transvestites living as women" (see figure 2.8). However, before this photo was published in *Das. 3 Geschlecht*, it had already been used twice as the cover image for *Die Freundin*, and given the stylish outfits of the figures, it is possible that it came from a fashion magazine. When it was first published in *Die Freundin*, a magazine addressed to lesbian readers, the same photo was given the caption "Girlfriends."[37] This image migration from the lesbian to the transvestite magazine is thus a case of relabelling: while the figures

were first presented as lesbian women, in *Das 3. Geschlecht* they are described as men wearing women's clothing.[38] It is possible that the reason for this repeated usage of the same photo was an initial lack of fashionable images available for publication, forcing the magazine to resort to simple tricks. But since this photo had been published in three successive years with the different ascriptions, and since the readers of *Das 3. Geschlecht* may have also been familiar with the special supplement for transvestites in *Die Freundin*, we can assume that at least some of them noticed the game of deceptive captioning.

And yet this photo is one of the very few in which the figures (assuming they were men) appear to successfully pass, which is of course unsurprising if they were actually women. The reader, mentioned above, who cut the image out of the magazine and constantly carried it around with them found the picture so appealing because of the figures' fashionable appearance and perfect feminine staging. Perhaps this person was familiar with the earlier instances in which the image had been used and saw through the trick, or perhaps it was exactly this uncertainty that excited them?

Unlike most other images in the magazine, this one is given a concrete location in the caption. Yet there are actually no points of reference in the background of the image that would allow the location to be identified. By mentioning only a few cities such as Berlin, Paris, and New York – three metropolises of fashion and modernity – the editors localize transvestitism as a primarily big-city phenomenon, while the text contributions

Voo-Doo

Some trans individuals during the
Weimar period in Germany attempted
suicide, and doctors at the time often
interpreted these attempts as signs of
how seriously these individuals desired
to change their sex. Doctors also cited
these attempts as justification for
medical treatment such as castration.
This distinguished the understanding
of suicide for trans individuals
from its use in the context of early
homosexual movements, where tragic
suicides were framed as evidence
for the strength of social stigma and
the ruinous effects that came with
being known as homosexual.[1] Both
interpretations of suicide, however,
influenced Hirschfeld's depictions of a
"young transvestite Willy Pape" in the
illustrated volume to *Die Transvestiten*.

    We do not know if "this young
transvestite" consented to having
either their name or their attempted
suicide revealed. Both facts could
have been damaging to the public
reputation of the person depicted here,
especially since they reveal a hidden
past that – as Hirschfeld's caption
tells us – this "young transvestite" had
explicitly attempted to move beyond in
taking a new identity. The image also
does not tell us whether this identity
was something lived only on stage, or
whether this person also lived in public
as a woman or in another gender
identity different from the male identity
assigned to them at birth. Indeed,
the person depicted here was more

Tafel XVI

Der junge Trans-
vestit Willy Pape,
dessen Veranlagung
durch einen Selbst-
mordversuch in
Frauenkleidern
bekannt wurde. Seine
Eltern wurden vom
Verfasser über seinen
eigenartigen Zustand
aufgeklärt und ge-
statteten ihm dann,
zum Varieté zu gehen,
wo er seitdem mit
größtem Erfolge als
Schlangentänzerin
auftritt.

Figure 2.12: Willy Pape in the illustrated volume of Magnus
Hirschfeld's *Die Transvestiten*, 1912. "The young transvestite Willy
Pape, whose inclination became known when he attempted to commit
suicide in women's clothing. His parents received education about his
unique condition and then allowed him to go to the varieté, where he
has since appeared with the greatest success as a snake dancer."

849

Der Transvestit
Voo-Doo, einer
der bekanntesten
internationalen
Tanzsterne

(Photo
Gerlach)

FIGURE 2.13, 2.14 and 2.15:
Voo-Doo as a snake dancer
in Magnus Hirschfeld's
Geschlechtskunde, 1930;
Die Insel (aimed at gay
men), 1927 (caption:
"The transvestite Voo-
Doo, one of the most
internationally well-known
stars of dance"); and *Das
3. Geschlecht.* (caption:
"The dance phenomenon
who has achieved world
success as a woman in his
snake-dances").

Voo-Doo

*Das Tanzphänomen, der als Frau
in seinen Schlangentänzen einen
Welterfolg erzielte.*

widely known in public as the performer
Voo-Doo.[2] But we do not know how they
were called in their private life or in public
when not on stage.

The figure of a snake that sheds its
skin is a powerful motif for imagining
gender transition. We find Voo-Doo in this
role in a range of images from Hirschfeld's
publications and popular magazines
nearly twenty years later (figures 2.13
and 2.14). And this is a theme that also
appears elsewhere in *Das 3. Geschlecht*
(figure 2.15). The figure of a male-bodied
individual performing "snake dances" as
a woman is highly overdetermined, to say
the least. For one thing, it plays to Biblical

Michael Thomas Taylor and Rainer Herrn   53

Schlangentänzerin, von hervorragender körperlicher Gewandtheit, in elegantem Kostüm

FIGURE 2.16: "Snake dancer of exceptional bodily grace in an elegant costume." *Das 3. Geschlecht*, 1931.

Männlicher Artist, der als „Orientalische Tänzerin" Weltruf genießt

FIGURE 2.17: "Male Artist, who enjoys a worldwide reputation as an 'oriental dancer.'" *Das 3. Geschlecht*, 1931.

stories of original sin. Lucifer seducing Eve and Eve convincing Adam to partake of the forbidden fruit are obvious points of reference. Here, the transgressive potential of the seduction and the knowledge it might reveal – knowing both in a carnal sense and as a new awareness about the world – are heightened by the gender play. Seen in the context of its time, another aspect of the image is particularly prominent: Orientalist motifs that were associated with sexuality and eroticism. This is a motif repeated in other images printed in the magazines we are examining here, which reflects roles and performances common on stage at the time.

To be sure, such associations take us beyond what we concretely know about Voo-Doo's life story into the realm of imagination, fantasy, and mythology. Stage performances and images like these are liable to become screens for our own projections precisely because they do not convey real knowledge about real individuals' lives. And as is apparent from looking at how these images were used in publications, we see that more often than not they become screens for the projections of editors, scientists, doctors – and readers, too.

We also find Voo-Doo – without birth name – in Hirschfeld's *Geschlechtskunde*, published in 1930, but in an entirely different form (figures 2.18 and 2.19).

Several things are salient about these later images. We are provided with the stage name of the figure they

FIGURE 2.18: "Expressive drawing by Voo-Doo (compare photos opposite)." Hirschfeld, *Geschlechtskunde*, 1930.

FIGURE 2.19: "Feminine form of expression of the same person in dance".

depict, for one. Even more important is the fact that Hirschfeld combines this photograph with a drawing attributed to Voo-Doo and that both are described as "expressive." Voo-Doo's body, like Voo-Doo's art and Voo-Doo's clothing, are all depicted as expressions of their inner life and personality. And next to the photograph, the artistic drawing depicts a self that is psychologically richer, more fully alive, and more colourful. The drawing can moreover be read as a revelation precisely because of its juxtaposition to a self who is more fully clothed – but of course this is a revelation of a gendered identity that is more complex than the female figure depicted in the photograph. At the same time, a closer look at the photograph shows that it, too, has been altered: Voo-Doo's body has been retouched narrow their waist and exaggerate the snake-like curves of their dance.

FIGURE 2.20: Cover pages of all five issues of *Das 3. Geschlecht*.

are more likely to depict the "provinces" as places of refuge and recovery. In agreement with the self-image of transvestites as big city dwellers, there are only very few images of transvestites in rural settings, let alone in rural work clothing.[39]

Visual Rhetorics

There is another way in which playing with the images and attributions seems to represent a conscious decision about how to use images in *Das 3. Geschlecht*, as the cover photos make particularly clear. In contrast to the majority of illustrations in the inside pages, the cover photos advertise the magazine with explicitly erotic stagings of femininity. The clearly visible, well-formed breasts of the exotic cover girls in issues 1 to 3 seem to place these figures outside of any kind of gender ambiguity (see figure 2.20). Inside the magazine, however, the femininity of these figures was made more ambiguous. Here the images

were reprinted with captions calling our perception of femininity into question. The effect is almost absurd, because the captions so obviously contradict the visual evidence (see figure 2.21), particularly at a time when plastic surgery techniques had not advanced to point of being able to produce such perfect breasts. For example, the Egyptian dancer posing with what can only be viewed as a blatantly obvious phallus symbol in issue 1 is presented inside the magazine as a "hermaphrodite." The figure dressed as an attractive revue dancer on the cover of issue 2 is presented with a caption that asks: "Woman or Man??" – as if there could be any doubt about the figure's unambiguous sex. In a combination of the gender irritations found in issues 1 and 2, issue 3 adds a caption to its cover girl: "Hermaphrodite? Woman? or Man?" On the cover of issue 4, we see the back side of a nude figure with a cloth draped over their shoulders like a drape or a veil. What stands out is the graceful posture together

with the somewhat affected position of the fingers in the opened hands. The lighting gently underscores the feminine contours of the hips and shoulders, while the hairstyle and jewelry reinforce the unambiguous gendering. Within the issue itself, the same image now appears with a caption pointing to the supposedly "true" sex: "Nude figure of a male transvestite from behind." This is the only issue with a cover page depicting a person who is then explicitly described as a transvestite inside the issue.

On the cover of issue 5, by contrast, we see a woman posing half-naked from the side who is putting on boots, a pose that is vaguely reminiscent of sadomasochistic staging. The genitals and breasts are hidden by the pose. A glance in the slightly tilted hand mirror lying on the bootjack is perhaps intended to arouse viewer's voyeuristic interest in unambiguously determining the figure's sex. But the image's caption inside the issue leaves the question of the figure's apparently evident sex up to the beholder to decide: "Woman or man?" The photo seems to be modelled on the pose that Marlene Dietrich made famous in the 1930 film *The Blue Angel* when she lasciviously sits on top of a barrel on the stage to sing the line: "From head to toe, I'm ready for love." Perhaps the caption is to be read as an allusion to the ambivalence of Dietrich's sex appeal, which had an effect on both sexes?

We can only speculate about the reasons why this image was made more enigmatic inside the magazine. Perhaps this was the editors' strategy to legitimize the decision to print erotic photos on the cover. In any case, it was not a self-evident choice for a magazine that was sold openly on the street to have such cover images.[40] At the same time, with their references to the number of images inside the magazine, these covers and their layouts make a promise about the magazine's contents that is not fulfilled inside the pages.

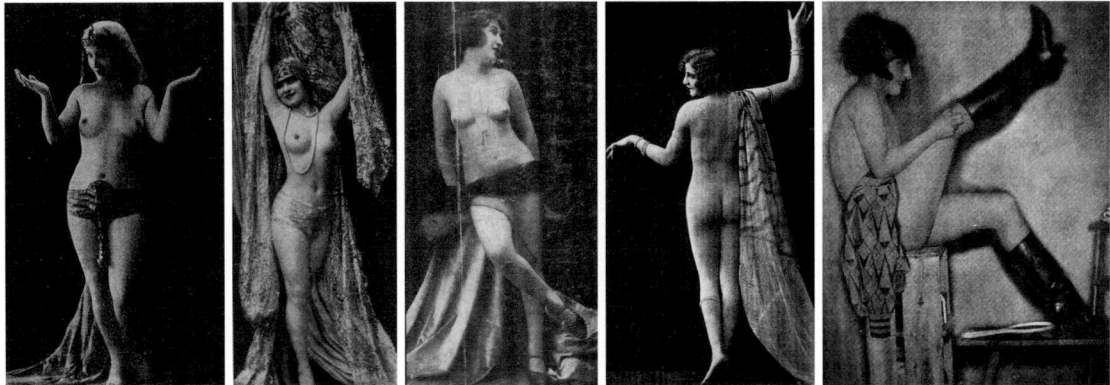

FIGURE 2.21, The same cover girls inside the magazine: "Hermaphrodite," "Woman or man??," "Hermaphrodite?," Woman or man?," "Nude figure of a male transvestite from behind," and "Woman or man"? from *Das 3. Geschlecht* 1 (1930): 27; 2 (1930): 17; 3 (1931): 17; 4 (1931): 23; and 5 (1932): 30.

These speculations aside, this play with gender had a history. The strategy was introduced by Magnus Hirschfeld, who in 1904 already presented images of the Chevalier d'Éon in women's clothing and men's clothing, at a conference of German natural scientists and physicians. The chevalier, of whom you can find an image in the gallery devoted to "Gender Play," was an eighteenth-century French aristocrat, soldier, and spy who later lived as a woman and who had become an icon for the transvestite movement by the early twentieth century. Hirschfeld asked his colleagues to answer the question – "Man or woman?" – to prove that people whom he categorized as "sexual intermediary stages" could be equally convincing in the clothing of either sex.[41] In *Die Insel*, Radszuweit transformed this practice into a popular quiz with a "prize question, homo- or heterosexual?" Photos of men and women, in both female and male clothing, were presented under this question, and readers were asked to identify the homosexuals.[42] What is notable in this photo collage is the arrangement of images and their visual language. Above a row of four bust portraits of young men in inconspicuous, solidly bourgeois outfits, and for whom it was presumably not possible to immediately determine their sexual orientation, the editors place a young man with a clearly homosexual appearance; he is wearing women's clothing and assumes an affected pose (grasping for her pearls, as it were), which functions in this context as a negative antitype. Beneath the row of four images, we see a young woman in riding clothes with a hat and a raised whip.[43]

This and other collages of images in *Die Insel* rely on the same canon of bourgeois values of conspicuous/inconspicuous self-presentation while also reflecting the conventional assumption against which heterosexual transvestites were fighting, namely that men who wear women's clothing and women who wear men's clothing were all homosexual. Whether the editors intended this or not, the visual subtexts in *Die Insel* and *Das 3. Geschlecht* are similarly ambivalent.

Gender Play

Hirschfeld's first scientific book, *Geschlechts-Übergänge* (Sexual transitions) elaborated his thesis that the gender of each person was a unique combination of masculine and feminine traits. Hirschfeld took the motto for his book, printed prominently on its front cover, from the German philosopher and inventor of calculus, Gottfried Wilhelm Leibniz (1646–1716), who famously said that "Everything in nature comes in degrees and not in leaps."[1]

Writing about a juxtaposition of two photos in this book captioned "Mann oder Weib?" (man or woman), Kathrin Peters concludes that "gender/ sex [*Geschlecht*] exists as a riddle and not as a solution; nothing about it is simply visible – always already given."[2]

Despite Hirschfeld's intentions of illustrating sexual diversity, the fact that he and others located *Geschlecht* in and on the body is what fuels the expectation that the truth of these figures' *Geschlecht* might lie, ready to be revealed, beneath their clothing. Yet as Peters argues, these images are also evidence of an idea central to contemporary gender studies: that clothing might produce gender identity, not just express it or allow it to be seen.

Hirschfeld plays the same game with other images, such as the depictions of the Chevalier D'Éon – a seminal figure for emerging transvestite movements in Europe.

FIGURE 2.22: Plate 39: "Man or woman?" Magnus Hirschfeld, *Geschlechts-Übergänge*, 1905.

But a key point in D'Éon's biography was that he/she was known as a spy – a master of disguise. Here, too, clothing hides rather than reveals *Geschlecht*.

Hirschfeld's locating of *Geschlecht* in/on the body becomes more explicit in other photos from this same volume that he takes from the German photographer Wilhelm von Gloeden, who often photographed nude Sicilian youth. Although the story of the person represented in figure 2.24 is not told in *Geschlechts-Übergänge*, we know from other sources that he lost his genitals in combat.[3] His presence here is thus somewhat jarring in the context of Hirschfeld's natural-scientific argumentation, although this fact remains hidden. It also

Tafel XXVIII.

68.   69.

70.

Mann oder Weib?

FIGURE 2.23: Plate 28: "Man or woman?" Unnamed images of the Chevalier D'Éon, Magnus Hirschfeld, *Geschlechts-Übergänge*, 1905.

points to the crucial role that warfare played in the development of plastic and reconstructive surgery. These techniques were perfected during the First World War and were then adapted for use in gender-affirming surgeries in the 1920s. The First World War in particular had paradoxical effects on popular conceptions of gender difference; the many wounded soldiers and the German defeat produced fears that masculinity was

in crisis while also fostering a popular culture more open to the idea that the boundary between genders was permeable.

Moreover, it is precisely in the use of von Gloeden's photographs that we can see how medical authorities turned to neo-classical aesthetics to construct ideally "feminine" bodies as a new norm for new nonbinary conceptions of gender that replaced earlier notions of monstrosity or hermaphroditism.

After the First World War, as gender play became more generally

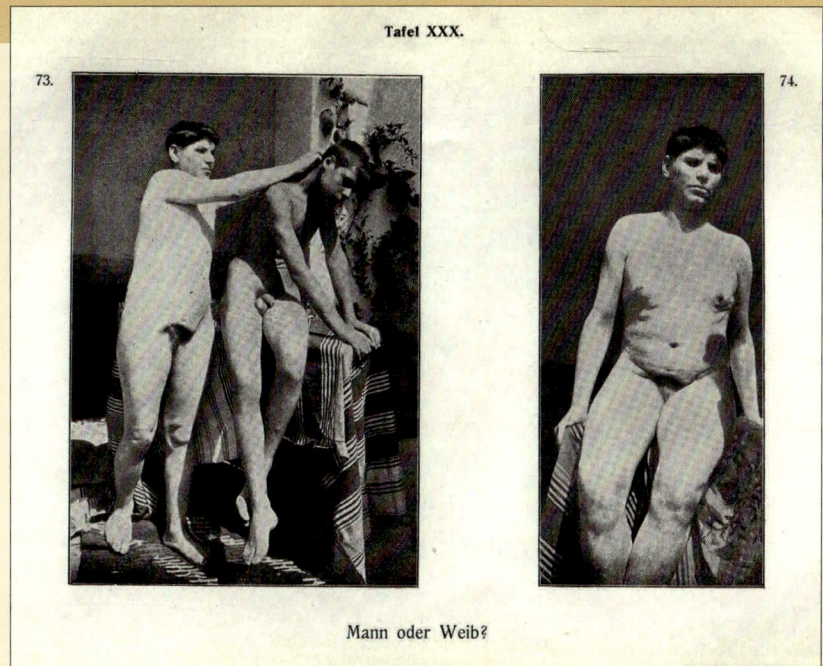

FIGURE 2.24: Plate 30: "Man or woman?" Magnus Hirschfeld, *Geschlechts-Übergänge*, 1905.

FIGURE 2.25: "Prize question: ??Man or woman??" *Die Insel*, 2, 1927.

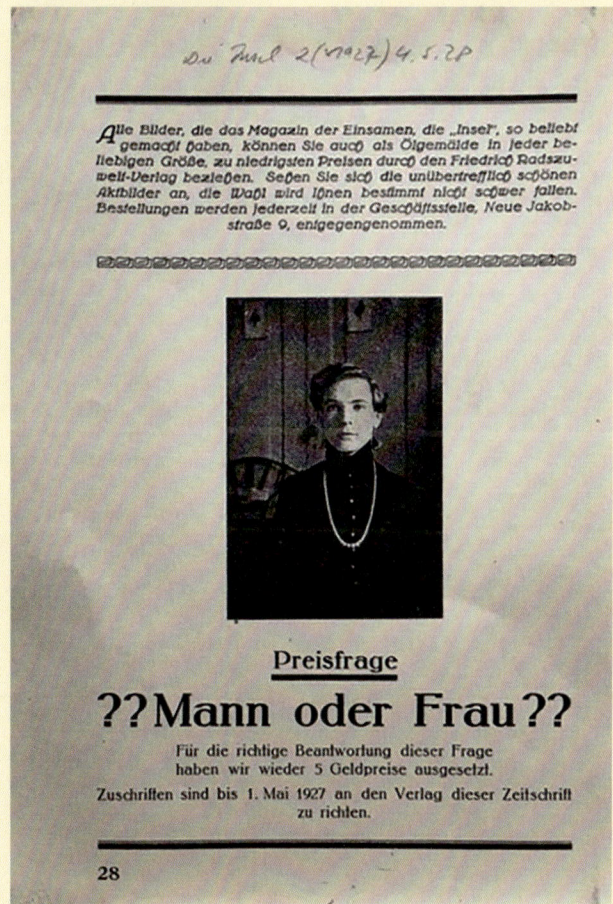

widespread and acceptable in popular culture, the same gestures appear in popular publications, such as the magazine *Das 3. Geschlecht* (figure 2.25).

To see how this gender play could also be celebrated in a theatrical context, one can examine a selection of images of the same figure – the theatrical performer Hansi Sturm – from across a range of publications (figure 2.26).

As Rainer points out, readers of *Das 3. Geschlecht* complained about the preponderance of theatrical figures in public representations of transvestitism. These complaints likely also reflected the wider social prejudice that nonconforming gender identity was indeed a matter of acting and performing – with the unspoken assumption that cis-bodied binary gender identity was natural, genuine, and authentic.

Die Insel 1 (1926) 2.1.16

Hansi Sturm

der jugendliche, ebenso be-
kannte wie beliebte Damen-
darsteller, dessen Auftreten
in vielen deutschen Städten
Aufsehen erregte, gastiert zur
Zeit mit großem Erfolg in
Magdeburg.

Unsere Bilder

zeigen den begabten elegan-
ten Schauspieler als Herr
und Dame.

16

Die Welt der Transvestiten
(Sonderteil der Zeitschrift „Die Freundin")

Die sexuelle Uranlage ist bei beiden Geschlech-
tern ein und dieselbe, d. h. das männliche und das
weibliche Geschlecht hat sich aus Organen, welche
beide Geschlechter gemeinsam haben, entwickelt.
Nach den neuesten Forschungen sind z. B. die
Sexualanlagen bei acht Wochen alten menschlichen
Embryos dieselben, und erst in der folgenden Zeit
beginnt die Entwicklung nach der männlichen oder
weiblichen Seite.

Jedenfalls ist es eine unleugbare Tatsache, daß
der Mann neben seinen spezifischen männlichen Organen auch die weiblichen Merkmale besitzt, und
daß die Frau auch die männlichen Organe hat. Jeder
Mann, selbst der normalste, hat immer etwas vom
Weibe und das Weib immer etwas vom Manne. Dadurch ist aber schon bewiesen, daß jeder Mensch,
gleichviel ob Weib oder Mann, in mehr oder weniger
entwickelter Form beide Geschlechter in sich ver-
eint und daß es demnach keinen absoluten Mann
und kein absolutes Weib geben kann.*)

Erst die Mischung und das Mischungsverhält-
nis der verschiedenen sexuellen Merkmale bestimmt
den Sexualcharakter des Menschen. Überwiegen die
männlichen Elemente gegenüber den weiblichen, so
bezeichnen wir das Wesen als männlich, im umge-
kehrten Falle als weiblich. Da die Mischung
zwischen dem männlichen und weiblichen Element
sehr verschieden sein kann, so ergeben sich viele

Die Transvestitenfrage / Elly R.

Vor einiger Zeit wurden unter dem Titel: „Ein
Mann erschießt sich im Brautkleid seiner Frau",
zwei Fälle veröffentlicht, in denen die großen Tages-
zeitungen, welche vorher zwei Selbstmorde von
transvestitisch veranlagten Männern ohne jedes
Kommentar brachten, eine weitere Erklärung über

Junger Artist gastiert erfolgreich als Mann und als Frau

kann. Aber ein Arzt kann doch Winke geben, wie der junge
Mensch vor den Gefahren, welche die abnorme Veranlagung für jeden Mann in sich birgt, nach Kräften durch Auf-
klärung, liebevollen Rat und Eingehen in die Interessensphäre
des jungen Menschen gemindert werden kann.

(Der vorstehende Artikel ist dem Buche „Mannweiber und
Weibmänner" entnommen und kann zum Preise von Mk. 2.—
durch den Friedrich Radszuweit-Verlag, Berlin S 14, Neue
Jakobstr. 9, bezogen werden. Redaktion.)

7

FIGURE 2.26: Selection of photos of Hansi Sturm. Left
caption: "Hansi Sturm, the young, equally famous and
beloved female impersonator, whose appearance in
many German cities aroused great interest, is currently
performing in Magdeburg with great success. Our
photos show the talented, elegant actor as a man and a
woman." *Die Insel*, 1926. Caption, above right: "Young
transvestite in female clothing. Young female artist
(female transvestite) who lives in her home entirely as
a man. *Die Freundin*, 1927. Right caption: "A young
visiting artist performing successfully as a man and a
woman." *Das 3. Geschlecht*, 1930.

Visual Effects

And yet the re-depiction of the cover girls inside the pages of *Das 3. Geschlecht* along with irritating captions likely had other effects on the readers, because they are placed directly next to photographs of clothed transvestites. In this way, both their questioning of gender attribution and their eroticizing effects are transferred to the tableaux of photos that surround them, perhaps leading the reader to ask if the same seductive female bodies might not in fact be hidden beneath the clothing of the transvestites.

Why shouldn't the "male transvestite in the countryside," who appears so plain, not have an equally magnificent female body underneath her apron as does the "Revue girl" posing in complete contrast next to her (see figure 2.27)? Or why should this "New York transvestite" with a hat, little bag, blouse, and jacket not be hiding as perfect a body as the bare-breasted neighbouring figure with a pearl necklace (see figure 2.28)?

The possible meaning produced by cross-referencing the photographs placed next to each other in this way is strengthened by a further category of image, namely photos depicting male bodies. As I have noted, the cover image from issue 4 – "Rear view of a male

above FIGURE 2.27: "The male transvestite in the countryside" and "Woman or man?" *Das 3. Geschlecht* 2 (1930): 17.

below FIGURE 2.28: "Hermaphrodite? Woman? or man?" and "A New York transvestite gives us his image for publication." *Das 3. Geschlecht* 3 (1931): 17.

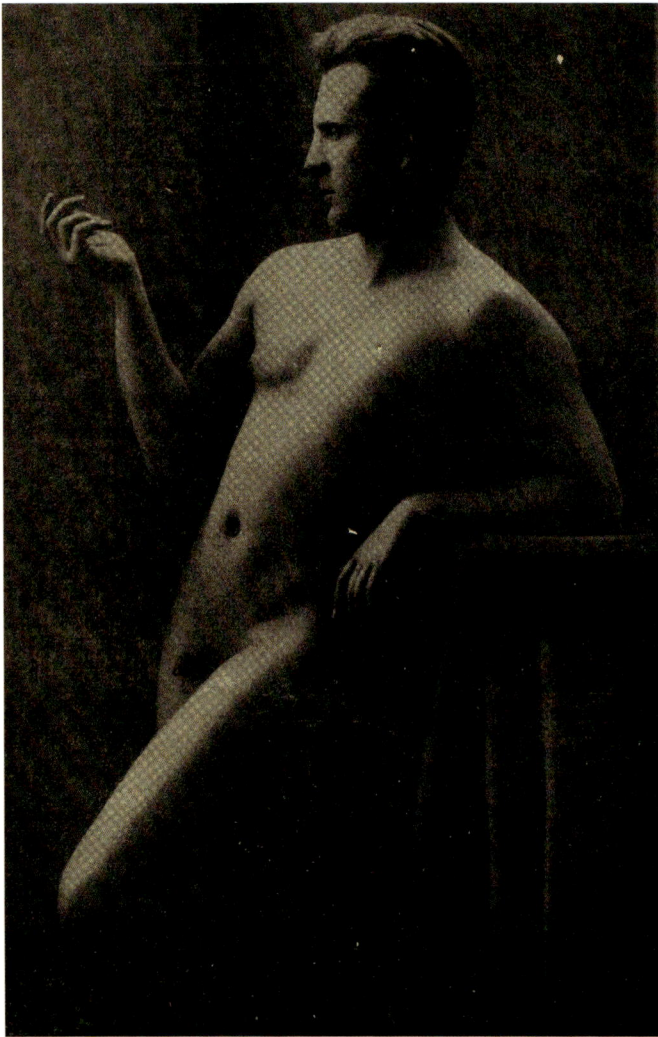

FIGURE 2.29: "Male transvestite with pronounced female bodily forms; note especially the beginnings of a breast." *Das 3. Geschlecht* 3 (1931): 10.

transvestite" – reveals a perfectly embodied femininity, as do the covers of the previous issues. Inside issue 3, however, we find a "male transvestite with pronounced female bodily forms" (see figure 2.29).

Here, the male genitals clearly mark the bodies as male, but other aspects of the image render the bodies feminine: the pose, the lighting on the breast and the hips, and the extensive retouching of the penis (making it less prominent and recognizable)

prompt us to imagine a mixed-gendered body. Rather than emphasizing the incongruity of the male body with the feminine figure, as is common for image practices of the time meant to illustrate sexual difference, the placing of these photos next to images of perfect femininity underscores the similarity of these bodies with those of the women. In all five issues, we find similar photos of naked men with captions that emphasize their subjects' feminine breasts and body forms or what they identify as female facial features (see figure 2.30).

It is worth noting in passing that depicting these supposed transvestites in the nude is itself a further paradox, since transvestitism was at the time defined by the wearing of clothing, and these photos had all been published previously with different captions and ascriptions in the homosexual magazine *Die Insel*. In *Das 3. Geschlecht*, however, they served as illustrative examples of bodily gender-mixing (*körperliche Mischgeschlechtlichkeit*), thus providing visual evidence for the argument that transvestites comprised a physically distinct and yet "natural category of gender" – a "third sex," as Magnus Hirschfeld emphasized again and again.[44] The male nude, which appears so strangely out of place, nevertheless conveys harmonious agreement between the form of the body and the inclination of the figure's soul, which is also reflected in a different way in the private photos of transvestites wearing clothing.

As overwrought as these captions appear, they nevertheless conformed to the vital interests of many male transvestites, namely the desire to move about "inconspicuously" in public or to be a woman. In order to get closer to this goal, some transvestites not only strove to appear feminine in their clothing and habitus but also to have a female bodily form. For this purpose, many underwent "breast injections," as one reader writes, in order to also "appear to be a woman in one's body."[45] In this sense, the visual rhetoric of images that emphasize feminine bodily forms marks a displacement of transvestitism from clothing as a second skin to the first skin of the body. This displacement corresponded to the desires for medical changes of sex that we find documented from 1910 onward.[46] And it points to a further group of individuals who were, at the time, beginning to differentiate themselves from the transvestites: those whom Harry Benjamin and others would later call "transsexuals" and who appear as "total" or "extreme" transvestites in Hirschfeld's sexological writing.[47]

The illustration practice of *Das 3. Geschlecht* gives rise to several considerations that may be of interest to further historical researchers. First, we should note that visual representation plays a special role for strategies in the self-empowerment and self-reassurance of transvestites, a role that is different from that played for members of other sexual and gender minorities. This is the only way to understand why so many individuals submitted their private photos for publication in the magazine. But there have been no other analyses of the image practices in the other magazines addressed to homosexual women and men produced

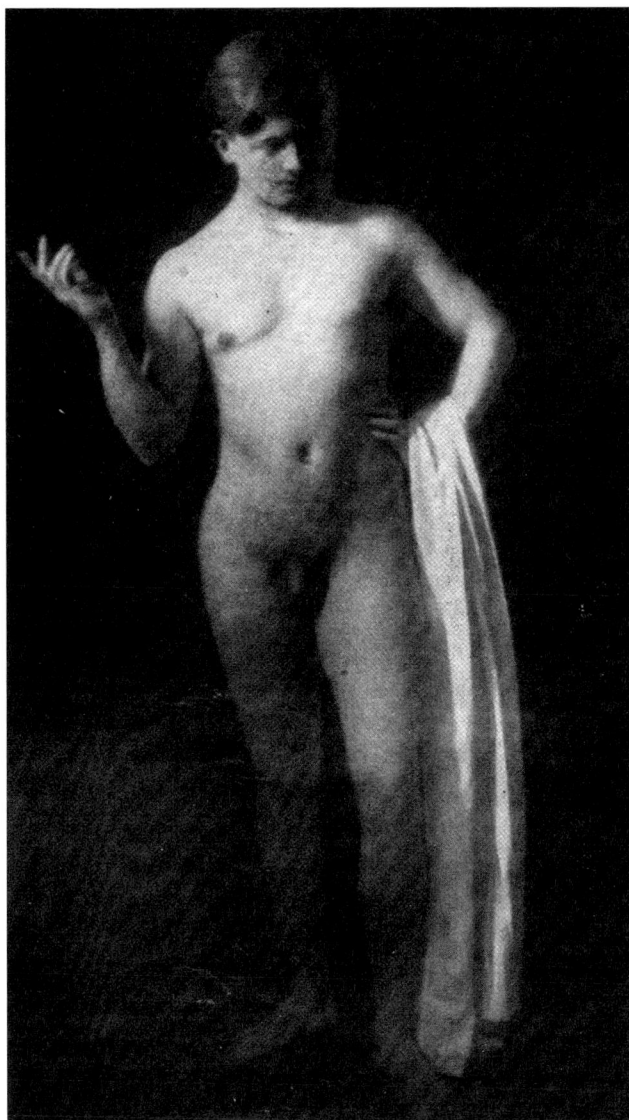

FIGURE 2.30: "Especially note the girl-like face and the female bodily forms." *Das 3. Geschlecht* 2 (1931): 10.

by this or other publishers. In contrast to *Das 3. Geschlecht*, however, we can already say that none of these other publications contain private images sent in by private readers.

It would furthermore be interesting to examine more closely the reasons for the establishment of different factions, divided according to sex and sexual orientation, which eventually determined the conditions for the increasing dominance of self-images of heterosexual transvestites over the course of the magazine's five issues. This would also lead to the overarching historical question of how gender and sexual minorities dealt with each other. In addition to the frictions I have discussed here: were there also groups that valued each other, had common interests, undertook common activities, or showed solidarity with each other? Looking at the clientele in the Institute for Sexual Science, we can say that the interactions between homosexuals, transvestites, and individuals who were intersex was largely determined by existing social norms and structures of prejudice.[48] That Friedrich Radszuweit, a publisher whose magazines were mainly addressed to homosexual men and women, had decided to initiate a transvestite magazine such as *Das 3. Geschlecht* can nevertheless certainly be understood as an act of solidarity. In the end, the significance of commercial interests appears to have been secondary. Even more important than the commercial failure, this project was an unsuccessful attempt on the part of Radszuweit's press to transfer the organizing model of homosexuals to male and female transvestites.

How images migrated between homosexual and transvestite magazines produced by the same publisher, along with the corresponding relabelling of photos, certainly points to a certain permeability of the barriers between these minorities. At the same time, the editors of *Das 3. Geschlecht* largely consisted of homosexual men who chose the images and gave them captions and thus expressed judgements about the staging of heterosexual

transvestite readers. However, this normative commentary ultimately derived from the same petit-bourgeois set of values that also shaped the text contributions written by the transvestites themselves. Seen in this way, the homosexual editors of the magazine operated at the boundary between the production of images representing self-perception and the perception of the self by others.

GALLERY NOTES: Lotte Hahm

1   Information about Lotte Hahm's biography is taken from Jens Dobler, *Vom anderen Ufer: Geschichte der Berliner Lesben und Schwulen in Kreuzberg und Friedrichshain* (Berlin: Bruno Gmünder Verlag GmbH, 2003), 111–16, 228, and 250; Heike Schader, *Virile, Vamps und wilde Veilchen: Sexualität, Begehren und Erotik in den Zeitschriften homosexueller Frauen im Berlin der 1920er Jahre* (Königstein/Taunus: Helmer, 2004), 76–7; and Claudia Schoppmann, *Nationalsozialistische Sexualpolitik und weibliche Homosexualität* (Pfaffenweiler: Centaurus, 1997), 166.

GALLERY NOTES: Voo-Doo

1   See Samuel Clowes Huneke, "Death Wish: Suicide and Stereotype in the Gay Discourses of Imperial and Weimar Germany," *New German Critique* 46, no. 1 (2019): 127–66; Clowes contrasts this use with masculinist writers who depicted gay suicides sympathetically.

2   See Dobler, "Der Travestiekünstler Willi Pape alias Voo-Doo," as well Jens Dobler, *Von anderen Ufern: Geschichte der Berliner Lesben und Schwulen in Kreuzberg und Friedrichshain* (Berlin: Bruno Gmünder Verlag, 2003), 155–63.

GALLERY NOTES: Gender Play

1   "Motto: Tout va par degrees dans la nature et rien par sauts. Leibniz"; Magnus Hirschfeld, *Geschlechts-Übergänge: Mischungen männlicher*

*und weiblicher Geschlechtscharaktere
(sexuelle Zwischenstufen)* (Leipzig: Verlag
der Monatsschrift für Harnkrankheiten und
sexuelle Hygiene, W. Malende, 1905).

2 "dass Geschlecht als Rätsel und nicht als
Lösung existiert"; Kathrin Peters, *Rätselbilder
des Geschlechts: Körperwissen und Medialität
um 1900* (Zurich: Diaphenes, 2018), 9. Peters
traces the origins of these images, as well
as one later use of this them in 1995, in an
essay where the montage was altered, as an
entrée into thinking about masculinity and
femininity as a "Maskerade, als Positionen
innerhalb oszillierender Zuschreibungen von
Geschlechtsidentitäten, die jedes Subjekt schon
immer spalten" (masquerade, as a position
within the oscillating designations of gender
identities that have always divided every
subject), 11.

3 Hirschfeld, *Sexualpathologie*, Bd. I (1921, 2nd
edition), Tafel V.

NOTES TO CHAPTER 2

1 The first important publications devoted to
the medical and/or emancipatory practices of
illustration for gender and sexual minorities
in the German-speaking world are Katharina
Sykora, "Umkleidekabinen des Geschlechts:
Sexualmedizinische Fotografie im frühen
20. Jahrhundert," *Fotogeschichte* 24, no. 92
(2004): 15–30; Kathrin Peters, *Rätselbilder des
Geschlechts: Körperwissen und Medialität um
1900* (Zürich: Diaphenes Verlag, 2010); Susanne
Regener and Katrin Köppert, "Medienamateure
in der homosexuellen Kultur," in *privat/
öffentlich: Mediale Selbstentwürfe von
Homosexualität*, ed. Susanne Regener and
Katrin Köppert (Vienna: Turia & Kant, 2013),
7–17, esp. 11. See also Michael Thomas Taylor,
Annette F. Timm, and Rainer Herrn, eds, *Not
Straight from Germany: Sexual Publics and
Sexual Citizenship since Magnus Hirschfeld*
(Ann Arbor: University of Michigan Press,
2017).

2 Another exception in this regard is Magnus
Hirschfeld's publication practices, which
attempted to provide evidence for his
"Zwischenstufentheorie" (theory of gender
and sexual intermediary stages) through visual
argumentation beginning as early as 1904.

Magnus Hirschfeld, *Geschlechts-Übergänge:
Mischungen männlicher und weiblicher
Geschlechtscharaktere (sexuelle Zwischenstufen)*
(Leipzig: Verlag der Monatsschrift für
Harnkrankheiten und sexuelle Hygiene, W.
Malende, 1905).

3 Rainer Herrn, *Das 3. Geschlecht: Reprint
der 1930–1932 erschienen Zeitschrift für
Transvestiten* (Hamburg: Männerschwarm
Verlag, 2016). In addition to comments on
illustration practice, the volume's afterword
also contains detailed considerations of the
texts sent to the magazine by readers, and to
the various attempts made to found transvestite
associations.

4 I have largely avoided the medical term
"transvestite" in this article, using the neutral
term "cross-dresser" instead, although many
readers of the journal *Das 3. Geschlecht*
explicitly referred to themselves as male and
female transvestites and were also addressed as
such by the editorial staff.

5 This asymmetrical dialogue was in fact
initiated by men who considered themselves
"sexually normal," meaning heterosexual.
In instances where women were involved, I
use feminine pronouns; in instance where
men were involved, I use male pronouns.
Magnus Hirschfeld, *Die Transvestiten:
Eine Untersuchung über den erotischen
Verkleidungstrieb* (Berlin: Alfred Pulvermacher
& Co., 1910).

6 Only later did Hirschfeld notice the existence
of homosexual transvestites and what he called
"mixed-sex" transvestites, or individuals
identifying with other nonbinary genders;
Magnus Hirschfeld, *Sexualpathologie: Ein
Lehrbuch für Ärzte und Studierende*, vol. 2
(Bonn: A. Marcus & E. Webers Verlag, 1918),
esp. 139–78.

7 Rainer Herrn, *Schnittmuster des Geschlechts:
Transvestitismus und Transsexualität in
der frühen Sexualwissenschaft* (Giessen:
Psychosozial-Verlag, 2005), 31–42.

8 Hirschfeld, *Sexualpathologie*, 142.

9 Magnus Hirschfeld, *Sexualität und Kriminalität*
(Vienna: Interterritorialer Verl. "Renaissance,"
1924), 42. This is not only the single reference to
the association by name that has been found. It
also marks, in general, the tentative beginning

of movements to organize, even if accompanied by exclusionary measures.

10   Lothar Goldmann, "Über das Wesen des Umkleidungstriebes," *Geschlecht und Gesellschaft* 12 (1924–25): 281–96 and 334–78, esp. 294.

11   Goldmann, "Über das Wesen des Umkleidungstriebes," 353.

12   Ibid.

13   Ibid., 349.

14   Ibid., 353–4.

15   Radszuweit was chair of the Bund für Menschenrecht, editor of the most widely circulating homosexual magazines, author of homosexual trivial novels, bookseller, and also an event organizer. For an account of the relationship between his various functions, see Jens Dobler and Kristine Schmidt, "Die Bewegung der Weimarer Republik beginnt in Pankow," in *Verzaubert in Nord-Ost: Die Geschichte der Berliner Lesben und Schwulen in Prenzlauer Berg, Pankow und Weißensee*, ed. Jens Dobler (Berlin: Gmünder, 2006), 43–51; and Jens Dobler, "Nachwort," in Männer zu verkaufen: *Ein Wirklichkeitsroman aus der Welt der männlichen Erpresser und Prostituierten* (Hamburg: Männerschwarm Verlag, 2012), 159–78.

16   After a great deal of research among private collectors and antique booksellers, I was able to acquire all five issues of *Das 3. Geschlecht*; the facsimile edition appeared in 2016 with Männerschwarmskript publishers. Herrn, *Das 3. Geschlecht*. I would like to thank the publisher of the series, Wolfram Setz.

17   Magnus Hirschfeld and Max Tilke, *Der erotische Verkleidungstrieb (Die Transvestiten)*, vol. 2: *Illustrierter Teil* (Berlin: Alfred Pulvermacher & Co., 1912).

18   Hirschfeld, *Sexualpathologie*, 166. Hirschfeld gave his 1910 monograph about transvestites the subtitle "Eine Untersuchung über den erotischen Verkleidungstrieb" (An examination of the erotic drive to cross-dress) – a blanket generalization that many transvestites rejected. See Hirschfeld, *Die Transvestiten*.

19   Regener and Köppert, "Medienamateure in der homosexuellen Kultur," 13.

20   See *Das 3. Geschlecht* 1 (1930): 1 and 2 (1930): 11. For more on Von-Doo, see Jens Dobler, "Der Travestiekünstler Willi Pape alias Voo-Doo," *Invertio – Jahrbuch für die Geschichte der Homosexualitäten* 6 (2004): 110–21.

21   Two parts of a series about "Gender Disguise on Stage" were even included in the issues of the special supplement *Transvestit*. The authorship was noted as "nach Sanitätsrat Dr. Hirschfeld" – "According to Medical Counselor Dr. Hirschfeld." See "Geschlechtsverkleidung auf der Bühne," *Die Freundin* 1, no. 4 (1924): n.p. This text consisted of excerpts from the chapter with the same title from Hirschfeld's monograph, which Radszuweit had perhaps used for the magazine without Hirschfeld's permission, since the series suddenly stops after the second instalment.

22   Dr. Wegner, "Männer als Frauen–Frauen als Männer," *Das 3. Geschlecht*, 1930, esp. 2.

23   *Das 3. Geschlecht* 1 (1930): 7 and 2 (1930): 9.

24   Verlag und Redaktion, " *Das 3. Geschlecht* Geschlecht,' Heft II erscheint demnächst!" *Die Freundin*, n.d.

25   Yet it is worth noting that these requests for images did not appear in *Das 3. Geschlecht* but in the special supplement to *Die Freundin*.

26   Ema Katero, "Stimmen aus dem Leserkreis über *Das 3. Geschlecht*," *Die Freundin*, 1930, emphasis in the original.

27   See the unnumbered advertisements page of *Die Freundin* 8, no. 19 (1932).

28   Vera von Roman, "Sehr geehrte Redaktion!" *Die Welt der Transvestiten*. Sonderteil der Zeitschrift *Die Freundin*, 1930, emphasis in the original.

29   Herrn, *Schnittmuster des Geschlechts*, 61–4 and 116–19; Geertje Mak, "Hirschfeld und die Transvestiten: Warum es nie was geworden ist zwischen Frauen in Männerkleidern und der Sexualwissenschaft," in *Dokumentation einer Vortragsreihe in der Akademie der Künste:100 Jahre Schwulenbewegung*, ed. Manfred Herzer (Berlin: Rosa Winkel, 1998), 157–69.

30   Ein Transvestit aus der Provinz, "Stimmen aus dem Leserkreis über *Das 3. Geschlecht*," *Die Freundin*, 1930.

31   The word *Sache* has a multivalent meaning. It could simply be read as "issue" or "cause,"

but it is likely that the writer meant this to refer to actual activism: a public campaign for acceptance.

32 Anna Maria H. E., "Etwas zum 'Sammeln,'" *Die Welt der Transvestiten*. Sonderteil der Zeitschrift *Die Freundin*, 1931.

33 On the changing editorial influence of Friedrich Radszuweit and his adoptive son Martin Radszuweit and its effect on the profile of these publications, see Heike Schader, *Virile, Vamps und wilde Veilchen: Sexualität, Begehren und Erotik in den Zeitschriften homosexueller Frauen im Berlin der 1920er Jahre* (Königstein: Helmer, 2004), 44–178. On Radszuweit's social associations, see Dobler, "Nachwort," 159–78.

34 Rainer Herrn, "Transvestismus in der NS-Zeit," *Zeitschrift für Sexualforschung* 26, no. 4 (2013): 330–71, esp. 332. Moreover, in larger cities the police maintained a transvestite registry that contained information about biological sex, sexual orientation, and the reason for the person's registration by the police – especially in the case of punishable acts (Herrn, "Transvestismus in der NS-Zeit," 334).

35 See, among other sources, *Das 3. Geschlecht* 3 (1930): 24 and 5 (1930): 31, bottom right.

36 Grete M., "Transvestiten über sich selbst, Gedanken zum Transvestitismus," *Das 3. Geschlecht*, 1932.

37 See *Die Freundin* 4, no. 10 (1928): cover. Only with this first publication of the image is the photographer named as Manuel Frères. For the second publication, see *Die Freundin* 5, no. 5 (1929): cover.

38 Similar image migrations with instances of relabeling can also be found in sexological publications; on this point, see Rainer Herrn, "Bildergeschichte(n): Metamorphotische Inszenierungen der sexualwissenschaftlichen Fotografie," *Mitteilungen der Magnus-Hirschfeld-Gesellschaft*, 104–8, nos 37–38 (2007).

39 See *Das 3. Geschlecht* 3 (1931): 17, and 5 (1932): 32.

40 For the magazine *Die Ehe* (Marriage), published at the same time by an employee of the Institute for Sexual Science, Ludwig Levy-Lenz, two cover images were used: an openly erotic image for distribution by mail, which was covered up by a more "decent" cover page intended for public sale.

41 Magnus Hirschfeld, *Geschlechts-Übergänge: Mischungen männlicher und weiblicher Geschlechtscharaktere (sexuelle Zwischenstufen)* (Leipzig: Max von Spohr, 1913), http://edoc.hu-berlin.de/docviews/abstract.php?lang=ger&id=37433, Plates XXXVII–XXX. On this point, see Peters, *Rätselbilder des Geschlechts*, 7–8.

42 "Preisfrage, homo- oder heterosexuell?," *Die Insel* 1, no. 1 (1926): 17.

43 While the man in women's clothing with the changing captions was also published in other contexts in *Die Freundin* and *Das 3. Geschlecht*, the woman with the whip is found "only" in *Das 3. Geschlecht*.

44 See, for instance, the nude photo from the front in issue 2, page 10, which was captioned with the words: "Especially note the girl-like face and the female bodily forms." In issue 3, page 10, we read regarding another photo: "Male transvestite with pronounced female bodily forms; note especially the beginnings of a breast." And in issue 3, on pages 29 and 31, we find three similar stagings of bodies.

45 Hilde Baronin Rotenburg, "Die Not der Transvestiten," *Die Welt der Transvestiten*. Sonderteil der Zeitschrift *Die Freundin*, 1929.

46 Beginning in 1910, we also have evidence of the removal of primary sexual characteristics for this purpose, either by transvestites themselves or with the help of doctors, until actual sex changes were demanded beginning in 1916. This was spurred on by research into hormones and genital surgery, and was actually carried out beginning in 1920–21. On this point, see Rainer Herrn, "Die operative Geschlechtsumwandlung als Experiment am Menschen," in *Sexualität als Experiment? Identität, Lust und Reproduktion zwischen Science und Fiction*, ed. Nicolas Pethes and Silke Schicktanz (Frankfurt am Main and New York: Campus Verlag, 2008), 45–70.

47 Hirschfeld, *Geschlechtskunde*, 592.

48 Rainer Herrn, "Ge- und erlebte Vielfalt – Sexuelle Zwischenstufen im Institut für Sexualwissenschaft," *Sexuologie: Zeitschrift für Sexualmedizin, Sexualtherapie und Sexualwissenschaft* 20, nos 1–2 (2013): 6–14.

3

"I am so grateful to all you men of medicine": Trans Circles of Knowledge and Intimacy

Annette F. Timm

"I am so grateful to all you men of medicine who have been so good to me." These words of appreciation appear in a January 1954 letter from a 49-year-old trans woman, Carla Erskine (pseudonym),[1] to the German-born American endocrinologist Harry Benjamin, whom she had first met in California in 1953 and who had helped advise and treat her before and after her gender-affirming surgery at the University of California, San Francisco, in December 1953.[2] Between 1953 and 1956, Benjamin and Erskine exchanged close to 100 letters, discussing every detail of her physical transformation and her relationships with other "transvestites" (the term she generally used) in California. She was friends with Louise Lawrence, known to historians as a central figure in the network of trans individuals in 1950s America.[3] The two of them were part of a close-knit group in San Francisco and surroundings, and they cooperated with Benjamin to find research subjects for Alfred Kinsey's planned book about transsexuality – a project interrupted by his death from a heart ailment and pneumonia in 1956.[4] Unlike Christine Jorgensen, the glamorous ex-GI

"The more medical people sympathetically interested in transvestism the better."

FIGURE 3.1: Carla E. KILSC-HB 17. Copyright © 2017, The Trustees of Indiana University on behalf of the Kinsey Institute. All rights reserved.

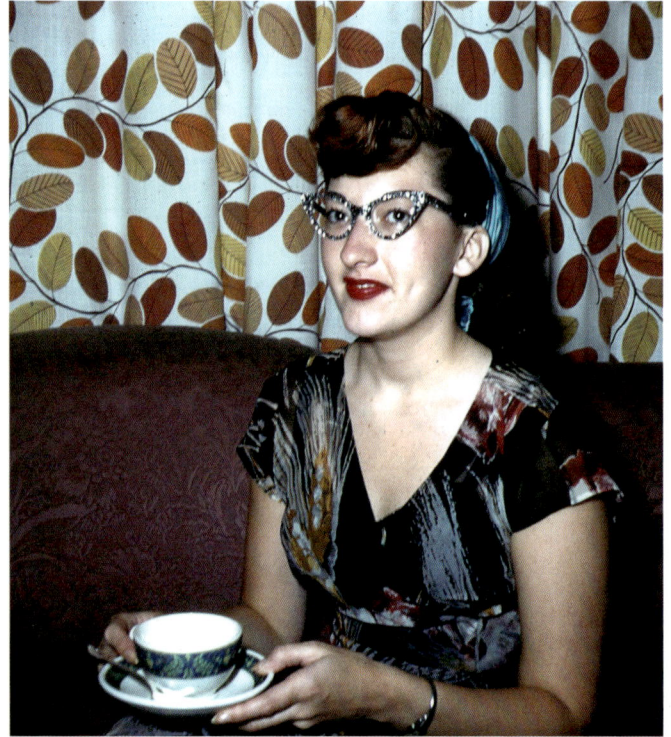

FIGURE 3.2: One of Carla's friends, KILSC-HB 17. Copyright © 2017, The Trustees of Indiana University on behalf of the Kinsey Institute. All rights reserved.

who had become a media sensation in late 1952 after American newspapers began publishing sensationalized reports about her surgery in Copenhagen, Carla purposely and successfully preserved her anonymity. She was one of very few transgender Americans to have procured surgery – some in the U.S. but most abroad – in defiance of the rulings of state and district attorneys in Wisconsin and California,[5] who had relied on an obscure British common-law statute meant to prevent the self-maiming of soldiers to describe genital surgery on healthy tissue as "mayhem."[6] Carla's desperation led her to take matters into her own hands – with a sharp knife – an act that ultimately eased her path to receiving

reconstructive surgery.[7] Although she saw herself as a pioneer, she had no interest in fame. Having just visited Louise and another trans friend in October 1954, Carla wrote to Benjamin: "Couldn't the news paper [sic] have made a sensation of the meeting of the three of us? If they'd have known. As near as we can figure we almost had a quorum. 3 out of 9 in the U.S. as near as we could think."[8] Carla later became a professional photographer, but she had no intention of sharing the stereoscopic slides that she took of her trans friends with the press.

Hoping to help Benjamin and Alfred Kinsey with their collaborative effort to better understand what they were most

Harry Benjamin's Use of Photographs of Carla Erskine

In Benjamin's files we have copies of the releases that all of his patients signed granting permission for their photographs to be used in *The Transsexual Phenomenon*, including a release from Carla. These releases give Benjamin total control over where and how to use these images, under the condition that the anonymity of the signer be protected:

> I ___ do hereby give permission to Harry Benjamin, M. D., to use any photographs and any materials related to my case history in any publication he may see fit to present said material. It is understood that my identity will not be revealed and that proper procedures are followed to insure my anonymity. There is to be no financial compensation to me for this permission.

Yet Benjamin did not publish these photos in the main part of his book. Rather, they were printed in a separate supplement to the book that could be obtained only by writing to the publisher on medical stationery. It is hard to say why these photos of Carla (figures 3.3. and 3.4) were published in this supplement. Benjamin's book confines photographs of genital surgery to the supplement, but these photographs of Carla do not fall into that category. And the photographs published in the main part of the book do include nudity. Given what we know about Carla's wishes to remain private, perhaps this was a decision to lessen the impact of their publication? In *The Transsexual Phenomenon*, Benjamin speaks of his "patient" with the pronoun "he," but we will use "she" since that is how she wanted to be known and that is how Benjamin in fact addressed her in their correspondence.

In the introduction to this book, we have reproduced the color, stereoscopic slide that was used to produce the photograph of Carla sitting on the couch (figure 1.2) we see here in the leftmost image of figure 3.3. Benjamin's use of this image here in his book, with his caption, tells a very different story than we might glean from the image itself. Benjamin's arrangement of four images subordinate the moment of private, even dignified self-presentation we find in the original slides to a clinical interpretation. One thing that is immediately striking is that in both of the clothed photographs, Carla's face has been blocked out – a common technique in medical photography meant to protect her privacy, but which also has the effect of depersonalizing her. Perhaps for similar reasons, the photograph of her naked body in the centre does not include her head, as it does in the original colour version. But the effect of depersonalization in Benjamin's book is more brutal. It reductively forces a focus on Carla's naked body – on the tattoos and male

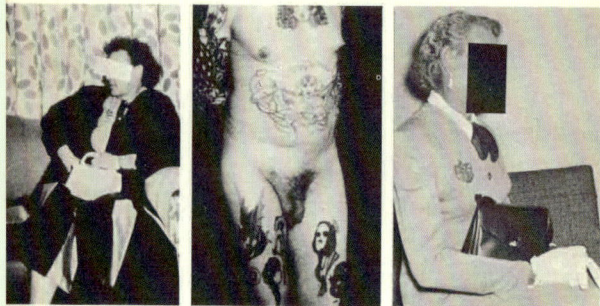

45-year-old, masculine-looking male transsexual, before sex reassignment operation. Note hypogonadal state. Tattoos were acquired in futile attempt to masculinize himself. After failure to do so, he began to live and work as a woman. Conversion operation was in 1953 (at age 45). Since then, patient has led a reasonably contented life as a woman (see case history in Chapter 7, Part II).

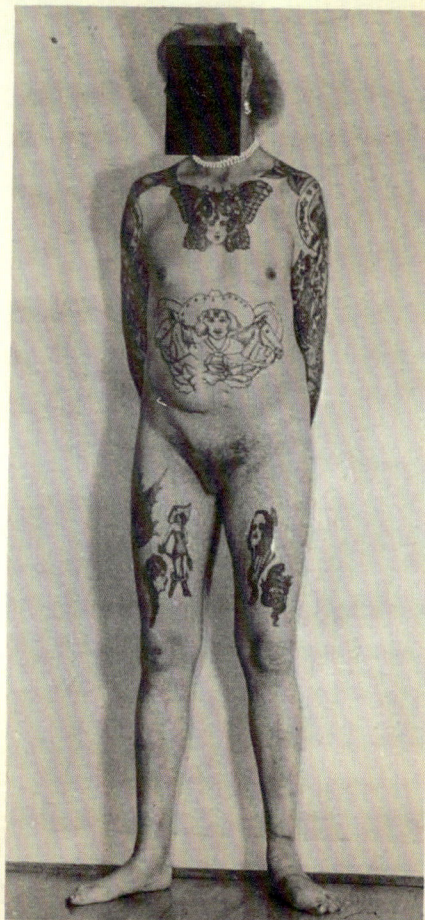

FIGURE 3.3 and 3.4: Left and right pages from the special image supplement to *The Transsexual Phenomenon*, 1966. Caption: "45-year-old, masculine-looking male transsexual, before sex reassignment operation. Note hypogonadal state. Tattoos were acquired in futile attempt to masculinize himself. After failure to do so, he began to live and work as a woman. Conversion operation was in 1953 (at age 45). Since then, patient has led a reasonably contented life as a woman (see case history in Chapter 7, Part II)."

genitals – as though this were the true evidence revealing her gender, evidence that is ostensibly covered up or hidden in the photographs in which she presumably passes as a woman. What we see in this triptych, then, is a message reinforced by figure 3.4: a contrast between photos of Carla dressed as a woman and the hidden "truth" of her body – and her history – exposed when the clothing is removed.

The caption is a further lynchpin for both this clinical framing and the power it claims to expose the truth we are meant to see. Benjamin directs us to gaze at Carla's genitals and tells us that the tattoos are signs of a history of suffering – suffering imposed by her male body and by her attempts to make her body more masculine by getting sailor's tattoos. But here, too, the power claimed by the caption also goes beyond this revelation. In contrast to these apparently doomed efforts of the patient, it also provides a narrative of successful treatment carried out by a doctor.

Following this narrative, the clinical framing for the larger image (figure 3.4) draws our attention to Carla's altered genitals (also offering a justification for showing them – another defense against charges of obscenity). But perhaps what stands out most in this photograph is that Carla is wearing a pearl necklace and earrings. These pieces of jewelry are unmistakable markers of femininity and beauty that push back against the clinical framing and demonstration of Benjamin's intentions. As objects that Carla quite intentionally chose to keep wearing despite being otherwise unclothed, they also prompt us to think more carefully about Carla's tattoos as forms of decoration.

Several similar photographs of these tattoos, also color slides, exist in Benjamin's papers.

As was just noted, in *The Transsexual Phenomenon*, Benjamin describes these tattoos as an unsuccessful attempt at masculinization. Yet one might also say that they have very feminine motifs: like the pearl necklace, they might also be read as aesthetic adornment. They are beautifully feminine and carry clear symbolic meaning – of transformation, with feminine motifs; even of feminine strength or empowerment. Acquired at a moment in Carla's life when there were no treatment options, not for her at least, we can read this decision to decorate her body in this way as

an expression of agency and a willful remaking of her body to be how she would like it. Unlike Benjamin, who reads them only as suffering and failure, we might read them as an assertive act by Carla to claim power over her own body.

Moreover, Benjamin gives no indication of why he reads them in this way – we are not told whether this is his own judgement, or that of his patient. Knowing that Carla was a sailor for a time is important information to put these tattoos in context. In one history of how tattoos entered into and became celebrated in American culture, for instance, Margo DeMello points to what she calls the "golden age of the tattoo" between the world wars, when it was primarily among sailors that tattooing became established as an almost exclusively working-class male practice, and to the period after the Second World War, when mainstream, middle-class prejudices against tattooing solidified.[1] DeMello notes these cultural boundaries meant that tattooing could also be appropriated by lesbians. That description does not apply to Carla, but this shared history is again reflective of how the same cultural practices and markers could be appropriated by very different groups that shared the fact of being stigmatized for not fitting into heterosexual binary gender models – and also of how carefully we as cultural scholars must be in reading these signs in the context of personal life histories, as best we can. Moreover, in the style of this period so clearly reflected here,

which consisted of stock characters or motifs that were easily readable and often had literal meaning in referring to events in a sailor's life or identity, the butterfly carries a particular significance. One recently published collection of photographs of sailor tattoos from this period describes the motif we also find on Carla's chest thus: "Butterfly. Aside from the aesthetic interest of this tattoo, it embodies transformation, the fulfilment of one's destiny and resurrection. It is also considered as embodying the soul of whoever wears it."[2] It depicts a metamorphosis.

With that intention in mind, consider another image of Carla, which Benjamin did not publish (figure 3.5). This image reflects a moment in which she is showing her tattoos to the camera.

One of the reasons this photograph is ambivalent is that we cannot see Carla's face. We can't say whether she is being playful and coy, or whether she is being asked to reveal herself in a way that is uncomfortable or painful. The intended audience of the photograph is also unclear. Was this image meant only for the photographer and Carla? For friends? For Benjamin? For his book? We cannot say.

commonly calling "transvestism," Carla sent her slides to Benjamin. It was the discovery of these beautifully evocative slides in a box of vacation photos in the Benjamin Collection at the Kinsey Institute that provided part of the inspiration for the exhibition *TransTrans*, which I curated with Michael Thomas Taylor and Rainer Herrn at the Nickle Galleries at the University of Calgary in spring 2016. The images led us to Carla, and Carla, her friends, and their predecessors have much to tell us about the intimate and personal networks that provided the foundation for knowledge about trans identities and their medicalized definitions in the United States and Europe in the mid-twentieth century.

Carla was one of Benjamin's first trans research subjects and a key source for his 1966 book *The Transsexual Phenomenon*, the book that would solidify his reputation as a foremost researcher of all aspects of what we would today call transgender or trans identity. The distanced, medicalized, and sometimes quite judgmental tone of this book belies the warmth and understanding exhibited in Benjamin's correspondence with his trans patients. It is difficult to gaze upon the photos of genitals or read the harsh captions describing individual self-presentation in Benjamin's book without feeling that his research subjects had been exploited or unwillingly placed in biological categories of someone else's devising. The title of the book alone is probably enough to raise the suspicions of readers who are today much more sensitive about terminology and to the necessity of allowing trans individuals to speak for themselves.[9] I will argue, however, that

despite the depersonalized tone typical of 1960s medical writing, Benjamin's book and Kinsey's research have to be understood as the culmination of a long history of trans people advocating for themselves and demanding help from medical science. Rather than focusing only on what these experts said about their subjects, in other words, we need to go behind the scenes of the texts themselves and ask what trans individuals *taught* medical researchers. What did Benjamin – and through him Kinsey – learn from Carla and her friends and how did strategies for gathering information about trans identities arise from relationships that were by no means as clinical as the word "transsexuality" or the era's medicalized descriptions and taxonomies might suggest? In what follows, I will first provide some justification for the argument that intimate and personal networks have always been a key feature of trans history. Beginning in early twentieth-century Germany, I will describe such relationships and their cross-Atlantic dimensions over half a century before exploring the intimacy of the letters that Carla wrote to Benjamin in the early 1950s.

From Germany to the United States

As with many other realms of biological knowledge, the period immediately following the Enlightenment witnessed a dramatic expansion in medical interest in sexual behaviour and a growing conviction that what had previously been categorized only in religious terms – as various degrees of sin – should now be investigated using scientific methods. With some interventions from Italy, France, and Great Britain, it was primarily German, Swiss, and Austrian doctors who began to categorize human sexual desire and behaviour and to formulate a discipline of sexual science in the mid-nineteenth century.[10] Sexological findings arose out of the increasingly sexually tolerant atmosphere in cities such as Berlin, where thriving sexual subcultures became the incubators for sexual rights movements. This connection between sexological investigation and legal reform efforts was most evident in the work of Magnus Hirschfeld. Hirschfeld co-founded the Scientific Humanitarian Committee in 1897 – often considered the world's first gay rights organization – and he authored numerous influential books and articles about the spectrum of human sexual diversity. Joanne Meyerowitz, Susan Stryker, and others have pointed out that Benjamin provided a link between Hirschfeld and Kinsey and that the openness to gender-affirming surgeries that he had acquired while still in Berlin inspired him to cooperate with Kinsey's project of cataloguing all aspects of human sexual variation.[11] After emigrating to the United States during the First World War, Benjamin spent most of his postwar summers in Germany, and he often accompanied Hirschfeld on his research jaunts through Berlin's famously gender-bending nightlife.[12] Benjamin notes that it was as "a young student at the Berlin University" that he first met Hirschfeld, in 1906 or 1907.[13]

These connections between scientists are an important feature of trans history.

And yet I will argue that the usual way of describing this transmission of knowledge has produced a de-emotionalized and therefore inaccurate narrative that has purposely underplayed the role of intimate relationships and the agency of those who have been most affected by this research. Although motivated by an understandable attempt to preserve the privacy of incredibly marginalized and persecuted individuals, later historians have sometimes unconsciously repeated the de-personalizing and quantifying tendencies of mid-twentieth-century medical researchers.

The fact that our research began with the intention of staging an exhibition rather than writing a book has had a significant impact on the shape of my argument. Knowing that one will have to tell compelling and concise stories – with few words and no footnotes – focuses one's mind on finding the most significant threads of transmission and on tracking interpersonal connections that might be meaningfully presented to gallery visitors, who, like all humans, have a finite amount of tolerance for the physical exertions of standing and reading. But with this chapter I have the space to argue that zeroing in on personal connections is more than simply a strategy of engagement; it is critical to understanding how knowledge – perhaps particularly knowledge about sexuality – is created.

We began, as historians too often do, with the idea of following a thread of knowledge transmission from one prominent man to another.[14] But the archival research that Michael and I conducted quickly revealed both the impracticality and the inadvisability of this way of framing things. For one thing, Kinsey was not a collector of his own correspondence or notes, so retracing the steps he took to arrive at his new project was not entirely possible. More importantly, however, we uncovered an entirely new story in his correspondence with Harry Benjamin – a story that revealed the active involvement and influence of trans individuals. The deeper we looked the more obvious it became that a very few highly motivated individuals, some of whom had their own personal connections to Germany, were responsible for bringing Benjamin and Kinsey together and for transforming their views on the diagnosis and treatment of individuals who wished to change their gendered self-presentation and their legal sex.

Our initial instincts that Kinsey must have known about Hirschfeld's research on transvestites were correct. His library contained a growing collection of Hirschfeld's publications, and he relied upon a German-speaking staff member, Hedwig Gruen Leser, to translate relevant passages, which he cited in both of his two monumental, best-selling books *Sexual Behavior in the Human Male* (1948) and *Sexual Behavior in the Human Female* (1953) – hereafter referred to as the *Male* and *Female* books.[15] But Kinsey was actually fairly dismissive of this early German sexological work. It was only after he began his collaboration with Harry Benjamin that a significant German influence on Kinsey can be said to have taken hold – too late for Kinsey to have worked through the implications or to

include this perspective in any published work. Yet even though Kinsey did not live long enough to publish his research on transsexuality, how and why he embraced the subject at all has much to tell us about the scientific study of sex in the twentieth century. Investigating precisely how he arrived at this subject turns out to be as interesting as what he might have written about it had he lived. As we will see, Kinsey did not *find* "transsexuality" as a subject of scientific investigation; individuals who wanted to be investigated found him. As Carla's case exemplifies, they often found Kinsey by first finding Harry Benjamin, who had himself come to the topic because trans individuals sought him out for his endocrinological expertise. In other words, to accurately track the transmission of knowledge about transsexuality, we have to give up our tendency to view sexuality as something that can be "discovered" by medical experts and ask more focused questions about the life stories and desires of trans people themselves. Even though the structure of what follows will still partially track the flow of ideas from one male expert to the next, the true agency lies elsewhere within the narrative.

From Hirschfeld to Benjamin

Histories of how trans individuals sought to live authentic lives in the twentieth century have generally been told through the lens of the work, writing, and private musings of medical experts.[16] There is a certain inevitability to this perspective, since, particularly in the first half of the century, it was most often the scientists and doctors who categorized and quantified, who made pronouncements about the need for legal reform, and who were consequently the targets of those who decried any change to the dominant social and cultural paradigm of cisnormativity. But as Edward Dickinson and Richard Wetzell have argued of the history of sexuality more generally, a particular reading of Michel Foucault's description of the development of new scientific understandings of sexuality in the modern era has often placed too much emphasis on the *Deutungsmacht of bourgeois medical experts*" – the power of self-appointed opinion leaders and specialists in human sexual behaviour to single-handedly produce sexual categories and identities.[17]

This *Deutungsmacht* still risks influencing us, as we remain tempted to conflate sex, sexuality, and gender and to ignore the subjective experiences of individuals within their social settings and intimate relationships. As Foucault implies in his introduction to the tragic story of the nineteenth-century "hermaphrodite" Herculine Barbin, the modern insistence that people only have one "true sex" (there being supposedly no such thing as a real mixture of the sexes) means that people we would now call intersex were only ever considered "pseudo-hermaphrodites" – not *real* hermaphrodites or a true mixture of the sexes but imperfect versions of one sex or the other. Meanwhile anatomical investigations that purported to determine which biological sex was predominant in the genitals were read as ipso facto evidence that the opposite sex of the "true sex"

should be the one that the individual in question desired.[18] Under this biopolitical regime, which still governs many public discussions and popular opinions about intersex and trans people, sexuality (the sexual desire of the individual) is secondary to biology and to a biopolitical combination of heteronormative and cisnormative dictates. As will become concrete in my biographical discussion of Carla Erskine below, these socio-medico structures make it imperative to pay attention to two taxonomical dichotomies and how they intersect: sex/sexuality (the match or mismatch between anatomy and choice of love object) and sex/gender (the match or mismatch between one's anatomy and one's social presentation and comportment). Even as the categories are manifestly blurred in lived lives, medical and psychological authorities – not to mention social mores and legal systems – have sought to keep them intact. As Gill Frank and Lauren Gutterman have argued, well into the 1970s and to some degree up to the present, "the messier realities of trans peoples' lives, including queer desires or gender queer identities, needed to be smoothed out for them to be accepted by physicians and a wider public."[19]

All of this helps to explain the frequent erasure of intersex individuals in narratives of trans history, since the tendency to think about ourselves (and therefore also people of the past) as having one true sex is still common. Even researchers like Kinsey and Benjamin who accepted that there could be a mismatch between sex and sexuality (that same-sex love was natural) or between sex and gender (the "transsexual phenomenon" in Benjamin's formulation) could not quite accept that there might not be one "true sex" to be found.

Foucault's insistence on debunking the "true sex" in his discussion of Barbin makes it clear that reductive readings of what he meant by sexuality have been unhelpful. As Franz Eder has argued, the "positive and productive building of the 'sexual subject' and his [sic] 'desire'" has helped to revise the top-down approach that a simplistic reading of Foucault produced.[20] In other words, we must pay attention to how the various experts who sought to scientifically categorize sexual identity in the twentieth century were both operating within very specific paradigms of scientific argument *and* being influenced by the subjects of their research.

Harry Oosterhuis's study of Richard von Krafft-Ebing is a model of this approach, since he reveals the "dialogical" process through which one of the first sexologists reached his conclusions. Oosterhuis argues that despite the fact that Krafft-Ebing's *Psychopathia Sexualis*, first published in 1886, began as a list of sexual pathologies and thus "enabled medical treatment and other forms of restraint … it also opened up the possibility for the individuals involved to speak out, to find a voice, and to be acknowledged,"[21] making "both patients and doctors … agents of culture at large."[22] That the patients influenced the doctors in this earliest era of the medicalization of sexuality is made clear in Krafft-Ebing's increasing tolerance towards homosexuality, which he first viewed as a pathology but later fought to decriminalize. He was one of the

first signatories to Magnus Hirschfeld's petition for the abolition of section 175 of the German penal code, which outlined punishments for "unnatural" indecency or fornication (*widernatürliche Unzucht*) and that applied primarily to sexual acts between men.[23]

Sensitivity to the desires and needs of patients became a hallmark of sexological research, at least in Germany, where Magnus Hirschfeld's founding of the Institute for Sexual Science in Berlin in 1919 was motivated not only by the pursuit of medical knowledge but also by the larger effort to advocate for legal reform and social tolerance for sexual minorities. This activist role, however, meant that Hirschfeld and virtually all researchers in the field of human sexuality who followed him were acutely sensitive to the public furore that their work might produce, and they tended to rigorously conform to shifting norms of scientific argument. While the case-study approach dominated all forms of sexual science in the late nineteenth century – most famously in the work of Krafft-Ebing and Sigmund Freud – by the turn of the century, Hirschfeld became convinced that only statistical studies of the broad spectrum of human sexual presentation, self-understanding, and behaviour would convince the public to accept human sexual and gender diversity. In 1899, he began to publish the results of his Psycho-biological Questionnaire, an approach to gathering information about sexual behaviour that eventually gathered information from about 10,000 individuals and was later emulated (with little attribution) by Alfred Kinsey.[24] But Hirschfeld also cultivated close relationships with anyone who conceived of themselves as sexually nonconforming, and he continued to rely on detailed case histories to formulate his arguments about sexual diversity. This is most apparent in his 1910 book *Die Transvestiten* (*The Transvestites*), which was based on the life stories of seventeen individuals who wrote to him about their desire to live in the clothing or the body of the other sex and who might never have made themselves known to medical authorities had they not been exposed to Hirschfeld's work and generally sympathetic attitudes through trusted personal networks.[25] In the opening pages of *Die Transvestiten*, Hirschfeld admits that the life stories of these individuals initially took him aback. Despite his openness to the idea of sexually mixed types (*Mischungsarten*, or what he also called *Zwischenstufen* – intermediary stages) he did not initially know what to make of these "strange people" (*seltsame Menschen*) who "despite totally normal sexual drives display strong physical tendencies of the other gender." In all seventeen cases, the individuals had voluntarily contacted Hirschfeld, who then encouraged them to write autobiographies. He remained in contact with these people for up to twelve years. While he had at first been convinced that these individuals were living in a state of "self-delusion," his personal connection to them eventually convinced him to supplement his "objective observation of large data sets" with more focused attention to a small group of individuals.[26]

Without detailing precisely how he met each individual, Hirschfeld notes that all but two of his contacts (who were referred from other doctors) came to him directly, either in writing or "orally" (*mündlich*). This vague description is likely an allusion to the fact that Hirschfeld spent considerable amounts of time visiting the various bars and cafés of Berlin's vibrant sexual subcultures.[27] This methodology for finding research subjects conflicted, of course, with the scrupulously scientific aura that he sought to project to the world in the interests of presenting himself as an objective scientific voice. In other words, behind the scientific atmosphere projected in public lectures and other outreach activities, the research of the Institute for Sexual Science depended upon the trust that sexually nonconforming individuals placed in Hirschfeld (who divulged his homosexuality only in intimate settings) and his colleagues.[28] The authors of this book and others have elsewhere detailed how this trust turned the institute into something more than a venue for scientific research.[29] The picture on the facing page (figure 3.6), about which we know very little, visually depicts how intimate contacts had become central to the collection of information and the advocacy for individuals who could not conform to the heteronormative culture of early twentieth-century Germany.

Hirschfeld's ability to use intimate personal connections for his research would have been virtually unimaginable in almost any other city in Europe or North America. The degree to which early twentieth-century Germany – and particularly Berlin – represented a new form of tolerance for sexual diversity is clear if we investigate Hirschfeld's close cooperation with the police. As Jens Dobler

FIGURE 3.6: The Institute of Sexual Science as refuge ca. 1919. Photographer unknown. Copyright: Magnus-Hirschfeld-Gesellschaft.

has argued, there was an astounding degree of cooperation between Berlin police, the Scientific Humanitarian Committee, the publisher Friedrich Radszuweit's Bund für Menschenrechte (League for Human Rights, another organization campaigning for the repeal of §175), and Hirschfeld himself.[30] The Department for Pederasty (Päderastenabteilung) was founded within Berlin's police department in 1885, and its four successive directors – Leopold von Meerscheidt-Hüllessem (1885–1900), Hans von Tresckow (1900–1911), Heinrich Kopp (1911–1923), and Bernhard Strewe (1923–1933) – displayed what Robert Beachy has called an attitude of "qualified toleration" for sexual minorities and their specific social and legal problems right up to

the beginning of the Nazi era.[31] Throughout the late nineteenth and early twentieth centuries, the *Päderastenpatrouille* (pederast patrol) engaged from ten to twelve constables whose official duties included the investigation of male prostitution and infringements against §175. In this atmosphere, laws meant to undergird heteronormative understandings of acceptable self-presentation and sexual activity made individuals living a closeted sexual life of any kind vulnerable to a blackmailer's threat to turn them over to police. The relatively progressive impulses of the four successive directors of the Päderastenabteilung meant that police efforts tended to concentrate on prostitution and on protecting individuals

FIGURE 3.7: A 1928 *Transvestitenschein* (transvestite pass). Courtesy of the Magnus-Hirschfeld-Gesellschaft. Following advice from Hirschfeld, Berlin police officials issued this *Transvestitenschein* (transvestite pass) to Eva Katter (who called himself Gert and was a carpenter) on 6 December 1928. The card reads: "The worker Eva Katter, born on 14 March 1910, and residing in Britz at Muthesisushof 8, is known here as someone who wears male clothing. Strewe, Police Commissioner." Katter was a patient at the Institute for Sexual Science and was occasionally presented to visitors as a "demonstration case" (medical specimen). While living in the former German Democratic Republic, he was one of the few institute patients to establish contact with the Magnus Hirschfeld Society. In donating his records, Katter reclaimed his history and made it part of the institute's archive. He died in 1995.

from being blackmailed for their self-presentation or consensual relationships, which in practice created a remarkably tolerant atmosphere in the city.[32] This atmosphere fostered Hirschfeld's research, since it allowed for the flourishing sexual subculture that provided the venue for his encounters with a diverse spectrum of visitors to the restaurants and cafés frequented by "urnings" (a short-lived word for homosexuals) and other gender-questioning individuals in Berlin. He estimated that there were already twenty or so of these establishments in Berlin in 1904.[33] Hirschfeld often visited these places in the company of police constables.

He later praised Meerscheidt-Hüllessem as a "champion of light and justice" who "with word and deed selflessly stood by hundreds and saved many of them from shame and death," and he described Hans von Tresckow as having "saved hundreds of homosexual men from despair and suicide" by prosecuting their blackmailers.[34] The close cooperation between sexologists/activists and the police is best exemplified in Hirschfeld's creation of what he called "transvestite passes" – certified pieces of identification that were recognized by the Berlin police department and that therefore protected cross-dressers from arrest under laws against "causing a public nuisance" or impersonation.

I have dwelled on the importance of Hirschfeld's immersion in the nightlife of Berlin's sexual subcultures because this turns out to have been a very important factor in transmitting knowledge about transsexuality from Germany to the United States: it created the conditions for Harry Benjamin to learn from Magnus Hirschfeld. Benjamin was still a medical student in Germany when police inspector Heinrich Kopp, who was a mutual friend, introduced them. In his "Reminiscences," written in 1970, Benjamin describes Kopp as a "sympathetic and serious student of the homosexual and other sexual problems." "A couple of times," Benjamin writes, "I was invited to accompany Hirschfeld and Kopp, who were good friends, on tours through a few gay bars in Berlin. The most famous was the Eldorado where mainly transvestites gathered, and female impersonators performed."[35]

Benjamin started going back to Berlin in 1921, visiting the Institute for Sexual Science and meeting with Hirschfeld and his colleagues on a yearly basis. Bemused that the "courageous" but famously grumpy and stingy Hirschfeld had earned the nickname Tante Magnesia (Aunt Magnesia)

FIGURE 3.9: Harry Benjamin with Magnus Hirschfeld in New York (KILSC photo collection KIDC60151).

instead sought out those who might help them, and the patients themselves taught these men what their personal experiences might mean for our larger understanding of the spectrum of human sexual and gender experience. After coining the word "transvestite," Hirschfeld was forced to realize that the term could not fully describe many of the individuals who sought him out in Berlin's bars and night clubs. (As we discuss in the closing chapter on terminology, there is no German equivalent for the term "cross-dresser.") It was these trans people, most of whom never became household names (but some of whom we have already met in Rainer's chapter in this book), who were also responsible for creating the networks of knowledge that began to span the Atlantic in the early twentieth century.

Otto Spengler

The likelihood that doctors would encounter trans people only through personal relationships also had a long history in the United States.[38] The earliest description we have found of the personal networks that began to form between self-described transvestites in the United States appears in a 1914 article by New York gynecologist Bernard S. Talmey, in the *New York Medical Journal*.[39] Talmey describes an exchange of letters between five transvestites (one German, three American, and one British) in the first decade of the twentieth century. He explicitly refers to Hirschfeld's recent book about "transvestism" – *Die Transvestiten* – then only published in German, and it

from the adoring patrons of these clubs,[36] Benjamin took mental notes on how scientific knowledge about sexual diversity could be gathered through unconventional personal contacts with gender-questioning individuals. Although Benjamin never denied the influence of his German mentors, he would later obscure Hirschfeld's impact on his own thinking by claiming to have invented the term "transsexuality." (We will discuss the use of this term in the final chapter on "Historicizing Transgender Terminology.") Even Kinsey might have been exposed to Hirschfeld's terminology through his acquaintance with Benjamin, because the word "transsexuality" appears in the *Male* book in 1948, long after Kinsey and Benjamin had met.[37] But the point is that none of these men *discovered* sexual diversity. Sexually diverse individuals is therefore perhaps no accident that the "first patient" described in the article is, like Talmey himself, a German immigrant; we now know that this was Otto Spengler.[40] (See figures 1.6–1.12 and 3.10–11.)

Although the correspondence between the transvestites Talmey describes deploy the pseudonym *"Miss* S.," he refers to this person only as *"Mr.* S.," and he continues to use words like "masquerade" when describing the clothing practices of these individuals.[41] Nevertheless, we can surmise that it is only personal sympathy that led Talmey to write about this subject at all, because he admits that he had known Mr. S. "in a social way" for years without having ever "detected any outward suggestion of femininity … [or] discover[ing] any delusional state in his psyche."[42] The tone of both the article and the slightly revised version of the story that Talmey includes in his 1919 book about love is nonjudgmental. He simply reprints Spengler's autobiography and provides excerpts from the very intimate and private correspondence between these individuals, including personal biographical detail and descriptions of their motivations for wearing female clothing. Mr. S, we learn, always dressed like a man in public and was "the proprietor of a big business and himself takes charge of it." Noting that Mr. S expressed a wish for castration in order "to live as a woman absolutely," Talmey does not diagnose the condition as pathological, describing this desire as "in no way a mere fancy" but rather as "an important anomaly."[43] In its emphasis on Spengler's emotional stability, business success, intellectual abilities, and

standing in the community, this implicitly sympathetic account strikingly diverges from the conservative tone of Talmey's other writings, which include diatribes against masturbation and other forms of "degenerate" sexual expression. Although he does call transvestism a "psychoerotic pathology," there is far less vitriol and judgement here than in his other books, some of which – such as *Woman: A Treatise on the Normal and Pathological Emotions of Feminine Love* – already reveal their prejudices in their titles.[44] Indeed, rather than exploring the relationship between transvestites' clothing practice and their sexual desires, Talmey describes cross-dressing as arising from the "esthetic sensibility" of a man who "harbors exalted ideas and is striving to secure artistic enjoyment in the appreciation of the beautiful."[45] This was, he argues, following Havelock Ellis, "a sexo-esthetic inversion of pure artistic imitation" – a kind of clothing fetish – that has nothing to do with homosexual attraction.[46]

Talmey's long-term personal relationship with Spengler seems to have motivated a surprisingly nonjudgemental description of the phenomenon of cross-dressing. Since we know that Spengler actively searched for connections and sympathetic reactions from the medical community (he carried on a long correspondence with the U.S. Army Surgeon Dr. Mary Walker, who had a large archive of images and letters from cross-dressing individuals),[47] we have to assume that Spengler had carefully cultivated the relationship that accounted for Talmey's accepting reaction to the revelation that his friend was a cross-dresser. In short, that Spengler and his correspondents became the first transvestites to be discussed in the medical literature in the United States had much to do with the personal relationships within New York's German immigrant community.

Of course, Talmey's sympathies only went so far, and he cannot be considered a true advocate for the acceptance of trans people. Although we cannot be sure what Spengler would have wanted, it is instructive that Talmey insistently used male pronouns for Mr. S. Spengler's story also forces us to acknowledge that the possibilities for socially transitioning were clearly more limited in early twentieth-century New York than they were in Hirschfeld's Berlin. American cities had begun imposing municipal ordinances restricting cross-dressing in the 1850s, and police often resorted to older laws against the use of public disguise.[48] Spengler hoped to influence these policies. Appearing under the pseudonym Rudolph von H. in psychiatrist George W. Henry's massive study *Sex Variants: A Study of Homosexual Patterns*, Spengler reported: "Several times I went to the police department to get permission to wear women's clothes but I didn't succeed. In Berlin I went out on the street dressed as a woman. I even did that here occasionally. If you don't make yourself obnoxious nobody noticed it."[49] As Talmey notes, Spengler lived out his desires primarily at home. Spengler's wife, Helene (née Wasbutzky), whom he married in 1898, was at first tolerant of the "masquerading"; she shared lingerie, sewed dresses, and bought gifts of clothing and perfume for

her husband.[50] Spengler's three children – Valerie (1900), Hildegard (1906), and Alfred (1908) – were accustomed to their father dressing in female attire. Hildegard apparently called her father "papa-lady."[51] All of these details strongly indicate that we should view Spengler not as a "cross-dresser" but as trans.

Nonetheless, since we know that Spengler could not live a public life as a woman in a city where tolerance for trans identities was virtually nonexistent outside of marginalized subcultures, and because we do not know what female name might have been used in the home, I have avoided using any gendered pronouns in these passages. There is of course a case to be made that present-day understandings and ethical practices must be brought to bear on our analyses of trans history, and debates about ethically sensitive gendered language are unlikely to ever cease. But as historians we cannot erase their effects on lives as they were actually lived, and we must be careful not to use terminology that exaggerates the individual agency and life possibilities of our historical actors.

With that proviso aside, one might still profitably investigate precisely how this one individual used interpersonal connections to have far-reaching influence on the self-declared experts who were investigating the lives and desires of trans individuals in twentieth-century America. Spengler was extremely active in the German community in New York.

Having emigrated to the city in 1892 as a nineteen-year-old with two dollars in his pocket, he quickly established himself in the press clipping industry and opened his own company, Argus Pressclipping Bureau, in 1902. Argus provided businesses with the service of finding press clippings on subjects of interest. Alongside his successful business, Spengler was the founder or active member of various German immigrant associations in New York. In 1913, as part of his "efforts to promote German culture and science," he compiled a compendium of the achievements of German immigrants in New York, *Das deutsche Element der Stadt New York* (The German element of the city of New York).[52] His interest in archaeology led him to take a trip to "the Orient" (it is unclear which countries he included in this term) and to museums in Europe in 1906, and he likely used the opportunity to visit Berlin, where he had lived since the age of seven. As noted above, this was the same year that Benjamin met Hirschfeld. Might the three men have met in one of the gender-bending bars that were already common in the city? We can only speculate, but it is certainly possible.[53] Benjamin later described having met Spengler "in the early 1920s."[54]

This was during a period when Benjamin was trying to establish himself as an expert in rejuvenation therapies – hormonal treatments, inspired by the research of the Austrian physiologist Eugen Steinach, that were meant to counter the effects of aging. Steinach had performed a series of famous experiments on guinea pigs, which involved the transplantation of gonads in order both to rejuvenate the animal and to transform its gender characteristics.[55] He then developed an alternative technique to achieve the same ends: vasoligation (sometimes called

vasoligature), a form of vasectomy that he promised would increase vitality and sexual potency. His procedure was all the rage in the 1920s and 1930s, attracting patients such as William Butler Yeats and Sigmund Freud.[56] These primitive forms of hormonal treatment struck Benjamin as a new panacea for aging, and he became the most well-known American exponent of the benefits of getting "Steinached," eventually performing as many as 500 of these operations.[57] Benjamin first introduced the procedure to an American audience by giving a lecture to the New York Academy of Medicine in 1921, and in 1923 he arranged for a screening of the documentary film that popularized Steinach's research.[58]

Either of these public events could have attracted Spengler's interest, particularly since Steinach's fame could not have escaped someone with German language skills and such a personal interest in the subject.[59] Spengler visited Benjamin's office to request a prescription for the estrogenic hormone known as "Progynon." Benjamin overcame his initial hesitations, and "a mild gyneocomastia was produced to the infinite delight of the patient and with emotional improvement."[60] In other words, it was Spengler who insisted upon treatment for the purposes of sexual transformation. Spengler's autobiography in Henry's book describes the procedures that Benjamin performed: "In trying to become feminine, I went through rejuvenation, the American Steinach operation. I had this when I was fifty-two. A doctor who specializes in it x-rayed my testicles to make me sterile. I wanted to get more feminine. I wanted to

Otto Spengler. Director Argus Presscipping Bureau

Ein bekannter
New Yorker Transvestit

FIGURE 3.10: Spengler in Otto Spengler, ed., *Das deutsche Element der Stadt New York: Biographisches Jahrbuch der Deutsch-Amerikaner New Yorks und Umgebung* (New York: Spengler, 1913).

FIGURE 3.11: Spengler in *Das 3. Geschlecht*, 1932. The caption reads: "A well-known New York transvestite."

develop female breasts and shoulders. I also took a great deal of progynon to develop my breasts and it succeeded quite well. I've got the hips of a regular woman."[61] Since progynon was not on the market until 1928, it is likely that the hormonal treatment began only a few years after the operation and x-ray treatment. This was a period when Benjamin was regularly spending time in Berlin in order to remain up-to-date on both Steinach and Hirschfeld's research.[62]

But there were even more direct and personal conduits for this transatlantic transmission of information. It is clear that by the 1930s, Spengler had developed close contacts with the transvestite community in Berlin and was contributing private photos to the Berlin magazine *Das 3. Geschlecht.* A comparison of the figures in the Otto Spengler sidebar in the introduction (figures 1.6 to 1.12) and the two images of Spengler above makes it clear that the "New York transvestite" was Otto Spengler.

Henry does not appear to have been aware of these images, but they certainly would have provided fodder for his uncharitable assessment that Spengler should be categorized as a "narcissistic" case. Without using a control group, Henry and his collaborator, the gynaecologist and artist Robert Latou Dickinson, had set out to discover the "constitutional deficiencies" ("structural, physiological, and psychological") that distinguished "the sex variant [who] seems to be in part a by-product of civilization," from the "normal" heterosexual.[63] Spengler, perhaps naively, was willing to provide both personal and physical data for the project. As Henry's opening description notes: "Rudolph [Spengler] maintains his interest in promoting a more tolerant attitude toward the transvestite and he is ready at any time to present himself for study and demonstration."[64] Henry's commentary is considerably less sympathetic than Talmey's, though this might have something to do with the fact that by the time Henry interviewed Spengler (likely in the early 1930s), there had been a significant social and economic decline. The once thriving news clipping business had fallen on hard times, and Spengler now lived alone. "He dwells," Henry observed, "in a world of classical fantasy, indifferent to the dirt and poverty of his immediate surroundings."[65] Summarily dismissing Spengler's claims to have been an influential historian,[66] Henry attributes Rudolph's identification with a bronze statue of Narcissus and his desire to wear women's clothing as indicative of "exhibitionistic" tendencies and vanity; in short, he diagnoses Spengler as a narcissist.

It is intriguing that Spengler fails to mention visiting places that might have provided solace for his feelings of social isolation. The interview with Henry is silent about what George Chauncey describes

as the "massive drag (or transvestite) balls that attracted thousands of participants and spectators in the 1920s" and the beer gardens of the Bowery, where, as a visiting medical student put it in 1890, "male perverts, dressed in elaborate costumes, 'sat for company'" and earned commissions on drinks.[67] It is likely that Spengler's dreams of social mobility led him to look down his nose at such venues during the time of his life when he was still married and economically successful. It is also possible that the very visibility of gay men in New York,[68] who had adopted female dress and labels like "fairy" and "queen" primarily to signal their sexual interest in other men, would have scared Spengler away. The self-consciously middle-class German likely did not run in the same social circles as those who had formed the secret club Cercle Hermaphroditos and met in a room above the "fairy" bar Paresis Hall, where they stored their female clothing and hid from New York's laws against cross-dressing in public.[69] In other words, Spengler's own bourgeois self-understanding likely increased his social isolation.

Entirely ignoring these social dynamics, Henry also underplayed the importance of the educational efforts undertaken by "sexual variants" themselves. Digging even deeper, we find that another relationship Otto Spengler cultivated had a significant impact on the transmission of knowledge about sexual diversity. Along with his own business, Spengler also worked on the editorial staff of *Der Deutscher Vorkämpfer*, a magazine about German pioneers in the United States, which was founded by Louis Viereck, a former German member

FIGURE 3.12: George Sylvester Viereck. United States Library of Congress's Prints and Photographs Division. Public Domain.

of parliament for the Socialists Workers' Party, who had emigrated to the U.S. in 1896.[70] Louis's son, the poet and closeted homosexual George Sylvester, wrote propaganda for the German government during both world wars, and he authored popular science tracts such as the 1923 book (published under a pseudonym) *Rejuvenation: How Steinach Makes People Young.*[71] Having become famous as a poet and journalist, Viereck took advantage of Hirschfeld's 1930 trip to the United States to publish widely syndicated newspaper articles about "the Einstein of Sex … Dr. Hirschfeld," wisely capitalizing on the popularity of his previous interview with Albert Einstein.[72] Viereck and Hirschfeld used the familiar "Du" form of address in

correspondence to each other. Just before leaving for New York, Hirschfeld wrote to Viereck as a fellow "cultural freedom fighter," asking that Viereck cooperate with Benjamin to plan a "worthy reception" for his arrival.[73] Viereck agreed to do advance publicity for Hirschfeld's trip, and he acted as Hirschfeld's travel agent, accompanying him on stops in Chicago, Detroit, and California after a six-week stay in New York.[74]

What makes this relationship extremely strange is that by the time of this trip, Viereck was already involved in pro-German propaganda activities that one would have expected Hirschfeld to adamantly reject. After all, Hirschfeld had embarked on the world tour that began in the United States and continued to Asia and the Middle East in part to escape the anti-Semitic and homophobic vitriol that the Nazi party was fomenting against him.[75] Viereck, meanwhile, had sympathetically interviewed Adolf Hitler in 1923 and had been "dazzled" by someone he described as a "widely read, thoughtful, and self-made man."[76] By 1933, the *Jewish Daily Bulletin* was already calling Viereck the "Chief Nazi Propagandist in the U.S."[77] In 1942, Viereck was convicted of acting as a Nazi propagandist without having registered with the U.S. Department of State as a foreign agent. After serving five years in jail, he became a supporter of Senator Joe McCarthy and never entirely repented for his Nazi sympathies.[78] It may seem paradoxical that he combined his pro-Nazi activities with a keen interest in the work of German sexology and its Jewish practitioners (another of his famous interviewees was Sigmund Freud).[79] His own homosexuality was clearly at play here, but it is particularly interesting that he later revealed, albeit anonymously, an interest in transsexuality. In a 1937 article that Viereck wrote under the pseudonym Donald Furthman Wickets, he describes how Mary Weston, shot-put record holder for Great Britain, later became Mark Weston.[80] Citing Steinach's research and other famous cases of gender transition (such as the life of the Chevalier d'Éon), Viereck/Wickets implicitly supported the notion of a spectrum of human sexual identity, writing that "My friend, the late Dr. Magnus Hirschfeld, of the Institut für Sexualwissenschaft in Berlin (suppressed by the Nazis), calculated that the number of different sexual types equals 46,046,721, or three raised to the sixteenth power."[81] In 1945, Benjamin shared Viereck's autobiography with Alfred Kinsey, who thought it was "interesting and definitely important in our own study [of sexual behaviour]."[82]

So Viereck, a German nationalist and later Nazi sympathizer likely became sympathetic to the plight of trans individuals both through his connections to Hirschfeld and to Spengler, whom he certainly knew through his father and other contacts in the German community in New York. In 1930, both Viereck and Benjamin were instrumental in bringing Hirschfeld to New York, and we know from Henry's account that Spengler (who had by this time been treated by Benjamin) was a "prominent visitor" to Hirschfeld's New York lectures and even presented himself publicly as an example of a transvestite on

these occasions.[83] What we cannot know is how intense the relationship between Spengler and Viereck might have been. Spengler told Henry of two homosexual encounters. In both cases, Spengler had been "flattered" into accepting the passive role in the sexual act, partly out of curiosity, but with no significant sexual response.[84] The second encounter, when Spengler was forty-six, involved a man "ten years younger," who had long been attracted to Spengler but "hadn't dared mention it."[85] Could this have been Viereck? Quite possibly, I would submit, since Viereck was indeed ten years younger. But even if this is unjustified speculation, it is quite clear that the dense network of personal connections influenced all involved and likely produced considerably more tolerance towards trans identities than would otherwise have been the case. These threads of knowledge transmission reached to the most important sexological researcher of the post-Second World War period: Alfred Kinsey.

Viereck's release from prison in 1947 came just as Kinsey was finalizing publication of the *Male* book and beginning research for the *Female* book. It is thus perhaps instructive that Benjamin and Kinsey corresponded about both Viereck and Spengler in that year. In June 1947, Kinsey told Benjamin that he would be happy to meet Viereck, and in October Benjamin reminded Kinsey to return the file *and* the "many photos" of Otto Spengler that he had lent him.[86] By this time work on Kinsey's *Male* book, which contains very little reference to transvestism, would have been finalized, while research on the *Female* book had just begun. Between the 1948 publication of the former and the 1953 publication of the latter Kinsey's view of the subject underwent a rather radical transformation. When, in 1950, Kinsey first interviewed the person for whom Meyerowitz provides the pseudonym Val Barry, he encouraged someone he still absolutely considered to be male "to undertake homosexual relations as a means of learning to value his genitals."[87] In contrast, the *Female* book prominently cites Talmey's *Love: A Treatise on the Science of Sex-Attraction*, where the description of Spengler and the four other "transvestites" published in the 1914 *New York Medical Journal* article is repeated.[88] Kinsey must therefore have been familiar with Talmey's arguments, and he must have relied on these five case studies to make his unsupported (and now very unconvincing) claim that transvestism resulted from clothing fetishism and was thirty or forty times more likely in males. Given the correspondence with Benjamin, it is also certain that he had made the link between Talmey's "first patient" and Otto Spengler. This one individual was thus enormously influential in starting a conversation about sexual transition in mid-twentieth-century America.

Although he left behind no definitive statements on the subject, the evidence I have presented strongly suggests that even Kinsey had begun to at least entertain the possibility that trans identities were within the spectrum of "normal." By 1949, he and his primary collaborators – Wardell Pomeroy, Clyde Martin, and Paul Gebhard – were explicitly trying to tear down preconceptions of "normal" human sexual

development. They argued, for instance, that the term "crimes against nature" had no scientific grounding:

> [The law] proscribes [sexual acts which do no damage to property or to person] on the ground that they are crimes against nature – that is, abnormal or perverse behavior – and punishable because they are so rated. They are punishable without respect to the mutual desire of the parties involved to engage in such activities and irrespective of the fact that the persons immediately concerned may find satisfaction in their performance. In all the criminal law, there is practically no other behavior which is forbidden on the ground that nature may be offended, and that nature must be protected from such offense. This is the unique aspect of our sex codes.[89]

Given this line of argument and Kinsey's sympathetic reaction to the trans women he was meeting through Harry Benjamin in the early 1950s, it seems unlikely that he could have continued to reject the validity of their desires. The transition in Kinsey's thought is visible in the few paragraphs he wrote about transvestism in the *Female* book. This second volume adds to the *Male* book by providing at least a brief definition of transvestism (he notably does *not* use the word "transexuality"), and it coyly alludes to research underway "to secure a sample which will ultimately allow us to estimate the number of transvestites in the United States."[90] But the book was published in

1953, just before he and Harry Benjamin started corresponding about the circle of trans women around Louise Lawrence in San Francisco. It is not surprising, therefore, that Kinsey's understanding of the people he only called transvestites was dependent upon his understanding of the fundamental difference between males and females and his assumption that "males are more liable to be conditioned by psychologic stimuli."[91] Kinsey's fundamentally binary understanding of gender roles made it difficult for him to understand trans identities, and we cannot know whether the collaboration with Benjamin and his contacts with trans women would have changed his mind. But there are at least hints that it might have.

The Benjamin–Kinsey Collaboration

Exploring the Benjamin–Kinsey collaboration helps us to understand the importance of personal networks in the history of sexology. After beginning to correspond with Alfred Kinsey in Spring 1944, Benjamin finally met the famous biologist "sometime around 1945,"[92] and the two men began comparing notes about gathering sexual data through personal contacts and visits to bars and night clubs.[93] In 1949, Kinsey referred an effeminate boy who wanted to become a girl to Benjamin,[94] and they began sharing files of people they generally referred to as "transvestites." In September 1949, at precisely the same time that Benjamin started to address his letters to Prok (Kinsey's nickname) rather than to Dr. Kinsey, the correspondence between

the two men became much more intimate, with frequent descriptions of the personal lives, medical quests, and intertwined social networks of the small but growing number of Americans who were seeking hormone treatment and surgery. Throughout the early 1950s, Benjamin reported to Kinsey on his frequent visits with the circle of intimates around Louise Lawrence during his yearly summer residence in San Francisco (he ran a summer clinic on Sutter Street), and he forwarded information about his contacts to Kinsey. Kinsey then travelled to take these individuals' histories, and he became intimately acquainted with a group of primarily trans women, mostly in San Francisco, Chicago, and New York. Whenever Benjamin and Kinsey were in the same city, the two men went out to explore establishments they thought most likely to be "sexologically interesting." Benjamin led the way. Their common interest in this type of participant-observer research is apparent in their letters, such as the one dated September 1951, where Benjamin reported that he had taken a fascinating tour of the seedy bars of Mexico City and had seen "the lowest type of prostitution." Although his lack of Spanish skills and the extreme class divisions of the scene made it impossible for him to have a truly "sexiting" trip (as Albert Ellis, who was then working on his book *Sex without Guilt*, had wished him), he hoped that Kinsey would join him on a return trip. In other words, Benjamin was following in the Hirschfeld tradition, and he had found a kindred spirit in Kinsey, whose loitering in seedy areas of Chicago and other cities had already gotten him arrested (or nearly so) on several occasions.[95]

Kinsey's writing does not provide any details about this methodology, which might be categorized as a type of anthropological fieldwork. He described his interview method in great detail in various interviews and publications, but he says nothing about how he found many of his most "sexologically interesting" interview partners. As Donna Drucker, Elizabeth Stephens, and Peter Cryle have argued, Kinsey's self-perception was as a taxonomist – a gatherer of masses of data that could then be categorized and analyzed.[96] But the fact that he could find so few trans individuals to investigate means that his planned volume on transsexuality could only have been written with a less stringent reliance on statistics. He simply did not have the numbers for a reasonable sample. He clearly knew this, but he was also eager to address the critique he had received for failing to investigate the significance of cross-dressing in past publications; he left it out of the *Male* book entirely and only added a few paragraphs on "transvestism" to the *Female* book.[97] Despite the small pool of subjects, Kinsey's collection of material about trans cases was meticulous: he took extremely detailed case histories and travelled long distances to meet with just one or two individuals. (For instance, he had a four-hour-long interview with Carla Erskine – double the usual length – who "found him to be a lovely and sympathetic man").[98] Despite his antipathy for psychoanalysis, his methods of investigating transsexuality were much more personal than statistical, and in his early speculations about categorizing these individuals, he tended to opine that "no two of them are very much alike" – a judgement that would have complicated any neat taxonomy.[99] The subject of transsexuality might even have forced him to at least somewhat revise his views on what Hirschfeld would have called the "intermediaries" – the various shadings between male and female.

In other words, his encounter with trans people was a difficult learning process that contradicted his instinctual reaction to gender difference. In the *Male* book, Kinsey had rejected the idea of fixed sexual types. He particularly detested "unscientific" uses of the word "bi-sexuality," indignantly objecting that it was being "used to imply that these persons have both masculine qualities and feminine qualities *within* their single bodies."[100] He refused to ever speak in terms of fixed sexual identities, writing only about "homosexual acts," never about "homosexuals," and despite his own creation of a scale of human sexual difference, he placed far more emphasis than Hirschfeld on social conditioning. Kinsey insisted that terms like "intersex" and "bisexual" could only be used for humans in ways analogous to biological descriptions of animals who possessed both male and female anatomical structures. Those who engaged in homosexual behaviours, then, were not physical or sexual intermediates but rather examples of the limitless human capacity for variety in sexual comportment. This was a rejection of Hirschfeld's "theory of sexual transitions" (*Zwischenstufenlehre*), which posited that variations in sexual organs, physical build, sex drive, and emotional makeup produced a clearly categorizable – if also theoretically infinite – variety of sexual types.

Hirschfeld's insistence on this spectrum implied that the notion of solely male or female forms was illusory.[101]

Kinsey acknowledged Hirschfeld's pioneering efforts and was particularly respectful of the German sexologist's use of surveys (for instance Hirschfeld's 1904 distribution of forms to 3,000 technical college students and 5,721 metal workers), but he ultimately dismissed all early studies on sexual behaviour as failing to meet the sampling standards of scientific population analysis. Kinsey scoffed that much of Hirschfeld's information was "nothing more than gossip,"[102] and he seems to have ignored Hirschfeld's theory of sexual transitions altogether. Given what we know about Kinsey's rather selective reading habits,[103] this might merely have been a matter of failing to ask his translator to read the relevant works. As Heike Bauer has argued, Kinsey's reactions to Hirschfeld's work were almost certainly also influenced by the fact that "for Kinsey Hirschfeld's own homosexuality disqualified the German from scientific authority."[104] It is nevertheless instructive that Kinsey cites but does not comment on Hirschfeld's 1910 book *Die Transvestiten*. Kinsey was clearly uncomfortable with any theories of sexual diversity that might threaten a gender order based on sexual dimorphism: the "natural" distinction between male and female. He acknowledged that men and women are "alike in their basic anatomy and physiology,"[105] but as Janice Irvine has argued, his insistence on the "biological imperative" has the ring of someone desperate to justify the double standard.[106] As Kinsey put it in

the *Female* book: "The human male's interest in maintaining his property rights in his female mate, his objections to his wife's extra-marital coitus, and her lesser objection to his extra-marital activity, are mammalian heritages."[107] Women, he insisted, had less sexual capacity and were less malleable to social conditioning; they had less "conditionability" than men and were therefore less likely to seek a variety of sexual experiences.[108] He had no problems finding ways of making the massive amount of data he collected fit these preconceptions. But as he and Benjamin began to collect information about "transvestites," and as they participated in long-term relationships with some of these individuals, Kinsey in particular was faced with dilemmas that would challenge both his insistence on mass data collection and his sexually dimorphic worldview.

By the time Kinsey died in 1956, there was only a handful of publicly acknowledged transsexuals in the United States. These individuals undoubtedly represented a tiny fraction of trans Americans. We can guess this because Christine Jorgensen and others who had undergone public transitions received hundreds of letters from desperate people. (Jorgensen alone received "some twenty thousand" letters.)[109] Benjamin and Kinsey were determined to find as many of these people as possible, and they believed that they knew of all of the medically registered cases in the United States. But by the time of his death in 1956, Kinsey had only one hundred histories of trans women and eleven trans men, and he knew of only ten cases where surgery had been performed (only one more than Carla had reported six years earlier.)[110] This was nothing like the data set that he had relied on to write his *Male* and *Female* books, which were collectively based on 18,200 case studies and for which Kinsey developed a punch-card system for data analysis.[111]

Kinsey's extensive involvement with Benjamin and the long correspondence between the two men about every aspect of the lives of trans women they knew in the early 1950s makes it clear that this was a far more intimate and personal form of research than Kinsey had conducted in the past. Kinsey's interest in these individual cases and his rather undocumented reliance on them in the *Female* book indicate how important it is to understand the role of personal networks in the formulation of knowledge about sexuality. When it came to his research on transsexuality, Kinsey was forced to follow the theoretical, case-study approach more common to his German predecessors and their American followers rather than maintaining the taxonomical rigour he had pursued in his previous work. Given the much smaller sample size, and given his own sympathetic tendencies, he was forced to listen to the words of individuals and appreciate their self-representations in all of their complex and sometimes contradictory richness. He was dependent upon the social network between these people simply to *find* his research subjects, and both he and Benjamin inevitably became involved in the tensions, joys, and disappointments of people forced to live secretive and emotionally intense lives.

In 1951, Kinsey wrote to a person seeking surgery with the opinion that "A male cannot be transformed into a female through any known surgical means. In other words, it would be very hopeless to attempt to amputate your male organs and implant a vagina." This summed up his belief in the sexual binary and the fixity of sexual identity. "We humans," he wrote, "are either heterosexual or homosexual."[112] While it is impossible to predict where his new research would have led him had he lived, there are hints in the correspondence with Benjamin (whose belief in human bisexuality and whose support for the benefits of surgical intervention were already well established in the 1950s) that Kinsey could not have easily sustained his conviction that transsexuality was just one more example of male/female sexual dimorphism.[113] At the very least he would have been forced to acknowledge that his initial assumptions about the predominance of male-to-female transsexuality had been wrong. We now know that trans people who had been assigned female at birth likely existed in equal numbers but were less likely to think that they could be helped by medical science and therefore less likely to make themselves known to researchers like Benjamin and Kinsey.[114] But it is most important for my purposes in this chapter that this very personal involvement between scientists and an extremely marginalized sexual minority demonstrates the unique way that knowledge about transsexuality was assembled and transmitted in this era.

If we look a little deeper into the pages of the *Female* book, we can uncover the transformation that was in progress in

Trans Men

There are relatively few images or stories of trans men in the sources we used for *TransTrans*, and even these stories are often evidence of the comparative invisibility of trans men in history – both despite and because of the relative ease with which women could dress in men's clothing and pass as men.[1] Hirschfeld's case studies in *Die Transvestiten*, for instance, include sixteen "male transvestites" and only one "female transvestite" (to use Hirschfeld's terms). In another section of the book, the "Differentialdiagnose" (differential diagnosis), Hirschfeld also gives the story of a female transvestite whom Hirschfeld speaks of with female pronouns: Katharina T. or "Miss T.," as Hirschfeld calls him.[2] Born in 1885, Katharina T. considered himself "to be a man completely," although Hirschfeld identifies Katharina as a homosexual, meaning a woman who is attracted to women. Hirschfeld and his psychoanalyst colleague Karl Abraham personally intervened as medical authorities to procure a certificate from the Berlin Police attesting that Katharina was known to the police as a cross-dresser and that Katharina had no improper or dishonest motives. In our exhibition in Calgary, we depicted Katharina T.'s story with a blank panel that read "no image" because we have none – a choice we also made to underscore the relative invisibility of trans men in this history.

Felix F.   Max Sch.   Ernst K.
Fall 4   Fall 7   Fall 6

FIGURE 3.13: Photograph from the dissertation by Hans Abraham, *Der weibliche Transvestitismus* (Female transvestitism), 1921. Reprinted in Hirschfeld, *Geschlechtskunde*, 1930). Caption: "Felix F. Case 4; Max Sch. Case 7; Ernst K. Case 6; (photographed by the author)."

Other extant photographs of trans men come from Hans Abraham's 1921 dissertation *Der weibliche Transvestitismus* (Female transvestitism).[3] These photographs are powerfully reminiscent of the social typographies produced in the 1920s by August Sander, and other images we find in Hirschfeld and Benjamin's later

797

798

799

Frauen der Arbeiterklasse, die als Männer leben

550

Female transsexual before any operative procedure or treatments.

FIGURE 3.14: "Women from the working class who live as men," Hirschfeld, *Geschlechtskunde*, 1930.

FIGURE 3.15: Sole image of a "female transsexual" in Harry Benjamin's, *The Transsexual Phenomenon*, 1966. University of Victoria Libraries, Transgender Archives collection. Harry Benjamin, *The Transsexual Phenomenon*. New York: Ace Publishing Corp, 1966. Special Collections call number RC560 C4B46 1966.

publications show how these styles traveled across cultures and time periods (figures 3.14 and 3.15).

Benjamin insisted in *The Transsexual Phenomenon* that "the frequency of female transsexualism is considerably less than that of the male"[4] – a misjudgement, Annette argues, that he shared with Alfred Kinsey and others. Benjamin included several pictures of "male transsexuals" (male-to-female/ transwomen) dressed as both men and as women, but he includes only this single photograph of a "female transsexual before any operative procedure or treatments," and we see him dressed only as a man – continuing a photographic practice we find in Magnus Hirschfeld's work, where "female transvestites" (trans men) are generally depicted only as men when they wear clothing. Yet

FIGURE 3.16: "Female transvestite" in *Das 3. Geschlecht*.

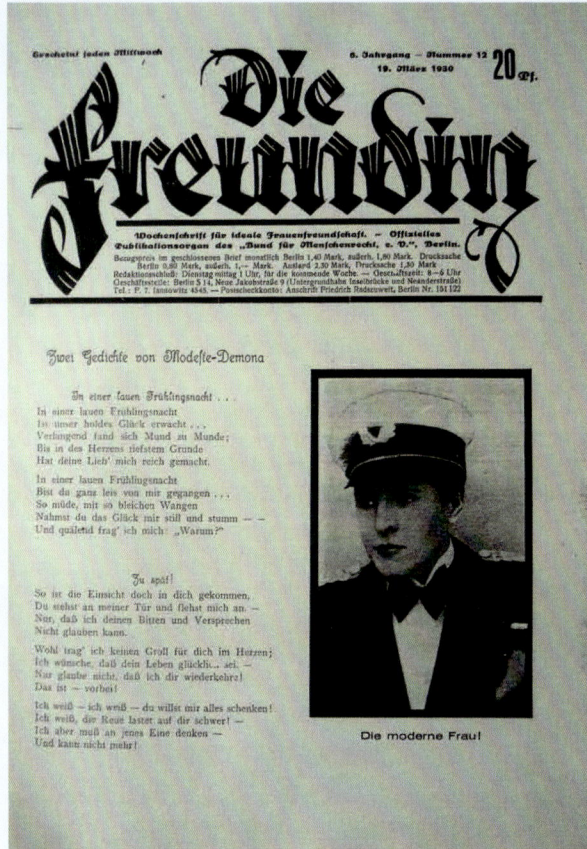

FIGURE 3.17: Cover of *Die Freundin* (March 19, 1930), captioned "The modern woman."

we also see, in these photographs, a continuity of visual representation and self-presentation that must have been visible and obvious to those who employed it.

Many masculine or cross-dressing women were also presented as lesbians; and as Rainer shows, the same image was often used in different contexts to depict different identities. Sailors was one prominent style, as we see in this single image (figures 3.16 and 3.17) reproduced in both *Das 3. Geschlecht* (aimed at transvestites) and *Die Freundin* (aimed at lesbians).

The social implications of this theme are explored in more detail in the image gallery on sensationalism.

Kinsey's approach to transsexuality and its implications for his understanding of the gender spectrum. In this book, as opposed to the first volume, Kinsey felt compelled to address – although skeptically – the science of endocrinology, which was Benjamin's medical specialty and also provided the original basis for gender-affirming surgery through the experiments of Eugen Steinach. While admitting that endocrinologists were among the "special consultants" for the project and that "hormones may have more effect on bodily functions than any other mechanism except the nervous system,"[115] he warns that popularized knowledge about the impact of hormones was "quite incorrect":

> Journalistic accounts of scientific research, over-enthusiastic advertising by some of the drug companies, over-optimistic reports from clinicians who have found a lucrative business in the administration of sex hormones, and some of the discussions among state legislators and public administrators who hope that hormone injections will provide one-package cure-alls for various social ills, have led the public to believe that endocrine organs are the glands of personality, and that there is such an exact knowledge of the way in which they control human behavior that properly qualified technicians should, at least in the near future, be able to control any and all aspects of human sexual behavior.[116]

He then goes on to minimize the effect of hormones in general and to decry the common usage of distinguishing "male" and "female" hormones.[117] His purpose in fostering doubt in the science of endocrinology, however, becomes clear when he alludes to *another* of his ongoing research projects: "institutional sexual adjustment" – in other words, sex in prisons, mental institutions, boarding schools, and the like. For Kinsey, the conviction that hormones drove sexual behaviour had led to the "unwarranted opinion that anything associated with reproduction must, ipso facto, be associated with an animal's sexual behavior, and it had justified intolerable abuses, such as the castration of sex offenders."[118] This skeptical approach to hormone treatment must have led to numerous debates with Benjamin. Given how central hormone preparations were to Benjamin's treatment of trans patients, it also means that two of the five major projects Kinsey was working on when he died were on a collision course. (The other three projects were sexuality in art, sexual factors in marital adjustment, and the influence of drugs on sexual behaviour.) It is of course difficult to say how this conflict would have played out. Would Kinsey have been persuaded by his intimate relationships with a relatively small number of trans people who were desperate for hormone treatment and who thrived once it was administered? Or would he have insisted on maintaining his taxonomic and statistically rigorous methods until the birth control pill came to shatter his preconceptions about female sexual capacity? Who knows. But it certainly seems clear that we need to be more cognizant of these intimate relationships to understand how knowledge about sexuality has been constructed.

Carla Erskine

Perhaps no other relationship better exemplifies how trans individuals themselves accelerated the learning curve for medical experts than that between Carla Erskine and Harry Benjamin. In an active correspondence of at least four years in the early 1950s, the patient wrote to the doctor with increasing trust, but also with measured insistence that she be understood as a complete and rational human being. Benjamin wrote back somewhat more concisely, but also with a degree of personal concern and engagement that certainly exceeded the boundaries of most doctor-patient relationships. There are breaks in the correspondence during the summers, when Benjamin lived at the Hotel Sir Francis Drake in San Francisco and met with his Californian patients in person. For this reason, we do not have any letters discussing Carla's self-performed orchiectomy in August 1953, since Benjamin would have been in the city and would have seen her in person. When the threads of correspondence were picked up in the fall, it becomes clear that Benjamin was informed not only of medical issues but also about the complex relationships between Carla and a close circle of friends around Louise Lawrence.

Like Lawrence, Carla viewed herself as "doing missionary work for our cause." She described how happy she was to speak to

the "psychiatric interns [who] sometimes become well known and prominent psychiatrists" and who had flocked to her bedside after her 1953 surgery. "The more medical people sympathetically interested in transvestism the better," she wrote to Benjamin in 1954.[119] She regularly offered (through Benjamin) to put Kinsey in touch with any "transvestites" she had met,[120] and she even considered the idea of compiling a scrapbook (like the one Louise Lawrence was working on for Kinsey) with which she hoped to be able to "furnish a small hit towards the understanding and acceptance of this problem."[121] But Carla soon realized that fame was not for her. "I see nothing in publicity for me except trouble," she wrote.[122]

As she was still recovering from the gender-affirming surgery that she received at the University of California Hospital on 30 December 1953, she wrote to Benjamin complaining that "the newspapers have somehow got hold of the fact that I have had this surgery."[123] The gossip columnist Herb Caen had tried to get information out of Carla's surgeon, Frank Hinman Jr., but Hinman had quickly quashed these efforts, drawing on his influence in the larger medical community to convince the muckrakers to back off. In Carla's words, Hinman argued that it "was not to the best interests of medicine, the public or myself to publish and that this case was not enough like Christine's to have sensational news value," by which she likely meant that unlike Christine Jorgensen, she had no intention of becoming a famous entertainer.[124] The resulting article was thus typically titillating but mercifully brief, with incorrect initials (for which Carla thanked Hinman) and no promise of future information: "Medical Insidem: A successful "Christine-type" operation has been performed on a man (initials L. C.) at U. C. Hospital by one of the town's topmost surgeons, who wants anonymity. The transformed male is now living as a woman in Redwood City. 'A much truer case than Christine's' is all the doctor will say."[125] Since Carla's story has remained so hidden, Hinman's efforts to maintain confidentiality seem to have had a lasting effect. I suspect (but have been unable to verify) that her ability to keep her story a secret rested upon personal relationships with Herb Caen and other newspaper columnists.[126] I will return to this story below.

The decision about whether to seek publicity faced all trans people, and in the United States all trans people in this period lived under the cloud and the glow of Jorgensen's fame. While some were eager to achieve something similar, they also knew that publicity would make it impossible to lead a normal life. Having first met Christine through Louise Lawrence in the spring of 1954, Carla had enormous respect for the famous woman's success and influence on public opinion. "She's changing public opinion greatly,"[127] Carla wrote to Benjamin, and she was impressed that despite some "false polish" gained from a career in show business, Christine was not being spoiled by fame and was generally having a salutary effect on their cause to garner public acceptance for sexual transition.[128] But Carla was not a performer, and she realized that any publicity would destroy her plans to work as a nurse.[129] She

was devastated when she lost a nursing job for no apparent reason, strongly (and realistically) suspecting that the secret of her past life had been exposed.[130]

It is clear that Benjamin evaluated Carla as an entirely rational person, quite unlike some of the other trans people he and Kinsey had interviewed, who they often assessed as unstable. In the tables of all of his trans patients, Benjamin later categorized Carla's "psychological health" as "very good," which placed her just below a few others, whom he described as being in "excellent" psychological health, but above the majority of his patients, who were described as "poor," "doubtful," "fair," or just "satisfactory." Despite Benjamin's general support for Carla's view that seeking fame was not advisable, by the time he was compiling the data for his 1966 book, he accepted that even trans women who became entertainers, such as Christine Jorgensen and Aleshia Crenshaw (who later became a successful – passing – actress under the name Aleshia Brevard) could be described as being in "excellent" psychological health.[131] But in the 1950s, both Benjamin and Kinsey seemed particularly suspicious of those seeking fame, and they were more likely to link psychological health with some kind of respectable employment. Although Carla's difficulty in keeping a full-time job and the fact that she frequently complained to Benjamin about her money problems and her inability to budget likely contributed to his slight downgrading of her psychological health,[132] her desire to remain a private person certainly met with his approval.

This desire for secrecy and privacy certainly gives the historian – in other words me, the person who just happens to be reading Carla's private correspondence – pause. I can only hope that this enterprise is ethically justified as being part of precisely the kind of enlightenment that Carla sought to bring about. Her path was not the path of publicity, and yet I hope that detailing her story several decades after her 1976 death will inspire those still struggling with the obstacles to social and medical transition and reveal to cisgender readers that these stories also affect them. The history of how Carla came to receive treatment and how she was treated by medical science is both heartening and troubling. It is only by being precise about the details that we can understand both how far we have come and how far we still have to go in honouring individuals' own sense of sexual and gender identity. With this stated, I will spend some time exploring the more intimate details of Carla's life and her correspondence with Benjamin.

In the nine-page autobiography that Carla composed for Harry Benjamin, she outlines a troubled childhood and a difficult young adulthood.[133] In this document, she cites her birthdate as 13 January 1910, but census data (and subsequent pronouncements of her age) make it clear that she was actually born in 1905 in Casper, Wyoming.[134] Having been born with a genital anomaly (Benjamin later diagnosed this as hypospadias),[135] she was initially raised as a girl. Benjamin's diagnosis conflicts with the decision of the doctor who attended her birth to tell Carla's parents that she should be raised as

a girl. It also complicates our assessment of whether the baby would today be classified as intersex. We must therefore be very careful not to discount this possibility, since, as I noted earlier, the tendency to erase the history of intersex people remains strong.[136] As I will discuss in more detail below, there is conflicting evidence about what Carla herself thought. She consistently called herself a transvestite, but she also described the female physical characteristics that were present long before she received any hormonal treatment. Of her time serving in the navy during the Second World War, she said: "Heavens knows [sic] my breasts were larger then than now," in 1953.[137] Carla grew up convinced she was a girl and by the time she had reached her fifties, she was calling herself a transvestite and was desperate to erase all signs of maleness from her body. In some sense her story provides us with emotional insight for both experiences: the experience of being an intersex child who was lied to about her body throughout her childhood and the experience of a trans person who was eager to receive medical help that would help her live an authentic life. That she could only use the words available to her at the time to express the various ruptures in her sexual/gender identity only underlines the importance of historically contextualizing all terminology related to the trans and intersex experience.[138]

But back to the narrative of Carla's autobiography. At some point in her childhood (the timing is unclear) an accident on a staircase prompted her parents to bring her to a doctor, who informed them that their little girl was in fact a boy and performed (unspecified) surgery. This led to a traumatic deterioration of her relationship with her parents, particularly her mother, who seemed to think that she now had a "monster" in her home. Carla fled the family home and made her way to Galveston, Texas.[139] Working as a sailor for two years, she lived for a time in Tahiti and then made her way back to the United States "on an Australian cattle boat," arriving in San Francisco in July 1925. After landing a temporary job playing the cornet with Ringling Brothers circus, she "decided to try to live as a girl" and fled to Mexico City, where she took the name Marie Ciel Campbell. Although she does not explicitly say so, it is likely that she chose Mexico for legal reasons. As Clare Sears has documented, San Francisco and many other American cities where she might have been accepted by other trans women had passed laws against cross-dressing in the late nineteenth and early twentieth centuries. Fearing her ability to pass as a woman under the constant threat of police attention would have made Mexico a much more comfortable place for her to live.[140] She did successfully pass in Mexico City, even entertaining a proposal of marriage, until she was discovered by "a pawing drunk" and fled back to the United States to avoid humiliation.

She moved to Milwaukee, where a brief marriage to a woman named Ruth ended in frustration despite the birth of a son. "God knows I tried to be a man," Carla writes, "but even my best tries ended in embarrassment. Still when Jack was born I thought that perhaps I had succeeded once at least." (She later discovered that she had always been sterile and could not have been Jack's father.) Ruth's alcoholism and serial adultery, but particularly her tendency to proclaim Carla's sexual shortcomings loud enough for the neighbours to hear, led to divorce and a move to California. Carla then claims to have served in the U.S. Navy between 1941 and 1943, where her "physical abnormalities," particularly her breasts, were overlooked, but where her pre-existing and ongoing morphine addiction was discovered, leading to her discharge for fraudulent enlistment. Two brief relationships (with a more sexually tolerant woman and an apparently asexual man) were followed by suicide attempts and the eventual decision to medically confirm what she had always known: her feminine identity. "Due to the facts of my birth and the upbringing and due to the development of my breasts and due to the lack of body hair and the female pattern of its distribution and due to my narrow shoulders and small bones, I have always thought that there was more wrong with me than just sexual impotence and I made up my mind that if this were the case and in the same category, I would find out and if possible I would have this done. It seemed that if it were a possibility it would open up life itself again to me." But Carla's search for medical help was frustrated by doctors' reticence to undertake such a transition so late in life.

In 1953 she decided to take matters into her own hands. On 19 August 1953, the *San Francisco Examiner* reported on Carla's desperate act under the headline "Sex Operation on Self Fails":

The case of a Half Moon Bay man who masueraded [sic] for six weeks as a female nursing home attendant and performed a crude operation to change his sex was disclosed yesterday by Sheriff Earl Whitmore. The man, who gave his name as [Carla Erskine], 43, attempted vainly to emasculate himself last Saturday. He explained to Palo Alto hospital attendants that "I wanted to be like Christine." He was treated for shock and loss of blood, and was released Monday, Whitmore said. [Erskine], a former fisherman who declined to give his male forename, had worked for the past six weeks as a domestic in a Menlo Park home for elderly persons. An official of the home commented last night that "[Erskine is] no longer is with us."[141]

Luckily for Carla, the article did not ignite the flurry of press attention that she so feared. But her self-surgery was certainly known in the trans circles of the day.[142] She later tried to dissuade others from following her example, and she refused requests that she help them do so, on the grounds that she had herself almost bled to death.[143] Carla met Benjamin very soon after this episode. Benjamin would have been in California for his summer sojourn and, given that he kept a close watch on any newspaper articles about trans people, it is possible that the *San Francisco Examiner* article motivated the contact and that it was Benjamin who introduced Carla to Louise Lawrence. Carla's correspondence with Benjamin begins on 1 July 1953 with

a mention of their meeting at Lawrence's house, and it includes exact physical measurements, demonstrating Carla's desire to be both Benjamin's patient and his research subject.[144] Carla's case clearly influenced Benjamin, who later prided himself on being able to prevent "attempts at suicide or self-mutilation" through hormonal treatment and sympathy. He must have been referring to Carla when he noted in the introduction to Richard Green and John Money's book *Transsexualism and Sex Reassignment* that the "few instances of attempted self-castration by definitely nonpsychotic individuals impressed me greatly. Their desperation as well as the entire clinical history with their vain search for help, often from childhood on, made me realize that the medical profession truly treated these patients as 'stepchildren.'"[145]

But Benjamin also repeatedly told Carla that her case was quite different. "Yours is as unsimilar as can be" from the Jorgensen case, he told Carla when they were discussing the Caen article about her surgery.[146] It is difficult to tell exactly what he meant by this. He clearly did not believe that Carla was intersex, because he refused her request to describe her as a "pseudo-hermaphrodite" in order to patch up relations with her son, who could not accept her transition. Benjamin demurred, noting that one would have to add the term "psychic" to the term "pseudo-hermaphrodite" and that this "would be a very controversial diagnosis. You have had undescended testicles for which you were operated. [Benjamin is presumably describing the operation performed on Carla as a child.] They were then in a normal position, but not capable of forming sperm cells."[147] Carla pushed back: "I think this [using the word "pseudo-hermaphrodite"] would be no falsehood, and it would settle questions in an uninformed and somewhat immature mind that he couldn't possibly understand otherwise – I realize my own condition perfectly but to quite some few people who have to know of this change, the idea of hermaphroditeism [sic] is easier to explain and understand than is transvestism."[148] By this time, the diagnosis of "intersexuality" that was listed on Carla's hospital entrance form in December 1953 and that she found "interesting terminology" had disappeared from the discussion.[149] Since the relationship with her son was permanently broken (there is no evidence that he ever wrote to Benjamin) we cannot know what Carla decided to tell him.

There is also great uncertainty about how Carla represented herself to nonmedical professionals. Even before her surgery, she volunteered to speak to the San Francisco branch of the Mattachine Society, a gay rights organization that had been founded in 1950 in Los Angeles. This was yet another indication of her desire to educate at least the more tolerant portions of the public. Her talk was promoted with the following flyer, distributed only to members:

We have made special arrangements to have a true transvestite
give a prepared lecture on this most
interesting topic entitled:
WHAT IS TRANSVESTISM?

Our speaker has a fascinating story to tell, and we want you all to be there to enjoy this delightful personality. This talk will go into detail and be most revealing, not only from a physical but also from a historical standpoint, citing famous cases from history. The meeting is under direction of Mac and will be held at: 516–55th Street, Oakland, Apt. B. on Thursday evening, December 10, at 8 PM.[150]

Carla reported to Benjamin that the talk was well received and that she repeated it at least one other time, but she sadly did not take him up on his offer to have it transcribed and published in *The International Journal of Sexology*, the journal in which Benjamin was to publish what he claimed was the "very first medical article on transsexualism," and which folded in 1955.[151] Given the usage of the day, however, the language ("true transvestite") suggests that Carla was representing herself as someone who had been male but was transitioning to female. Leaving aside the genital malformation and even her own physical self-description as having "more wrong with me than just sexual impotence," I believe that this is the way that we should describe and understand her. Carla's friends also very clearly understood her to be a male-to-female transsexual (though they did not use this terminology until later).

As I have mentioned, Carla and her friends thought of themselves as a very small group of pioneers. They openly compared surgeries,[152] and they communicated with other trans individuals

FIGURE 3.18: Carla sent this portrait to Harry Benjamin for his "transvestite" files in the fall of 1954. From back row: Angela D., Louise Lawrence, Judy S., Carla Erskine. Photo by Alvin Harris. KILSC-HB-25, folder 10. Copyright © 2017, The Trustees of Indiana University on behalf of the Kinsey Institute. All rights reserved.

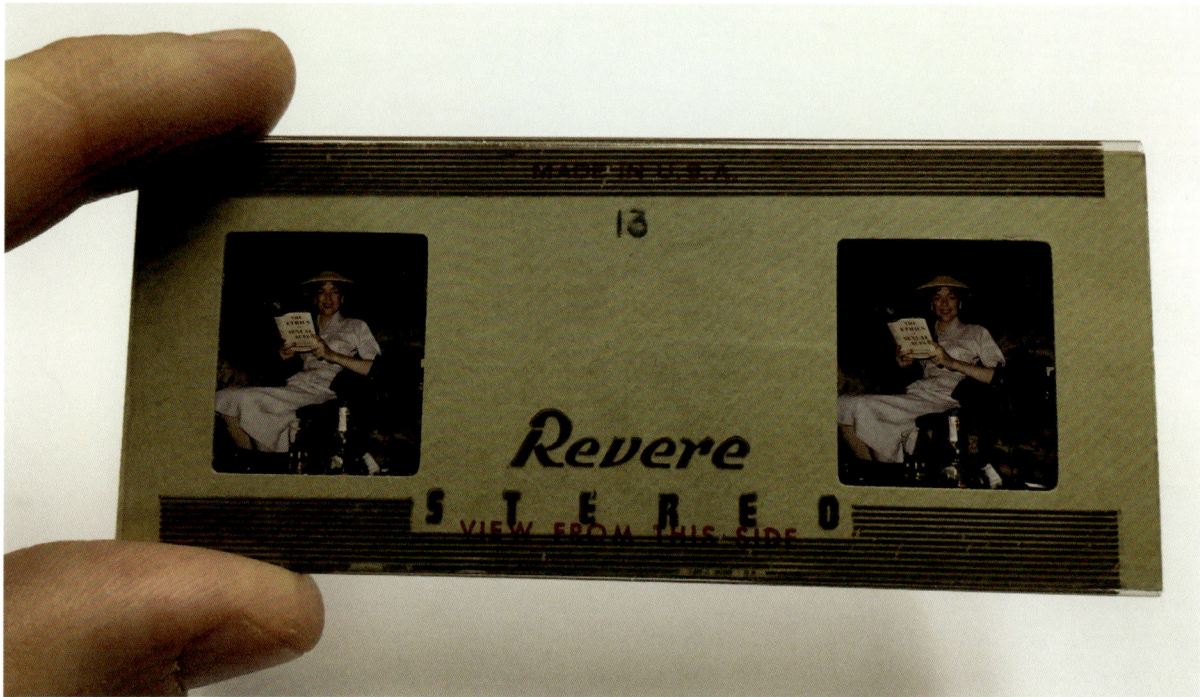

FIGURE 3.19: Stereoscopic slide (likely taken by Carla Erskine) of Christine Jorgensen, KILSC-HB 18. Copyright © 2017, The Trustees of Indiana University on behalf of the Kinsey Institute. All rights reserved.

across the world to discuss their social, medical, and cultural struggles.[153]

Some of these relationships ended in heartache. Carla told Benjamin of her bafflement that two of her trans friends, Angela D. and Judy S. (pseudonyms, see figure 3.18) had stopped speaking to her, and she was suspicious that they might have broken off the relationship in order to profit from their collaboratively developed idea to invent a new epilator.[154] Despite these disappointments, both Carla and Louise Lawrence were constantly on the lookout for other trans women to refer to Benjamin and Kinsey. In some cases, this led them to individuals who were clearly trying to emulate Jorgensen's path to fame. Carla told Benjamin that she and her friends quickly rethought the idea of contacting Bunny Breckenridge. Breckenridge was a troubled actor and millionaire; his 1954

announcement that he planned to undergo a sex-change operation in Denmark appears to have been nothing but a publicity stunt, and he later served time in prison for committing "perverse acts" with two young boys.[155] Carla quickly sensed Breckenridge's deception, calling him a "publicity seeking dilettante."[156] She had a much longer relationship with another troubled soul, Dixie MacLane, whom Susan Stryker describes as "a burlesque performer [who] tried to ride the wave of publicity about her surgery" (succeeding to some small degree in the 1950s) and about whom Alex will say more.[157] Carla's letters to Benjamin detail her growing frustration with Dixie's emotionally demanding personality and desire for publicity. Benjamin described Dixie as "emotionally deeply unbalanced" and therefore unlikely to be able to obtain surgery.[158] Carla complained that Dixie was "blowing her cork all over the place," threatening suicide, and displaying too much faith in the ability of surgery to transform personality. "She expects to be a woman and when she finds that the only thing gained will be the dubious legal right to dress in female attire, I am afraid for her."[159] Carla broke off the friendship when Dixie forwarded her letters and those of Louise Lawrence to Dr. Frederik Hartsuiker in the Netherlands.[160]

Another incident that contributed to the breakup with Dixie involved the police and makes it clear just how important passing was for trans women in 1950s California. Having travelled to Los Angeles in the spring of 1955 for psychiatric testing with Frederic G. Wordon at the University of California Medical Center in Los Angeles, Carla was apprehended by officers from the Los Angeles Police Department (LAPD), an experience for which she blamed Dixie:

> As usual when I come in direct contact with Dixie, I got mad at her and, as usual about her ideas on publicity she expects and hopes to get when she gets home. I think it was because of the company I kept in Los Angeles (Dixie and [Karen] sure look "queen" letting their hair grow out etc.), but when they met me at the station a plain clothesman cornered me and told me he thought I was masquerading. I told him lets go to police Doctor and settle question [sic], which we did. Took only one minute and I was appologized [sic] to an politely

excorted [sic] to my hotel in style. The policeman wanted to be sure that I had no hard feelings as he said he was only doing his job – and that the two people (Dixie and [Karen]) who met me at the station were known homosexuals and because of my heighth [sic] and rather deep voice the "mistake" was an easy one to make. So everything ended nicely and this little episode has probably done a great deal to reassure me. I wonder if Dr. Kinsey might like a report of this incident? And I wonder if a written statement from you or Dr. Hinman might not save trouble and a bit of embarrassment if such an occasion should arise again. What do you think?[161]

In post-Second World War Los Angeles, moral authorities viewed cross-dressing as a provocation that threatened the city's reputation and contributed to a cosmopolitanism they viewed as threatening. As the collectively authored book *Lavender Los Angeles* explains, the LAPD therefore "relentlessly cracked down on LGBT expression … [They] raided gay bars, entrapped gay men, and arrested LGBT people who cross-dressed."[162] As Carla's description of this episode demonstrates, trans people craved medical protection from this harassment (they would have been thrilled to have access to the kind of medical authorization that Magnus Hirschfeld's "transvestite passes" provided), and they quickly recognized that genital surgery could offer some security. The tone of Carla's letter to Benjamin and her concern about how Dixie and her other trans friend Karen might be endangering her cause by appearing disreputable in public make it clear that she was desperately trying to appear deserving of medical treatment in Benjamin's eyes.

Another area of concern for trans patients was how their sex lives might be assessed. Carla told Benjamin that she thought Dixie was unsuitable for surgery because her friend "has and enjoys some kind of sex life and ... would be very unhappy to give this up even tho [sic] she thinks it doesn't mean much to her now."[163] This one sentence hints at an extremely sensitive subject that is very rarely explicitly mentioned in the correspondence, perhaps for fear that it might fall into the wrong hands, but likely also because of an awareness that stress on erotic desire could only harm the cause of increasing tolerance for transitioning individuals. Well into the 1990s, it was common for trans advocates to try to silence any discussion of erotic desire to avoid awakening a moral backlash.[164] During the 1950s, Benjamin was still describing trans women – people he was then calling "transsexualists" – as "the most disturbed group of male transvestites."[165] He thought that their sexuality was largely "nongenital" and that the creation of an artificial vagina could aid the sexual satisfaction only of their male partners.[166] But he was also beginning to create a distinction between transvestites and "transsexualists" – the former, he insisted, derived sexual pleasure from their genitals while the latter viewed these body parts with disgust.[167] This background, and the likelihood that Carla and Benjamin

discussed these theories, provides an additional twist to Benjamin's argument that Carla was unlike Jorgensen and MacLane. But there were clearly tensions surrounding this subject even at the time.

Richard Ekins has meticulously detailed how Benjamin's advocacy – his understanding of the "art of the possible" – led him to transform an early acceptance of human sexual variety (with Hirschfeldian undertones) into a more heteronormative categorization of surgery as a path to "normal" gender relations.[168] But this analysis crucially leaves out the influence of Alfred Kinsey and (more understandably) the sexual inclinations of those investigating trans lives. It is instructive that during a brief marriage to a heterosexual man, Carla wrote to Benjamin about her surprise that she was achieving sexual satisfaction and that she was proud to be satisfying her husband, despite the fact that she did not have a vagina. She asked Benjamin to report on this experience to Kinsey.[169] Kinsey, she must have known, had been initially disapproving of surgical intervention to remove the penis, because he simply could not imagine why anyone would want to remove an organ of such massive orgiastic potential. This obsession with counting orgasms has not escaped the notice of those who have analyzed his *Male* and *Female* books.[170] Kinsey defined sexuality as the potentially unlimited capacity for sexual release or "outlet" – a potential upon whose fulfilment culture and society only acted as negative forces in the form of moral prescription and repression. But his own repressed childhood (his father railed against masturbation) and troubled early marriage (he and his wife needed medical advice to consummate their marriage) probably contributed to his valorization of the male orgasm as the most obvious (not to mention countable) manifestation of human sexual capacity.[171] These preconceptions were likely the origin of his initial reluctance to accept the existence of transgender individuals, especially because he (and initially Benjamin) assumed that the desire to change one's sex was an almost exclusively "male" (i.e., male-to-female) phenomenon.

Kinsey's own sex life has been the subject of much fascination and was a key theme of the 2005 film about his life directed by Bill Condon. Benjamin has yet to receive the same biographical treatment, and we have only hints about how his own sexual practice might have influenced his views of the sexual lives of his trans patients. Aside from the discussions of nightlife that I have already mentioned, I have found only one cryptic yet revealing note from Benjamin to Kinsey that seems to be a description of sexual activity: "Did I tell you I have trouble with my girl?" Benjamin wrote in September 1951. "She has just reached the age of consent, and now she starts refusing. Any advice?"[172] We cannot know what Benjamin might have meant, and what appears to be an allusion to sex with an underage partner is certainly disturbing. There is also a hint in one of the interviews that Susan Stryker conducted with Aleshia Brevard Crenshaw that Benjamin might have had extramarital sexual relationships. Crenshaw, who began her transition as a female impersonator at Finoccio's bar in San Francisco,[173]

describes herself as becoming one of Harry Benjamin's "girls." Crenshaw met with Benjamin soon after receiving a diagnosis that would later allow her to have surgery. (From her biography, we can glean that she met Benjamin in 1958 and had surgery in 1962.) Crenshaw told Stryker that Benjamin "added me to his little list. You know how there are RGs – real girls? Well he always said there were RGs, and His – his girls."[174] Benjamin, Crenshaw noted to Stryker's nonsurprise, "had his own quirks … He had a fetish for very thin girls with very long hair. He had a hair fetish. So that was his quirk." Stryker admitted to having heard this before, and Crenshaw responded with the reflection that "these are the sorts of things we don't want out. We try to build a mystique about transsexuals. I guess it's time to let the truth be out there though."[175] Given the incredible service he provided for so many desperate individuals, it is understandable that Benjamin's mystique has lasted this long. But in our era of increasing understanding of the incredible plasticity and variability of human sexual identity, it strikes me as illogical to continue to try to cleanly separate scientific understandings of sexuality from the researcher's own emotional responses.

Everything I have said so far about the close personal relationship that Carla and Benjamin cultivated after 1953 helps us to read the images that we displayed in the two iterations of the exhibition *TransTrans* in 2016 and 2019–20. Between 1953 and 1955, Carla sent Benjamin stereoscopic slides of her friends, most of whom were sitting on a couch in Louise Lawrence's living room. This aspect of her "missionary work" was

so important to her that she prioritized developing and mailing the slides despite a near-constant state of poverty.[176]

She and her friends clearly hoped that these photographs would portray their successful integration into everyday life. They wanted to convince Benjamin and Kinsey that their desires were valid and that medical intervention could be successful. Carla's devotion to the cause of scientific inquiry is evident in her willingness to have nude pictures of herself published in Benjamin's 1966 book. This is the context for the middle image in the triptych in Benjamin's book (figures 3.3 and 3.4). Carla gave Benjamin permission to use her images in order to foster knowledge about transsexuality.[177] I would argue that the intrusion into Carla's private life that republishing these pictures represents is justified by the fact that it helps us to understand how adamantly Carla and her friends tried to convince Benjamin of their own "normality." The slides from Louise's couch call out for us to accept the "normality" of those photographed.

The images are personal, playful, intimate, and they express the joy of transformation and personal fulfilment. But it must also be said that the images are not particularly good photographic portraits. Carla's attempt to make a living with a portrait studio lasted a little over a year, collapsing in December 1955.[178] She had already been complaining to Benjamin about her renewed financial difficulties and about how she had been thinking of making

> a large selection of photomicro-
> graphs of biological specimens
> [from the oceanside near her home]
> and purvey them to the educa-
> tional system as aids to teaching
> … I have given up trying to con-
> duct business for myself as I know
> from past experience that Im [sic]
> not able to manage the sales and
> business management end of it …
> It always comes back to this basic
> problem, that I do not understand
> financial affairs and am not capable
> in realizing on my work. So here I
> am sitting with a brand new and
> beautiful life and dont [sic] know
> what to do about it. I am in a rut
> and life is passing me by. How does
> one break out of a rut?[179]

I have made several efforts to discover precisely the details of Carla's "beautiful life," but I have only been able to find a few very tantalizing hints about how about how she turned this interest in micro-photography into a successful career. In November 1972, Herb Caen, the San Francisco gossip columnist who had first encountered Carla when he wrote about her self-surgery in 1953, asked his readers: "You know the Avenue Theatre on San Bruno Avenue, which plays silent movies? Well, [Carla Erskine], who made her fortune in

Figure 3.21: One of Carla's friend with child on Louise Lawrence's couch, KILSC-HB 17. Copyright © 2017, The Trustees of Indiana University on behalf of the Kinsey Institute. All rights reserved.

electronics, bought it because she's mad for that big organ. Quite a woman is [Carla]; not only does she own a gullwing Mercedes and a white Rolls, she just qualified – at age 68! – to fly solo in her Skyhawk plane."[180] From this, we can gather that Carla became wealthy in the decade after she stopped writing to Harry Benjamin. "She came to the rescue," Vernon Gregory, the owner of Avenue Theatre told *Oakland Tribune* reporter Elinor Hayes in July 1969. "She is a living genius who has made a fortune in her own electronic business and has installed an organ in her home."[181]

How did she achieve this dramatic reversal in her economic fortunes? The details have been difficult to determine. The

FIGURE 3.22: A couple on Louise Lawrence's couch, KILSC-HB 17. Copyright © 2017, The Trustees of Indiana University on behalf of the Kinsey Institute. All rights reserved.

only extended description of her life that I have been able to uncover is in a blog post written by the plastic surgeon Donald R. Laub. In "Many People, Many Passports," Laub provides entertaining stories about his illustrious career as a plastic surgeon in California. He served as the chief of plastic surgery at Stanford University School of medicine between 1968 and 1980, and he was the founder of Interplast (now called ReSurge International), an international charity providing life-changing operations for people in countries too poor to offer such services. The entry about Carla makes it very clear that despite a differently spelled first name and a few vaguely recalled details of personal history, Laub did indeed meet Carla in 1963. She required surgery for a hernia, and she asked Laub, the still aspiring plastic surgeon, to "get that tattoo aligned exactly right when you do the suturing."[182] Laub later performed transgender surgeries himself,[183] and in his blog he describes how this early encounter began a long-term friendship and collaboration with Carla. Sadly, by the time I tracked down this story, I was told by a former secretary of Dr. Laub's that he was suffering from brain cancer, so I was unable to interview him.[184]

Carla had eventually found a new career. As Laub puts it "during the birth of Silicon Valley she was able to make microphotography negatives of the plans for a computer chip; the manufacturing process utilized silver salts in the negatives of her microphotos to etch silicon into chips." Having received shares in "one of the more prominent laser and computer companies in Silicon Valley," she had been able to build a beautiful Japanese-style home in the hills of Los Altos.[185] Laub later encouraged her to invent three-dimensional television (which she apparently did), and when her personal nurse, a man with whom she lived in an apparently platonic relationship, told him that she was becoming depressed in retirement, Laub employed Carla as a photographer for Interplast. By the 1970s, she was "worth several million" and had donated a large sum to Laub's research. Sadly, in 1976, Carla was diagnosed with metastatic cancer of the rib – a recurrence

of a previous bout with lung cancer. Upon hearing that she likely only had six weeks to live, Carla asked the young medical student who had delivered the news to hand over her purse. She then swallowed the cyanide capsules that she had brought with her to the hospital and died twenty-four hours later.

I tell this story, despite being unable to confirm the details, because the letters to Benjamin trail off in 1955, leaving the impression that Carla might not have been achieving a successful personal and professional life. (In his book, Benjamin misleadingly reproduces a picture of her working in a short-lived nursing job, although he certainly knew that she had become a "chemical" photographer by 1965.)[186] Laub's obvious affection for Carla, and his sadness-filled respect for her decision to end her life, makes it clear that she had found peace. She had, writes Laub, "display[ed] more wisdom than any of us, perhaps abandoning her beautifully ornamented body. She may have elected not to try another life. [Carla] was a friend. Not in the sense of a friend I considered 'close' or a friend I would ask to dinner or a friend I would introduce at a party, but as a friend who was a co-worker, a valuable and essential member of the team, and therefore, an extension of myself."[187] It was only when he wrote this blog entry thirty years later that Laub forgave the medical student for being so rashly honest in providing Carla with her cancer prognosis. In other words, she had continued to establish intimate networks of knowledge to the end of her life and beyond.

Conclusion

This chapter has demonstrated that three aspects of trans history require more concentrated reflection than they have previously been accorded: international connections, personal (and even intimate) networks, and the sexual self-understandings and practices of the researchers and popularizers themselves. Everything that I have said here adds weight to the work of historians who have begun to insist that historians pay more attention to emotions and intimacy as having causal effects on trajectories of knowledge, political developments, and patterns of both tolerance and prejudice.[188] Without the space to delve into this historiography, I would simply underline that productive discomfort in revealing intimate histories is not the same thing as voyeurism or sensationalism. I have alluded several times to the uncomfortable feelings I experienced while analyzing the intimate correspondence between doctors and patients and the erotic and otherwise extremely private images that trans women in the 1950s shared with men like Harry Benjamin and Alfred Kinsey – men in whom these individuals placed enormous faith and trust. In the next chapter, Alex will demonstrate that similar forms of compassionate care characterized the relationship between doctors and trans patients in Europe after the Second World War.[189] It is important to note that the social intolerance prevalent in many societies can still mean that revealing such intimate relationships or questioning the god-like objectivity of scientific research can create unjustifiable risks. Yet there has never been a time when secrets about sex improved the lives of those being persecuted for their desires and self-understandings. There has never been a time when it has truly helped anyone to act as if human sexual desire or subjective interpersonal relationships can be ignored in either politics or law without intensifying the mechanisms of repression. In revealing some of the most intimate desires of people like Otto Spengler and Carla Erskine, I have tried to demonstrate that the respect these people were accorded by scientists and medical practitioners like Harry Benjamin and Alfred Kinsey, as well as the varying degrees of happiness that these relationships produced, definitively overrules any objections that scientific objectivity was compromised when researchers took their trans patients' feelings seriously. The history of trans experience in Germany and the United States teaches us that intimate relationships are thus not necessarily inimical to scientific knowledge – that is, provided that these relationships are built on mutual respect and structured in ways that protect individual bodily integrity. Indeed without the interpersonal trust that developed across the Atlantic and over the course of several decades, the lives of trans people today would be immeasurably more difficult.

GALLERY NOTES: Harry Benjamin's Use
of Photographs of Carla Erskine

1   Margo DeMello, *Bodies of Inscription:
     A Cultural History of the Modern Tattoo
     Community* (Durham: Duke University Press,
     2000), 59–70.

2   See, for instance, the tattoos presented in
     Jérôme Pierrat and Éric Guillon, *Marins
     tatoués : portraits de marins 1890–1940;
     Portraits of Sailors 1890–1940* (Paris : La
     manufacture de livres, 2018), 112.

GALLERY NOTES: Trans Men

1   In reference to trans men in America around
     the turn of the twentieth century, Emily
     Skidmore has recently argued that they "often
     sought to pass as conventional men, aligning
     themselves with the normative values of their
     communities." See *True Sex: The Lives of Trans
     Men at the Turn of the Twentieth Century*
     (New York: New York University Press, 2017),
     3. This was a desire they shared with many
     trans women, who nevertheless found it more
     difficult to pass and, as Alex elaborates in his
     essay, were often relegated to spaces of theatre
     and prostitution.

2   Magnus Hirschfeld, *Die Transvestiten:
     Eine Untersuchung über den erotischen
     Verkleidungstrieb*, 192–8. Volker Weiß
     identifies him as "Katharina Kohnheim."
     See also Volker Weiß, *'mit ärztlicher Hilfe
     zum richtigen Geschlecht?': Zur Kritik der
     medizinischen Konstruktion der Transsexualität*
     (Hamburg: Männerschwarm Verlag, 2009),
     164, cited from Geertje Mak, "'Passing
     Women' in the Consulting Room of Magnus
     Hirschfeld: On Why the Term 'Transvestite'
     Was Not Employed for Cross-Dressing
     Women," *Österreichische Zeitschrift für
     Geschichtswissenschaften* 9, no. 3 (1998): 388.

3   Hans Abraham, *Der weibliche Transvestitismus*
     (Berlin: Ebering, 1921).

4   Harry Benjamin, *The Transsexual Phenomenon*
     (New York: Ace Publishing Corp, 1966).

NOTES TO CHAPTER 3

1   Joanne Meyerowitz's pseudonym for this
     woman is Caren Ecker. See Joanne Meyerowitz,
     *How Sex Changed: A History of Transsexuality
     in the United States* (Cambridge and London:
     Harvard University Press, 2002), 155 and
     elsewhere in this book. Carla died in 1976,
     and I have made several unsuccessful attempts
     to find descendants (or even good friends) to
     obtain permission to use her full name. As I
     will discuss in more detail below, Carla seems
     to have been entirely estranged from all family
     members when she died, and she actively
     attempted to avoid any publicity about her
     transition. Although, as is noted in the sidebar
     "Harry Benjamin's Use of Photographs of Carla
     Erskine," she gave permission to Benjamin to
     use her image and tell her story, revealing her
     identity clearly presents ethical quandaries. I
     am torn between my respect for her desire for
     privacy and my desire to also convey respect for
     her indomitable spirit and her contribution to
     the advancement of knowledge. While privacy
     is often critical to the safety and well-being of
     trans individuals, anonymization – particularly
     long after death – can also be a form of
     forgetting and belittling their contributions and
     life stories. In the end, I must follow the policies
     of the Kinsey Institute Library & Special
     Collections by maintaining her anonymity,
     but I have chosen to use first names in this
     chapter, because it better suits the atmosphere
     of intimacy I am addressing.

2   Letter from Carla Erskine to Harry Benjamin,
     22 Jan 1954, Kinsey Institute Library & Special
     Collections, Harry Benjamin Collection
     (hereafter KILSC-HB), Box 4, Ser. II C.

3   Lawrence's role as a pioneer and her
     "instrumental [work] in developing the trans
     community's connection to pioneering sex
     researchers such as Alfred Kinsey and Harry
     Benjamin" were recently honoured by the
     creation of an archive that carries here name.
     See Louise Lawrence Transgender Archive,
     https://lltransarchive.org/.

4   Carla describes her various friendships with
     Californian trans women in her letters to
     Benjamin. A letter dated July 1953 makes
     it clear that they originally met at Louise
     Lawrence's apartment in the early summer

of 1953, likely at the beginning of his yearly sojourn in San Francisco. Erskine to Benjamin, 1 July 1953, KILSC-HB, Box 4, Ser. II C.

5   Erskine to Benjamin, 5 Oct 1954, KILSC-HB, Box 4, Ser. II C.

6   For a somewhat more detailed account of these rulings, see Meyerowitz, *How Sex Changed*, 47–8.

7   Carla alludes to the fact that self-surgery had almost caused her to bleed to death in a letter to Benjamin on 5 Oct 1953, KILSC-HB, Box 4, Ser. II C. I will return to this episode below.

8   Carla was not including Louise Lawrence, who never underwent surgery. Erskine to Benjamin, 5 Oct 1954, KILSC-HB, Box 4, Ser. II C.

9   Julia Serano provides a concise and sensitive discussion of debates over terminology that has influenced my wording in this chapter: Julia Serano, *Whipping Girl: A Transsexual Woman on Sexism and the Scapegoating of Femininity* (Emeryville, CA: Seal Press, 2007), 23–34.

10   This is certainly not the place to rehearse the various stages of this history. For accessible summaries, see: Veronique Mottier, *Sexuality: A Very Short Introduction* (Oxford and New York: Oxford University Press, 2008); Robert A. Nye, ed., *Sexuality* (Oxford: Oxford University Press, 1999); and Anna Clark, *Desire: A History of European Sexuality* (New York: Routledge, 2008).

11   See Meyerowitz, *How Sex Changed*, 45; and Susan Stryker, *Transgender History* (Berkeley, CA: Seal Press, 2008), 38–40. The link between the two men has now become well enough known to be recorded in textbook narratives such as Ardel Haefele-Thomas's *Introduction to Transgender Studies* (New York: Harrington Park Press, LLC, 2019), 102–3. While it is not quite correct to call Benjamin Hirschfeld's student, as Haefele-Thomas does (Benjamin was a fully qualified endocrinologist by the time he met Hirschfeld in Berlin), they are very right to note that Benjamin's success in being named the first person to study transgender or transsexual people has much to do with the accessibility of his work, in contrast to that of Hirschfeld or particularly Richard von Krafft-Ebing, who purposely obscured his most sensitive writings from the public by writing passages in Latin (103).

12   For a description of this nightlife, see: Katie Sutton, "'We Too Deserve a Place in the Sun': The Politics of Transvestite Identity in Weimar Germany," *German Studies Review* 35, no. 2 (2012): 335–54; Robert Beachy, *Gay Berlin: Birthplace of a Modern Identity* (New York: Knopf, 2014); and Jill Suzanne Smith, *Berlin Coquette: Prostitution and the New German Woman, 1890–1933* (Ithaca, NY: Cornell University Press, 2014). On Benjamin's connections to researchers in Europe, see Friedemann Pfaefflin, "Sex Reassignment, Harry Benjamin, and Some European Roots," *International Journal of Transgenderism* 1, no. 2 (1997), https://cdn.atria.nl/ezines/web/IJT/97-03/numbers/symposion/ijtc0202.htm. Pfaefflin notes that Benjamin was "fully informed about Hirschfeld's work" and "eagerly soaked up every new finding of sexual endocrinology and sexual psychology years before he met the first transsexual patient."

13   Harry Benjamin, "Reminiscences," *Journal of Sex Research* 6, no. 1 (1970): 3–4.

14   We expected that Kinsey must have somehow drawn on the research of Hirschfeld, and we expected to base our exhibition on a small archival treasure – the "Hirschfeld Scrapbook" – which we knew was housed in the archives of the Kinsey Institute in Bloomington. We were disappointed to discover that the scrapbook (a scattered collection of letters, reports, and published documents from Hirschfeld's years as a researcher and gay-rights activist) had arrived at the Institute after Kinsey's death. (Someone had found it in Nice in 1959, long after Hirschfeld's death in 1935.)

15   Alfred C. Kinsey, Wardell R. Pomeroy, and Clyde E. Martin, *Sexual Behavior in the Human Male* (Philadelphia and London: W. B. Saunders Company, 1948); Alfred C. Kinsey, Wardell R. Pomeroy, Paul H. Gebhard, Clyde E. Martin, and John Bancroft, *Sexual Behavior in the Human Female* (Philadelphia and London: W. B. Saunders Company, 1953). His two books were an immediate sensation – the *Male* book had gone into its six printings ten days after it was released. See: Wardell Baxter Pomeroy, *Dr. Kinsey and the Institute for Sex Research* (New York: Harper, 1972), 265. Although tracking down sales numbers is a daunting task, it is clear that the two books together sold hundreds

of thousands of copies and were translated into many languages. See Ron Jackson Suresha, "'Properly Placed before the Public': Publication and Translation of the Kinsey Reports," *Journal of Bisexuality* 8, nos 3-4 (2008): 203–28.

16 Even the most well-known and influential trans and intersex memoirs of this period tend to emphasize the role of doctors or are narrated by others. The most obvious example is the biography of Lili Elbe, which is almost always called a memoir or an autobiography despite having been written by someone else. Niels Hoyer, ed., *Man into Woman: An Authentic Record of a Change of Sex*, trans. H. J. Stenning (New York: E. P. Dutton & Co., Inc., 1933). See also the sidebar "Photomontage of Lili Elbe" in Michael's chapter. Another example of medical intervention in the authorship of trans/intersex memoirs is Hirschfeld's influence in the publication of N. O. Body, *Memoirs of a Man's Maiden Years*, trans. Deborah Simon (Philadelphia: University of Pennsylvania Press, 2009).

17 See Michel Foucault, *History of Sexuality*, vol. 1: An Introduction (New York: Pantheon Books, 1978); and Edward Ross Dickinson and Richard F. Wetzell, "The Historiography of Sexuality in Modern Germany," *German History* 23, no. 3 (2005): 291–305, esp. 298–9.

18 Having lived her entire life as a female, Barbin was "discovered" to be male when she was twenty-two and was forced to change her gender presentation to male. This prevented her from continuing a relationship with her female lover. She committed suicide in 1868. Michel Foucault, *Herculine Barbin*, trans. Richard McDougall (New York: Vintage, 1980), esp. vii–xvii.

19 Gillian Frank and Lauren Gutterman, "Canary," *Sexing History*, accessed 1 July 2019, https://www.sexinghistory.com/episode-24.

20 Franz X. Eder, *Kultur der Begierde: eine Geschichte der Sexualität* (Verlag C. H. Beck, 2002), 17.

21 Harry Oosterhuis, *Stepchildren of Nature: Krafft-Ebing, Psychiatry and the Making of Sexual Identity* (Chicago: University of Chicago Press, 2000), 185.

22 Ibid., 12.

23 Harry Oosterhuis, "Sexual Modernity in the Works of Richard von Krafft-Ebing and Albert Moll," *Medical History* 56, no. 2 (April 2012): 133–55, 137. See also Richard von Krafft-Ebing, "Neue Studien auf dem Gebiete der Homosexualität," *Jahrbuch fur sexuelle Zwischenstufen* 3 (1901): 1–36. Krafft-Ebing argued that homosexuality should not be thought of as an indication of degeneration (2) and that it was more akin to a small physical deformity than to a depravity or sickness (5).

24 An analysis of some of the questionnaires can be found in Hirschfeld's medical journal, the *Jahrbuch für sexuelle Zwischenstufen*, but the originals were mostly destroyed when the institute was plundered by Nazi students on 9 May 1933. See Rainer Herrn, Michael Thomas Taylor, and Annette F. Timm, eds, "Magnus Hirschfeld's Institute for Sexual Science: A Visual Sourcebook," in *Not Straight from Germany: Sexual Publics and Sexual Citizenship since Magnus Hirschfeld* (Ann Arbor, MI: Michigan University Press, 2017), 64. The estimate of 10,000 questionnaires is from Vern L. Bullough, "Introduction," in Magnus Hirschfeld, *The Transvestites: The Erotic Drive to Cross-Dress* (Buffalo, NY: Prometheus Books, 1991), 11. In 1904, Hirschfeld conducted a survey of students and metal workers in Berlin, seeking to establish the proportion of homosexual and bisexual individuals in the population in order to campaign against anti-homosexual laws. His work experienced a setback when he was fined 200 Marks for sending survey postcards asking about sexual identification through the mail. See Magnus Hirschfeld, "Das Ergebnis der statistischen Untersuchungen über den Prozentsatz der Homosexuellen," *Jahrbuch für sexuelle Zwischenstufen* 6 (1904): 109–78. This is the only Hirschfeld questionnaire to which Kinsey refers. See Kinsey, Pomeroy, and Martin, *Sexual Behavior in the Human Male*, 691.

25 Magnus Hirschfeld, *Die Transvestiten: Eine Untersuchung über den erotischen Verkleidungstrieb* (Berlin: Alfred Pulvermacher & Co., 1910). This book was not translated into English until 1991.

26 Hirschfeld, *Die Transvestiten*, 4–5.

27 He describes some of these visits in detail in Magnus Hirschfeld, *Berlins drittes Geschlecht:*

Mit einem Anhang: Paul Näcke, Ein Besuch bei den Homosexuellen in Berlin, ed. Manfred Herzer (1904; repr. Berlin: Verlag Rosa Winkel, 1991). Even in this book, which was clearly meant for a popular audience, Hirschfeld maintains the voice of the objective (in other words nonparticipant) observer, yet the inclusion of information about intimate relationships and festive rituals are indications that these visits were neither fleeting nor impersonal.

28   Trust is central to political organization of all kinds. See Ute Frevert, "Does Trust Have a History?," in Max Weber Programme: Lectures Series (San Domenico di Fiesole: European University Institute, 2009), http://cadmus.eui.eu//handle/1814/11258. (I thank Katie Sutton for pointing me to this citation.) This is just one example of Frevert's work on the history of emotions, a subject that has recently gained more scholarly attention. For overviews see: Frank Biess, "History of Emotions," *German History* 28, no. 1 (1 Mar 2010): 67–80; and Monique Scheer, "Are Emotions a Kind of Practice (and Is That What Makes Them Have a History)? A Bourdieuian Approach to Understanding Emotion," *History and Theory* 51, no. 2 (2012): 193–220.

29   See the various contributions in Taylor, Timm, and Herrn, eds, *Not Straight from Germany*.

30   Jens Dobler, *Zwischen Duldungspolitik und Verbrechensbekämpfung: Homosexuellenverfolgung durch die Berliner Polizei von 1848 bis 1933* (Frankfurt a.M.: Verlag für Polizeiwissenschaft, 2008).

31   Beachy, *Gay Berlin*, 55.

32   Dobler, *Zwischen Duldungspolitik*, 399–406.

33   The estimate is from Hirschfeld, *Berlins drittes Geschlecht*, 74. Hirschfeld notes that it is difficult to give an exact number, because of the underground nature of these establishments.

34   Magnus Hirschfeld, *Die Homosexualität des Mannes und des Weibes* (Berlin: Louis Marcus Verlagsbuchhandlung, 1914), 1001–2.

35   Benjamin, "Reminiscences," 4.

36   Ibid.

37   Kinsey, Pomeroy, and Martin, *Sexual Behavior in the Human Male*, 612. Kinsey conflates various terms in a way that Benjamin would most likely have objected to: "The terms sexual inversion, intersexuality, transsexuality, the third sex, psychosexual hermaphroditism, and others have been applied not merely to designate the nature of the partner involved in sexual relation, but to emphasize the general opinion that individuals engaging in homosexual activity are neither male nor female, but persons of mixed sex."

38   For a history of the gay balls and drags in New York, see George Chauncey, *Gay New York: Gender, Urban Culture, and the Making of the Gay Male World, 1890–1940* (New York: Basic Books, 1994).

39   B. S. Talmey, "Transvestism: A Contribution to the Study of the Psychology of Sex," *New York Medical Journal* 99 (Jan–June 1914): 362–8. The account is reprinted, with some edits and exclusions in: Bernard S. Talmey, *Love: A Treatise on the Science of Sex-Attraction. For the Use of Physicians and Students of Medical Jurisprudence*, 4th rev. ed. (New York: Eugenics Publishing Company, 1919), 297–309.

40   This was first established, likely through personal communication with Benjamin, in: Leah Cahan Schaefer and Connie Christine Wheeler, "Harry Benjamin's First Ten Cases (1938–1953): A Clinical Historical Note," *Archives of Sexual Behavior* 24, no. 1 (1995): 73–93, 77. Benjamin alludes to Spengler very vaguely in Harry Benjamin, *The Transsexual Phenomenon: A Scientific Report on Transsexualism and Sex Conversion in the Human Male and Female* (New York: The Julian Press, 1966), 34. We can only make the identification through the footnote to Talmey.

41   Talmey, *Love*, 305–6.

42   Talmey, "Transvestism," 362.

43   Ibid., 363–5.

44   For example: Bernard S. Talmey, *Woman: A Treatise on the Normal and Pathological Emotions of Feminine Love* (New York: Practitioners' Publishing Company, 1908).

45   Talmey, "Transvestism," 368.

46   Talmey, *Love*, 297. Havelock Ellis first used the term "sexo-aesthetic inversion" in "Sexo-Aesthetic Inversion," *Alienist and Neurologist* 34, no. 2 (1 May 1913): 156–67. It

is likely that Talmey read the German version: Havelock Ellis, "Sexo-Ästhethische Inversion," *Zeitschrift für Psychotherapie und Medizinische Psychologie* 5, nos 134–162 (1914).

47   Schaefer and Wheeler, "Harry Benjamin's First Ten Cases," 78.

48   For a list of the imposition of such ordinances and a nuanced explanation of the sociological conditions that allowed them to gain popularity between 1848 and 1974, see Stryker, *Transgender History*, 32–6.

49   George W. Henry, *Sex Variants: A Study of Homosexual Patterns*, One-Volume (New York and London: P. B. Hoeber, 1948), 493. This book was first published in two volumes in 1941. Exactly when or how many times Spengler visited Berlin is unclear. As mentioned below, it is likely that one of these trips took place in 1906, but neither the Talmey nor the Henry biographies provide any additional detail.

50   Talmey, "Transvestism," 365.

51   Henry, *Sex Variants*, 493.

52   Otto Spengler, ed., *Das deutsche Element der Stadt New York: Biographisches Jahrbuch der Deutsch-Amerikaner New Yorks und Umgebung* (New York: Spengler, 1913), 250. The biographical details provided here are from his own, presumably self-authored, entry in this compendium.

53   Further circumstantial evidence of this meeting is provided by Benjamin's colleagues, who later wrote that Hirschfeld claimed Spengler to have been the inspiration for *Die Transvestiten*. Schaefer and Wheeler, "Harry Benjamin's First Ten Cases (1938–1953)," 77. Schaefer and Wheeler cite the English translation of the book, without providing a page number, and they do not provide any other convincing evidence for this assertion. Spengler's biography does not match any of the seventeen cases in *Die Transvestiten*. This all leads one to believe that this information was passed on orally from Benjamin (or perhaps even Spengler) and all authors were purposely obscuring the fact that the meetings had actually taken place in bars rather than in a respectable medical setting.

54   Harry Benjamin, "Introduction," in *Transsexualism and Sex Reassignment*, ed. Richard Green and John Money (Baltimore: The Johns Hopkins University Press, 1969), 1. I have not been able to determine a more precise date for this meeting, and this appears to be the only place that Benjamin wrote about it. It is clear that this was Spengler; we are introduced to "an elderly transvestite who owned a press-clipping bureau," and Benjamin's colleagues Leah Cahan Schaefer and Connie Christine Wheeler confirm this in "Harry Benjamin's First Ten Cases," 77.

55   Meyerowitz, *How Sex Changed*, 45. Benjamin's respect for Steinach's work is evident in his obituary: Harry Benjamin, "Eugen Steinach, 1861–1944: A Life of Research," *Scientific Monthly* 61, no. 6 (1945): 427–42.

56   Angus McLaren, *Reproduction by Design: Sex, Robots, Trees, and Test-Tube Babies in Interwar Britain* (Chicago: University of Chicago Press, 2012), 85–104.

57   Anonymous, "Harry Benjamin: Part 2 Rejuvenation," A Gender Variance Who's Who (blog) 5 Oct 2012, accessed 26 June 2019, https://zagria.blogspot.com/2012/10/harry-benjamin-part-2-rejuvenation_5.html. Even though the author of this blog remains anonymous, I have found the information it provides extremely helpful and impeccably researched. This is one of the few pieces of information I was not able to find elsewhere.

58   For a detailed description of the popularization of Steinach's research, see Rainer Herrn and Christine N. Brinckmann, "Of Rats and Men: The Steinach Film," in Thomas, Timm, and Herrn, eds, *Not Straight from Germany*, 212–34.

59   For more on how the popularization of Steinach's research encouraged those seeking sex affirming surgery to seek out information and request medical services, see Joanne Meyerowitz, "Sex Change and the Popular Press: Historical Notes on Transsexuality in the United States, 1930-1955," *GLQ: A Journal of Lesbian and Gay Studies* 4, no. 2 (1 Apr 1998): 159–87, esp. 166.

60   Benjamin, "Introduction," 2. Benjamin initially prescribed sterilization through x-ray treatments on Spengler's testicles. See Meyerowitz, *How Sex Changed*, 46.

61   Henry, *Sex Variants*, 495.

62   This does contradict however, the assertion of Benjamin's colleagues, Shaefer and Wheeler, that Spengler only became a patient in 1938. Schaefer and Wheeler, "Harry Benjamin's First Ten Cases," 77. It is also slightly at odds with the otherwise scrupulously researched blog "A Gender Variance Who's Who." The author does not cite Spengler's biography in *Das deutsche Element*, and has therefore not discovered the birth date of 1873. "Otto Spengler (1876? – 194?) Businessperson," A Gender Variance Who's Who (blog), 18 Nov 2016, accessed 26 June 2019, https://zagria.blogspot.com/2016/11/otto-spengler-1876-194-businessperson.html.

63   Henry, *Sex Variants*, 1023. For an overview of the project, see Jennifer Terry, "Anxious Slippages Between 'Us' and 'Them': A Brief History of the Scientific Search for Homosexual Bodies," in *Deviant Bodies: Critical Perspectives on Difference in Science and Popular Culture*, ed. Jennifer Terry and Jacqueline L. Urla (Bloomington: Indiana University Press, 1995), 129–69, esp. 143.

64   Henry, *Sex Variants*, 489.

65   Ibid.

66   Despite being poorly expressed, Spengler's claim had some merit. A 400-volume, 80,000-page clipping collection on the First World War is currently housed at the Library of Congress. Erin Allen, "World War I: A Wartime Clipping Service," webpage, Library of Congress Blog, 27 July 2016, accessed June 29, 2019, https://blogs.loc.gov/loc/2016/07/world-war-i-a-wartime-clipping-service/.

67   George Chauncey, *Gay New York: Gender, Urban Culture, and the Making of the Gay Male World, 1890–1940* (New York: Basic Books, 1994), 2, 40.

68   Chauncey counters the "myth of invisibility" in *Gay New York*, 3.

69   On the Cercle, see Jonathan Ned Katz, "Earl Lind: The Cercle Hermaphroditos, c. 1895," OutHistory.org, accessed 4 July 2019, http://outhistory.org/exhibits/show/earl-lind/related/cercle-hermaphroditos.

70   The senior Viereck's story is intriguing on its own. In 1886, he had served a nine-month prison term, along with August Bebel and other socialist leaders, for conspiracy to infringe against the law banning socialist organizing. His son later cultivated the rumour that his father had been the illegitimate child of Kaiser Wilhelm I. See Niel M. Johnson, "George Sylvester Viereck: Poet and Propagandist," *Books at Iowa* 9 (Nov 1968): 22–4, 28–36.

71   George F. Corners and A. S. Blumgarten, *Rejuvenation: How Steinach Makes People Young* (New York: Seltzer, 1923). A copy of the letter that Sigmund Freud wrote to Viereck, asking if he would write something similar about psychoanalysis, is in Harry Benjamin's files in the Kinsey Archive. See Johnson, "George Sylvester Viereck."

72   Tom Reiss, *The Orientalist: Solving the Mystery of a Strange and Dangerous Life* (New York: Random House Publishing Group, 2005), 285–7. Viereck later included a profile of Hirschfeld under this same title in George Sylvester Viereck, *Glimpses of the Great* (London: Duckworth, 1930).

73   Hirschfeld to Viereck, 22 Oct 1930, Magnus-Hirschfeld-Gesellschaft, "Magnus Hirschfeld – Brief an Sylvester Viereck," Magnus-Hirschfeld-Gesellschaft, accessed 5 Aug 2018, http://www.hirschfeld.in-berlin.de/frame.html?http://www.hirschfeld.in-berlin.de/hirschfeld/brief_an_viereck.html.

74   For an account of Hirschfeld's time in the United States and the reception of his public lectures, see Ralf Dose, *Magnus Hirschfeld: The Origins of the Gay Liberation Movement*, trans. Edward H. Willis (New York: Monthly Review Press, 2014), 88–93.

75   In fact, Hirschfeld never returned to Germany. Soon after the Nazis came to power in January 1933, Hirschfeld's institute was ransacked, and his friends strongly advised him not to return. He died of natural causes in 1935 in Nice.

76   Quoted in Phyllis Keller, "George Sylvester Viereck: The Psychology of a German-American Militant," *Journal of Interdisciplinary History* 2, no. 1 (1971): 59–108, 97 from a 22 September 1934 letter to Upton Sinclair. George Sylvester Viereck, "Hitler the German Explosive," *American Monthly*, Oct 1923. An edited version of the interview appeared in the *Guardian*'s "Great Interviews of the 20th Century" series: George Sylvester Viereck, "'No Room for the Alien, No Use for the

Wastrel,'" *Guardian*, 17 Sept 2007, https://www.theguardian.com/theguardian/2007/sep/17/greatinterviews1.

77 "Viereck Called Chief Nazi Propagandist in the U.S. Helmut von Gerlach Asserts Pro-German Agent of War Days Is Enacting Same Role for Hitler," *Jewish Daily Bulletin*, 17 Dec 1933.

78 His son, Peter Viereck, who became a successful poet, historian, and political philosopher, was in graduate school at Harvard during the war years, and he was so furious about his father's activities that the two did not speak for sixteen years. Elaine Woo, "Peter R. Viereck, 89; Pulitzer-Winning Poet Spurned by Fellow Conservatives," *Los Angeles Times*, 20 May 2006, http://articles.latimes.com/2006/may/20/local/me-viereck20.

79 On Viereck's support for McCarthy and his continued cultivation of Nazi contacts, see Ralph Melnick, *The Life and Work of Ludwig Lewisohn: A Touch of Wildness* (Detroit: Wayne State University Press, 1998), 513.

80 Donald Furthman Wickets, "Can Sex in Humans Be Changed?," *Physical Culture*, January 1937, 16–17, 83–5. For a general biography of Viereck, see Martin J. Manning, "Viereck, George Sylvester," in *Encyclopedia of Media and Propaganda in Wartime America*, ed. Martin J. Manning and Clarence R. Wyatt, vol. 1 (Santa Barbara, Denver, and Oxford: ABC-CLIO, 2011), 483.

81 Viereck also apparently became the exiled Kaiser Wilhelm II's ghostwriter, a fact that takes on particularly significance given the rumours about homosexuals in the Kaiser's social circle. See Norman Domeier, *Der Eulenburg-Skandal: Eine politische Kulturgeschichte des Kaiserreichs* (Frankfurt am Main: Campus Verlag, 2010). Melnick, *The Life and Work of Ludwig Lewisohn*, 189. Melnick describes the 1904 love affair between Viereck and the poet Ludwig Lewisohn. See esp. 95–105.

82 Kinsey to Benjamin, 18 June 1945, KA-Corr., Benjamin, Folder 1 (May 1944–December 1950).

83 Henry, *Sex Variants*, 497.

84 Ibid., 497 and 494.

85 It is thus extremely unlikely that this Otto Spengler is the same person who Jonathan Ned Katz has claimed was a director of the Berlin-based *Wissenschaftlich-humanitäres Kommittee* and who supposedly gave a talk on homosexuality to the German Scientific Society of New York in May 1906. This confusion has been repeated multiple times (including in Jennifer Terry, *An American Obsession: Science, Medicine, and Homosexuality in Modern Society* [Chicago: University of Chicago Press, 1999], 111), but the chances that Spengler, who had lived in New York since he was nineteen in 1892, had become a director of a Berlin-based organization are very slim indeed.

86 Benjamin to Kinsey, 19 June 1947 and Benjamin to Kinsey, 8 Oct 1947, in KA-Corr., Benjamin, Folder 1.

87 Quoted in Meyerowitz, *How Sex Changed*, 171.

88 See Talmey, *Love*, 297–309. The first edition was published in 1915 and now seems very difficult to find. Talmey does not mention Hirschfeld in the third edition. The sixth (or possibly seventh) edition was published in 1938.

89 Alfred C. Kinsey et al., "Concepts of Normality and Abnormality in Sexual Behavior,"in *Psychosexual Development in Health and Disease*, ed. Paul H. Hoch and Joseph Zubin (New York: Grune & Stratton, 1949), esp. 12. Later: "Wherever one finds contradictory interpretations of what is sexually normal and abnormal, one should consider whether philosophic, moral, or social evaluations, or scientific records of material fact are involved," 12.

90 Kinsey et al., *Sexual Behavior in the Human Female*, 681.

91 Ibid.

92 Benjamin notes that it was Robert Latou Dickinson who brought the two together. Benjamin, "Reminiscences," 9.

93 In a letter of 24 August 1946, Kinsey thanks Benjamin for "the splendid help you gave us while we were in the city. Your leads were valuable and it becomes very apparent that we must get San Francisco started before you give up spending your summers there. You could do worlds for us in helping us to know people." KA-Corr., Benjamin, Folder 1.

94 Benjamin, "Introduction," 3.

95 Quoted in Jonathan Gathorne-Hardy, Linda Wolfe, and Bill Condon, *Kinsey: Public and Private* (New York: Newmarket Press, 2004), 98–9, from Albert Deutsch, "What Dr. Kinsey Is up to Now!," *Look*, 8 May 1951.

96 Donna J. Drucker, *The Classification of Sex: Alfred Kinsey and the Organization of Knowledge* (Pittsburgh: University of Pittsburgh Press, 2014), 1 and 9; and Peter Cryle and Elizabeth Stephens, *Normality: A Critical Genealogy* (Chicago: University of Chicago Press, 2017), 336. On quantification in the life sciences and its influence on sexology more generally, see Howard H. Chiang, "Liberating Sex, Knowing Desire: Scientia Sexualis and Epistemic Turning Points in the History of Sexuality," *History of the Human Sciences* 23, no. 5 (2010): 42–69, esp. 50–2.

97 Meyerowitz, "Sex Research at the Borders of Gender," 77; and Kinsey et al., *Sexual Behavior in the Human Female*, 679–81. Of course, this critique was by no means the loudest that Kinsey's books elicited. He immediately became and remains a favoured subject of contempt for the Christian right. I am thinking particularly of the writings of Judith A. Reisman and Edward W. Eichel, which William Simon has accurately described as nothing but a paranoid assembly of "innuendo, distortion, and selective representation of decontextualized 'facts'" and which now only exists as a self-published ebook. See William Simon, "Review of Judith A. Reisman and Edward W. Eichel's *Kinsey, Sex and Fraud: The Indoctrination of a People. An Investigation into the Human Sexuality Research of Alfred C. Kinsey, Wardell B. Pomeroy, Clyde E. Martin, and Paul H. Gebhard*," *Archives of Sexual Behavior* 21, no. 1 (1992): 91–3.

98 Erskine to Benjamin, 14 Oct 1953, KILSC-HB, Box 4, Ser. II C. On the usual length of Kinsey's interviews, see Paul A. Robinson, *The Modernization of Sex: Havelock Ellis, Alfred Kinsey, William Masters and Virginia Johnson* (Ithaca, NY: Cornell University Press, 1989), 44.

99 Cited in Meyerowitz, *How Sex Changed*, 85 from Kinsey to Lawrence, 10 Oct 1949, KI, folder: Alfred C. Kinsey, Lawrence Collection.

100 Kinsey, Pomeroy, and Martin, *Sexual Behavior in the Human Male*, 656–7.

101 Hirschfeld, *Geschlechtskunde*, 599, cited in Rainer Herrn, "Magnus Hirschfelds Geschlechterkosmogonie: Die Zwischenstufentheorie im Kontext hegemonialer," in *Männlichkeiten und Moderne: Geschlecht in den Wissenskulturen um 1900*, ed. Ulrike Brunotte and Rainer Herrn (Bielefeld: Transcript Verlag, 2007), 173–96, 185. As Herrn points out, this notion of a spectrum did not protect Hirschfeld from privileging homosexuality over other intermediary variations. See also Darryl B. Hill, "Sexuality and Gender in Hirschfeld's *Die Transvestiten*: A Case of the 'Elusive Evidence of the Ordinary,'" *Journal of the History of Sexuality* 14, no. 3 (2005): 316–32, esp. 320.

102 Kinsey, Pomeroy, and Martin, *Sexual Behavior in the Human Male*, 691. Kinsey et al. were referring to Magnus Hirschfeld, "Das Ergebnis der statistischen Untersuchungen über den Prozentsatz der Homosexuellen," *Jahrbuch für sexuelle Zwischenstuffen* 6 (1904): 109–78.

103 As Donna Drucker notes, he privileged works that relied on scientific rather than religiously inspired argument, on face-to-face interviews or survey data, and on large sample sizes. While Hirschfeld's work would have satisfied the first three criteria and certainly had the advantage of also exploring nonmarital sex, Kinsey would certainly have considered it insufficiently quantitative. Drucker, *The Classification of Sex*, 74.

104 Bauer provides a fascinating and instructive textual analysis of Kinsey to further excavate the links between the two men. See Heike Bauer, "Sexology Backward: Hirschfeld, Kinsey and the Reshaping of Sex Research in the 1950s," in *Queer 1950s: Rethinking Sexuality in the Postwar Years*, ed. Heike Bauer and Matt Cook (New York: Palgrave MacMillan, 2012), 133–49.

105 Kinsey et al., *Sexual Behavior in the Human Female*, 641.

106 Janice M. Irvine, *Disorders of Desire: Sexuality and Gender in Modern American Sexology* (Philadelphia: Temple University Press, 2005), 47–8.

107 Quoted from Kinsey et al., *Sexual Behavior in the Human Female*, 412, in Irvine, *Disorders of Desire*, 28.

108 Ibid., 35.

109 Cited in Meyerowitz, *How Sex Changed*, 92–3, from Christine Jorgensen, *Christine Jorgensen: Personal Autobiography*, with an introduction by Harry Benjamin (New York: P. S. Eriksson, 1967), 189.

110 Meyerowitz, "Sex Research at the Borders of Gender," 80.

111 The figure of 18,300 case studies comes from Suzanne G. Frayser and Thomas J. Whitby, *Studies in Human Sexuality: A Selected Guide*, 2nd ed. (Englewood, CO: Libraries Unlimited, 1995), 103. On Kinsey's punch-card system, see Drucker, *The Classification of Sex*, esp. 107–15. Drucker cites the number of 18,000 case studies for both the *Male* and *Female* volumes. Ibid., 112.

112 Quoted in James H. Jones, *Alfred C. Kinsey: A Public/Private Life* (New York: W. W. Norton & Company, 1997), 622.

113 Meyerowitz argues that Kinsey's sustained contact and Lawrence's long campaign to change his mind about transvestism had "planted [the] seed of doubt" by the early 1950s. Meyerowitz, "Sex Research at the Borders of Gender," 75.

114 Genny Beemyn, "Transgender History in the United States: A Special Unabridged Version of a Book Chapter from *Trans Bodies, Trans Selves*, edited by Laura Erickson-Schroth," accessed 24 June 2019, https://www.umass.edu/stonewall/sites/default/files/Infoforandabout/transpeople/genny_beemyn_transgender_history_in_the_united_states.pdf. Beemyn also notes that the first female-assigned, nonintersexed person to have received hormonal treatment (in 1939) and genital surgery (in 1946) was the British physician Michael Dillon (11). (Alex discusses Dillon's story in this book.) Meyerowitz points out that while the ratios of reported cases have been very skewed towards trans women in the past, "today some doctors in the United States find roughly equivalent numbers of male-to-females (MTFs) and female-to-males (FTMs)." Meyerowitz, *How Sex Changed*, 9. See also the chapter "Have Female-to-Male Transsexuals Always Existed?" in Aaron Devor, *FTM: Female-to-Male Transsexuals in Society* (1997; repr., Bloomington: Indiana University Press, 2016); Emily Skidmore, *True*

Sex: The Lives of Trans Men at the Turn of the Twentieth Century (New York: New York University Press, 2017); and Geertje Mak, "'Passing Women' in the Consulting Room of Magnus Hirschfeld: On Why the Term 'Transvestite' Was Not Employed for Cross-Dressing Women," *Österreichische Zeitschrift für Geschichtswissenschaften* 9, no. 3 (1998): 384–99.

115 Kinsey et al., *Sexual Behavior in the Human Female*, 90 and 716.

116 Ibid., 721.

117 Ibid., 729.

118 Kinsey, Pomeroy, and Martin, *Sexual Behavior in the Human Male*, 727–8.

119 Erskine to Benjamin, 4 Jan 1953, KILSC-HB, Box 4, Ser. II C.

120 Erskine to Benjamin, 18 Nov 1953, KILSC-HB, Box 4, Ser. II C.

121 Erskine to Benjamin, 9 May 1954, KILSC-HB, Box 4, Ser. II C.

122 Erskine to Benjamin, 19 Jan 1954, KILSC-HB, Box 4, Ser. II C.

123 Ibid.

124 Erskine to Benjamin, 10 Feb 1954, KILSC-HB, Box 4, Ser. II C.

125 Herb Caen, "Baghdad-by-the-Bay," *San Francisco Chronicle*, n.d.

126 It seems otherwise inexplicable that Carla's name would appear in San Francisco gossip columns years later, with no reference to her gender. See: Herb Caen, "San Francisco: Herb Caen," *Honolulu Advertiser*, 18 Nov 1972 (a syndicated column) and Jack Rosenbaum's "Our Man on the Town" column in the *San Francisco Examiner*, 21 Mar 1970 and 30 Mar 1972.

127 Erskine to Benjamin, 18 Nov 1953, KILSC-HB, Box 4, Ser. II C.

128 Erskine to Benjamin, 3 Apr 1954, KILSC-HB, Box 4, Ser. II C.

129 Erskine to Benjamin, 22 Jan 1954, KILSC-HB, Box 4, Ser. II C.

130 Erskine to Benjamin, 15 May 1954, KILSC-HB, Box 4, Ser. II C.

131 Benjamin's notes in preparation for writing *The Transsexual Phenomenon*. See various copies of this table in KILSC-HB, Box 28 Series VI E. To Series VI. G.

132 See for example Erskine to Benjamin, 3 Dec 1953, KILSC-HB, Box 4, Ser. II C.

133 Typewritten document, titled only with "[Erskine], 1953," KILSC-HB, Box 4, Ser. II C.

134 Carla apparently told Donald R. Laub (a former doctor and later friend) that she was born in "Arabia," but, as noted above, this is contradicted by census records stating her birthplace as Casper, Wyoming. See Donald Laub, "The [Carla Erskine] Story," Many People, Many Passports, 11 Apr 2011, https://dlaub.wordpress.com/2011/04/11/.

135 Benjamin, *The Transsexual Phenomenon*, 52. Based on both his medical and personal relationship with Carla, Donald R. Laub diagnoses her as having had "grade 3 hypospadias, a birth defect in which the urine comes out just above the scrotum." Laub, "The [Carla Erskine] Story."

136 On the history of intersex and the ethics of speaking about it today, see: Alice Domurat Dreger, ed., *Intersex in the Age of Ethics* (Hagerstown, MD: University Publishing Group, 1999); Alice Domurat Dreger, *Hermaphrodites and the Medical Invention of Sex* (Cambridge, MA: Harvard University Press, 1998); Elizabeth Reis, "Divergence or Disorder?: The Politics of Naming Intersex," *Perspectives in Biology and Medicine* 50, no. 4 (2007): 535–43; Elizabeth Reis, *Bodies in Doubt: An American History of Intersex* (Baltimore, MD: Johns Hopkins University Press, 2010); Sandra Eder, "The Volatility of Sex: Intersexuality, Gender and Clinical Practice in the 1950s," in *Historicising Gender and Sexuality*, ed. Kevin P. Murphy and Jennifer M. Spear (Malden, MA: Wiley-Blackwell, 2011), 166–81; and Georgiann Davis, *Contesting Intersex: The Dubious Diagnosis* (New York: New York University Press, 2015).

137 "[Carla Erskine], 1953," KILSC-HB, Box 4, Ser. II C.

138 It also adds some fuel to current arguments that our obsession with gender classification in daily life has caused nothing but pain. See Heath

Fogg Davis, *Beyond Trans: Does Gender Matter?* (New York: New York University Press, 2017).

139 She claims that this occurred in 1923, which would have made her only thirteen had the birthdate of 1910 been correct. Given that she was really born in 1905, it seems unlikely that she would have run away at the age of eighteen. We can only surmise that the date that she fled was earlier than 1923.

140 Clare Sears, *Arresting Dress: Cross-Dressing, Law, and Fascination in Nineteenth-Century San Francisco* (Durham, NC: Duke University Press, 2014). In a newspaper interview, Sears notes that these laws were primarily passed in frontier towns keen to attract newcomers by projecting a respectable image. This motivated a crackdown on prostitution that affected cross-dressers, since "For a woman to dress as a man in some way communicated to other people that she was more adventurous, more sexually available." Tagawa, "When Cross-Dressing Was Criminal: Book Documents History of Longtime San Francisco Law," SF State News. San Francisco State University, Feb 2015, https://news.sfsu.edu/when-cross-dressing-was-criminal-book-documents-history-longtime-san-francisco-law.

141 "Sex Operation on Self Fails," *San Francisco Examiner*, 19 Aug 1953. Census data tells me that she was actually 48 at the time of this article, but she had begun lying about her age, perhaps in order to improve her chances of acquiring surgery.

142 In an interview with Susan Stryker, Don Lucas (a founding member of the San Francisco chapter of the Mattachine Society), names Carla as one of at least two individuals who had performed self-surgery. "Don Lucas Interview: Recorded at Lucas's Home in San Francisco," 13 June 1997, http://www.glbthistory.org.

143 Erskine to Benjamin, 5 Oct 1953, KILSC-HB, Box 4, Ser. II C.

144 Erskine to Benjamin, 1 July 1953, KILSC-HB, Box 4, Ser. II C. The letter sends along her precise physical measurements.

145 Benjamin, "Introduction," 3. It is possible but not clear whether Benjamin was consciously alluding to Richard von Krafft-Ebing's use of the term "stepchildren of nature" to describe

his patients. See Oosterhuis, *Stepchildren of Nature.*

146 Benjamin to Carla, 25 Jan 1954, KILSC-HB, Box 4, Ser. II C.

147 Benjamin to Carla, 25 Nov 1953, KILSC-HB, Box 4, Ser. II C.

148 Erskine to Benjamin, 30 Nov 1953, KILSC-HB, Box 4, Ser. II C.

149 Erskine to Benjamin, 7 Dec 1953, KILSC-HB, Box 4, Ser. II C

150 Carla forwarded this announcement to Benjamin. KILSC-HB, Box 4, Ser. II C.

151 Benjamin, "Introduction," 4. The article is: Harry Benjamin, "Transvestism and Transsexualism," *International Journal of Sexology* 7, no. 1 (1953): 12–14. In claiming this originality, Benjamin was certainly obscuring the inspiration he had received from the work of Magnus Hirschfeld.

152 Carla thought that Hinman's technique created a "far more natural" effect than that used for two of her friends. Erskine to Benjamin, 5 Oct 1954, KILSC-HB, Box 4, Ser. II C. However, according to Benjamin's table of surgeries, compiled for *The Transsexual Phenomenon*, this appears to be the only such surgery that Hinman performed. See KILSC-HB 28.

153 In October 1954, Carla attempted to make contact with the English trans woman Roberta Cowell, a former racing driver and Second World War fighter pilot whose autobiography proclaiming her the first British woman to have undergone reassignment surgery had by this time made her relatively famous. See *Roberta Cowell's Story* (New York: British Book Centre, 1954).

154 Erskine to Benjamin, 10 Nov 1954 and 24 Nov 1954, KILSC-HB, Box 4, Ser. II C. By the time the photo in figure 3.18 was taken in the studio of Alvin Harris (a friend of Louise Lawrence) in 1954, Angela had followed Carla's example by self-castrating. There is a small collection of photos of Carla (labelled under her real name) in the Harris-Wheeler Collection, part of the Vern and Bonnie Bullough Collection on Sex and Gender at Special Collections, California State University, Northridge. See Series III: Scrapbooks and Binders, 1949–54, Box 18, Folder 7. Richard F. Docter describes Harris as

a "lingerie fetishist." See *Becoming a Woman: A Biography of Christine Jorgensen* (New York: Routledge, 2007), 280.

155 "Obituary: John 'Bunny' Breckinridge," *SFGate*, 9 Nov 1996, https://www.sfgate.com/news/article/OBITUARY-John-Bunny-Breckinridge-2959951.php.

156 Erskine to Benjamin, 9 May 1954, KILSC-HB, Box 4, Ser. II C.

157 Aleshia Brevard Crenshaw Interviews, 2 Aug 1997, http://www.glbthistory.org. Dixie's public performances and her search for publicity justify providing her full name.

158 Dixie was the friend who begged Carla to perform surgery on her. Carla refused and called on Benjamin for support, demonstrating the triangular relationships at play (Benjamin to Carla, 15 Oct 1953, KILSC-HB, Box 4, Ser. II C.).

159 Erskine to Benjamin, 28 Feb 1954, 10 Feb 1954, and 8 Mar 1953, KILSC-HB, Box 4, Ser. II C. Benjamin, rather unethically, tells Carla that Dixie's case was being handled by Dr. Worden, a psychiatrist also treating Carla (Benjamin to Carla, 4 Mar 1954). Carla's enormous faith that Worden would handle these cases sensitively seems to have been unjustified, since his co-authored publication makes virtually no distinction between psychologically troubled individuals like Dixie and quite rational and stable trans women like Carla. Frederic G. Worden and James T. Marsh, "Psychological Factors in Men Seeking Sex Transformation: A Preliminary Report," *Journal of the American Medical Association* 157, no. 15 (9 Apr 1955): 1292–8. Benjamin later wrote to Kinsey: "The transvestites who have met him or have read his article are either disappointed, indignant, or very unhappy about it. I understand, of course, that Dr. Worden is not interested in these people except as material for some research. He has made valuable observations, but as a physician he has undoubtedly done more harm than good." Benjamin to Kinsey, 23 May 1955, KA-Corr., Benjamin, Folder 1.

160 Erskine to Benjamin, 3 May 1954, KILSC-HB, Box 4, Ser. II C.

161 Erskine to Benjamin, 7 Mar 1955, KILSC-HB, Box 4, Ser. II C.

162 Roots of Equality et al., *Lavender Los Angeles* (Charleston, SC: Arcadia Publishing, 2011). For more general histories of prohibitions against cross-dressing in the U.S., see: Peter Boag, *Re-Dressing America's Frontier Past* (Berkeley: University of California Press, 2011); and Vern L. Bullough and Bonnie Bullough, *Cross Dressing, Sex, and Gender* (Philadelphia: University of Pennsylvania Press, 1993). Like these two books, Carla Sears focuses on the nineteenth century in *Arresting Dress*.

163 Erskine to Benjamin, 8 Mar 1954, KILSC-HB, Box 4, Ser. II C.

164 For a fascinating discussion of the difficulties of discussing trans erotic desire in this period, see Aleshia Brevard Crenshaw Interviews. For an example of the tensions that raising the subject of erotic desire could produce even within circles of medical professionals who viewed themselves as experts on transsexuality and transgender identities in the 1990s, see the descriptions of two conferences provided in Richard Ekins, "Science, Politics and Clinical Intervention: Harry Benjamin, Transsexualism and the Problem of Heteronormativity," *Sexualities* 8, no. 3 (2005): 306–28, esp. 308–9.

165 Benjamin later described his use of the word "transsexualist" as unfortunate. Benjamin, *The Transsexual Phenomenon*, 16.

166 Benjamin, "Transvestism and Transsexualism," 13–14.

167 Harry Benjamin et al., "Transsexualism and Transvestism – A Symposium," *American Journal of Psychotherapy* 8, no. 2 (1954): 219–44, 220.

168 Ekins, "Science, Politics and Clinical Intervention," esp. 310.

169 Carla did not explicitly discuss the absence of a vagina in the letters, but Benjamin was certainly aware of this fact and would have passed the information on to Kinsey. Benjamin to Carla, 14 Apr 1955; 6 May 1955; and 19 May 1955, KILSC-HB, Box 4, Ser. II C.

170 On the "reification of orgasm" and Kinsey's role in it, see Annamarie Jagose, *Orgasmology* (Durham and London: Duke University Press, 2013), 29. Jagose notes that "Kinsey uses [orgasm's] alleged stability in order to quantify sexual practice: unless it ends in orgasm, sexual activity does not count, in the literal statistical sense, as an event." As Kinsey himself put it, there "is no better unit for measuring the incidences and frequencies of sexual activity." See Kinsey et al., *Sexual Behavior in the Human Female*, 46. See also Jennifer E. Germon, "Kinsey and the Politics of Bisexual Authenticity," *Journal of Bisexuality* 8, nos 3–4 (2008): 243–58, 252. For more on how Kinsey counted and classified orgasms, see Drucker, *The Classification of Sex*, 96–8 and 120.

171 As R. Marie Griffith has argued, "accounts of his stringently religious father … [are] habitually embellished well beyond documentary evidence." "The Religious Encounters of Alfred C. Kinsey," *Journal of American History* 95, no. 2 (2008): 349–77. She includes the most widely read biographies in this critique: Jones, *Alfred C. Kinsey* and Jonathan Gathorne-Hardy, *Sex the Measure of All Things: A Life of Alfred C. Kinsey* (Bloomington and Indianapolis: Indiana University Press, 1998). The fact that the Kinseys had trouble consummating their marriage is less controversial, though Jones's explanation that this was due to an "adherent clitoris" (Jones, *Alfred C. Kinsey*, 236) has also been challenged. See Sarah B. Rodriguez, *Female Circumcision and Clitoridectomy in the United States* (Rochester, NY: University of Rochester Press, 2014), 214n91.

172 Benjamin to Kinsey, 5 Sept 1951, KA-Corr., Benjamin, Folder 1.

173 Her memories of Finochio's are quite depressing: "It was great for someone in her late tweens and early 20s, and my God it was a far cry from Tennessee, but I saw enough of it to say, 'What a terrible – doomed, that's how you were in society back then, the drugs, sitting and praying in front of the mirror, crying about getting old – and they were every bit of thirty. You know. God.'" Aleshia Brevard Crenshaw Interviews, 30.

174 Aleshia Brevard Crenshaw Interviews, 31.

175 Ibid., 72–3. We speculate that Benjamin contributed to the very large collection of hair fetish photos in the Kinsey Institute's image collection.

176 There are numerous references to her financial situation in her letters to Benjamin. See for

example Erskine to Benjamin, 5 Oct 1954, 25 Dec 1954, and 27 Oct 1955, KILSC-HB, Box 4, Ser. II C.

177   KILSC-HB, Box 25-1, Permissions (1964).

178   Erskine to Benjamin, 27 Dec 1955, KILSC-HB, Box 4, Ser. II C.

179   Erskine to Benjamin, 10 Nov 1955, KILSC-HB, Box 4, Ser. II C.

180   Caen, "San Francisco: Herb Caen."

181   Elinor Hayes, "Old Films, Organ Revived," *Oakland Tribune*, 6 July 1969. For the story of the theatre, see Dewey Cagle, "What's New… on the Avenue?," *Theatre Organ Bombarde: Journal of the American Theatre Organ Enthusiasts*, April 1968. Carla is mentioned on page 16.

182   The words are as written/remembered by Laub in "The [Carla Erskine] Story."

183   A search of the rich documentary evidence housed at The Digital Transgender Archive pulls up at least twenty-nine hits on Laub's name, all glowing descriptions of his contributions to surgical techniques while he was at Stanford and his numerous presentations to the yearly symposium of the Harry Benjamin International Gender Dysphoria Association (now called the World Professional Association for Transgender Health). He is praised in trans publications such as *AEGIS News*, *Chrysalis Quarterly*, *Female Mimics International*, *Gender Review* (Canada), *Metamorphosis Magazine* (Canada), *Renaissance News*, *The Transsexual Voice*, *The TV-TS Tapestry*, and *TransSisters: The Journal of Transsexual Feminism*.

184   Just as this book was in copyediting, I did receive a brief email from Dr. Laub, who appreciating reading a draft of this chapter.

185   Laub seems to have slightly misunderstood Carla's business career. An obituary in the *San Francisco Examiner* describes her as the founder, in 1962, of Micro Science Associates, which I have tracked down as having been headquartered in Mountain View, California. (See "Deaths," San Francisco Examiner, 1 Dec 1976. She died in Santa Clara, California, on 19 Nov 1976.) An image of some of the chips the company produced is included in the "Integrated Circuit Engineering Collection" at the Smithsonian National Museum of American History. See "The Chip Collection – Artwork Series 11-100400 – Smithsonian Institution," National Museum of American History, accessed 12 May 2020, http://smithsonianchips.si.edu/ice/s11-100400.htm.

186   Handwritten list of "Occupations of Operated Male Transsexuals," 11 Jan 1965, KILSC-HB, Box 28 Series VI E. To Series VI. G.

187   Laub, "The [Carla Erskine] Story."

188   The literature on this subject is now vast and growing. I will simply repeat the citation to two useful overviews: Biess, "History of Emotions," and Scheer, "Are Emotions a Kind of Practice." I have developed this perspective in other places, including the unpublished conference paper: Annette F. Timm, "Queering Friendship: What Hirschfeld Could Teach Hegel and Arendt," Rethinking Amity: Workshop in Honour of Michael Geyer, University of Chicago, 20 April 2013.

189   Alex cites Copenhagen physician Christian Hamburger's description of his involvement with patients like Christine Jorgensen in "The Desire for Change of Sex as Shown by Personal Letters from 465 Men and Women," *Acta Endrologica* 14 (1953): 361–72.

4

In the Shadows of Society: Trans People in the Netherlands in the 1950s

Alex Bakker

When Christine Jorgensen's 1952 transition gave hope to hundreds of trans people around the world seeking a similar way to become their true selves, it seemed that the near future for trans persons looked bright, especially in the Western European countries of Denmark and the Netherlands. Harry Benjamin thought of the Netherlands as a country with "more enlightened attitudes in matters of sex" and hoped that gender-affirmation surgery could take place there.[1]

In reality, Dutch society at that time offered transgender people very little space, as I explain below. Trans men remained invisible, as they were in other Western societies, because they were hidden or not distinguishable. Indeed there are hardly any sources on trans men in the Netherlands dating before 1959. As a result, the unfolding of transgender history in this time frame largely focuses on the lives of trans women. Trans women did have some sort of recognized existence, though they often worked under precarious economic

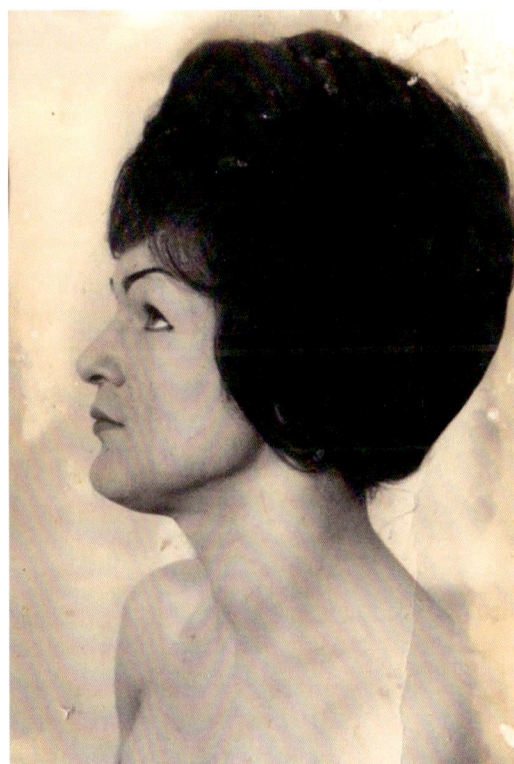

FIGURE 4.1: Aaïcha Bergamin, Dutch trans woman, around 1960 [private collection].

conditions in nightclubs and on the streets of red-light districts. Adult entertainment was often the only way of making a living for trans women who expressed their identity – and by becoming part of the night life, a trans individual was ostracized from the larger society and categorized as morally depraved and/or psychiatrically disturbed. Trans women who did not feel they were up for this life stayed in the closet. Some of them looked for help, talking about their feelings with a family doctor or a psychiatrist. Almost all medical doctors lacked understanding of and knowledge about transgender identities and interpreted the cry for help as a sign of a specific mental disorder – that is, the delusion of being of the opposite sex.

This description of the social situation for trans people will sound familiar to readers of the works of trans historians such as Susan Stryker, Joanne Meyerowitz, Aaron Devor, and Christine Burns about the realities of North America and the United Kingdom. So in which ways did the Netherlands stand out? Was Harry Benjamin right in his optimistic assessment?

Through archival research in the collections of Harry Benjamin and the Dutch psychiatrist Coen van Emde Boas, I traced a network that was formed between these two key figures – the latter in cooperation with Frederik Hartsuiker, who was the first Dutch psychiatrist involved. In the mid-1950s, for a year and a half, the Netherlands replaced Denmark as the place of refuge for trans women (mostly American) seeking gender-affirmation surgery. My guess is that around ten foreign

trans women had operations in Holland. How did these pioneering trans women experience their medical treatments; how were they treated by the doctors? What medical and personal views did these Dutch doctors develop? How did they understand or even explain the "transsexual phenomenon," and how did they diagnose and screen trans persons seeking gender-affirmation surgery? Later in this chapter I will explore the archival evidence about surgical options available to trans women in the 1950s.

Due to a lack of support from medical authorities, the route to the Netherlands stopped in 1955, to be followed by Casablanca as the new destination for trans women who wanted surgery. In the penultimate section of this chapter I describe the service Dr. Burou provided there, as well as the possibilities, limitations, and significance of this treatment for trans people around the world. Did Burou's clinic for gender-affirmation surgery, which lasted until the mid-1970s, qualify as an ideal solution? The last section deals with the first case of trans surgery performed within general, public health care in 1959 in the Netherlands. Remarkably, this surgery was openly presented to the public. How did this come about, and what was the response to it?

Transgender People in the Twilight

We know far less about transgender men from the 1950s and 1960s than we do of trans women. Possibly this is because trans men did not stand out, or possibly it is because they remained in the closet.² Transgender women could escape to society's shadows. Joining this subculture was not an option for transgender men, whose freedom of movement was limited by the gender designation on their official identification. People assigned female at birth were dependent on men in all sorts of ways. Until 1956, Dutch married women were prohibited from buying a car or a house, opening a bank account, or undertaking any other legal action without written permission from their husbands. Breaking out of this coercive mould required enormous fortitude. How far could one go? One common assumption is that trans men tried to establish their gender identity by behaving in the most masculine ways possible. Perhaps even some of those who – openly or not – identified as lesbians were in fact transgender men. This could include someone like the Dutch novelist Andreas Burnier, who wrote about androgyny and the struggle with gender identity, for instance in the 1969 novel *Het Jongensuur* (The boys' hour).³

Testosterone was identified as the crucial male sex hormone in 1935. Its use as a medical drug only became available in the 1950s, in particular for intersex patients and cisgender men who lacked male hormones. Unlike the female sex hormone estrogen, which was available in tablets and therefore relatively easy for trans women to acquire and consume, testosterone had to be injected intramuscularly. This is not something easy to do by yourself – another factor making it harder for trans men to self-medicate than it was for trans women. A similar difficulty faced trans men

seeking surgery. After having performed defeminizing surgeries in Berlin in 1912, Richard Mühsam noted that trans men were also more likely to seek surgery than trans women in the early twentieth century. Unlike trans women, who could surgically self-castrate with a reasonable chance of survival, trans men required a doctor's assistance to remove breasts or the uterus.⁴ Despite these complications, it is certain that there were transgender men in the 1950s and 1960s who underwent a physical transition. In 1956, Van Emde Boas asked the pharmaceutical company Organon to please send him a supply of the new medicine "sustanon," a brand name for testosterone: "In connection with the specific make-up of my practice, I deal with patients who require treatment with an androgen relatively frequently."⁵ We know that the trans man who was operated on in 1959 in Arnhem (see the final section of this chapter) had been on hormonal treatment for some years. Another source quotes the memory of a student who witnessed Van Emde Boas presenting a trans man with a full beard as an example of one of his transgender clients during a university class in the 1960s.⁶

A Trans Subculture

Fringe venues like nightclubs with transvestite shows and red-light districts were always part of big city life in Europe – particularly in cities like Amsterdam, Paris, Antwerp, or Berlin. Finding work within this subculture, which often meant resorting to prostitution, was a survival strategy and therefore an entirely rational

Hirschfeld's "Female Transvestites"

Medical sources devote comparatively little attention to people who at the time were called "female transvestites" (trans men), and many women who cross-dressed wanted to be recognized not as transvestites but as men. This is reflected in many of the life stories that accompany these images. For instance, in 1930 Hirschfeld reprinted the following two photos from Hans Abraham's 1921 dissertation *Der weibliche Transvestitismus* (Female transvestitism), the first publication dedicated to this topic.

Abraham tells the story of an aunt and niece. His main intention was to show that there were also what he called heterosexual female transvestites, i.e., women who liked to dress as men but who were sexually attracted to men. Today, we would speak of trans men who love men. But just as with Hirschfeld's earlier work *Die Transvestiten*, this attempt failed. What the book depicts is, to use its own terms, female transvestites who desired other women. When Hirschfeld retells this story of this "aunt and niece," he describes both of them as homosexuals and transvestites: as women (as he genders them) dressing as men who were attracted to other women (even if those women dressed as men or in masculine styles).

Hirschfeld reprints the image to underscore his theories that sexual traits or dispositions such as

Als Männer lebende Tante und Nichte
(Transvestiten)

Figure 4.2: "Aunt and niece living as men (transvestites)," Hirschfeld, *Geschlechtskunde*, 1930.

transvestitism or homosexuality are genetically heritable. The key point for this argument is that "aunt" and "niece" are related. Yet the story does not fit so easily within this framing. In noting that it was the niece who convinced her older relative to cut her hair and dress and live as a man, Hirschfeld was likely pushing back against common charges that homosexuals seduced the young. And in any case, the niece's act of social reproduction, as well as the obvious way in which both these individuals copy recognizable styles of dress and comportment (see the gallery on trans men), are plainly

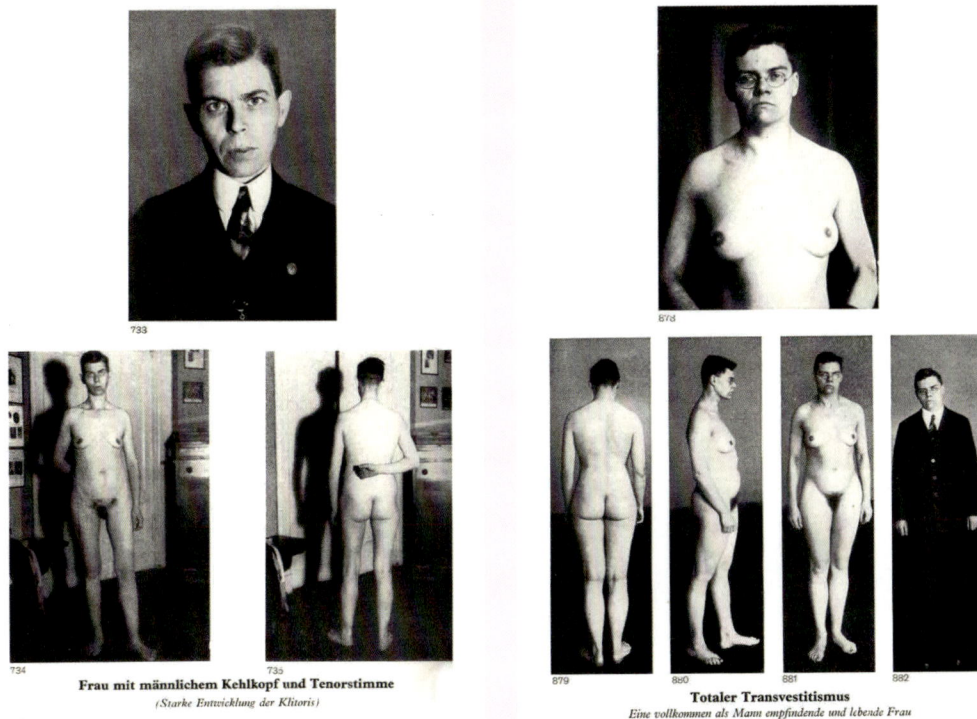

733

Frau mit männlichem Kehlkopf und Tenorstimme
(Starke Entwicklung der Klitoris)

734   735

879   880   881   882

Totaler Transvestitismus
Eine vollkommen als Mann empfindende und lebende Frau

FIGURE 4.3 and 4.4: "Woman with male Adam's apple and tenor voice (strong development of the clitoris)" / "Total transvestitism, a woman living and experiencing himself completely as a man." Hirschfeld, *Geschlechtskunde*, 1930.

visible as irritants – if not counterevidence – to this biological discourse. Looking at these two women who want to be men (as Abraham would put it), Hirschfeld explicitly tries to exclude social reproduction and focus on heredity. One might even say he willfully ignores the photographic evidence to define these "female transvestites" in terms of their bodies and to explicitly counter the idea that they might reproduce their kind socially, not biologically. Social reproduction can also be read here as a disruption or threat to the biological definition of females as tied to sexual reproduction.

Hirschfeld's attempt to focus attention in such cases away from cross-dressing and onto the body is evident in other images from *Geschlechtskunde* that repeat this visual gesture. These two sets of photos above (figures 4.3 and 4.4), captioned "total transvestism," were most likely taken in Hirschfeld's Institute for Sexual Science. Produced in the mode of clinical demonstration, they are difficult to view today because of the unequal power relations they reproduce and the way that they expose their subjects to our gaze.

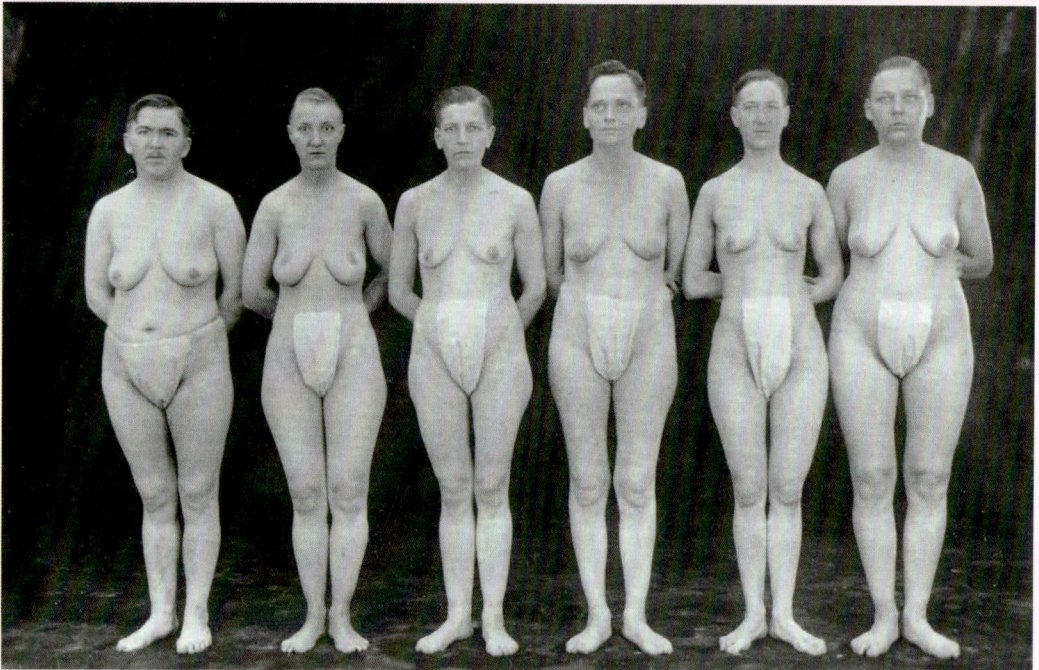

FIGURE 4.5 and 4.6: Two photographs categorized under "Nudism, German" in KILSC photo collection, KIDC56621 and KIDC56622. Copyright © 2017, The Trustees of Indiana University on behalf of the Kinsey Institute. All rights reserved."

They were meant to demonstrate that these individuals should be allowed to dress in men's clothing because their bodies supposedly display mixed-sex characteristics. Hirschfeld is attempting here to anchor an ethical and political argument about social norms in an understanding of the body as objective and natural, meaning that this truth should be immediately visible to the eye of the natural scientist and his readers. Hirschfeld's label "total transvestite" corresponds to what Benjamin later described as "transsexuals" – individuals who are "deeply unhappy as a member of the sex (or gender) to which [they were] assigned by the anatomical structure of the body." Benjamin's focus, however, was on individuals assigned a male sex at birth who wanted to live as women.

Figures 4.5 and 4.6 offer another juxtaposition of two photographs, so clearly similar in staging and style, found in Kinsey's archive. Their provenance is unknown, but they were donated by Harry Benjamin in 1958.

The photos were catalogued under the heading of "Nudist Photographs, German" – a decidedly odd categorization given that they are obviously meant to draw a contrast based specifically on how the figures are dressed. This might be taken as further evidence of the difficulty with which women who dressed in men's clothing fit into scientific-medical theories of transvestitism. Yet if read against the background of Hirschfeld's category of "total transvestite" and his use of similar images, it also suggests that whoever catalogued these photos – and perhaps the medical gaze of the camera itself – was in fact not concerned with clothing or cross-dressing at all, but rather with a notion of gender taken to be legible on the body itself.

This same scene appears in a very popular 1922 film about the work of Eugen Steinach (1861–1944), an Austrian endocrinologist whom Benjamin also revered and personally visited.[1] Steinach, who worked first in Prague and later in Vienna, believed that he had found the means to therapeutically manipulate aging and gender. He experimented on animals, transplanting testes into juvenile female rats and ovaries into juvenile male rats. He believed that he had found the causes of homosexuality and gender deviance – that there would be cells in the testes of homosexual men producing female hormones, and cells in the ovaries of women producing male hormones. His aim was to cure homosexuality and other "abnormal" variations of sexuality and gender through tissue implants from normal heterosexual men and women. His name even became a popular verb; having yourself "steinached" referred to a rejuvenation procedure meant to increase libido by either pinching off or severing the vas deferens of men or implanting foreign testes under the abdominal wall. The discourse of rejuvenation that grew out of this research was chiefly concerned with re-establishing male vitality.[2]

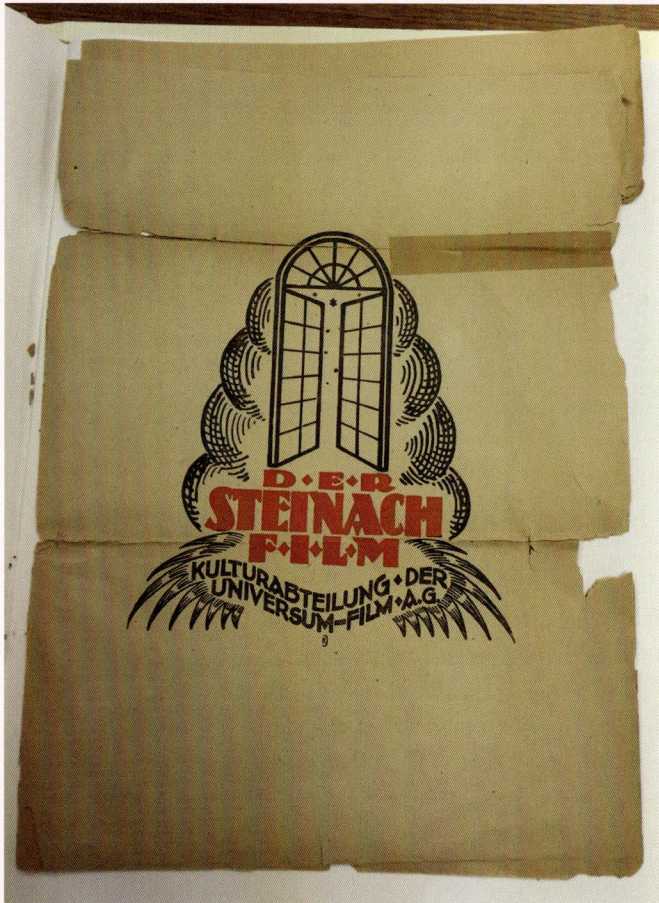

FIGURE 4.7: Benjamin's copy of the Steinach Film brochure in his files, KILSC-HB KILSC-HB HB 15-II B-58a. Copyright © 2017, The Trustees of Indiana University on behalf of the Kinsey Institute. All rights reserved.

In 1922, the German film studio Ufa produced a film, *Steinachs Forschung* (Steinach's research), as part of its new mission to distribute "educational films based exclusively on scientific knowledge." This earlier version was aimed exclusively at an expert audience, but a popular version was produced against Steinach's will and was released in 1923. The film was screened to enthusiastic audiences across German-speaking Europe and was spoken of elsewhere. The use of Steinach's research to treat transgender individuals was not its original purpose, nor was it the primary application of its results. The film nevertheless motivated many individuals, such as Otto Spengler, to seek hormonal and surgical procedures. As Annette reveals, in 1921 Benjamin lectured on the procedure at the New York Academy of Medicine and arranged for the film's screening there in 1923. But Benjamin's attempt to bring the film to mainstream American theatres was unsuccessful. His papers, however, include a – decidedly phallic – brochure for the film. The motif is evidence of the deeply masculinist, sexual shape of this rejuvenation discourse, its marketing and public perception, and its visual representation.

It was only when we hung these two photos (figures 4.5 and 4.6) in our exhibition next to a projection of an excerpt from the Steinach Film, however, that we discovered their appearance there. Archival research is always a combination of serendipity and diligence.

choice. As long as one's official papers did not match the gender in which one was living, it was not possible to live openly as a woman and get a "regular" job. Getting an income was crucial: legally, trans women were still men – men who had to provide for themselves. The nightlife of theatre and prostitution offered various ways of making a living and provided enough cash to pay for an attractive appearance, hormones, and perhaps surgery. Nevertheless, it required a fearless, daring character to survive in these surroundings, and it helped if trans women had some talent in singing, dancing, or at least entertaining. Bourgeois trans people who had the same transgender feelings but often lacked the required audacity or even willingness to enter this world, which so many considered "depraved," therefore often stayed in the closet. Hence the imagery and stereotype of trans women as sexual deviants – exciting and seductive or immoral and vile – was perpetuated.

Drag clubs were particularly common in Paris. Le Carrousel and Madame Arthur were well-established clubs with high-quality shows in the red-light district Pigalle. Some of the performing artists became true jet-set stars in the late 1950s, such as Coccinelle, Cappucine, Bambi, and April Ashley. It was widely known that the artists had been born as men – that was indeed the attraction for many of the men who came to see the performances. Cross-dressing had the reputation of being a form of theatre with a tantalizing amount of stylish nudity. After the show was over, some of the girls offered their services to the customers. That is how they made their money, and how the customers received the

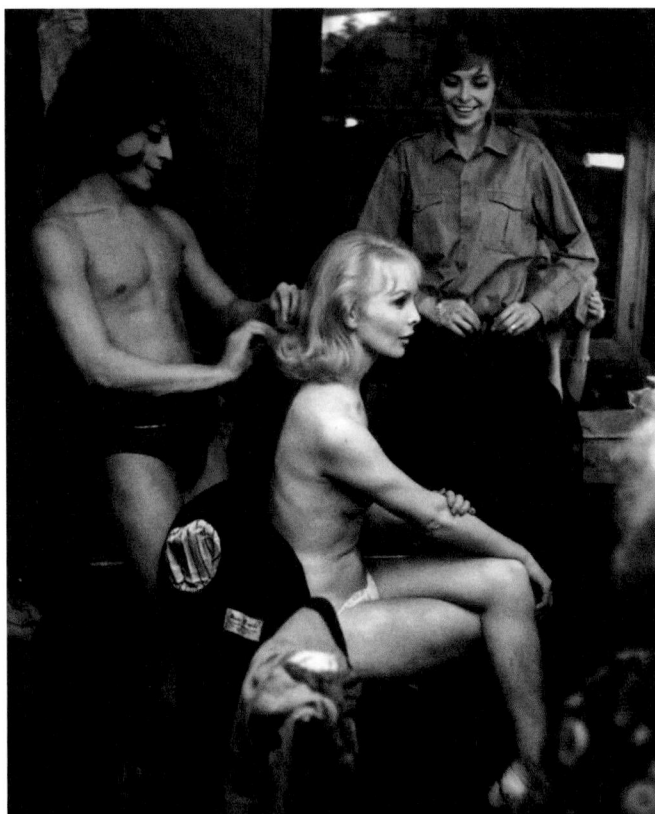

FIGURE 4.8: Bambi in the dressing room of Le Carrousel, Paris, 1960s [public domain].

pleasure they were seeking. Other big cities in Europe, such as Amsterdam, Antwerp, Hamburg, and Berlin had similar clubs. In the 1950s and 1960s, Dutch transgender women travelled to these cities, hoping to become stars themselves and to make lots of money, but mainly to be able to live as women. As Jill Pattiradjawane (a Dutch trans woman born in 1939), told me:

I was born as a boy in Jakarta, Indonesia. The news about Christine Jorgensen reached there as well. It immediately gave me a future. When I had seen Le Carrousel's cabaret, I was sure: I wanted to be part of that. I needed to get to

Europe, to Paris, Berlin, Amsterdam!

I've worked at Le Carrousel for years. It had to be perfect, and exactly the same every single night. Lower your left arm now, raise your right arm now, stand like this now, like that now. You couldn't afford to let go, even a little a bit. So, rehearsals every day, be present at eleven every morning. We were the mannequins and stood at the back of the stage. The lead characters were at the front and had their own acts. They were the stars. But we didn't look bad either, if I say so myself.[7]

There were also travesty clubs on the fringes of society, but these lacked the glamour of the more famous Pigalle clubs. In the red-light districts of the major cities, transgender people often combined their performances as artists with a life of prostitution. In Amsterdam "the life" largely happened around the Zeedijk. Good citizens did not visit this narrow street full of bars between Central Station and the Nieuwmarkt; here you would find all that was considered perverse and corrupt: sex workers (women, boys, transgender people), opium, so-called "Negro" music in jazz clubs, and a wide selection of seedy bars.

Life was often hard and grueling for transgender prostitutes, yet it also offered the freedom to live somewhat publicly as a woman. Within this subculture, transgender women were able to realize their identity; simply put: they could be themselves. By the mid-1950s, it was known to trans people in this scene that taking female hormones yielded the desired results: breast development, softer skin, and a feminization of body fat. In Amsterdam, a progressive family doctor with an office in the middle of the red-light district had no objections to prescribing hormones for transgender women. In other cities, women were able to source them on the black market.[8] The standing of these women in the world of pimps, police, and cisgender prostitutes was usually very low. Often, transgender women were limited to hustling, as it was difficult to obtain a "love room," i.e., a rented room to perform sex work. The madams knew that these women were vulnerable to the police and to the law, and demanded rents much higher than the market rate.[9] In Amsterdam, the infamous APV 105 (Algemene Plaatselijke Verordening, a local regulation with the force of law), otherwise known as the cross-dressing law, stated that it was forbidden to dress in the clothes of the opposite sex. The Netherlands was one of the very few countries to have such a law, and in the rest of Europe, particularly in Germany, cross-dressing was generally punished with laws against creating a public nuisance.[10] The police used this ruling as a means to bully transgender prostitutes they knew, to arrest them and bring them in to the station, where they were forced to undress and were humiliated, laughed at, and had their clothes taken away.[11] The police did this for fun on quiet nights, making clear that they considered transgender women fair game for their amusement. If your official gender did not match your looks, you had reason to fear the authorities.

Transatlantic Connections

"EX-GI BECOMES BLONDE BEAUTY" was the big headline on the front page of the *New York Daily News* on December 1, 1952. The sensational news spread far and wide, as far as the Far East. As Aaïcha Bergamin (1932–2014), a Dutch trans woman told me:

> You didn't even know it had a name. But then something appeared in the news. About a Christine Jorgensen, an ex-soldier of the American army who'd had an operation in Scandinavia to become a woman. All newspapers covered it and we went absolutely crazy, in those dressing rooms of our Paris nightclub. So, there were more options besides illegal hormones, besides hiding your penis between your legs. We immediately went to find out how we could get those operations as well.[12]

Jorgensen became a beacon of hope for transgender people in the 1950s after she had sex reassignment surgery in Copenhagen, Denmark. She received hundreds of letters from all over the world – from fans, from admirers, but mostly from other transgender people who had up until then believed that they were the only ones in the world with such "deranged feelings."[13] Jorgensen was the first transgender woman to receive such elaborate attention from the press.

Jorgensen's transition in the early 1950s had a profound impact on transgender people. In her book *How Sex Changed:*

FIGURE 4.9: Christine Jorgensen in Copenhagen, Denmark, December 11, 1952. Copyright © The Danish Royal Library.

A History of Transsexuality in the United States, Joanne Meyerowitz showed in detail the positive impact that this visible transition had on American trans people. After interviewing several older Dutch trans pioneers, I can confirm that this effect was not confined to the United States. As Aaïcha Bergamin and Jill Pattiradjawane make clear in the quotes above, the news stories about Christine had the same impact in the Netherlands that they had in the United States and other countries.[14]

But what did doctors in the Netherlands think of "the Jorgensen case"? It took a while before the medical field came up with

Sensationalism

Many of the images and stories from the sources we used in *TransTrans* are marked by sensationalism, which drew its power from a combination of sex, scandal, tragedy, and gender transgression. For instance, here is a story published by Hirschfeld in 1930 in *Geschlechtskunde* (figure 4.10). It tells of a woman who was impregnated by a sailor who threatened to report her as a cross-dresser unless she had intercourse with him.

Hirschfeld was both an advocate for marginalized communities and a scientist, and he constantly drew attention to the violence that sexual minorities faced. His decision to include the story of the sailor underscores the double vulnerability of this person as a biological woman and a cross-dresser.[1] Yet it is also significant that sailors were a social class perceived as being at the limits of respectability: even more rowdy, less socially disciplined or respectable than other workers, they were considered unrooted to any one place or family and had a reputation for sexual licentiousness. The scandal exists on so many levels: not only of a hidden pregnancy (an old trope and fact of social reality), or of a man proving to be a woman, but of a woman proving to be a sailor and the conflict of all of these scandalous facts with the bourgeois ideals of motherhood.

Friedrich Radszuweit's popular publications quite often openly exploited

Frauen als Männer aus dem Arbeiterstand

Frau, die als Matrose geschwängert wurde
(Ein Kamerad,¹ der ihr Geschlecht entdeckt hatte, drohte mit Anzeige, falls sie ihm nicht zu Willen wäre)

FIGURE 4.10: "Women as men from the working class. Woman who was impregnated as a sailor (a comrade who had discovered her sex threatened to report her if she did offer herself sexually)." Hirschfeld, *Geschlechtskunde*, 1930.

this sensationalism. These magazines include many examples of boulevard-style tales of sexual scandals and what were called *Lustmorde*, or murders of passion. One of his publications, *Das dritte Geschlecht* (1928–30) – which carried the same name as *Das 3. Geschlecht* (1930–32) but was written out – entirely consisted of sexual scandals. Yet the following example, at least, from *Die Freundin*, also uses personal tragedy and sensational

FIGURE 4.11: *Die Freundin*, 1928. Headline: "Killed her husband out of love for her girlfriend." Caption: "Vilma West, who murdered her husband out of love for her girlfriend (see the longer report inside)."

rhetoric to argue for social reform. The scandal is announced on the cover, and the report follows inside.

The full story:

She killed her husband out of love for her girlfriend!

Report from Brooklyn:

Velma West, an 18-year old girl from a good family, was forced by her family to marry a respectable young man. She lived with him for three months before her husband tried to separate her from her girlfriend, to whom she was bound by a great love. To prove to her girlfriend how great her love was, and because it was impossible for her to live at her husband's side, Velma murdered her young spouse with a hammer.

Had the case been reversed – had Velma murdered the young man because he had had an affair with another woman – then the sentence would likely have come to five years prison with possibility of parole. "Cherchez le femme" is what the judge would have said! But since this love was something unnatural, something dirty, hardly to be mentioned, Velma West had to pay for this misdeed with her life. This American way of thinking! Would it have not been more just to punish the parents (who forced the girl against her will into marriage, supposedly to make her "normal")?

When will America learn that same-sex love is not a vice but an appearance of nature? According to all appearances, never!

Die Freundin (1928)

Amerikanischer weiblicher Transevstit

FIGURE 4.12: "American female transvestite," *Das 3. Geschlecht*, May 1930.

This same drawing also appeared in *Das 3. Geschlecht*, where the figure is described as a woman dressed as a man – an "American female transvestite" – rather than as a lesbian:

The need to reuse the probably limited stock of photos that Radzuweit had, and of course to sell magazines, undercuts the authenticity of the story and any agenda of social reform we might glean from it. In short, it probably did more harm than good.

This fine line that *Die Freundin* is toeing here between emancipation, visibility, and pandering to the prejudices of its day is brought home by a comparison with these tabloids from the 1960s that Harry Benjamin collected (figures 4.13, 4.14, and 4.15).

Here, the intentions of connecting a community or giving it visibility are completely absent, replaced by nothing but prurient sex(ual) scandal. This comparison reminds us, however, that these later tabloids did not invent such tropes of sensationalism and scandal. Indeed, the tenor of shocking sexual revelation is almost constant in the histories we are looking at here precisely because it reflected social reality.

Figure 4.13, 4.14, and 4.15: Tabloids from the 1960s collected by Harry Benjamin. The National Insider, 19 July 1964, Volume 5, Number 3, cover, KILSC-HB 14-15 / The National Insider, 19 July 1964, Volume 5, Number 3, p. 4, KILSC-HB 14-15 / Midnight, 24 June 1963, cover, KILSC-HB 14-15. Copyright © 2017, The Trustees of Indiana University on behalf of the Kinsey Institute. All rights reserved.

a serious response. Only in 1954 did the authoritative medical journal *Nederlandse Tijdschrift voor Geneeskunde* (NTvG) review an article by Christian Hamburger, the endocrinologist from Copenhagen who had directed Jorgensen's treatment.[15] Hamburger's article reveals his excited fascination and his compassion for his patient. In his review of Hamburger's article, gynecologist Willem Paul Plate mirrors this perspective and literally copies Hamburger's closing sentence: "Doctors should regard it as their duty to do their utmost to make the lives of these men and women, who are deprived of a harmonious and happy life due to no fault of their own, as comfortable and easy as possible."[16] But Plate was one of very few doctors with this perspective. The prominent psychiatrist and university professor Eugene Carp called Jorgensen's transition a peculiar perversion of erotic feelings, and he labelled the people affected with these feelings "sufferers of the delusion of sex change." His conclusion was crystal clear: one should not use surgical intervention to "deform" the patients "into beings who, on the surface, show the characteristics of a female physicality."[17] Carp had published earlier about the so-called delusion of sex change in his 1951 textbook *Psychopathologische opsporingen* (Psycho-pathological investigations).[18] He explained the disorder as stemming from strongly suppressed homoerotic feelings, but he also found that the delusion occurred in "many sufferers of other perversions, in neurotics and some types of schizoid psychopathology."

Given guidelines for medical privacy, we cannot determine whether professor Carp's patients were indeed psychiatric patients or not. But these are not mutually exclusive concepts: these individuals could have been psychiatric patients *and* transgender. This may have starkly coloured Carp's perception and may perhaps explain in part his opinion that trans identities were "delusions." However, his texts do provide insights into the way an influential psychiatrist in the Netherlands of the mid-1950s would view this phenomenon – or at least, how he would write about it, as we will see below.

From the United States to Holland

Transgender people all over the world, especially from the United States, wanted doctor Hamburger's clinic in Copenhagen to also operate on them. The hospital in Copenhagen was unable to cope with all the requests and soon the Danish authorities decided that transgender people from abroad were no longer welcome. Harry Benjamin had by this time treated many trans people in his clinics in New York and San Francisco. When Denmark became inaccessible, Benjamin contacted his network and found psychiatrist Frederik Hartsuiker in Haarlem, who was known for his expertise in prescribing castration for sex offenders. (There is a striking parallel to the role of Hartsuiker with that of Karl Bowman in the United States, a psychiatrist who specialized in the castration of male sex offenders and ultimately came into contact with trans women and medical practitioners such as Harry Benjamin.)[19] Christian Hamburger, the Danish doctor who was responsible for Jorgensen's treatment, was already referring transgender women to him: there was, in other words, a direct line from Hamburger to Hartsuiker.[20]

The Dutch psychiatrist Hartsuiker and the American endocrinologist Benjamin first established contact over the case of Dixie MacLane early in 1954.[21] Hartsuiker had received a letter from MacLane, asking to be castrated by him. Hartsuiker responded by asking MacLane not to come to Holland before sending more information, such as the results of tests carried out by a psychiatrist or psychologist and a written life history, including a description of MacLane's sex life. Thinking that Harry Benjamin was MacLane's psychiatrist, Hartsuiker wrote to Benjamin asking for his advice in this case. It is not clear whether the doctors had previously met or known about each other, but the tone of the correspondence suggests some level of acquaintance. The Dutch doctor wrote to his colleague overseas: "Would there be good purpose to operate [on] this man? Is it possible that, for instance, we perform the castration here and that the further demasculinization is done in his own country?"[22] Benjamin responded by making it clear that he was not MacLane's psychiatrist, and he agreed with Hartsuiker's impression of MacLane as being very unstable and unrealistic in their demands. Benjamin was perhaps also influenced by Carla Erskine's analysis of Dixie and by the conflict between the two women that Annette describes. His belief that Dixie might become even more unstable if denied surgery certainly echoes

Carla's description of Dixie "blowing a cork all over the place" and threatening suicide.[23]

> It would be entirely up to psychiatrists like yourself to decide whether Dixie is a suitable subject for a de-masculinization operation. I am afraid however that a blunt refusal may precipitate an acute psychotic state. The recommendation of "chemical castration" with large doses of estrogen and accompanying psycho-therapy may be the next best way to help him. I think Dixie is a more serious problem than many other transsexualists and it is really often difficult to decide which is the lesser of the two evils: to operate or to refuse operation.[24]

Hartsuiker decided not to proceed with providing care for MacLane;[25] however, this interaction with Benjamin led to their collaboration in helping other transgender women from the United States in the Netherlands. In response to a request from Violet C. to come to the Netherlands for surgery, Hartsuiker wrote to Benjamin in March 1954, asking that Benjamin arrange for a psychiatric evaluation, which should include a life story written by the patient and the results of Rorschach and Szondi tests.[26] His request was meant to save Violet C. from incurring additional costs for testing in the Netherlands. Hartsuiker gave a price estimate of 200 to 300 Dutch guilders for the procedure and twelve to fifteen guilders a day for the hospital stay (an amount equivalent to approximately 200 US dollars).[27] After receiving this information, Benjamin answered transgender women seeking his help, such as Shelly W., by explaining: "If you are interested in an operation, I must explain to you that such would not be feasible in this country because it is illegal. The operation can and has been done repeatedly in Holland and I have the necessary contacts there."[28] Benjamin also gave Shelly W. information about how he prepared patients for the trip to the Netherlands: he placed them under observation and treatment for at least three months; he gave them hormone injections at least once a week; and some possibly also received hormone pills, a consultation with a psychiatrist, and several psychological tests. Patients were to visit Benjamin once or twice a week and would be charged ten to fifteen dollars for each visit.[29]

Dr. Hartsuiker, however, had in the meantime developed some doubts about transgender surgery. He was skeptical of the idea that men could really become women, which was how he was conceptualizing such surgical interventions. With this specific group of patients, he simply recognized an extreme desire for castration, and he had been willing to assist with that in an expert manner. But after the exchange with Benjamin, he started backtracking, writing:

> In recent months so many transvestites have come to Holland, especially from England and America (and several without announcing their arrival), seeking demasculinization. Among them were so many unbalanced and hysterical figures, that the surgeons refuse to carry out operative treatment any longer. I believe that from a psychiatric point of view there are indeed some objections to this treatment for these mentally so very much disturbed patients.[30]

Harry Benjamin responded immediately, afraid that the Holland connection was falling away. He tried to convince Hartsuiker that the four people he wanted to send overseas were completely balanced psychologically and that a "sex change" operation was the only appropriate option for them – it was the right thing to do. He also objected that they had already made all the preparations for their trip to the Netherlands. Benjamin agreed with Hartsuiker that there was no indication for surgery, as traditionally understood, for the majority of the transvestites, but for some "we must consider surgery as a calculated risk and perhaps as the lesser evil." He referred to an article he was about to publish in the *American Journal of Psychotherapy*.[31]

The debate between the two doctors continued in an elaborate correspondence. Hartsuiker suggested an alternative: send the candidates to surgeon Daniel Lopez Ferrer in Mexico, which would be a more appropriate place for them than the Netherlands. Once again, the source of Hartsuiker's resistance reveals the paradox that characterized notions of transgender identity at the time. The patients were blamed for being too effeminate and for showing homosexual tendencies. It is clear that they were still being seen as men – men who wanted to undergo castration.

This conflation of homosexuality and transsexuality, both of which Hartsuiker viewed negatively, was quite common in the 1950s, as Meyerowitz has argued.[32] Hartsuiker told Benjamin that

> In the hospitals here there have been some rumour [sic] about the operative treatment of transvestites. People do not feel it ethically justified. The patients-transvestites themselves caused this opinion. Some of them behaved themselves very hysterically, showed unpleasant homosexual tendencies and acted at the men's ward in such an effeminate way that the other patients protested against their being there. The result is that the surgical department will not take them up for the time being.[33]

Despite his skepticism, Hartsuiker wrote a letter to Coen van Emde Boas, a well-known progressive psychiatrist and sexologist from Amsterdam, the same day, asking if Van Emde Boas would be willing to treat a few English and American "transvestites." Coen van Emde Boas was the embodiment of sexology in the Netherlands in the 1950s, often occupying himself with sensitive issues, such as homosexuality, birth control, and abortion. In his home-based practice he saw people with what were then called paraphilias or sexual disorders, including transvestites. Van Emde Boas answered Hartsuiker positively: "I've been interested in the transvestites' issue for many years now, but my material base is still very small and I

FIGURE 4.16: Coen van Emde Boas, famous Dutch psychiatrist and sexologist

also believe that we should help these tragic figures as much as we possibly can."[34]

Demasculinization and Feminization Procedures

Backed up by Van Emde Boas and the arguments Benjamin continuously supplied, Hartsuiker eventually agreed to admit more American transgender women for treatment, though he now mostly served as an intermediary for Van Emde Boas and only saw patients once or twice, for diagnostic support. Van Emde Boas became the attending physician for these cases. It proved very hard to find a replacement for the surgeon who had been doing the operations up to then, Dr. Nauta of the Diaconessenhuis in Haarlem. Hardly anyone wanted to step in. Only the Amsterdam-based general surgeon H. C. Koch Jr. was willing to help. Koch performed the surgeries at the Boerhaavekliniek, a small hospital in the heart of Amsterdam with a capacity of only sixty patients. Hartsuiker made one final exception for patient F., who had already been to see him and Nauta in 1953 and who had been promised that the duo of doctors would continue the treatment.

What did the procedure entail? The candidates for operation had already been using female hormones, which generated a somewhat castrating effect. The wish these transgender women shared was to get rid of their male genitalia, and preferably then undergo vaginoplasty, though this was a secondary consideration. The immediate goal was demasculinization by castration. As already mentioned, in the United States this procedure was viewed as mutilation and was legally prohibited on those grounds ("mayhem"). This judicial status, which had come about after the decision in a 1949 legal case of a trans woman seeking medical care, blocked further gender-affirmation surgery in the United States for years to come. According to Susan Stryker, only a few dozen operations were secretly performed by urologist Elmer Belt in Los Angeles.[35]

The legal reasoning of mayhem in regard to gender-affirmation surgery did not apply in the Netherlands. Basically, there were four possible surgical phases for transgender women: 1) castration of the testes; 2) penectomy (penis amputation); 3)

plastic reconstruction of the empty scrotum into a female exterior and 4) vaginoplasty.

The first two procedures were available in the Netherlands during this period, with the surgical techniques that had been developed after ample experience with castration of sex offenders. However, procedures number three and four were not available in the Netherlands. To further femininize their genitalia, transgender women tried their luck in Denmark. Although Christine Jorgensen's doctors had officially announced that they were no longer taking on foreign patients, they made some exceptions if patients had already been castrated. This was the case for J., for example, who went to Copenhagen a few weeks after her castration and penectomy in Amsterdam in order to convince the doctors to perform the next procedure. She succeeded, and shortly after she was admitted to the local hospital for procedures to lower the urethra and remove part of the scrotum; the remainder was fashioned into a likeness of the labia majora, but no vaginoplasty was performed.

Many American women went back to the United States for vaginoplasty, even though this technique was still in its infancy. Benjamin knew a number of plastic surgeons, such as Elmer Belt in Los Angeles, who were willing and able to do this. Because the procedure did not qualify as mayhem it was not illegal, which cleared away the legal hurdles that had prevented doctors from operating. It is interesting to note that in terms of eligibility for transformational procedures the situation in Europe and the United States was completely inverse: the main obstacle, demasculinization, was possible in the Netherlands, but further steps towards femininization were not, whereas feminization procedures were much more available in the United States.

In early 1955, Van Emde Boas wrote to J. about the option of a vaginoplasty: "that such surgery as this hadn't proved effective, to his knowledge. He said that the opening had a tendency to grow together and lose its depth. However, he said he based his opinion on a couple of cases in Germany about twenty-four years ago."[36] But phase three, the plastic reconstruction of the empty scrotum into a female exterior, also turned out not to be an option in the Netherlands – to the bitter disappointment of F., who had stayed on for a long time, waiting for the promised operation. This made Benjamin furious. As he wrote to the prospective patient Rosa F.:

> I don't know whether I feel more sorry or more bitter about this utterly indefensible attitude of those Holland clinics. Are they trying to outdo us in hypocrisy, puritanism, cowardice or whatever you may call it? All you can do at the present is to wait for further word from Dr. Hartsuiker and be patient. After all, nothing is lost. The operation can and will be performed, if not abroad, then here. The annoying part is merely the uncertainty of time and place.[37]

The Dutch doctors presumably reasoned that further care for these foreigners was not their responsibility, given that they

had already provided access to castration with great difficulty. After all, feminization treatment was available (both legally and in practice) in the patients' home countries. The Dutch doctors only wanted to heed the most urgent requests. What might also have played a role here is that the treating physicians were focused on keeping the transgender women in the Netherlands for the shortest possible time. They always feared publicity or problems with the police. Van Emde Boas later wrote that the police told him that "if we continued treating these people we could end up coming into conflict with the law ourselves for intentional infliction of grievous bodily harm."[38] Writing to Benjamin in April 1955, J. explained the atmosphere in the following terms:

> It seems that Dr. Emde Boas is reluctant to approve more than the orchidectomy and peotomy[39] for foreign patients and has made a sort of "gentlemen's agreement" with his colleagues and with the police that no plastic surgery will be approved for foreign patients after the aforesaid castration and peotomy. Dr. Emde Boas apparently feels that the patient's own country, should grant him the extra surgery. Moreover, if there should be any publicity, the entire blame for the feminizing operations won't fall on Holland if the plastic work is done elsewhere.[40]

The stance of the treating physicians in the Netherlands with regard to secrecy was

FIGURE 4.17: News clipping from United Press, 1954

related to what had happened in the case of Tamara Rees. Rees is considered to be the third American transgender woman after Christine Jorgensen to have received gender confirmation surgery, the second being Charlotte McLeod.[41] Rees contacted Dr. Hartsuiker in Haarlem through Hamburger in Copenhagen, and she received the notification in the fall of 1953 that she was welcome to come to the Netherlands for treatment. In her memoirs, which are certainly not factually reliable,[42] Rees describes Hartsuiker as very likable. She

remembered his continuous warning that the choice was irreversible and that positive outcomes were not guaranteed. Hartsuiker undertook psychiatric analysis, which spanned several hours of examination. After receiving a green light, Rees was operated on by surgeon Nauta in the Diaconessenhuis in Haarlem on January 5, 1954, where she underwent castration and possibly penectomy (amputation of the penis).

Tamara Rees stayed in Amsterdam for almost a year. The exact circumstances surrounding this stay are unclear, but while there she came to the attention of the (immigration) police. According to Rees, she was followed by the police, who thought she must be a prostitute. In September 1954, she was arrested and put in jail, possibly because she went out dressed in women's clothes. Hartsuiker had advised the police in Amsterdam and the American consulate to allow Rees to dress as a woman, which they did for several months before inexplicably changing their policy. Rees was deported back to the United States in November 1954, escorted by the police. Her story got some publicity in the American press,[43] very much to Dr. Hartsuiker's annoyance, as he was quoted as Rees's psychiatrist without having spoken to the press himself – and despite his agreement with Rees to stay clear of any publicity. He uttered his frustration in a letter to Benjamin, saying: "Up to now I have had only unfavourable experiences with these patients concerning their reliability in many respects,"[44] and he once again expressed his wish not to continue these treatments. Benjamin replied: "You are quite right that many of these patients are utterly unreliable. After all, nature has made them misfits. The tragedy is that some of the reliable and reasonably balanced patients (like F. and J.) have to suffer for the sins of the others."[45]

Following the problems surrounding Tamara Rees, Van Emde Boas was strict: the candidates had to be absolutely willing to remain under the radar of the press while they were undergoing the entire procedure. Transgender women had to arrive in the Netherlands with their masculine appearances and had to stay that way until they left the country again. They were not allowed to dress in female attire in public, since this was against the local law and might lead to trouble with the police – something that the women were already very much familiar with in their home countries.

So these transgender women were by no means out of the closet – in fact, they were invisible. The feminizing effects of the use of hormones were there, in varying degrees, but these remained unnoticed against a background of male clothing and male voices. They were addressed with "he" and "him" by the doctors, and, as we know from their letters, they used male pronouns when referring to each other. The concept of the "real life test": a certain period of time, mostly a year, to prove to the medical caregivers that one was ready for gender affirming surgery, was definitely not yet part of medical practice. This would only become protocol from the 1970s on. For now, the order of the steps was the opposite: first (castration) surgery, then at a chosen moment, coming out and starting life as a woman. Describing this need to stay undercover, F. wrote to Benjamin that "Under the circumstances it was not an easy task for Dr. Nauta to make arrangements to maintain the secrecy of the operation to be performed, which was done in a Catholic Hospital and I was accommodated with two other patients. Helpful, was my not understanding the Dutch language – so they could not ask me any questions."[46] Only when someone had had the "conversion" and presented herself as a woman to the outside world did these women and the doctors introduce and use the female

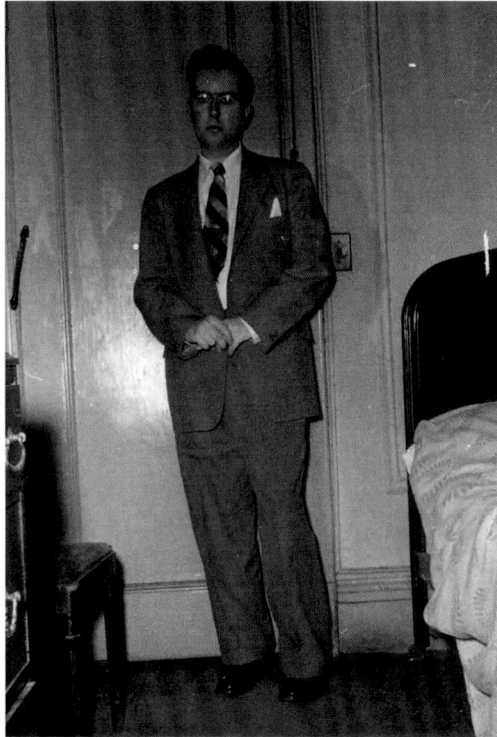

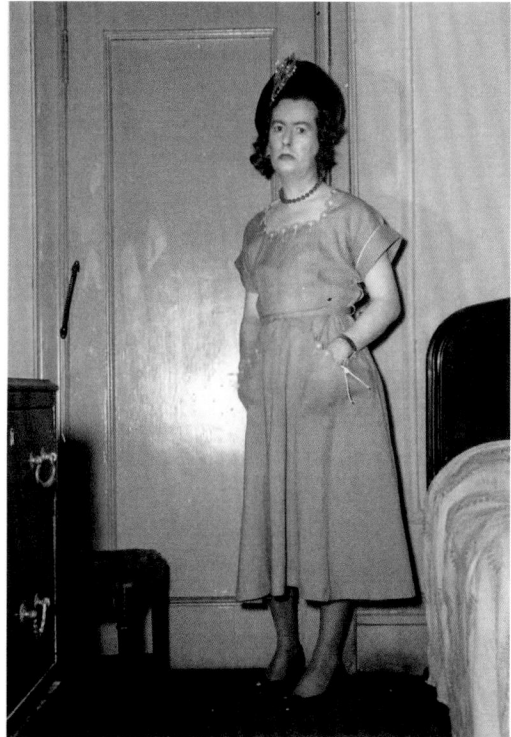

Figure 4.18 and 4.19: Pictures (possibly self-taken) of Catherine J. KILSC, Harry Benjamin Collection, KILSC-HB 5. Copyright © 2017, The Trustees of Indiana University on behalf of the Kinsey Institute. All rights reserved.

name and the pronouns "she" and "her." Some trans women tried to obtain a female identity document by showing a letter from the doctor and psychiatrist that they should be considered a female to the American embassy in the Netherlands. In some cases they succeeded and were able to safely travel back to the United States as women, but others were forced to wait until they were home to take this step.

In the first months of 1955, Violet C., Rosa F., Catherine J., and Daphne P. came to the Netherlands in the hopes of obtaining surgery. C., J., and P. already knew each other very well and they looked after each

other after their operations. The trans women stayed together in the little hotel Hegra on Herengracht 269 in Amsterdam, "so they would not become lonely, at least not emotionally," as Van Emde Boas described it years later.[47] The hotel was affordable, simple but comfortable. The owners of the hotel were aware of their guests' situation and were very discreet and helpful during their unusual stay. Apart from the doctors and other medical staff, they were probably the only people who knew that these surgeries had taken place. As J. wrote to Benjamin in one of her many letters: "My family still doesn't know about me. They think I've gotten a leave of absence from my job in order to enjoy an extended vacation in Europe. I've sent them post cards regularly, and also an occasional letter, all telling of the marvelous time I'm having sightseeing. During those times I was hospitalized I had [Daphne] or the nurses mail the cards for me."[48]

It was an intense trajectory: for the actual operation, the transgender women were dependent on Van Emde Boas for permission. Unlike Hartsuiker, Van Emde Boas wanted to reexamine everything himself. They were expected to appear in his practice almost every day. He did extensive psychological and physical examinations assisted by endocrinologist Grad Hellinga, a prominent expert in the field of andrology, among others. The psychological and sexological examinations investigated how patients viewed homosexuality or masturbation, whether they had suicidal thoughts, and whether they would be able to sustain themselves financially after transition.

Van Emde Boas also demanded that they present themselves once in female attire at his office, and he expected them to appear at an educational seminar that he organized for students at his home. C. and J. spoke to a group of about fifteen students and a few college professors about their transgender feelings. During the first part of the evening they were dressed in a masculine manner, during the second part, in a feminine. Much like Carla Erskine, they were happy to answer the many questions in the interests of contributing to the development of

knowledge and understanding.[49] The four transgender women wrote to Harry Benjamin throughout their entire stay in the Netherlands; Benjamin very much wanted to stay abreast of how they were doing. Van Emde Boas also corresponded with Benjamin during this period, repeatedly telling him that he had to ease up on sending new people over and that these people had to be stable, inconspicuous, and able to dispose of sufficient resources. Benjamin asked more questions about concrete details, so he could sufficiently inform future patients before they left for the Netherlands – for example, about the costs. The total costs minus travel added up to about a thousand dollars (which would be about 10,000 dollars today): 500 dollars for medical expenses and 500 for transportation costs and room and board.[50]

Patients arrived in the Netherlands approximately five to six weeks before surgery. The reason for their admission to hospital was kept a secret; the other patients and the nursing staff who were not directly involved in their care were not informed. Hospital staff not directly engaged with the medical care viewed the patients as just ordinary men who had the bad luck to be suffering from a hernia or appendicitis while on holiday. As J. described things to Benjamin:

> The average Dutchman apparently knows nothing of the demasculin-ization operations that are per-formed in his country. Certainly, the procedure is not generally known. When I was lying in bed

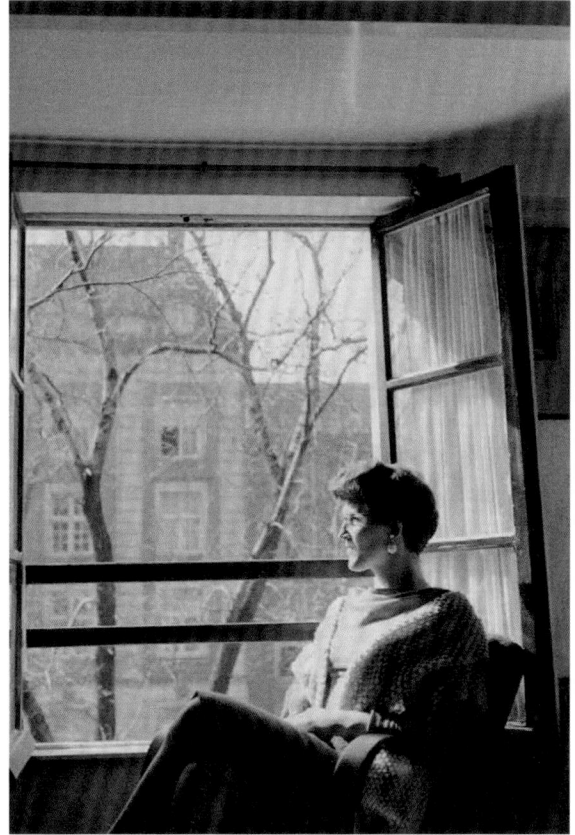

FIGURE 4.20 and 4.21: Pictures of Daphne P., taken at Hotel Hegra, Amsterdam, 1955. KILSC-HB 5. Copyright © 2017, The Trustees of Indiana University on behalf of the Kinsey Institute. All rights reserved.

the night before my operation a nurse asked me if it was my appendix that troubled me. I told her I had a growth in the joint that had to be removed. Other nurses during the past ten days have sympathized with me because my "holiday" was spoiled by my sudden illness while in Holland.

One of my night nurses asked me if I suffered much pain before the operation. I told her not very much. Generally speaking, the nurses are not curious at all. Their observations about my "sudden illness" were apparently prompted merely by sympathy. Still, I can't help but feel that some of them might be a bit suspicious, but all this is of relatively small moment. For the most part, I myself am "playing dumb."[51]

Disconnection of the Dutch Route

This organized transatlantic route for trans women wanting sex reassignment surgery would not last long. When Van Emde Boas was organizing these procedures, it had been possible for surgeons to perform surgeries under their own authority in private clinics. The surgeon was hardly accountable to anybody – not to the anaesthesiologist, not to the assistant, not to the nurse, but only to the hospital director. The surgeon Koch performed a number of operations under these conditions in the Boerhaavekliniek in Amsterdam, until the hospital director found out and prohibited the procedures in April 1955. According to Van Emde Boas the last patient was literally removed from the operation room.[52] Van Emde Boas's assistant wrote to him while he was on holiday in April 1955, noting that since no other clinic was willing to conduct surgery of this kind, Koch had decided to perform the operation on this last patient under local anesthesia in his home office.[53] "Everything went well," the assistant continued:

> He/she is now being nursed at Huize Ardina, Keizersgracht 280, the owner is a friend of Hotel Hegra, the daughter of the family is a nurse ...Do we have to write to Benjamin that the arrival of the next patient will have to be postponed for a while, in view of the stance of the hospital boards? I don't think it's very useful to have them come here for examinations

> and then be sent back without surgery. And Koch didn't seem willing to help every next patient the same way he helped P. To the contrary. This was an emergency solution.[54]

Benjamin was consequently informed that he should not send new patients for the time being. This provisional decision became permanent, ending the official route from the United States to the Netherlands for transgender patients.

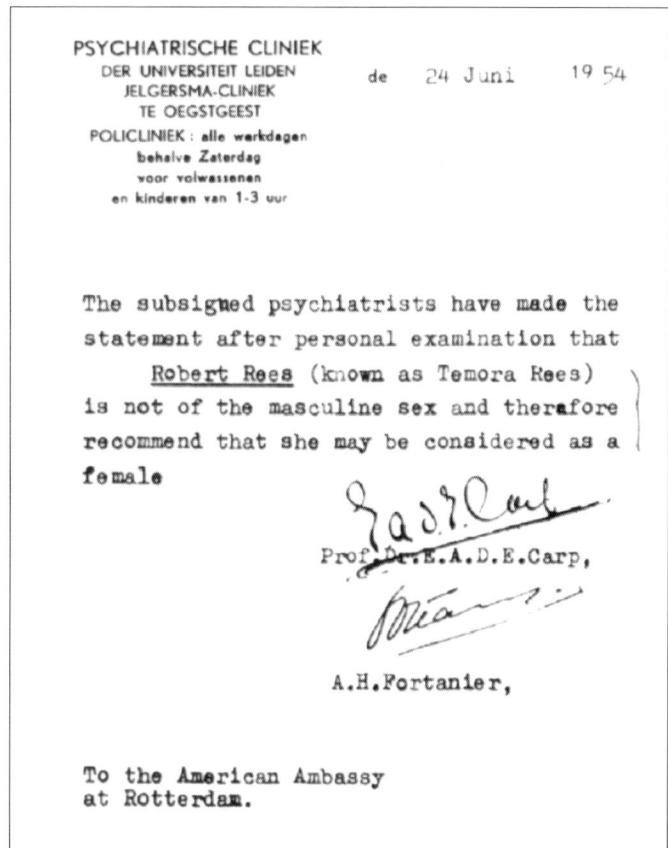

> PSYCHIATRISCHE CLINIEK
> DER UNIVERSITEIT LEIDEN
> JELGERSMA-CLINIEK
> TE OEGSTGEEST
> POLICLINIEK : alle werkdagen
> behalve Zaterdag
> voor volwassenen
> en kinderen van 1-3 uur
>
> de 24 Juni 19 54
>
> The subsigned psychiatrists have made the statement after personal examination that
>
> Robert Rees (known as Temora Rees) is not of the masculine sex and therefore recommend that she may be considered as a female
>
> Prof. Dr. E.A.D.E.Carp,
>
> A.H.Fortanier,
>
> To the American Ambassy at Rotterdam.

FIGURE 4.22: *Psychiatrische Cliniek* on Robert Rees. Copyright © Tamara Rees, Reborn (1955).

Small Circles

The small circle of trans women who sought surgery in the Netherlands sent frequent letters back and forth, and they were also in constant contact with Benjamin, who kept them informed about the shifts in medical policy. As the other chapters of this book have demonstrated, his relationship with trans women seems to have been close, intense, and sincere. It is evident that these women put their trust in him and felt support from both him and his wife, to whom they kept sending their best wishes. The image of Benjamin as a compassionate doctor has been noted before, for instance by Pat Califia in her analysis of Harry Benjamin as one of the first "Gender Scientists."[55]

Even with Benjamin's warm support and extensive involvement, however, the transgender women had to convince the Dutch doctors of their wishes. They were thoroughly questioned, examined, and tested physically and psychologically. In practice, the standard protocol involved transgender people moving heaven and earth to convince the treating physician. By pushing back strongly, the treating physicians tested the urgency of the desires of the patient in question. Nevertheless, the transgender women who kept Benjamin informed mainly wrote very positively about the Dutch treating physicians. They describe these doctors as sympathetic, caring, and highly interested. F. was even taken by Hartsuiker on tourist trips in his car, and they went out to dine. It is possible that the reports back to Benjamin tended to be positive because the women were dependent on the doctors. But their drive to supply Benjamin with accurate information seems authentic. Only C. was angry that she was not allowed to wear female attire in public, and she blamed the treating physicians for this. In contrast, J. wrote: "The whole procedure in Holland is hardly a cut and dried one … As it is, enlightened men like Drs. Emde Boas, Hartsuiker, Kijzer and Koch are in the minority in Holland … Once again, however, I'd like to emphasize that I for one am more than grateful to Holland for what has been done in my case up to now."[56]

It is hard to evaluate the level of compassion that Hartsuiker and Van Emde Boas had as doctors. Based on their writing, it seems to me that they were more authoritarian figures and more professionally distant than Benjamin. Their opinions demonstrated a limited medical-psychiatric perspective that framed trans women only as interesting cases. They did want to be kept informed about the well-being of the women when they returned home and exchanged letters. But their interest was not so much personal or humane; rather, the transgender phenomenon was a fascinating new field of study for them, and they needed the information that only trans people themselves could provide.

Moreover, there seems to be some contradiction in the way doctors behaved on a personal level versus how they wrote about trans people in general. Public writing was often less caring. A prime example comes from professor Carp of

Leiden University, whose official statement on the validity of transgender identities was very negative. He condemned transgender people as having a psychiatric disorder that should not be physically treated.[57] In practice, however, Carp backed Hartsuiker's decision to perform a castration on Tamara Rees and wrote her a note to hand to the American embassy, stating that he "recommend[ed] that she may be considered a female."[58] Carp was also consulted for the surgical treatment for F. and granted his support.[59] We can conclude that Carp, as a leading psychiatrist in the Netherlands, conformed and even contributed to professional peer pressure to authoritatively reject medical treatment for trans people even as he acted differently in the privacy of his own clinic.

Van Emde Boas as a Sexologist

It was not only trans women from the United States whom Van Emde Boas helped; others came to him from England, Germany, and of course the Netherlands. In 1955 he examined at least thirteen people.[60] Because Coen van Emde Boas played such a large role in the care of transgender people in the 1950s, it is essential to focus on the criteria he used.

To Van Emde Boas, the feminine or masculine look of transgender people, based on extensive observations, was very important. His assistant at the time, Margreet Groot, remembers him explicitly asking her opinion: did the patient, upon entering the waiting room, come across as predominantly male or female?[61] He wanted

to hear her views as a woman, and he regarded it like a second opinion.

The value Van Emde Boas placed on the appearance of transgender people went beyond makeup and dresses. If a transgender woman was unlucky enough to be unable to physically conform to common standards of feminine presentation due to her height or heavy build, for instance, Van Emde Boas would refuse to recommend treatment. Van Emde Boas also imposed a number of conditions before he would recommend surgery. Psychotherapeutic solutions had to be exhausted, and the candidate had to be mentally stable and free of any "exhibitionistic tendencies à la Jorgensen."[62] Relying on a report of the Dutch Health Council from 1966, which I will discuss in more detail below, we can glean an understanding of the treatment norms that were prevalent at the time Van Emde Boas was practicing. The report describes the criteria that the small international network of psychiatrists-sexologists, including Van Emde Boas, relied on in the 1950s:

> Pro-indications: The existence of constitutional transsexism that brings subjective intolerable suffering to the patient, resulting in the danger that he or she will slide into suicide, automutilation or a social psychiatric untenable situation. Contra-indications: Insufficient intelligence; insufficient ego-strength; malign progression in demands; insufficient insight into the fact that plastic surgery does not mean a change of sex; exhibitionistic

tendencies; absence of willingness to live a virtually asexual and
partnerless life; looks, voice and
demeanor unsuitable for the desired
sex; familial and other social complications.[63]

Van Emde Boas himself never mentioned
demanding asexuality from his patients,
but he was concerned about "malign
progression in demands," meaning that
patients would desire more and more far-
reaching and unrealistic transformative
procedures. He only agreed to treat
transgender people when he felt that the
diagnosis was beyond doubt. In a letter
to his colleague, Professor Urban of the
University Clinic of Innsbruck, Austria,
Van Emde Boas formulated it like this:
"Je ernster der Wahn, desto besser die
Prognose" (the more serious the delusion,
the better the prognosis).[64] He did use the
term "delusion," but he meant it in the
psychiatric sense current at the time, not in
the sense of a misguided illusion.

The discussion was never about
hormonal treatment; the doctors only spoke
about surgical interventions. Its irreversible
aspect instilled so much fear that chances
of success had to be 100 per cent. Van Emde
Boas basically delinked his diagnosis of
transsexuality from his recommendation
for an operation. It was not about being
trans or not: what mattered was being
suitable to undergo the transition.

Besides diagnostic criteria, Van Emde
Boas developed his theories about the
foundation of the transgender phenomenon
as a psychiatrist and sexologist. He initially
distinguished between constitutional and
neurotic transsexists, even using the term
transvestites. He had introduced the term
"transsexists" to counter the increasingly
commonly used term "transsexuals."
He stated that the treatment for these
individuals involved evaluations of people's
sex, not of their sexuality. Harry Benjamin
recognized the reasoning but did not adopt
this term, because he found it "a bit of a
twister for the American tongue."[65] As
we mention in our "Note on Transgender
Terminology," Benjamin did come close to
Van Emde Boas's usage by briefly employing
the word "transexualist."

Constitutional transsexists, according
to Van Emde Boas, were born with a
condition that left their brain insensitive
to their own sex hormones. Recent animal
testing with rats served as preliminary
proof of his theory. The logical consequence
of this condition, he averred, was that
the child was destined to develop the
identity of the other sex. But because
this was not visible on the outside, the
child would still be recognized by others
as the sex that had been designated at
birth. Neurotic transsexists did not suffer
from the same innate condition. In their
case, psychological development was the
villain. But if psychotherapy proved to be
unsuccessful, Van Emde Boas believed
that the "therapeutically resistant neurotic
transsexist" nevertheless deserved gender-
affirmation surgery. He made a further
distinction between different versions of the
neurotic transsexist: there were real ones
and fake ones. Real neurotic transsexists
could be suffering from a primary
condition, acquired in early childhood, or
a secondary one, acquired after an initial

masculine development. The fake neurotic transsexists were to be found in show business and prostitution, and they only wanted to transition in order to garner professional benefit.

That Van Emde Boas referred only to the initial masculine development in his description of neurotic transsexists was no accident. He did not ascribe a biological foundation to transgender men at all and believed that their condition was the result of "disastrous environmental influences in early childhood," such as a family setting in which the child had been given a masculine role.[66] With both types, the constitutional and the neurotic transsexists, he believed that psychiatric testing was of the utmost importance. He considered extensive diagnostics, based on psychiatric and clinical psychological research and a long trial period of functioning successfully in the role of the other sex, to be necessary.

Casablanca and Georges Burou

After surgical procedures became impossible in Copenhagen and Amsterdam, a new location coincidentally emerged: Casablanca, where the French gynecologist Georges Burou had his Clinique du Parc. A front door with gold-plated handles and wrought-iron ornamentation contrasted with the somewhat less classy back door. Women who came for regular gynecological appointments entered through the front door; those who did not want to be seen went in through the back. Burou was known as a doctor for "secret procedures." He did abortions, he helped women deliver

babies to be put up for adoption, and he likely also reconstructed hymens for unmarried women whose desire to appear to be living by Islamic moral standards caused them to seek help in having their virginity "restored" before marriage.[67]

In 1956, someone called on him with a desperate cry for help to change male genitalia into female. Burou, who had a passion for inventions and was totally unaware of previous such work in the world,[68] developed the technique of the penis inversion: turning the skin of the penis inside out to create a hole and make a vagina. This turned the procedure into a one-stage operation – a big step forward from the four stages that were used up until then: castration, penectomy, reconstruction, and creation of an artificial, shallow vagina.[69] Burou's technique turned out to be the gold standard for vaginoplasty and is still used today.

Unlike Hamburger, Benjamin, Hartsuiker, and Van Emde Boas, Georges Burou was not part of any medical network and, like colleagues in Mexico and a few other parts of the world, he worked in relative obscurity and isolation.[70] In 1970, Burou made first contact with Benjamin, and only in 1973, towards the end of his career, did he present his knowledge at the Second Interdisciplinary Symposium on Gender Dysphoria Syndrome at Stanford University Medical Center in Palo Alto, California. For trans people, the crucial distinction between accessing care from one of the doctors in the network of the Danes, Americans, and Dutchmen and coming to Burou's practice was that with Burou they could get immediate surgery.

FIGURE 4.23: Daphne P., possibly recovering in Hotel Hegra, Amsterdam, 1955. KILSC-HB 5. Copyright © 2017, The Trustees of Indiana University on behalf of the Kinsey Institute. All rights reserved.

No screenings, no diagnoses, no talks with psychiatrists to try to convince them of the urgency. Burou did show a humane understanding of the needs of trans people, and he respected their identity, as he himself stated in a newspaper interview.[71] But he was not committed to understanding the psychological background of the transgender phenomenon, nor did he care about social standards regarding trans men and women being able to pass. He gave trans women full autonomy over their own decisions, including the financial, psychological, emotional, and medical risks that came along with surgery.

Trans women knew how to find Burou; news travelled fast in the right circles. One of his first patients was Coccinelle, the famous star of the French drag clubs. Soon, patients started to arrive from all over the world, including possibly a few dozen from the Netherlands. They handed a note with

the clinic's name to a taxi driver – that was enough information. Payment was due upon arrival at the clinic: an amount ranging from 2000 to 5000 dollars,[72] preferably in French francs, American dollars, or travellers' cheques. A few basic medical tests followed to determine whether the patient could safely be operated upon. The operation was then scheduled for the next day. Burou's clinic had eight to ten beds, half of which were reserved for transgender women. The Dutch trans woman Colette Berends (1934–2012) remembered:

For me, having the operation in Casablanca was a huge and scary step to take. Positive as well as negative stories about Doctor Burou were circulating in our circles. One day you'd hear he was a butcher, the next that he was a good surgeon. That's why I decided to accept a two-month contract with a cabaret over there, so I had the time to properly find out what kind of man this Burou actually was and assess the clinic for myself. I had a conversation with him and got a favorable impression. I had also asked him: "Does it hurt badly when you come around?" He said: "No, don't worry, we'll make sure it doesn't." That positive impression turned out to be correct as I had a good operation and received good care.

One Sunday evening I had myself admitted. The nurse noticed that I was very nervous and sedated me. I only woke up the next morning to undergo the surgery. After the operation, I came around and found myself, arms tied, in the bed. No pain at all. I asked: "When will it start?" "Madame, it's already happened." I then cried and cried, and the next day again. All the tension was released. And I was overcome with joy.[73]

Burou stopped working around 1975, when he was sixty-five years old. In the meantime, gender surgeons had opened offices in other places in the world, so the options for gender-affirmation surgery remained available for transgender women,[74] that is to say, for those who could afford it. A sum of 2,000 to 5,000 US dollars was a lot of money in the mid-1970s, comparable to 20,000 to 50,000 today. And this only covered the surgery part of the trip; travel and possible extra accommodation costs (after or before the time in the clinic) had to be added. Such costs thus excluded trans women who had no means to obtain such a large amount of money. In a recent book on the subject of transsexual surgery, Aren Aizura argues that this was a privilege of white middle-class trans women.[75] I would instead say that this kind of surgery was a privilege of people with money, full stop, since I know that a number of Burou's patients were part of the subculture of drag shows and prostitution, and some were people of colour, such as Jill Pattiradjawane, who remembered that she had to work and even had to go without food to be able to save the money for her trip to Casablanca.[76]

In the space of twenty years, Burou performed an estimated 1,000

vaginoplasties. He focused almost solely on transgender women; it was very rare that a transgender man turned to him for help. One of those exceptions was from the Netherlands. After reading about Burou's practice in a magazine in 1972, a Dutch trans man (who wishes to remain anonymous) took the train and boat to Casablanca to ask for surgical help. Burou said he did not have the expertise to create a penis, but was willing to surgically remove the uterus and breasts.[77] One or two years later, Burou performed three phalloplasties but then stopped, because he was not content with the results, despite the fact that, according to *Paris Match*, the trans men themselves were.[78]

The generally good results of Burou's vaginoplasties did not mean that there were no complications. The downside of Burou's clinic, besides the exclusionary effect of the high price, was the total lack of aftercare. Patients came flying in and usually left straight after their hospital stay – which normally lasted seven to fourteen days – flying back to Paris, Amsterdam, Antwerp, Berlin, New York, or wherever they came from. They had to deal with any problems that developed afterwards themselves, at home, or hope that the local hospital would understand their situation and offer medical care.

One of the people who developed post-operative complications was Ms. B. from the Netherlands. When she arrived back home, she noticed she was losing a lot of blood, and the surgical site had become infected. She was urgently admitted to the Wilhelminagasthuis in Amsterdam, where the doctors treated her with some disdain.

She stayed in the hospital for months – in the psychiatric ward. This could be because she was indeed not quite herself after all that had happened, but it might also have been because at the time, transgender people were generally treated as being psychologically disturbed by definition.[79]

1959: Operation in Arnhem

On April 7, 1959, at the Municipal Hospital (Gemeenteziekenhuis) in Arnhem, plastic surgeon Siebren Woudstra operated on a thirty-four-year-old transgender man. This was likely the first female-to-male operation in the Netherlands. It was certainly the first transgender operation in the Netherlands that happened openly, in a general hospital.

The trans man who would play such an historic role was the thirty-four-year-old German Gert M. Gert M. was an instrument manufacturer by profession who had been living as a man for quite some time. A couple of years earlier, he had been tested by an international team of sexologists and psychiatrists at the university clinic in Hamburg. Apparently, his gender dysphoria had been so obvious and compelling that the doctors recommended plastic surgery. He had undergone a mastectomy in South Africa,[80] but he also wanted to have his uterus removed and a phalloplasty performed. To obtain these procedures, Van Emde Boas, who was part of the international team, required him to submit to an intense four-month observation in 1958. Van Emde Boas's assistant Margreet Groot remembers him very well:

Gert was the first woman-to-man transsexual we had. A gentle boy, he looked a bit boyish for his age, short, with stubble. He hated not being able to pee standing up and was very scared that people would notice that his pants were empty when he was playing sports. A nice, very modest man, with a steady girlfriend, a nurse whom he later married. He managed very well in daily life. Coen did his thorough analysis, and in all the sessions Gert's story remained solid. So, in the end it was a straight-forward case.[81]

Van Emde Boas arrived at the conclusion that people like Gert could benefit from medical assistance, and he referred Gert to a plastic surgeon, Woudstra. Woudstra was one of the first plastic surgeons in the Netherlands, and he enjoyed an excellent reputation. It is unclear what his motivation was to perform this daring procedure. It could not have been about the money, as the operation did not take place in a private clinic. It is likely that Woudstra was guided by the diagnosis of the psychiatrists in question and that he subsequently honoured the patient's request on ethical grounds. On the other hand, he may have been professionally excited by the new and technically challenging elements of the surgery. Woudstra had been asked to remove the uterus and vagina and to construct a penis that Gert could urinate with – an even more complex surgical challenge. Woudstra was able to fall back on existing techniques developed for cismen who needed penis reconstruction after some kind of trauma. He also studied the case of the English transgender man Michael Dillon, who underwent a series of phalloplasty surgeries performed by Harold Gillies between 1946 and 1949.[82] Gillies had constructed a penis with a big tubular piece, in which a smaller tubular piece was attached to serve as a urinary tract, forming a tube within a tube.[83]

The team meeting discussing the surgery at the Gemeenteziekenhuis Arnhem was published almost in its entirety in the *Nederlands Tijdschrift voor Geneeskunde* (Dutch journal of medicine),[84] but the gynecologist refused to cooperate. Plastic surgeon Woudstra was disappointed: "Who are we – nonexperts – to refuse to help." He meant "nonexperts" in comparison to the expertise of the two psychiatric institutions that made the initial diagnosis. The diagnoses indicated that it was best to continue on the path of transformation as far as possible. The reasoning was pragmatic: a process of transformation had already begun, so now it would have to continue to "complete" the person as much as possible.

Despite the fact that the German patient had been living as a man for years, the doctors consistently used the word "woman" and the pronouns "she/her." Obviously, they perceived the transgender man to still be a woman, albeit a woman wanting to live as a man. Almost all attending doctors said they could not understand the woman's wishes, but they could see that the patient was seriously ill and needed help. They trusted the psychiatrists' assessment that medical treatment was indicated. The treatment consisted of several operations and

encountered some complications. When asked if he still would have done it knowing how hard it was going to be, the German transgender man answered wholeheartedly: yes.[85]

The extensive report in the *NTvG* did not receive a warm welcome from readers. A barrage of heated letters to the editor ensued. Very few spoke in favor of the Arnhem team and the individual with the wish to change their sex. Responses included the following:

> I therefore want to only say one word: Insane!

> … deliberate infliction of serious bodily harm … bizarre operations, mental aberrations …

> If the procedure would have the desired results, do we then not need to consider the possibility that this "man" may develop masculine feelings for our daughter? Then I am glad that I don't live in Arnhem, because I have two daughters.

A plastic surgeon called it indefensible that a psychosis was being treated with a dummy treatment and found the entire idea downright ludicrous. "Surely, there won't have been anyone suggesting to her that she could become a 'real' man!"[86] And another: "All mutilating operations raise aversion, and to mutilate a normal female body in this way is so disgusting that it almost makes one sick to the stomach … We therefore have to hope or pray (depending on one's religion) that psychiatry will find

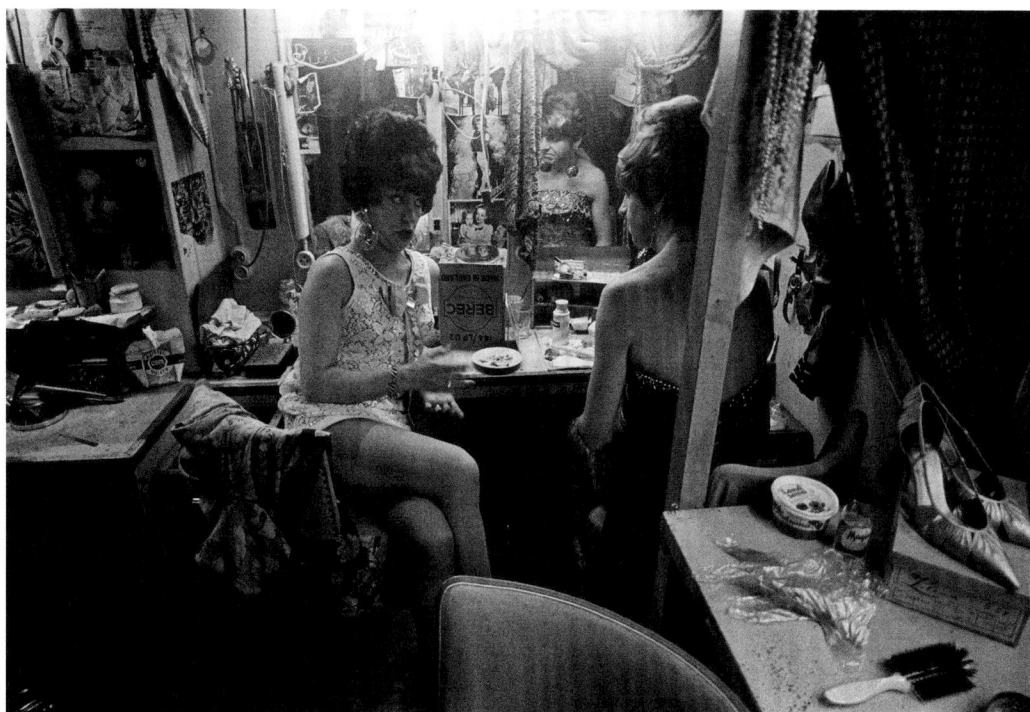

FIGURE 4.24: Trans women backstage at Bar Oporto, Warmoesstraat, Amsterdam, 1967. Aaïcha Bergamin (not in this picture) performed at it and later managed the bar. Copyright © Cor Jaring/Amsterdam City Archive.

an adequate therapy for these kinds of horrible 'freaks of nature.'"

Plastic surgeon Woudstra also had to go before the medical disciplinary council. All those involved made statements except the patient.[88] Woudstra was cleared of neglect and medically unethical behaviour because he had performed his operations under the authority of renowned psychiatrists and sexologists. The medical uproar did not go unnoticed and led to parliamentary questions being posed to the Minister of Justice. According to a national newspaper the operation even created "widespread" turmoil.[89] Meanwhile, the Minister of Social Affairs and Public Health requested a formal opinion from the Health Council on this medical-ethical problem. The question was: "Can it, in all fairness, be stated that in some cases we may expect a transformation to yield (psycho) therapeutic results?"[90] A committee was appointed, consisting of professors of psychiatry, psychology, a professor of criminal law, the chief inspector for Public Health, and a few doctors. It took the committee five years to formulate an opinion. In January 1966, its report was made public, ironically in the same year that Benjamin's more sympathetic *The Transsexual Phenomenon* was published.[91]

The committee's opinion was adamantly negative. The committee took it for granted that transsexuality stemmed from a mental disorder and its assessment of psychotherapy as a solution (albeit a limited one) followed from this predisposition. The argument that you should not cut into a healthy body carried a lot of weight. Between the lines, the committee also painted transgender people as unpleasant – freaks, even – who did not behave as good patients and were out to manipulate doctors. Examples of the positive effects of operations were simply rejected. The committee drily mentioned that it had rejected the idea of consulting any transgender people at all, simply conducting a literature review and interviewing two psychiatrist-sexologists: Coen Van Emde Boas and Herman Musaph. The final decision followed Musaph's psychoanalytical vision. This formal government statement effectively banned the provision of medical assistance to transgender people, making it all but illegal.[92] No doctor dared to touch this field anymore. Transgender people were once again confined to psychoanalytical sessions on the couch. In some cases, electroshocks were even applied.[93]

Waiting for Better Times to Come

And that is what life looked like for transgender people in the Netherlands in the mid-1960s. Out-of-the-closet transgender women were largely sent into the shadows of society, into a subculture of prostitution and nightlife – a hard and unsafe life. The outside world – be it the police, landlords, or municipal services – had the power to intimidate trans people, particularly because their identification and official registration generally failed to match their self-presentation. No physical change was possible other than the effects of taking hormones, unless one was brave and wealthy enough to go to Casablanca.

What about those who remained in the closet? Their transgender feelings must have left them in a state of confusion and frustration. Christine Jorgensen and other celebrity transgender women may have been role models, but not for everyone. Many transgender people in the Netherlands believed themselves to be crazy, sick, or sinners. Some transgender men believed that a transformation was only possible from man to woman and did not know it could also happen the other way around. The lack of future perspective kept people in chains. Many transgender people had internalized the stigma that they were dirty and vile, and they felt that they had to fight their desire to transition. They all had to wait for better times to come. As Aaïcha Bergamin put it:

> When they say to me: "Well, you'll understand that to normal people you ..." et cetera, then I immediately think: Right, normal people, and I'm opposite as abnormal. You'll always be marked, abnormal, perverse, sick, mentally ill. Especially psychiatrists give you that feeling. They're mostly brief visits. I don't have the impression that they begin to understand us. They're staring

at you like you're a miracle of God, and you can sense that they think you're some sort of idiot, a mad person.[94]

Conclusion

The Netherlands made a start in offering medical care to trans people as early as 1954. Within an international network that was largely constructed by liberal psychiatrist Van Emde Boas, doctors started treating transgender women from abroad who were seeking gender-affirmation surgery. The surgical treatment for American trans women focused solely on castration, this being the critical intervention they were not allowed to undergo in the United States. This early form of transgender care reflects normative social and medical views of the era that now feel quite narrow minded. As Susan Stryker writes: "medical science has always been a double-edged sword – its representatives' willingness to intervene has gone hand in hand with their power to define and judge."[95] The goal was to integrate trans people back into society, to have them lead a normal, inconspicuous, invisible life without anybody knowing about their history, not even potential partners. The Dutch approach was in sync with that of Harry Benjamin, about whom Pat Califia noted critically: "He seems completely unaware of any damage it might do a reassigned transsexual woman to hide her past from intimate partners … But Benjamin was not in the business of critiquing social sex roles or revolutionizing society's concept of womanhood. He

was in the business of helping disturbed and upset people fit into society as much as possible, to lead lives that were as contented as possible."[96] In my opinion this concept of transgender medical care can best be characterized by the word "detranssexualization" – a word commonly used by trans health care providers in the Netherlands in the 1970s and 1980s. It formed the core of the doctors' involvement: if a post-operative trans woman would have gone on living a life in the subculture of queer circles, my guess is that most of these doctors would have been quite disappointed.

Trans surgery was anything but easily accessible: the accessibility relied heavily on psychiatric concepts and on the psychiatrists' assessment of how well the individual passed, with an underlying assumption that the ultimate goal was to prevent desperate people from committing suicide. One of Van Emde Boas's criteria was that the candidate should no longer be susceptible to psychotherapy. Again, Califia's analysis points out the similarity to Benjamin: "Benjamin claims that in the absence of surgery, transsexuals will engage in self-mutilation or suicide. This makes it sound as if the surgeon is morally compelled, almost blackmailed, into operating, lest he contribute to self-destruction. In order to justify removal of male sex organs, the doctor must be seen to be as helpless in the face of this 'disorder' as the transsexual."[97]

Although Van Emde Boas and Benjamin shared many views towards the transgender phenomenon, there were also significant differences between them, possibly stemming from the fact that the Dutchman was a psychiatrist and the American was an endocrinologist. Benjamin located the etiology of "transsexualism" (as did the Danish doctors) as hidden in the body, not in the mind.[98] Van Emde Boas did not agree, and his disagreement is evident in his psychoanalytic theories. Nevertheless, such psychoanalytic interpretations did not stop Van Emde Boas from offering help and medical care.

In a way, the start of gender-affirmation surgery in the Netherlands was linked to a quite specific and body-negative form of health care: surgical castration as a form of relief for people suffering from what was considered a problematically high sex drive. Trans women contacted those with medical expertise in the castration (voluntary or nonvoluntary) of sex offenders. Removing the testes as a source of unwanted sex drive meant demasculinization, and that was the first step to becoming female. In general, one could argue that pioneering efforts to gain access to transgender care succeeded only by relying on very negative views about trans peoples' states of mind. In my interpretation of the Dutch case, these pioneers managed to persuade the few doctors willing to help not by achieving truly empathetic understanding but only because the doctors viewed gender-affirmation surgery as the lesser of two evils. But even this option remained closed to most: the accessibility of this medical care was restricted, because it relied primarily on the ability to pass. It was based on the concept of gender normativity and required integration into society. Some trans women

had no problem with this, because it was exactly what they wanted for themselves.[99] We have to realize, however, that the heteronormative and cisgendered norms excluded others from any consideration.

A number of Dutch trans women also went to Casablanca. The absence of gatekeeping in Dr. Burou's clinic empowered trans people to make autonomous decisions. The surgery itself was a big improvement for trans women, The option of having gender-affirmation surgery in the Netherlands through Van Emde Boas was not available anymore – had they even heard of it. The milestone male gender-affirmation surgery for Gert M. in Arnhem sadly backfired, in that it led to a storm of upheaval among medical peers and in society, which resulted in the Dutch commission's decision that no therapeutic success could be expected from transgender care and doctors should stay clear of these ostensibly severely disturbed patients. With this public statement of official government policy, the recognition of transgender people and their rights came to a full stop. Despite the fact that the door had been opened a crack, trans people in the Netherlands continued to be defined by limitations and exclusions. This would last until around 1970 before the first new attempt at trans health care came about. In line with the Arnhem case, trans health care was to be part of general health care, ultimately leading up to one of the biggest centres for trans care in the world, the Gender Team of the VU Medisch Centrum, Amsterdam (1975–present, total number of patients around 10,000).

GALLERY NOTES: Hirschfeld's "Female Transvestites"

1   On the Steinach Film, see Rainer Herrn and Christine N. Brinckmann, "Of Rats and Men: Rejuvenation and the Steinach Film," in *Not Straight from Germany: Sexual Publics and Sexual Citizenship Since Magnus Hirschfeld*, edited by Michael Thomas Taylor, Rainer Herrn, and Annette F. Timm, 212–34 (Ann Arbor: University of Michigan Press, 2017). Four major recent work on Steinach are Sonja Walch, *Triebe, Reize und Signale: Eugen Steinachs Physiologie der Sexualhormone; vom biologischen Konzept zum Pharmapräparat, 1894–1938* (Vienna: Böhlau Verlag, 2016); Michaele Lindinger, *Sonderlinge, Aussenseiter, Femmes fatales: Das "andere" Wien um 1900* (Vienna: Amalthea, 2015); Cheryl A. Logan, *Hormones, Heredity, and Race: Spectacular Failure in Interwar Vienna* (New Brunswick, NJ: Rutgers University Press, 2013); and Heiko Stoff, *Ewige Jugend: Konzepte der Verjüngung vom späten 19. Jahrhundert bis ins Dritte Reich* (Cologne: Böhlau, 2004). On the notion of the "glandular self" as it developed in the United States, see Michael Pettit, "Becoming Glandular: Endocrinology, Mass Culture, and Experimental Lives in the Interwar Age," *American Historical Review* 118, no. 4 (2013): 1052–76.

2   Michaela Lindinger argues that Harry Benjamin was the only doctor specialized in the rejuvenation of women, and that this work was "centered on (re-)establishing femininity as such": "Im Zentrum stand die '(Wieder-) Herstellung der Weiblichkeit an sich'"; *Sonderlinge, Aussenseiter, Femmes fatales*, 148.

GALLERY NOTES: Sensationalism

1   This photo likely depicts the person whose story was told in Case 15 in Hirschfeld's *Die Transvestiten* (116–27).

NOTES TO CHAPTER 4

1   Harry Benjamin, *The Transsexual Phenomenon: A Scientific Report on Transsexualism and Sex Conversion in the Human Male and Female* (New York: The Julian Press, 1966), 147.

2   For more about the invisibility of trans men and their separation from LGBT communities during earlier periods in the United States, see Emily Skidmore, *True Sex: The Lives of Trans Men at the Turn of the Twentieth Century* (New York: New York University Press, 2017). Susan Stryker has written that "'Transgender women who survive by participating in sexual street subcultures have long bonded together for mutual support, whereas transgender men often lived without being part of a larger transgender community." *Transgender History* (Berkeley, CA: Seal Press, 2008), 79.

3   For more background, see Elisabeth Lockhorn, *Andreas Burnier, metselaar van de wereld* (Amsterdam: Atlas Contact, 2015).

4   Richard Mühsam, "Chirurgische Eingriffe bei Anomalien des Sexuallebens," *Therapie der Gegenwart* 67 (1926): 451–5.

5   Coen van Emde Boas, translation from a letter in personal archives, 8 Nov 1956.

6   Dick Swaab, *Wij zijn ons brein: Van baarmoeder tot Alzheimer* (Amsterdam: Olympus, 2010), 96.

7   Interview with Jill Pattiradjawane, 2017.

8   Alex Bakker, *Transgender in Nederland: Een buitengewone geschiedenis* (Amsterdam: Boom Uitgevers, 2018), 43.

9   Otto de Vaal, *Man of Vrouw? Dilemma van de Transseksuele Mens* (Amsterdam: Wetenschappelijke Uitgeverij, 1971), 83.

10   There was not even a law against cross-dressing in the Third Reich. Another exception was the United States. As Clare Sears has documented, in the period between 1848 and the First World War, laws against cross-dressing were passed in forty-four American cities. She focuses particularly on San Francisco, which passed such a law in 1863. Clare Sears, *Arresting Dress: Cross-Dressing, Law, and Fascination in Nineteenth-Century San Francisco* (Durham: Duke University Press, 2014).

11 Local laws like these existed in many cities around the world. Susan Stryker describes the possible origins of these laws in the United States, dating back to the 1850s, in *Transgender History*, 32–5.

12 Interview with Aaïcha Bergamin, 2013.

13 Christine Jorgensen Collection, Archives Royal Danish Library, Copenhagen.

14 I have written about this in my book *Transgender in Nederland: Een buitengewone geschiedenis* (Amsterdam: Boom Uitgevers, 2018).

15 Christian Hamburger, "The Desire for Change of Sex as Shown by Personal Letters from 465 Men and Women," *Acta Endrologica* 14 (1953): 361–72.

16 W. P. Plate, "Het verlangen om van geslacht te veranderen," *Nederlands Tijdschrift voor Geneeskunde*, 13 Mar 1954, 726–7.

17 E. A. D. E. Carp, "Transvestitisme," *Nederlands Tijdschrift voor Geneeskunde*, 29 May 1954, 1474–7.

18 E. A. D. E. Carp, *Psychopathologische opsporingen* (Amsterdam: Strengholt, 1951) "Over het psychisme van de waan van de verandering van geslacht," 118.

19 Susan Stryker, *Transgender History* (Berkeley, CA: Seal Press, 2008), 43, 44.

20 It is likely that Hamburger knew Hartsuiker as a fellow medical expert on the impact of sex hormones.

21 I am providing MacLane's full name here because she sought fame as a burlesque performer under this name.

22 Letter from Frederik Hartsuiker to Harry Benjamin, 9 Feb 1954, Kinsey Institute Library and Special Collections, Harry Benjamin Collection (hereafter KILSC-HB), Box 5, Ser. II C – Hartsuiker, Dr. F.

23 Carla Erskine to Harry Benjamin, 28 Feb 1954, 10 Feb 1954, and 8 Mar 1953, KILSC-HB, Box 4, Ser. II C.

24 Benjamin to Hartsuiker, 15 Feb 1954, KILSC-HB, Box 5, Ser. II C – Hartsuiker, Dr. F.

25 We know from Benjamin's statistical lists and tables, compiled for *The Transsexual Phenomenon*, that Dixie MacLane ended up getting surgery with Dr. Ferrer in Mexico. See KILSC.

26 The Rorschach and Szondi tests are both so-called projective personality tests, designed to let a person respond to ambiguous stimuli, presumably revealing hidden emotions and internal conflicts projected by the person into the test. The Szondi test had images of gender variant people in it from the Hirschfeld's collection.

27 Hartsuiker to Benjamin, 10 Mar 1954, KILSC-HB, Box 5, Ser. II C – Hartsuiker, Dr. F. With the 1954 rate of 1 guilder for 3.8 American dollars, this seems to be quite low. In 1955, the price mentioned by Catherine J. to Harry Benjamin was around twice as high.

28 Harry Benjamin to Shelly W., May 3, 1954, KILSC-HB, Box 8, Ser. II C – W., Shelly.

29 Benjamin to W., 7 May 1954, KILSC-HB, Box 8, Ser. II C – W., Shelly.

30 Hartsuiker to Benjamin, 12 May 1954, KILSC-HB, Box 5, Ser. II C – Hartsuiker, Dr. F.

31 Benjamin to Hartsuiker, 18 May 1954, KILSC-HB, Box 5, Ser. II C – Hartsuiker, Dr. F. "Transsexualism and Transvestism as Psycho-Somatic and Somato-Psychic Syndromes," *American Journal of Psychotherapy* 8, no. 2 (1954): 219–30.

32 Meyerowitz, *How Sex Changed*, 82.

33 Hartsuiker to Benjamin, 12 June 1954, KILSC-HB, Box 5, Ser. II C – Hartsuiker, Dr. F.

34 Personal records of Van Emde Boas, correspondence with F. Hartsuiker, 24 June 1954.

35 Stryker, *Transgender History*, 45.

36 Catherine J. to Harry Benjamin, 30 Jan 1955, KILSC-HB, Box 5, Ser. II C – J.

37 Harry Benjamin to Rosa F., 31 Oct 1955, KILSC-HB, Box 4, Ser. II C – F., Rosa.

38 C. van Emde Boas, "De behandeling van transseksisten in Nederland 1953–1973: Een les van 20 jaar attitudeschommelingen," *Medisch Contact* 29 (1974): 475–8, here 475.

39 Peotomy is synonym for penectomy.

40 Catherine J. to Benjamin, 1 Apr 1955, KILSC-HB, Box 5, Ser. II C – J.

41 Meyerowitz, *How Sex Changed*, 82.

42 Tamara Rees, *Reborn: A Factual Life Story of a Transition from Male to Female*, n.p., 1955. Correspondence between Benjamin and Hartsuiker shows that Rees's story about having had a second and third genital operation in the Netherlands is not true.

43 "Boston Traveler," 8 Nov 1954, 15 and "Omaha World Herald," 8 Nov 1954, 7.

44 Hartsuiker to Benjamin, 19 Nov 1954, KILSC-HB, Box 5, Ser. II C – Hartsuiker, Dr. F.

45 Benjamin to Hartsuiker, 24 Nov 1954, KILSC-HB, Box 5, Ser. II C – Hartsuiker, Dr. F.

46 F. to Benjamin, 5 May 1955, KILSC-HB, Box 4, Ser. II C – F., Rosa.

47 Van Emde Boas, "De behandeling van transseksisten in Nederland," 475.

48 J. to Benjamin, 27 Apr 1955, KILSC-HB, Box 5, Ser. II C – J., Catherine.

49 J. to Benjamin, 11 Mar 1955, KILSC-HB, Box 5, Ser. II C – J., Catherine.

50 J. to Benjamin, 3 Mar 1955, KILSC-HB, Box 5, Ser. II C – J., Catherine.

51 J. to Benjamin, 11 Mar 1955, KILSC-HB, Box 5, Ser. II C – J., Catherine.

52 Van Emde Boas, "De behandeling van transseksisten in Nederland," 475.

53 In the Netherlands, it is quite common for doctors to have a home office as a practice.

54 The letter is stored in the personal records of Van Emde Boas.

55 Pat Califia, *Sex Changes: The Politics of Transgenderism* (San Francisco, CA: Cleis Press, 1997), 53.

56 J. to Benjamin, 1 Apr 1955, KILSC-HB, Box 5, Ser. II C – J., Catherine.

57 E. A. D. E. Carp, "Transvestitisme," 1474–7.

58 Rees, *Reborn*, 37.

59 F. to Benjamin, 6 May 1955, KILSC-HB, Box 4, Ser. II C – F., Rosa.

60 Note in personal archive Van Emde Boas.

61 Interview with Margreet Groot, by Alex Bakker, 2017.

62 Personal archives of Van Emde Boas, correspondence with Prof. Dr. Urban, Innsbruck, 14 June 1956.

63 Gezondheidsraad, "Rapport betreffende plastisch-chirurgische geslachtstransformatie: Verslagen en Mededelingen betreffende de Volksgezondheid," January 1966, 28.

64 Personal archives of Van Emde Boas, correspondence with Prof. Dr. Urban, Innsbruck, 14 June 1956.

65 Benjamin, *The Transsexual Phenomenon*, 30.

66 C. van Emde Boas, "Transseksisme: wat is dat eigenlijk?" *Medisch Contact*, 5 Apr 1974, 443–5. The article stems from 1974, but Van Emde Boas stated that he had developed this concept already in the 1950s.

67 Interview with Dutch plastic surgeon and Burou specialist Joris Hage, by Alex Bakker in 2017.

68 Donald R. Laub and Patrick Gandy, *Proceedings of the Second Interdisciplinary Symposium on Gender Dysphoria Syndrome* (Stanford, CA: Stanford University Medical Center, 1973), 247 (see https://catalog.hathitrust.org/Record/003521724 and http://ai.eecs.umich.edu/people/conway/TS/Burou/Burou.html, accessed 28 June 2019).

69 It should be noted that Burou's procedure remained unknown to doctors practicing elsewhere in the world as late as 1972, the year that Canary Conn (who later wrote an autobiography and appeared on various television interview shows in the United States) was operated on by Jesus Maria Barbosa (whom she anonymizes as Dr. Lopez) in Tijuana, Mexico. Her surgery, which she describes as having taken place in horrendously unsanitary conditions, was in two stages: castration and labiaplasty followed by penectomy and vaginoplasty. See Canary Conn, *Canary: The Story of a Transsexual* (Los Angeles: Nash Publishing, 1974). On "Lewis's" real name, see Sandy Stone, "The Empire Strikes Back: A Posttranssexual Manifesto," in *The Transgender Studies Reader*, ed. Susan Stryker and Stephen Whittle (New York and London: Routledge, 2006), 233n22. A fascinating interview that Conn gave to *Psychology Today* in 1977 has recently been made publicly available in a

podcast by Gillian Frank Lauren Gutterman. "Canary." Sexing History. Accessed 1 July 2019. https://www.sexinghistory.com/episode-24.

70   A discussion of gender-affirming surgery in Mexico awaits future research. Barbosa's name first appears in Benjamin's table of surgeries in 1966, while Burou (initially misspelled "Bureaud") first appears for a 1962 surgery. A later version of the table (clear because the spelling has been corrected), lists a Burou-performed surgery in 1957. See KILSC-HB 28.

71   "De gynaecoloog die vrouwen maakt," *Nieuwsblad van het Noorden*, 15 June 1974, 37.

72   Interview with Dutch plastic surgeon and Burou specialist Joris Hage, by Alex Bakker in 2017.

73   Interview with Colette Berends, by Alex Bakker, 2010.

74   J.Joris Hage, Refaat M. Karim and Donald R. Laub, "On the Origin of Pedicled Skin Inversion Vaginoplasty. Life and work of Dr Georges Burou of Casablanca," *Annals of Plastic Surgery*, (Dec 2007), 723-9.

75   Aren Z. Aizura, *Mobile Subjects: Transnational Imaginaries of Gender Reassignment* (Durham, NC: Duke University Press, 2018).

76   Interview with Jill Pattiradjawane, Dutch trans woman (born 1939), by Alex Bakker, 2017.

77   Interview with anonymous trans man, by Alex Bakker, 2015. See: Bakker, *Transgender in Nederland*, 48.

78   V. Merlin, "L'homme qui change le sex," *Paris Match* (1974): 37–9.

79   Interview with Ms. B. by Alex Bakker, 2010.

80   B. Haeseker and J-P. A. Nicolai, "De eerste geslachtsveranderende operatie van vrouw naar man in Nederland, 1959/'60," *Nederlands Tijdschrift voor Geneeskunde* (3 Mar 2007): 548–52.

81   Interview with Margreet Groot by Alex Bakker, 2017.

82   Gillies and D. Ralph Millard Jr., *The Principles and Art of Plastic Surgery*, vol. 2 (London: Butterworth & Co., 1957), 368–84.

83   Haeseker and Nicolai, "De eerste geslachtsveranderende operatie," 550.

84   "Nuttige notities No. 9 Verslag van een bespreking op een stafvergadering van het Gemeente-Ziekenhuis te Arnhem," *Nederlands Tijdschrift voor Geneeskunde* 103 (26 Dec 1959): 2647–9.

85   H. R. Bax, "Letter to the Editor," *Nederlands Tijdschrift Voor Geneeskunde*, 6 Feb 1960, 303. Bax was a surgeon at the *Gemeenteziekenhuis Arnhem*.

86   W. H. Beekhuis, "Letter to the Editor," *Nederlands Tijdschrift Voor Geneeskunde*, 12 Mar 1960, 536.

87   A. E. Nordholt, "Letter to the Editor," *Nederlands Tijdschrift Voor Geneeskunde*, 9 Apr 1960, 742.

88   Haeseker and Nicolai, "De eerste geslachtsveranderende operatie."

89   "Commissie zegt 'neen' tegen geslachtstransformatie," *Het Vrije Volk*, 1 Oct 1966.

90   Gezondheidsraad, "Rapport betreffende plastisch-chirurgische geslachtstransformatie," 3.

91   Gezondheidsraad, "Rapport," 4.

92   Archives Foundation Netherlands Gender Centrum (NGC): Frans van der Reijt, "De bejegening van transsexuele mensen in Nederland in de jaren 1960 tot 1990," 1993.

93   Interview with Henk Asscheman, endocrinologist at the Vrije Universiteit Medical Centre, Amsterdam, 2016.

94   De Vaal, *Man of Vrouw?*, 88.

95   Stryker, *Transgender History*, 36.

96   Califia, *Sex Changes*, 59.

97   Ibid.

98   Meyerowitz, *How Sex Changed*, 103.

99   See Meyerowitz, *How Sex Changed*, 12, on the risk of misinterpreting trans pioneers as activists against traditional norms.

5

Visual Medical Rhetorics of Transgender Histories

Michael Thomas Taylor

This story begins with a journey across the Atlantic, presented here as another introduction to a history that has no single starting point: the story of a woman who was known at least by some, in private, as Joanna when she lived in San Francisco, whom Hirschfeld names as John O. We do not know what name or names she used in public; in this case, the desire we might have to find a clear declaration of identity or self-naming simply cannot be fulfilled by history. I will thus refer to her here as J. She is the earliest protagonist in *TransTrans* whom we find crossing the Atlantic – first as she emigrated to America in 1882, and then as her photographs were published in Europe in 1912, in the illustrated volume to Magnus Hirschfeld's book *Die Transvestiten.*

These photos illustrate a life story that Hirschfeld told two years earlier as "Case Study 13" in *Die Transvestiten.*[1] What we know from Hirschfeld is that J. was born in Bavaria in 1862. Her practice of wearing women's clothing and living as a woman aroused social condemnation, which caused her to flee to Switzerland, to France, and – in 1882 – to New York. She managed to pass as a woman and hold down jobs as an embroiderer, a cook, a maid, and a governess in Jersey City,

But the mask has transformed into something else: a gesture, a piece of clothing, and a kind of second skin.

Der amerikanische auf Seite 100 der „Transvestiten" beschriebene Transvestit.

FIGURE 5.1: John O. in Magnus Hirschfeld's illustrated volume to *Die Transvestiten*, 1912. The captions in the image read: "Figure 1: As a young newspaper boy; Figure 2: In nudo; Figure 3: As a naked transvestite; Figure 4: In his female outfit."

Fig. 1. Als junger Zeitungsverkäufer.

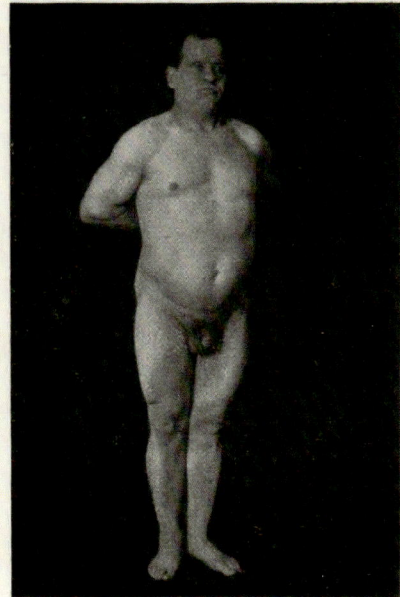

Fig. 2. In nudo.

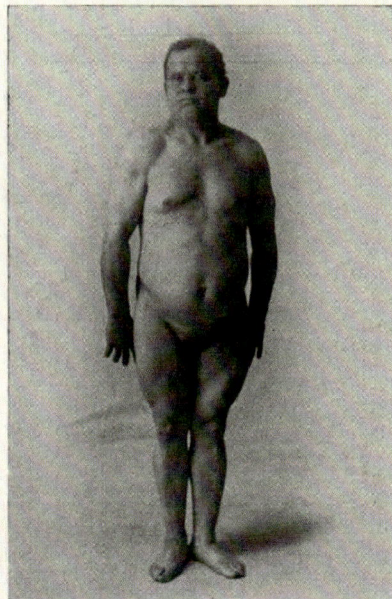

Fig. 3. Als nackter Transvestit.

Fig. 4. In seinem Frauenkostüm.

4*

Milwaukee, and Montana. But each time she was eventually discovered, and finally in 1885 she fled to San Francisco. In 1905, she began writing letters to Helene Stöcker – founder of the *Bund für Mutterschutz* (League for the Protection of Mothers), and a leader in the radical wing of the German women's movement who had also publicly advocated for free love – to seek support. Having received no reply, J. turned to Magnus Hirschfeld. She demanded of Hirschfeld that scientists finally take note of those who were "effeminate" rather than paying attention only to homosexuals and categorizing all cross-dressers as homosexual. Pressure from cross-dressers like J. motivated Hirschfeld to rethink his earlier theories and formulate new categories of identity. More recently, Susan Stryker includes J.'s story as told by Hirschfeld in her book *Transgender History*, using it to exemplify Hirschfeld's work with transgender persons and early transgender histories.[2]

A closer look at these images provides insight into the kinds of stories we have aimed to tell in this book and in the *TransTrans* exhibitions, especially the need we faced to look beyond biography, to the dynamics of seeing and being seen, of self-presentation and recognition or categorization by others, and to the communities that were created through sharing images. This is a shift embedded within the history of sexology itself, which moved around 1900 from its initial reliance on written, often literary, biographies and sources to visual evidence. Hirschfeld's arrangement of images and text in fact tells several stories – not all of them necessarily

intended. When read sequentially like a text, for instance, J.'s photographs tell a life story that accords with her biography: born and raised as a boy, the "young newspaper boy" took off this male identity like a cloak and then claimed a desire to dress in the clothing of – and in fact to become – a woman. This teleology and Hirschfeld's arrangement of the images also matters for how we read the naked bodies in the images. On one level, the images reinforce the overall biographical narrative. J. is noticeably younger in the first two of the images; and in the image in the second row in which she is naked, representing a later stage in her life, she poses in ways that make her look more feminine. Yet on another level, the images can be read as clinical demonstrations. Seen thus, the photographs on the top row stage a process of disrobing that reveals a body naked of any clothing or other cultural markers – a body "in nudo" that appears to naturally speak for itself by revealing the apparent biological sex of its subject. Conversely, the images on the bottom row can be read sequentially as a process of cross-dressing that retrospectively transforms this body – with her genitals hidden between her legs – into a paradox: the body of a naked transvestite.

In Hirschfeld's sense, however, this term is not a paradox, because Hirschfeld defined transvestitism as a *desire* or *drive* to dress in the clothing of the opposite gender/sex (the German word *Geschlecht* means both, although any history concerned with this category will be about changes in its meaning; we discuss this in more detail in our chapter on terminology). In *Die*

Transvestiten, Hirschfeld introduces this newly coined category as designating

the powerful urge to live in the clothing of the *Geschlecht* to which the person concerned does *not* belong according to the form of their body. For the sake of brevity, we will call this drive transvestitic (from trans = opposite and vestis = clothing). But in using this term, we must emphasize that clothing does not appear here "as a *dead thing*," that the kind of clothing a person wears is no arbitrary expression of a capricious whim but a *form of expressing one's inner personality*, a *sign* of one's disposition.[3]

Hirschfeld's arrangement of J.'s photographs reflects a dilemma or double bind in this definition. For it is only by dressing and undressing an individual that Hirschfeld can present them as a transvestite on his definition, i.e., that he can present a conflict between a desired gender expressed in clothing and a sex that is ostensibly visible on the body. And this procedure itself does violence to a part of their personality by forcing them to dress against their desires, robbing them of a living part of who they are.

The arrangement of J.'s images also reflects Hirschfeld's practice of representing individuals as examples of "sexual intermediary stages" (or *sexuelle Zwischenstufen*) by showing them naked with supposedly androgynous bodies and also dressed as a man and a woman. But there is a crucial difference: here, we do not have one ostensibly sexually ambiguous body presenting, when clothed, as male and female. We have, rather, two naked bodies, which function in different ways on each row. We have a transition, in other words, instead of something that is suspended as "either/or" and "in-between." This is one aspect of the arrangement that distinguishes it from other medical images of the period. There are others.

In analyzing medicalized photographs of nonbinary bodies from this period, for instance, Kathrin Peters has pointed especially to the staging and elicitation of shame that comes with a focus on subjects' genitals.[4] I will return to Peters's arguments below, but here I simply want to note that these photos of J. stand out if viewed in that context, because at least the clothed photographs were not obviously or definitively made for clinical purposes, and it is not clear to me that the naked photos were either. (They were manifestly made in a studio, but we cannot say with or by or for whom.) Moreover, the unclothed photos stand out as being the only photographic representation of nudity in Hirschfeld's book, and unlike other clinical images that Hirschfeld himself produced and used, one could argue that they are *not* focused on sexually ambiguous genitals.[5] They are presented as photographs of a *transvestite*, concerned with *clothing* and how clothing represents an inner sense of *Geschlecht*. Indeed, even in the nude images, and in contrast to other nude images that Hirschfeld used in medical contexts, I find there is modest dignity reflected in J.'s posture here – a kind of propriety, or even seemliness. The posing does not strike me as a coerced or forced exposure, or as marked by shame at all. Just as J. hides her genitals so too, one might say, does the photograph – but confidently, self-assuredly. Hirschfeld wants us to see one thing – a demonstration of a sexual type, the transvestite – stripped down to its nude physical form.[6] But J. perhaps wants us to see another – perhaps *not* to focus on this nudity and her genitals at all. She is showing her body, and asking Hirschfeld, at least, to look at *all of it*, together with her clothing, as an expression of who she is.

Finally, it is worth noting that Hirschfeld comes to his "analytical" definition of transvestitism only after recounting 158 pages of life stories. This is characteristic of his use of images in that he separates out case studies from photographs and other visual materials. Such a practice likely reflected conditions of how his works were published, but it also continued sexual scientific methods from the late nineteenth century. By contrast, for instance, as Annette discusses, Bernard S. Talmey integrated life stories and his own diagnoses with the photographs in his 1914 article, which directly responded to Hirschfeld's work. While Hirschfeld intimately knew many of his patients, he tried to carefully separate out his personal relationships from his scientific and medical arguments, in part to guard against charges of being biased and against the common assumption – often used as an attack – that he was homosexual. Talmey's article is much more upfront about the fact that his friendship with his "first patient," Otto Spengler, changed his views about transvestites and motivated him to advocate on their behalf. Hirschfeld's shift from written life stories to

photography is thus to be read as another strategy to achieve objectivity apart from the subjective framework of biography. Yet in the arrangement of these images of J., biography reasserts itself only to take on a new and subversive shape. The images stage a linear story and the gender conflict around which it pivots. But they also undermine this construct by showing how various selves, genders, and identities can exist simultaneously, as depictions of the same person.

Viewed from the perspective of contemporary scholarship, the dynamic staged by these photographs represents one example of the "before-and-after" genre of photography that Jordan Bear and Kate Palmer Albers have called "a strategy so commonplace that virtually every disparate photographic discourse has enlisted it."[7] Bear and Albers argue that before-and-after collages relate both to what the images depict and to a third "unseen event" that renders duration visible and thus relies on a viewer's imagination of what happens outside the frame; in this way, they argue, the genre also offers "a critique of common assumptions about photographic indexicality" that interrogates the conditions governing all photographs.[8] These photographs of J. can be read in this light, because the "truth" they aim to depict escapes the index of any single photograph, or perhaps of what photography as a medium can reveal. In coining the term "transvestite," Hirschfeld attempted to give such an "unseen event" a name. But its status as an epistemic object remained uncertain: is it a story of transition, conflict, or resolution? A drive or an identity? A misrepresentation of J., or a revelation of her truth?

These uncertainties are particularly significant when read within the wider history of how photography was used in the late nineteenth and early twentieth centuries. Complicating earlier interpretations of photography as a democratizing technology, recent scholars have emphasized two main trends in these histories: on the one hand, the use of photography to construct typologies of character and bodily difference centred on categories of race, class, gender, and nationality; and on the other hand, its use as a medium for self-expression, for depicting and disseminating styles and fashions, and for building community. To cite the terms of Alan Sekula's seminal essay "The Body and the Archive," photography developed both as an archive of bourgeois portraiture and as a "shadow archive" of marginal figures, of zones of deviance and respectability.[9] Subsequent work building on this insight has continued to examine how photography has been used in various contexts (medicine, science, anthropology, and ethnography, as well as popular culture) to categorize limits of respectability and representability.[10] Shawn Michelle Smith's work on photography and race, for instance, contrasts photography's use as a technology of knowledge, categorization, and surveillance with the ways in which mostly middle-class individuals became photographic practitioners in fashioning their own identities, exploiting both photography's claims of indexicality or objectivity as well as its power to construct reality, or even to lie.[11]

Smith's work reflects a perspective taken by many contemporary scholars who point attention beyond photographic images themselves to the contexts that shape how photographs have been used, viewed, and produced. As Donna West Brett writes: the "re-uses and interpretations of photographic images unsettles the self-evident reality of their visual field or historical location."[12] And in exploring the function of ethnographic or anthropological images in museums, specifically, Elizabeth Edwards argues that we view photographs as objects that "re-acquir[e] a living context instead of being arrested moments" and are thus "active" in performing their own meaning.[13] These perspectives, too, are significant for *TransTrans*. As historians and curators, we felt an obligation to tell the life stories of the individuals we encountered as faithfully as possible and to make visible the complex, contradictory, or fragmented qualities of these images. Yet we are also situating these images within *transgender* history, which we understand as a genealogy that is marked by the concerns of our present point of view, and that is attentive to moments of rupture and friction rather than one that seeks out linear progression.[14]

We were also keenly aware of another aspect of photography that many scholars have emphasized (following the work of Roland Barthes and Susan Sontag): the power photographs have to evoke feelings or affect.[15] In the introduction to this book, we already pointed toward the issue of viewing "difficult photographs." As we noted there, the images we discuss in this book encompass power relations inherent to medical or scientific situations, normative judgements and framings, and – in the context of sexuality – evocations of shame or sexual excitement, as well as scenes of voyeurism or exhibitionism. But beyond the ethical stance these difficulties imply for us as beholders and witnesses, such emotions have played a constitutive part in the history of photography. Looking specifically at photography in the late nineteenth and early twentieth centuries, for instance, Elspeth Brown and Thy Phu have emphasized the role that affect played in arguments about the medium, as well as the tensions in the medium itself that these debates reflected.[16] Brown and Phu argue that these understandings of photography developed in relation to discourses of intimacy and sentiment, as well as to norms of beauty and respectability, and that the medium's power to document and/or reveal shocking realities (as one sees in the photographs of Jacob Riis) reflects widespread concern at the time with the political efficacy of feeling. At the same time, they argue, the focus on "effect" rather than "affect" in these photographs has "effectively marginalized its shadow subjects."[17] They suggest a new critical focus on feeling that is not limited by these bourgeois values and might support a different kind of history – a queer history with a deeper awareness of how photographic archives function to mediate both absence *and* presence, remembrance *and* forgetting.[18]

And finally, our approach to these photographs was also shaped by work – such as that of Sabine Kriebel and Andrés Mario Zervigón – that emphasizes "doubt" as an epistemic category for thinking about photography. Doubt in this sense means

a "set of experiences including ambiguity, ambivalence, confusion, paradox, enigma."[19]

For photographs of "uncertain sex" around 1900, these issues come together in what Kathrin Peters discusses as "*Rätselbilder des Geschlechts*," or "riddle images of gender/sex."[20] As medicine came to hold "interpretational sovereignty" over matters of sex, Peters argues, medical photographs came to play a crucial part in this discourse by "producing visibilities and representations." She outlines a dual movement in this history. On the one hand, she writes, the sciences concerned with sex used these images to

> arrest what had not been captured, make visible what was invisible, and to disambiguate what was ambiguous. But precisely when it became possible to look more and more closely, increasingly large areas of nonknowledge or not-yet-knowledge, of nonvisibility, simultaneously opened up; and these, in turn, were meant to be made accessible with new techniques of visualization. In this process, sexual ambiguities represented cases of precedence, as it were, on the basis of which it should be possible to make general statements about the "essence" of sex.[21]

As I noted above, Peters focuses on the production of shame in analyzing images in which subjects are prompted by medical authority to show their genitals to have their sex diagnosed.[22] Her intention is to push back against work that has focused on an inherently "voyeuristic structure" of the technology or apparatus of the camera, realized in an objectifying gaze that is seen as congruent with the authoritative gaze of medicine or science. Instead, she emphasizes the "conditions under which the images were made": scenes of examination defined by acts of exposure and uncovering, of photographing and being photographed.[23] She thus contrasts shame to voyeurism as a moment of subjectivity, as a scene characterized specifically by power relations between subjects: "One who is ashamed knows quite precisely that he or she is being seen, which is different than the voyeur, who assumes that his gaze is not being returned, that he himself is not visible (or perhaps he is after all?)."[24]

This perspective is crucial for many of the photographs we are discussing here, especially the medical photographs. Peters' approach prompts us to move beyond blanket assertions of how photography replicates an objectifying, authoritative gaze to ask about the complex interplay of subjectivity – and the scenes that produced it – that is reflected in these images. Indeed, as the other essays in this book make clear, photography has always offered transgender individuals a medium to represent themselves as they would like to be seen, and to share those images with others to create supportive communities. Photographs were and still are used to represent how one should or would like to dress, how to comport and hold oneself or do makeup, or in order to gain recognition and understanding.[25] They also enact socially recognizable styles and ideals. For instance, the magazine *Das 3. Geschlecht*

is evidence of the fact that in Berlin and other large cities during the 1920s, studios emerged that catered to the needs and desires of individuals who called themselves transvestites. Trans individuals often modelled themselves after historical images or fashion photos, just as publications drew images from historical sources, fashion photography, and the theatre. Photographs were also important tools for self-advocacy with doctors and other authorities, and for gaining access to medical treatment.

And yet as Jay Prosser emphasized some twenty years ago, as transgender identities were emerging and transgender studies was just taking shape as a discipline, the truths depicted in these photographs were ephemeral and fleeting – moments captured that often stand at odds with how individuals most often presented themselves or were perceived by others.[26] At least until the 1990s, transgender history was in large part a history of passing or desiring to pass – a history of individuals who wanted to live and be perceived as a particular sex. This fact invests many transgender photographs with the intention of hiding their history of transition, which also complicates our work as historians.[27] For instance, the only reason that Annette and I suspected that first slide she found among Benjamin's vacation photos (figure 1.1) might be a picture of a trans woman is because we were looking for pictures of trans women. When it comes to photography, as Jennifer Blessing also argued in the 1990s, the medium's "strong aura of realism and objectivity promotes a fantasy of total gender transformation, or, conversely, allows the articulation of incongruity between the posing body and its assumed costume."[28]

We hope the many images we have discussed in this book have already begun to communicate a picture of the life stories at the centre of *TransTrans*, and of how they have been told, archived, or made public. We have also provided some clear indications of how we approached these images as historians and curators. Here, I now turn to the visual consequences of the medical framings that underpin so much of this history: to the categories of transvestite and transsexual introduced by Hirschfeld and Benjamin and to depictions of cross-dressing that these men drew from in their publications. I will examine how Hirschfeld and Benjamin attempted to reread existing practices of cross-dressing in terms of medicalized visual rhetorics – and also how these existing, and evolving, practices of gender presentation resisted, appropriated, and transformed their authoritative framings.

Transvestite/Transsexual

Harry Benjamin opens *The Transsexual Phenomenon* with a brief historical overview, and the history he tells begins with Magnus Hirschfeld.[29] Explaining that Hirschfeld was probably the first to use the term "tranvestism as a medical diagnosis," Benjamin describes Hirschfeld's interaction with "many of these persons" and notes the destruction of Hirschfeld's institute by the Nazis. Benjamin also explicitly reveals his own personal role in this history as a visitor to the Institute for Sexual Science. But the overall gesture

of Benjamin's reference to Hirschfeld is to distinguish himself from Hirschfeld's earlier model of "transvestitism" in order to then introduce a new category, "transsexualism."[30] Both Hirschfeld and Benjamin wanted their work to contribute a broader agenda of furthering public knowledge. For Hirschfeld, that agenda was "enlightenment": the achievement of social reform and increased visibility for sexual minorities based on an understanding of natural human sexual phenomena. For Benjamin, however, this agenda included not only a new paradigm for understanding what he called transsexualism but also a new model of treatment closely connected to his own work as a medical doctor. Hence even as Benjamin admits his personal and scientific debt to Hirschfeld, he emphasizes how his model of treatment supersedes this earlier history.[31]

This intention is especially visible in the way that Benjamin uses images. Take, for example, the repetition of this motif from the illustrated volume to *Die Transvestiten*,[32] published in 1912 (see figures 5.2 and 5.3).

There is no doubt that Benjamin knew Hirschfeld's book well, and I suspect that he intentionally chose these two images, with their undeniable visual symmetry to Hirschfeld's arrangement of images. In that case, even Benjamin's choice of images underscores his claim to supersede Hirschfeld, because a closer comparison shows that the two similar sets of images tell contrasting stories.

Hirschfeld's sorrowful transvestite ostensibly tells the story of an unhappy identity conflict ending in suicide. Given the caption, the diptych undoubtedly means

FIGURE 5.2: "A transvestite from the people who died by suicide," Plate 33 in Hirschfeld's illustrated volume to *Die Transvestiten*, 1912.

Ein Transvestit aus dem Volke, der durch Selbstmord geendet hat.

X was an actor and is now an actress. There are five years between these pictures of male and female, as well as a conversion operation and estrogen treatment during most of that time.

FIGURE 5.3: Harry Benjamin, *The Transsexual Phenomenon*, 1966, photograph section. University of Victoria Libraries, Transgender Archives collection. Harry Benjamin, *The Transsexual Phenomenon*. New York: Ace Publishing Corp, 1966. Special Collections call number RC560 C4B46 1966.

to say that this person's desire to dress in the clothing of one gender is at odds with their biological sex. But the images themselves are not so equivocal. For one thing, it is not entirely clear whether the clothing in the first image is masculine or feminine. It seems the buttons are in the front, and women's clothing would have likely had buttons in the back; but how should one read the cravat-like piece of clothing around the neck? Is this already an attempt to dress more femininely, or androgynously? The clothing in the second image, by contrast, is clearly marked as feminine by the headscarf and the knit sweater; the way the figure is holding her cup is also quite feminine, evidence of an alignment in gender identity between clothing and comportment that we are certainly also meant to read as being in tragic conflict with the figure's biological sex. The diptych thus stages a tragic conflict precisely by suggesting and then frustrating any interpretation of before and after. It is worth noting, as well, that the trope of tragic suicide was common in discussions of homosexuality in the first decades of the twentieth century, where it was often used rhetorically to elicit support for

Photomontage of Lili Elbe

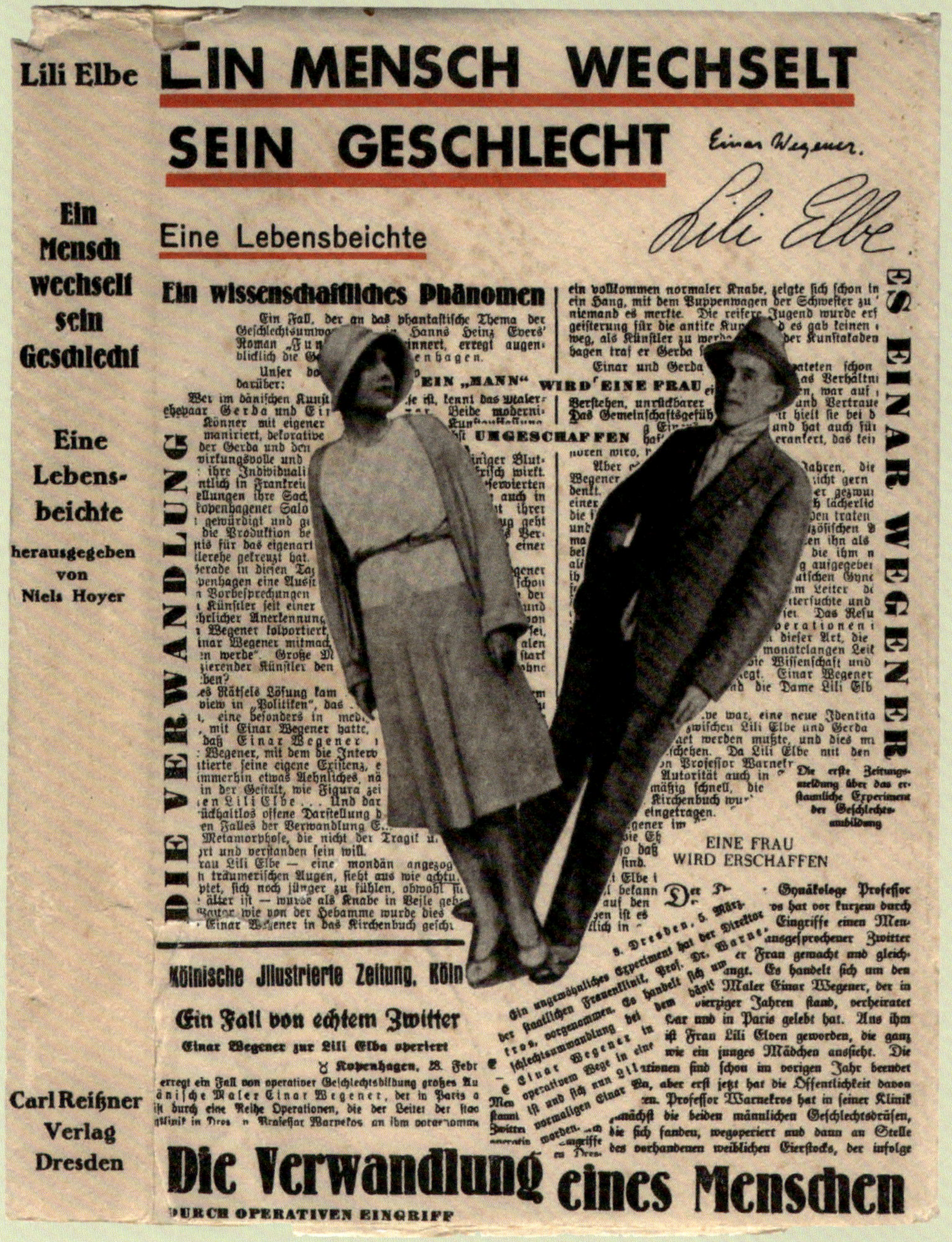

FIGURE 5.4: Cover to German edition of *A Person Changes Their Sex: A Life Confession*, edited by Niels Hoyer," with further text reading "A Person's Transformation through Operations," with signatures from Einar Wegener and Lili Elbe, 1932.

Both the visual gesture of before-and-after and photomontage are used in one popular depiction of a story that can be considered foundational because of its public impact and how it has come to be canonized in history – that of Lili Elbe. Here is the cover of a German version of a 1932 book edited by Niels Hoyer and purporting to be Lili Elbe's autobiography. The title can be translated as *A Person Changes Their Sex: A Life Confession*, but it was published in English in a modified form as *Man into Woman: An Authentic Record of a Change of Sex* and was republished in 2004 with the title *Man into Woman: The First Sex Change: A Portrait of Lili Elbe: The True and Remarkable Transformation of the Painter Einar Wegener*.[1]

Lili Elbe (born Einar Wegener in Denmark in 1882) underwent four gender-affirming surgeries in 1930 and 1931, the first in Berlin (under Hirschfeld's supervision) and the other three in Dresden, carried out by Kurt Warnekros. Particularly since the 2015 film *The Danish Girl*, Elbe has entered popular memory as the most visible person to undergo an early sex change operation. But she was not the first. Earlier operations were performed in 1920–21 by the Berlin surgeon Richard Mühsam for a patient who went by the name Dorchen.[2] Ideals of femininity linked with motherhood were deeply entrenched in the culture, leading to unrealistic expectations of what surgery might be able to achieve. These drove medical innovations that were particularly dangerous: Elbe died of organ rejection after a uterus implantation. The autobiography described above was not written by Elbe, but by Ernst Ludwig Hathorn Jacobson (under the pseudonym Niels Hoyer) after Elbe's death. As Sabine Meyer has conclusively demonstrated, although Elbe commissioned Jacobson to write the book and despite its later influence on trans readers, its status as an authentic account of how she would have described her life should be questioned.[3] Still, despite its somewhat dubious authenticity, this was the first account of a trans individual to gain widespread attention.

As with Hirschfeld and Benjamin, the visual rhetoric of this particular cover (there were others in other languages, which were much more staid) disrupts any simple biographical narrative. The book is titled "A Person Changes Their Sex" and subtitled "A Life Confession." Yet the cover also names three separate authors: the name "Einar Wegener" in a readable block script, a signature that reads "Lili Elbe," and an indication that the book has been edited by Niels Hoyer. We hardly need any tools of deconstruction or theoretical awareness about the complex authenticity of confessions to see that the "author" of this life history is plainly fragmented – personally and visually – just as the cover also fragments its columns of printed text.

homosexuals and (ideally) mobilize efforts for social and legal reform.[33] Here, this trope is similarly meant to elicit support for the tragic situation of transvestites. But it also underscores the overlap between the categories of homosexual (which had been circulating popularly for some time) and Hirschfeld's new category of the transvestite, despite Hirschfeld's attempt to now differentiate them.

Benjamin's photos, by contrast, depict clearly defined scenes of before and after. Even more importantly, the clinical ability Benjamin claims – of being able to change the bodies of his patients by changing their gender – now appears to resolve the underlying problem illustrated by Hirschfeld's transvestite. Benjamin's treatments turn the earlier tragic situation into a happy ending. The repetition of the motif appears to say (if only slyly, for those who also know Hirschfeld's work): while Hirschfeld can only document the tragic fate of those forced to act and dress against their own sense of their gender, Benjamin can now do something about it. Hirschfeld's book announces its author on the title page as "Dr. Magnus Hirschfeld, Special Doctor for Nervous and Psychological Diseases in Berlin." The German word for disease here, *Leiden*, also means "suffering." In Hirschfeld's work, it remains unclear whether this desire is itself pathological or a consequence of a society that cannot accept it. But in any case, in Benjamin's images the suffering that Hirschfeld aims to depict has been replaced by a new notion of subjectivity based on hormonal treatment, which Michael Pettit has termed the "glandular self."[34] This new self, Pettit

argues, was not immediately visible to the eye: "With its emphasis on the invisible secretion of chemicals, the glandular self likewise located the essence of human nature just beyond the threshold of ordinary and unassisted perception."[35] One consequence of Benjamin's arrangement of these photographs is to push back against this epistemic invisibility. As the treating endocrinologist, he moreover claims this glandular self as his own field and object of work, and its subjects as his own creation.

There is one more context crucial for reading these photographs of an actor/actress, namely the fact that it was precisely the accusation of impersonating or masquerading that was historically used to discredit those who cross-dressed and to bring legal charges against them. The possibility of arrest that transvestites in Hirschfeld's time faced was real, though it varied by country. Indeed, when Benjamin mentions Hirschfeld, his comments focus on his predecessor's work in helping to procure "transvestite passes" from the police in Germany to protect transvestites from arrest, with the explanation that this was the reason most transvestites came to visit Hirschfeld. "In the majority of cases," Benjamin writes, "this permission was granted because these patients had no intention of committing a crime through 'masquerading' or 'impersonating.' 'Dressing' was considered beneficial to their mental health."[36] Here again, Benjamin underscores the paradigm shift his book is meant to illustrate. Whereas Hirschfeld tried to solve this problem of masquerading with a police certificate, here again Benjamin will now apparently solve the problem altogether through medical, hormonal intervention.

Seen in this context, Benjamin's choice to represent an actor/actress is highly significant. Alex's essay underscores how it was only in theatrical spaces or on the streets in red-light districts in large cities that society offered trans women space to appear; this survival strategy meant working as prostitutes, with the accompanying effect of rendering invisible more bourgeois transgender women. Moreover, this coding of trans women as exciting sexual deviants drew from long-standing, explicitly bourgeois views of female actors as necessarily vulgar or sexual. In this view, the very appearance of women on stage was subject to a double-bind: it exposed femininity that was defined specifically in terms of chastity and modesty or, in its most extreme form, as something not to be seen in public at all.[37] As Alex explains, popular perceptions of trans women in the 1950s exacerbated these prejudices, which must had have added extra weight to accusations that transvestites were acting and hence untrustworthy. No doubt to counter this danger, Benjamin's emphasis on the happy outcome of his treatment suggests that we can now trust this person's gender presentation to accord with who they are. That is to say: we can trust that this actress is not acting when she presents in her new gendered self; because her gender performance now accords with her body, she must no longer "masquerade" or "impersonate." Furthermore, we can now clearly tell her gender performance apart from her professional abilities as an actress, giving both her gender and her professional identity a new kind of security and authenticity.

Benjamin's repetition of this motif also opens up a class difference to Hirschfeld's image. Hirschfeld's transvestite is explicitly marked as being "from the people" and appears in peasant garb. On the one hand, this, too, might be read as a strategy to insulate this person from charges of acting, particularly given that the photo seems quite staged and theatrical: to be from among the people might be read as being simplistic and naive, and therefore as genuine or incapable of guile. Hence even if the photo clearly appears to depict a person acting out a stock role or emotion, the simplicity of its protagonist might be taken as protection from charges of having nefarious intentions. Yet on the other hand, of course, the bourgeois suspicion against lower-class frauds and tricksters could equally apply here. Both possibilities are stereotyped projections of class difference, and it is only the figure's suicide that ultimately proves the genuineness of their suffering. The effect of Benjamin's image, by contrast, is to entirely do away with this problem for his actress. Now she can be confident in her professional identity without it threatening her gender identity, and vice versa. What's more, her profession as an actress gains middle-class respectability: in its authenticity, it is distanced from the various transvestites and female impersonators the public largely associated with transvestites.

Ultimately, however, like Hirschfeld's arrangement of J.'s photographs or sorrowful transvestite, Benjamin's

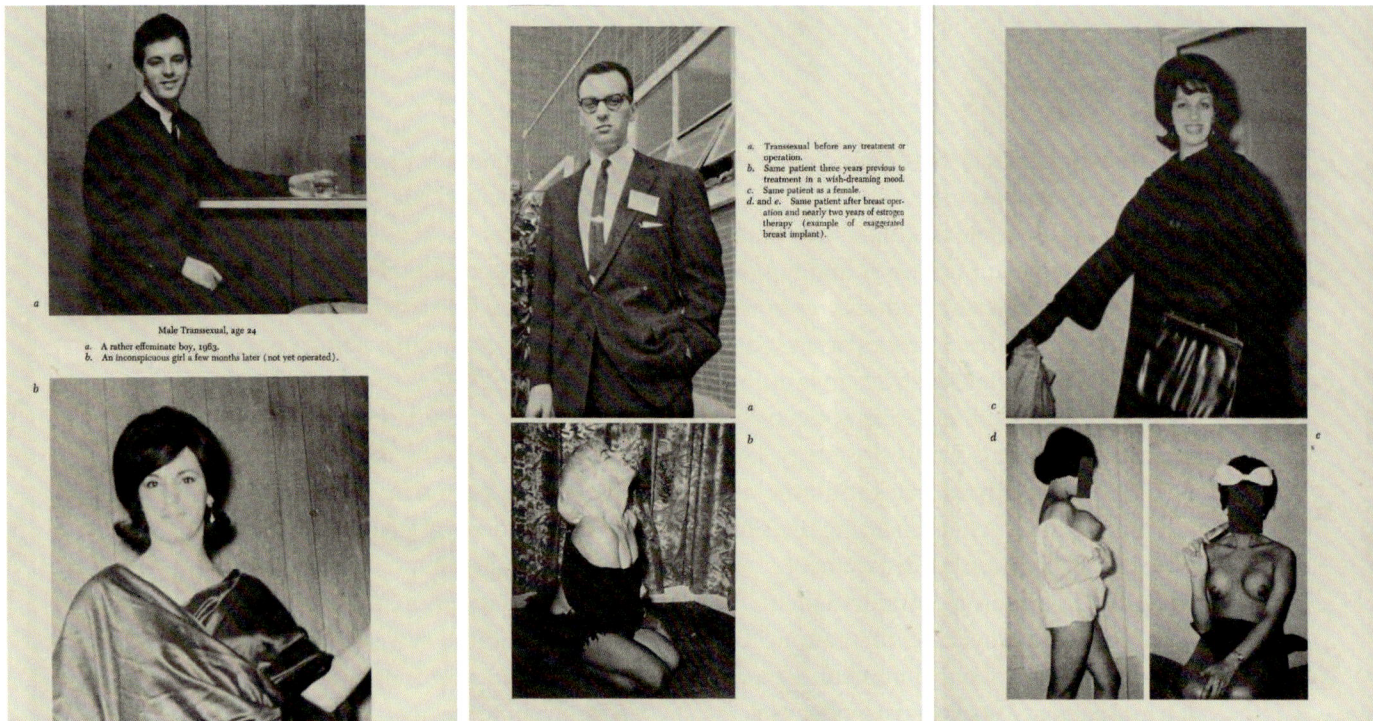

FIGURE 5.5: Progression of images in Harry Benjamin's *The Transsexual Phenomenon*, 1966. University of Victoria Libraries, Transgender Archives collection. Harry Benjamin, *The Transsexual Phenomenon*. New York: Ace Publishing Corp, 1966. Special Collections call number RC560 C4B46 1966.

photographs say more than he himself perhaps intended to convey. First, Benjamin refers to his patient apart from her gendered professional identity (actor/actress) and her personal gender presentation only as "X" – thus avoiding any reference to her sex. The effect is to make sex a kind of floating variable under the control of the doctor who names it and changes it. And regardless of what Benjamin says, I find the nature of these images quite ambivalent. Are they portraits? Publicity shots? Production stills? If the point of Benjamin's treatment is to make it so that transsexuals no longer have to masquerade, it remains a striking choice to illustrate that success with photos in which we cannot tell, and in which it is not clearly explained, whether we are seeing a person acting out a role or acting

out themselves. Indeed, knowing that this person has happily transitioned to a woman means that, at least in the first image, they must be acting out this inauthentic identity of being a man. Finally, it is likely that none of these photographs were staged for Hirschfeld or Benjamin, though we cannot be sure. What is clear is that their intentions go beyond or diverge from what Hirschfeld and Benjamin want us to see. With these photos from *The Transsexual Phenomenon*, I would say that the images even stand at odds with Benjamin's intentions.

The tensions we find in a juxtaposition of the images from these two books play out on a larger scale in Benjamin's choice of images overall. For if we look at the place of the actor/actress in relation to these other photographs, we find that the image

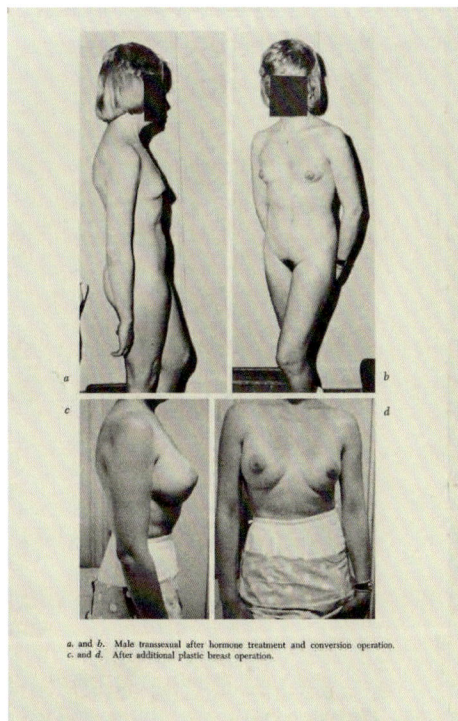

a. and b.   Male transsexual after hormone treatment and conversion operation.
c. and d.   After additional plastic breast operation.

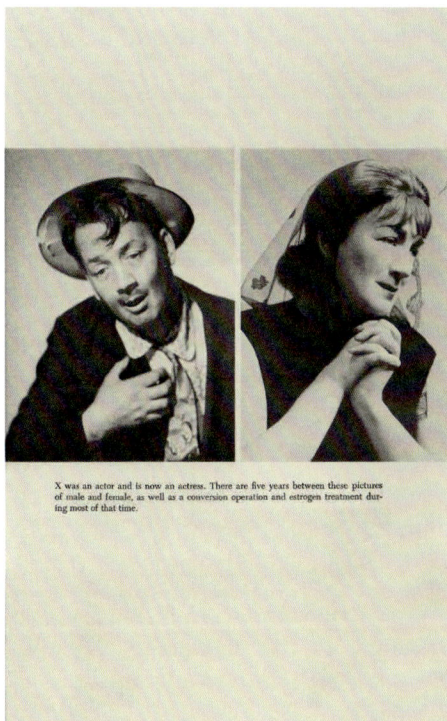

X was an actor and is now an actress. There are five years between these pictures of male and female, as well as a conversion operation and estrogen treatment during most of that time.

occupies a crucial position. Benjamin's selection and arrangement of images tell a story of a progression (figure 5.5). First, we find a person depicted in male and female clothing before treatment. Second, across two pages recto and verso, we find a person depicted in male and female clothing in the process of transitioning through hormone therapy and surgery. Third, we are shown a person who has undergone surgical and hormone treatment, with a focus on the naked body. And fourth, we have the photographs of the actor/actress documenting a happy outcome of a successful treatment. We have here a process of undressing and re-dressing with treatment of the body in between.

If we look more closely at the central collage spread across two pages, we see that it too documents the transition of a transsexual, thus repeating *in nuce*

the overall story of this image selection (figure 5.6). The letters in Benjamin's captions direct us to read the photographs according to biographical chronology, and this chronology unfolds as if it were printed in a book, from right to left and top to bottom, one page at a time. First, we have an unassuming, ordinary person who presents in men's clothing. Then, we have a kind of revelation, perhaps of the truth hiding beneath this façade but also of a person described as being lost to their own fantasies, "in wish-dreaming mode." Third, we see this same person "as female," in a mirror image to the first photograph as the person as male. And finally, we see two images that focus on the medical aspects of the transition and the transformation of the body, which Benjamin nevertheless comments upon by noting the "exaggerated" breast implants.

FIGURE 5.6: Two facing pages from *The Transsexual Phenomenon*. The caption in the image reads: "a. Transsexual before any treatment or operation. b. Same patient three years previous to treatment in a wish-dreaming mode. c. Same patient as a female. d. and e. Same patient after breast operation and nearly two years of estrogen therapy (example of exaggerated breast implants)." University of Victoria Libraries, Transgender Archives collection. Harry Benjamin, *The Transsexual Phenomenon*. New York: Ace Publishing Corp, 1966. Special Collections call number RC560 C4B46 1966.

But here, again, the images say more. For one thing, the spread of photographs across two pages hardly limits itself to being read sequentially like a book and, by analogy, as a personal biographical narrative. The powerful correspondence in size and style between the images facing each other across the page is clearly intended to illustrate before and after. So even as we are shown the story of a successful transition, the images maintain an awareness of this person as a transsexual who has transitioned. Moreover, the clear contrast between the content of the top and bottom rows also generates meaning. Above, we see bourgeois respectability. Below, we see the plainly eroticized desires and fantasies that this person connects to their female self – the allegedly pathological transsexual desire hiding, as it were, beneath the clothing in the top row, just as the "exaggerated breasts" can be read as physical remnants of the earlier psychological disturbance this first revelation might insinuate. As with the photographs of the actor/actress, these images present an underlying point of tension or at least difference to the bourgeois stability and respectability that Benjamin means to produce and secure with his medical treatment.

Finally, and perhaps to state the obvious: a wide gap appears to open up between the intentions likely represented by the photographs in the bottom row and Benjamin's medical intentions with his book. Benjamin's reaction to the overtly erotic desire the photographs display is to pathologize it as transsexual and as psychologically out of touch with reality. But as Annette and Alex have shown in great detail, this was often a fear projected by medical authorities onto trans men and women of the time, reflecting worries the doctors had about how their work would be perceived in public; and the power that medical authorities had to shape or coerce the appearance and behaviour of individuals desperate for treatment was enormous. The psychological reality of these individuals was much more complex than what they showed to doctors or what doctors show us. When I look at these photographs, I wonder: how different is the desire they depict from the motivations that so many of us have today in taking explicit photographs of ourselves? The intention of expressing a gender that differs from the

one assigned at birth may be different, but other intentions reflected in this photograph are quite common: to look sexy, to stage a certain look, to live out a certain fantasy, and probably – if one is lucky – to get others' approval, attention, and maybe even love. Benjamin struggles (or perhaps it is more accurate to say: does not even try) to integrate these aspects of the photographs with the evident claims they also make to represent this person's gender identity.

Benjamin's medical reframing of this cross-dressing is exemplary for the difficulties that both he and Hirschfeld encounter in using images to illustrate their categories of transvestite and transsexual. What the photos evince is simply more complicated and varied than these two categories and their medical reframings allow for. Both Hirschfeld and Benjamin turn to arrangements of photographs to illustrate the complexity of gender identities that cross over between male and female. Both men attempt to frame these images in narrative terms, but the images themselves – and their arrangement – open up layers of meaning that fail to conform to this framework. Some of these meanings reflect the complexity of these individuals' lives, and others reflect prejudices projected onto them. But for both doctors, it is moments of gender conflict or transition that remain difficult to depict photographically. Hirschfeld wants us to see, in and on the body, a conflict between a desire or drive and how a person dresses and acts. That is what the label "transvestite" is meant to capture. But what we see instead are narrative tropes of biography and tragic tropes of suffering and suicide. While

Hirschfeld's "Male Transvestites"

As in the magazine *Das 3. Geschlecht*, the images of "male transvestites" used by Hirschfeld often focus on fashion. We find figures posed in elegant dresses, artists, transvestites "from among the people" and – with John O. (as Hirschfeld calls her) – a single collage presenting a life story of gender transition. But unlike "female transvestites," who appear (when clothed) in a range of stock male social characters (as hunters, warriors, sailors, sportsmen), "male transvestites" are marked primarily by the social class of what they are wearing. This distinction obviously reflects gender norms about men and women, i.e., that women are primarily defined by their gender, men by their social role. And like the photographs of "male transvestites" printed in *Das 3. Geschlecht*, the dominant concern in the images published by Hirschfeld is with passing as women.

The first of these images is notable as a photo of Baron Hermann von Teschenberg, one of the four founders – with Hirschfeld – of what is probably the world's first gay rights organization, the Wissenschaftlich-humanitäres Komitee (Scientific-Humanitarian Committee) in 1897. (When Hirschfeld first published this image of Teschenberg in 1902, with a signed dedication indicating Teschenberg's gender and social status as a baron and his willingness for

FIGURE 5.7: "Two transvestites from aristocratic circles. Hermann Freiherr v. Teschenberg. N. N. from Rome. Hirschfeld's illustrated volume to *Die Transvestiten*, 1912.

the photo to be published, however, Hirschfeld presents Teschenberg as a homosexual and not as a transvestite.)

Some of the photos that Hirschfeld publishes are quite stunning and beautiful in the sense that they pass as female (figure 5.8). Others point to moments of theatrical gender play – here also with evidence of Hirschfeld's transatlantic gaze (figure 5.9). And

Der Transvestit Adam Kl.

FIGURE 5.8: "The transvestite Adam Kl." Hirschfeld's illustrated volume to *Die Transvestiten*, 1912.

Ein italienischer und ein amerikanischer Student in Frauenrollen.

a) Student der Universität Pisa.

b) Student der Universität Yale.

FIGURE 5.9: "An Italian and an American student playing the roles of women. a) Student from the University of Pisa. b) Student from Yale University. Hirschfeld's illustrated volume to *Die Transvestiten*, 1912.

with some, it is hard to avoid the conclusion that the individuals they depict are being exposed as ridiculous, even if these individuals themselves might be in on the joke or have made it themselves (figure 5.10).

The normative judgement reflected in these photos appears again and again in the images exhibited in *TransTrans*. Rainer's essay traces these judgements in the popular magazine *Das 3. Geschlecht*. Annette and Alex both show how it appears in medical criteria for treatment and doctor's opinions that selected out unstable individuals, or individuals with "unreasonable" demands or expectations. It can also be found in Benjamin's emphasis of the exaggerated self-presentation and

Tafel XXXV

Transvestiten, die sich als Balleteusen am wohlsten fühlen.

FIGURE 5.10: "Transvestites who feel most comfortable as ballet dancers." Hirschfeld's illustrated volume to *Die Transvestiten*, 1912.

when they do not. We find a difference, however, in this dynamic when comparing single images with the many arrangements of images of the same person that Hirschfeld and Benjamin produce. Single images depict passing or ridicule by evoking a comparison with gender norms that are tacitly assumed and brought to bear by the viewer (thought of course also made clear or underscored in other images). Single images thus also move away from an explicit mode of comparison that would take both points of the comparison as equals and shift toward moments of emotional resonance that reflect and reinforce existing gender norms. The medical arrangements of photographs, by contrast, can be read as demonstrations of the gender performativity as repeated acts of stylization that Butler, for instance, theorizes as the truth of all gender. This remains true even as Hirschfeld and Benjamin emphasize the "before/after" perspective of treatment, try to make sense of nonbinary gender in terms of biographical transition or tragedy, or make an argument for how gender expressed in a choice of clothing is ostensibly visible on the body. Of course, Hirschfeld's intention in arranging these single portraits in pairs or groups was to show patterns or similar types within human diversity. But this also accentuates the individuality of each presentation within the category as a matter of style and self-fashioning.

sexual desires – the "wish-dreaming mode" – of the individual presented in Michael's essay in figure 5.6. It is also worth noting that the normative framework projected onto images of men cross-dressing as women is largely absent from images of women cross-dressing as men.

These normative framings come from the incongruence or congruence between the person's body, on the one hand, and their self-presentation and clothing, on the other. Beauty is a consequence of these two aspects existing in alignment; ridicule results

Benjamin offers a paradigm for treatment meant to solve this tragic conflict, his notion of success as passing forces a single interpretation upon the particular histories of his patients, hiding their desires beneath a veneer of bourgeois normalcy and respectability. In short, both medical paradigms struggle to depict cross-dressing as a complex expression of gender identity in its own right, just as they fail to fully recognize the power that clothing has to make gender in and on the body, rather than just express it.

To illustrate this even more clearly, I now shift to a wider consideration of images of cross-dressing from which Hirschfeld and Benjamin drew. Since both men were concerned with illustrating a long history of transvestitism and transsexualism, this also entails a perspective shift beyond photographs to other kinds of images.

Picturing Cross-Dressing

The trope of presenting the same person in male and female clothing was one foundational gesture of Hirschfeld's visual rhetorics and an innovation that he introduced to sexology. So, for example, we find in the illustrated volume of *Die Transvestiten* this reproduction of a painting depicting the Chevalier d'Éon, a cross-dressing French aristocrat who became famous in late-eighteenth century England for engaging in fencing duels while dressed in female clothing, and who then lived as a woman.

Hirschfeld had already used these two images, in a lecture in 1904 and in his 1905 book *Geschlechts-Übergänge*,

FIGURE 5.11: Plate 51, The Chevalier d'Éon from the illustrated volume to *Die Transvestiten*, 1912. The caption in the image reads: "The Chevalier Charles, Charlotte, Genevieve, Louise, Auguste, Andrée, Thimothée, D'Éon & Beaumont. As a young female courtier (35 years old). Based on a copy by Angelika Kaufmann of Latour from the collection of George Keate, Esq. As an envoy to the Russian court (1770). Painted by Huquier. Engraved by Burke."

to introduce his practice of representing "mixed-sex" individuals through arrangements of images of the same person wearing male and female clothing. (It is plate 28; we discuss this juxtaposition in more detail in the gallery "Gender Play," which accompanies Rainer's essay.) Hirschfeld's decision to again use this image in *Die Transvestiten* is an example of how he applied his evolving categories to reinterpret the same images, biographies, or individuals. He saw and showed different things as his categories changed, or depending on the audience he was speaking to. This juxtaposition of D'Éon is thus not so much or not just an illustration of a contrast or even transition between man and woman but much more broadly of how clothing can shape and reshape identity, and how this reshaping continually escapes the categories by which it is recognized. How one dresses does not express a truth about one's (gendered) self. It generates meaning through an interplay of expression and recognition, as a gender play between oneself – or selves – and others, between what is outwardly seen and what is kept private.

Hirschfeld's use of these images thus also exemplifies how his work aligned with, supported, and fed the needs of emerging movements for sexual minorities to find historical antecedents for their own identities – beginning with Hirschfeld's decision to publish the letters that Karl Heinrich Ulrichs wrote to his family in 1899 in the first issue of the newly founded *Jahrbuch für sexuelle Zwischenstufen* (Yearbook for sexual intermediaries).[38] Havelock Ellis's use of d'Éon to coin the term "eonism" – which Benjamin notes – was also received in this same light: the world's first organization for transvestites, Vereinigung D'Éon (Association D'Éon) was founded in Hirschfeld's Institute for Sexual Science. But in *Die Transvestiten*, Hirschfeld uses images depicting a range of (gender) play performed by d'Éon's cross-dressing that undercuts any simple

reduction to this modern medical framing, or to a binary of male and female identities. Immediately after the juxtaposition of d'Éon dressed as a man and a woman, Hirschfeld also includes three more images of the same person: "As an old woman," "As an Amazon," and "As a dragoner captain."

Finally, one key point in d'Éon's biography is that d'Éon was a spy – and spies, it goes without saying, cannot be trusted because they are experts at deception. To quote a description of this history that Benjamin published in an appendix to his book:

> He is reported to have made his debut into history in woman's garb as the rival of Madame de Pompadour as a pretty new mistress for Louis XV. When his secret was made known to the King, the latter capitalized on his initial mistake by turning the Chevalier into a trusted diplomat. On one occasion, in 1755, he went to Russia on a secret mission disguised as the niece of the King's accredited agent and the following year returned to Russia attired as a man to complete the mission. Following the death of Louis XV he lived permanently as a woman. There was great uncertainty in England, where he spent his final years, as to whether his true morphological sex was male or whether the periods in male attire were not, in fact, the periods of impersonation. When he died, the Chevalier d'Éon had lived forty-nine years as a man and thirty-four years as a woman.[39]

Figure 5.12: Joseph Meißauer. Hirschfeld's illustrated volume to *Die Transvestiten*, 1912. The captions in the image read: "Joseph Meißauer; before and after the police's approval. On the basis of the medical assessment of Dr. Dr. Magnus Hirschfeld and Iwan Bloch, Mr. Joseph Meißauer received permission from the Berlin and Munich police to constantly wear women's clothing in accordance with his disposition."

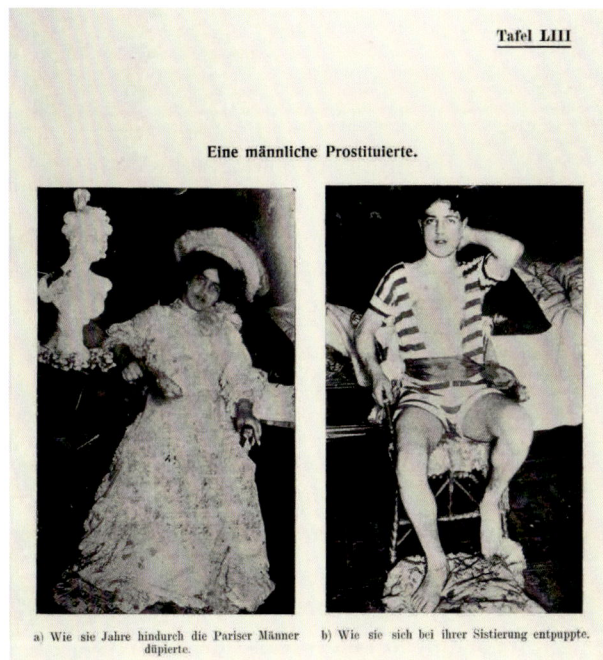

Figure 5.13: "A male prostitute." Hirschfeld's illustrated volume to *Die Transvestiten*, 1912. The captions in the image read: "A male prostitute. a) As she duped the Parisian men over years. b) As she was discovered upon her arrest."

Within the gesture of representing the same person as male and female that we find in these histories, we almost always also find the danger of masquerade and criminal dissimulation. The subtitle of Hirschfeld's book on transvestites is *Der erotische Verkleidungstrieb*, which is usually translated as "erotic drive to cross-dress" but could just as easily mean "the erotic drive to disguise oneself."

The contrast between an upstanding, bourgeois mode of cross-dressing and more criminal intentions is amplified by other images in Hirschfeld's volume. For instance, take these images of Joseph Meißauer (figure 5.12). As the caption indicates, Joseph Meißauer was one of the individuals to receive a so-called transvestite pass issued by the police, in this case on the basis of the medical assessment of Hirschfeld and Iwan Bloch. By contrast, some images emphasize the threat of dissimulation that this transvestite pass was meant to counter. An example is this set of photographs, which Hirschfeld placed immediately after the paintings of d'Éon, the spy (figure 5.13).

The history of photography from which *TransTrans* draws was deeply intertwined with such fears. It was to break the "professional criminal's mastery of disguises," Alan Sekula first argued, that nineteenth-century photography sought to employ the supposedly precise, objective lens of the camera.[40] Hirschfeld inherited these techniques and this objective understanding of photography. But just as his work hoped to free transvestites from the criminal bind forced on them by society, he interpreted what photography documents and reveals differently: as a tool for the natural scientist who observes, describes, and categorizes the phenomena that he sees. Throughout his career, Hirschfeld was keen to show the widespread manifestation of what he conceived as sexual variations – what we would today call variations of gender and sexual identity – across social classes and cultures. This followed an intention he established during the previous decade of describing the behaviour of cross-dressing in naturalistic terms, as a kind of camouflage or mimicry like that used or manifested by animals.[41]

Translating these intentions into a kind of social anthropology (a field just emerging at this time), Hirschfeld structured the illustrated volume of *Die Transvestiten* into two sections: an "Ethnographic Historical Section" and a "General Part."[42] Yet his selection of images does not correspond to what we might expect today of these conceptual distinctions. The ethnographic-historical section consists almost entirely of drawings made by a famous Berlin artist Max Tilke. The sole exception is one photograph of the back of an African woman (Plate 2), intended to depict "decorative scars of an ornamental character on the back of a *Janude* woman," as the caption indicates. I take the intention as being to show scarring as a practice of adorning the body similar to clothing, though this is not stated. But such an intention would have significant consequences for a notion of "transvestitism." Darwin, for instance, turned to practices of body modification or adornment to distinguish "savages" from civilized societies, in which these aesthetic practices are expressed through the impermanent fashions of dress.[43] One effect, then, of this sole photograph here – of a black woman's back, without a face, and hence entirely depersonalized – is that photography as an ethnographic tool becomes overdetermined as the medium for showing a body that is not only "savage" (to quote Darwin) but also feminine, black, and non-Western. Another, overall effect is to distinguish Hirschfeld's project and the various other sketched images of non-Western transvestites from such a purely racialized ethnography.

Indeed, in the second, "general" section (assembled by Hirschfeld alone), photography reappears in a more familiar, subjective form – as a medium of bourgeois portraiture, mixed in together with drawings and paintings that Hirschfeld meant to be read both as depictions of social reality and, as with his interpretation of the transvestite's clothing, an expression of an inner psychological identity. Yet there is more hidden in Hirschfeld's selection of images. As Rainer has pointed out, Tilke considered himself a transvestite and appears here, unnamed, wearing female clothing, as "a well-known artist in women's clothing" (Plate 23).[44] Like Hirschfeld, whose homosexuality was an open secret, Tilke is thus also to be seen here as a (closeted) reminder that the ostensibly objective, disinterested perspective that was claimed by sexology and instrumentalized in its arguments for social reform was also driven by deeply personal concerns.[45]

This ethnographic undertone nevertheless persists through both parts of the volume inasmuch as we are presented with figures from a range of cultures, classes, and historical periods. When projected onto non-European cultures, it produces fantastic forms of otherness – as in, for example, this projection of European mythology and mythic history onto these two "Amazons of our time" (figure 5.14). Like Tilke's "ethnographic" drawings in the illustrated volume, this projection represents a displacement of gender transgression away from Hirschfeld's own social world. In this sense, it contrasts markedly with the images that Hirschfeld shows of Western society, in which norms of passing and bourgeois respectability dominate.

One of these images, however, stands out because the "transvestite" it depicts has "glued his head onto a fashion photo" (figure 5.15). This photomontage – a practice that Sabine Kriebel has called "*the modern pictorial idiom*" – reflects popular practices of the time.[46] In introducing her analysis of John Heartfield's "revolutionary" montage practice, for instance, Kriebel cites a request sent to him that he "construct" a "portrait" of a soldier who had died, by

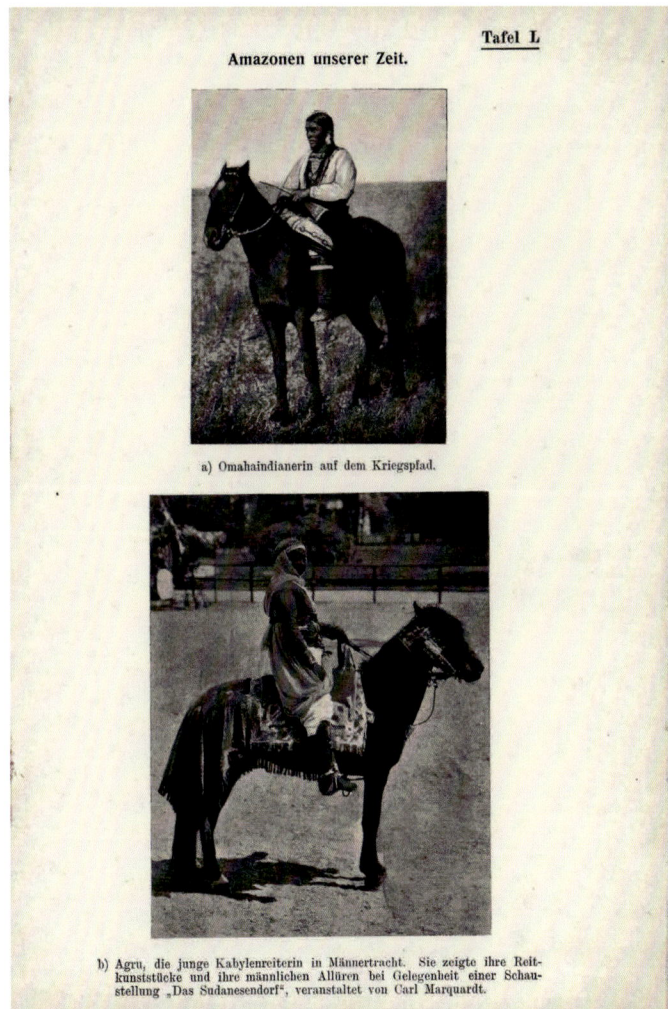

FIGURE 5.14: "Amazons of our time." Hirschfeld's illustrated volume to *Die Transvestiten*, 1912. The captions in the images read: "a) Omaha Indian Woman on the warpath; b) Agra, the young Kabul rider in male clothing. She shows her riding show tricks at the occasion of an exhibition 'The Sudanese Village,' organized by Carl Marquardt."

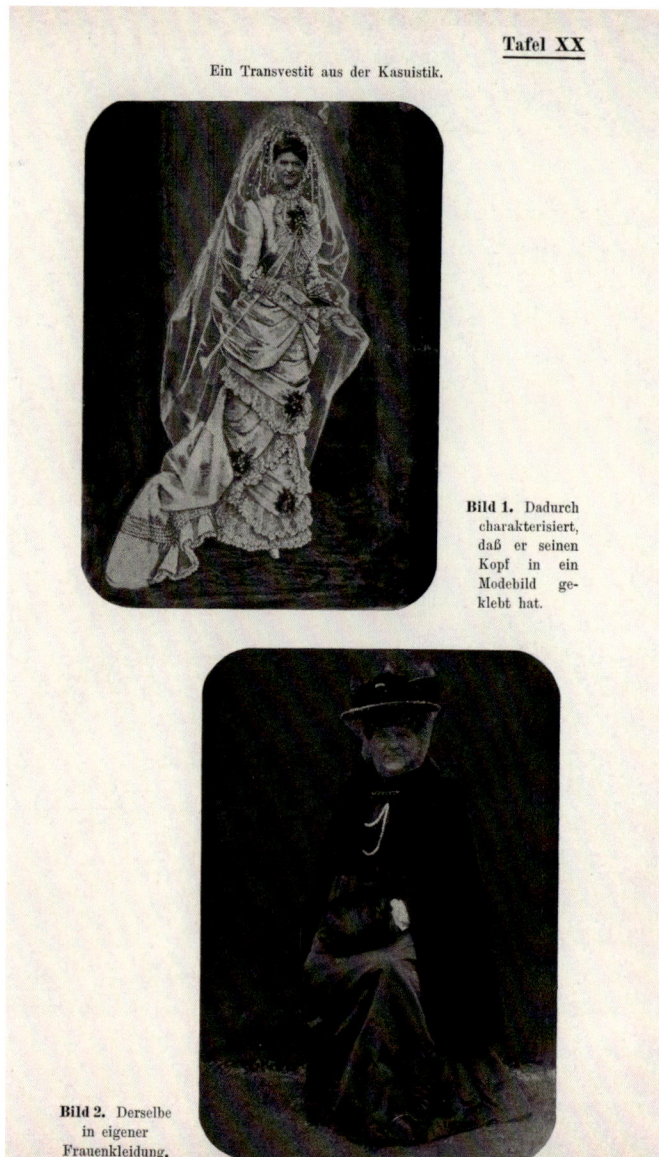

Tafel XX

Ein Transvestit aus der Kasuistik.

Bild 1. Dadurch charakterisiert, daß er seinen Kopf in ein Modebild geklebt hat.

Bild 2. Derselbe in eigener Frauenkleidung.

Figure 5.15: "A transvestite from the casuistic." Hirschfeld's illustrated volume to *Die Transvestiten*, 1912. "Image 1. Characterized by the fact that he has glued his head into a fashion photo. Image 2. The same transvestite in his own female clothing."

altering a photograph in which the soldier appears in military uniform, to instead present him in "cap, gown, and hood, and civilian clothes," thus satisfying the desires of his mother, who could not "'picture'" him in his military outfit. The request reflected, Kriebel notes, the "widespread wartime practice whereby infantrymen at the front affixed photographs of their faces to picture postcards of soldiers in uniform and sent them to family members back home."

Hence even before the war maimed so many bodies and spurred the development of the techniques in plastic surgery that would also have such far-reaching implications for transgender history, photomontage was already emerging with a kind of "magical" power analogous to surgery. For this particular transvestite, this power allowed her to literally picture herself in new clothing – a cutting-and-pasting confirmed as equivalent to reality in the second image in which she actually wears women's clothing. Photography here becomes a means to literally picture what this person has imagined, in a medium that claims to objectively record what it sees, even as the "suture" of photomontage (to use Kriebel's language) remains as a marker of this modern practice for reimagining reality. If we are meant to see past the cutting-and-pasting of the first image, which is how I take the intention behind the image, then the technical, material conditions of the photomontage appear to have disappeared – to have lost meaning, in light of photography's own power to picture identity.

Some of the photographs shown in *TransTrans*, however, mark a contrast to the works of art that Hirschfeld uses as illustrations. We have already discussed one example in two images of Voo-Doo from a later publication of Hirschfeld's that was intended for a popular audience, *Geschlechtskunde*, reproduced in the gallery accompanying Rainer's essay (figures 2.18 and 2.19). Hirschfeld first prints the "Expressive drawing by Voo-Doo," opposite "Feminine form of expression of the same person in dance." While the clothing in the photograph makes the image more unambiguously female, the emphasis on dance locates gender primarily in something performed with the body, rather than in/on the body itself; and while the drawing reveals a truth that the clothing hides, namely Voo-Doo's male genitals, it is also this image in which body, clothing, and self-expression most fully align as a creative fashioning of the self. In the image, the streamers in the drawing become extensions of Voo-Doo's body, the body becomes an exuberant expression of the self, and the drawing itself appears and is presented as an imaginative, creative act. When placed opposite this black-and-white photograph, it also has an effect similar to the erotic transferrals Rainer analyzes. It not only provides vibrant color lost in the medium of photography, which can be read as a critique – at perhaps the most obvious level – of the medium's supposedly mimetic veracity. The image's "expressiveness" also charges this reality with exuberant, imaginative energy, and the repetition of the pose in the photograph, but without clothing, codes the image as a self-revelation.

Two additional examples from Hirschfeld's *Geschlechtskunde* illustrate a similar dynamic, in which cross-dressing as its own mode of gender is recorded as works of art.

In the drawing (figure 5.16), the mask in the figure's left hand covers their breast, almost becoming part of the bodice or – with its shape and shading – a breast and a nipple. This is a mask that has been lowered from the face, plainly revealing the figure's identity while also pointing to the agency the figure has to make this choice. But the mask has transformed into something else: a gesture, a piece of clothing, and a kind of second skin. It thereby holds the potential to heighten gender ambiguity and erotic potential, affectively drawing viewers' attention and curiosity about the figure it depicts. Agency, behavior, clothing, and the body all come together here as intertwined markers of gender. Yet the drawing stages a revelation while calling its terms of identity and recognition into question.

The second image (figure 5.17), a painting, is notable for its signature, which gives this masculine self-presentation a name, "Joseph," and dedicates the work to Hirschfeld.

Hirschfeld reads these works of art as artistic productions of a "feminine" male artist and a "female artist inclined toward masculinity." This interpretation displaces gender creativity from the clothing to the art: in the first image, it is in the drawing itself that Hirschfeld labels "transvestitic"; and in the second, it is the painting that itself "projects" this soul into a body that, in colour and style, can hardly be told apart

Transvestitische Zeichnung eines femininen Künstlers

FIGURE 5.16: "Transvestite drawing of a feminine [male] artist." Hirschfeld, *Geschlechtskunde*, 1930.

from the figure's clothing and the painting itself.

Benjamin, too, followed Hirschfeld's tradition and turned to artistic sources for historical evidence of the natural "phenomenon" he was addressing. He includes an appendix to his book by Richard Green, M.D., on "Transsexualism: Mythological, Historical, and Cross-Cultural Aspects" that offers a broad overview of gender ambiguity, cross-dressing, and gender transformation across cultures, to conclude:

> Clearly, the phenomenon of assuming the role of a member of the opposite sex is neither new nor unique to our culture. Evidence for its existence is traceable to the oldest recorded myths. Diverse cultures present data demonstrating that the phenomenon is widely extant in one form or another and has been incorporated into cultures with varying degrees of social acceptance. Appraisal of contemporary clinical material regarding such patients assumes a fuller significance when cast against the backdrop of this historical and anthropological perspective. Ultimately a comprehensive understanding, evaluation and management of transsexualism will take into account the extensively rooted sources of this psychosexual phenomenon.[47]

Benjamin's book itself might be expected to offer some insight into how a clinically based approach might "take into account"

FIGURE 5.17: "A painting projecting the soul of a female artist inclined toward masculinity with the signature: 'Self-portrait as Joseph,' dedicated to Dr. Magnus Hirschfeld from Mark V., January 1927." Hirschfeld, *Geschlechtskunde*, 1930.

this history. What we find, however, is something quite different. First, Benjamin uses works of art to clearly distinguish his paradigm from earlier, supposedly mistaken attempts to explain the "transsexual phenomenon" and to differentiate it from other instances of nonbinary gender, such as "hermaphroditism." This is his intended use of this material. Second, we find that he uses art to quite literally project gender presentation onto his patients.

To see this, take the following series of images from *The Transsexual Phenomenon*

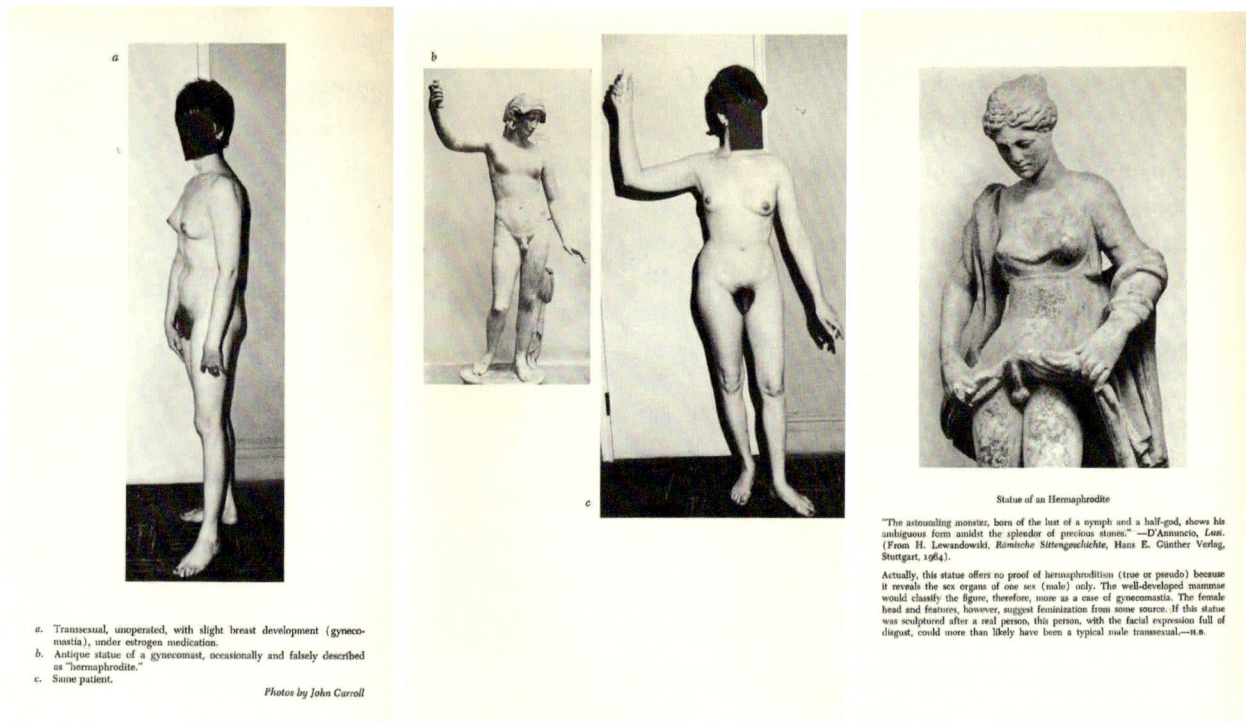

FIGURES 5.18: Three pages from the photographs published in *The Transsexual Phenomenon*, 1966. [left] Set 2: Photos by John Carroll. "a. Transsexual, unoperated, with slight breast development (gynecomastia), under estrogen medication. b. Antique statue of a gynecomast, occasionally and falsely described as a 'hermaphrodite.' c. Same patient. [right] Statue of a Hermaphrodite. Statue of a Hermaphrodite. 'The astounding monster, born of the lust of a nymph and a half-god, shows his ambiguous form amidst the splendor of precious stones.' —D'Annuncia, *Lust* [Desire]. (From H. Lewandowski, *Römische Sittengeschichte* [History of Roman morality], Hans E. Günter Verlag, Stuttgart, 1964). Actually, this statue offers no proof of hermaphroditism (true or pseudo) because it reveals the sex organs of one sex (male) only. The well-developed mammae would classify the figure, therefore, more as a case of gynecomastia. The female head and features, however, suggest feminization from some source. If this statue was sculpted after a real person, this person, with the facial expression full of disgust, could more than likely have been a typical male transsexual. – H.B."
University of Victoria Libraries, Transgender Archives collection. Harry Benjamin, *The Transsexual Phenomenon*. New York: Ace Publishing Corp, 1966. Special Collections call number RC560 C4B46 1966.

(figure 5.18). The statue on the right is an example of earlier traditions representing "hermaphroditism" that would have been well known by Benjamin. Benjamin grew up and was educated in Germany, where he – like Hirschfeld, only seventeen years older – received a classically steeped (medical) education.[48] Benjamin uses this image to push back against this tradition, citing it as a work of art to then discount its value as natural scientific evidence. Yet he does so, in fact, by misreading the work – by meaning to see through the claims it explicitly makes to uncover a different reality.

This becomes clear if we untangle the layers of references and citations that frame the image. Benjamin takes the photograph from a 1964-book written by

Herbert Lewandowski (which Benjamin references) – *Römische Sittengeschichte*, or "Roman moral history" – together with a quote that Lewandowski added to his own reproduction of the photograph: "'The astounding monster, born of the lust of a nymph and a half-god, shows his ambiguous form amidst the splendor of precious stones' – D'Annuncia, *Lust* [Desire]."[49] Benjamin does not offer any commentary of his own on this source or his decision to include Lewandowski's quote-as-gloss. This suggests Benjamin likely accepted at face value the claims the image and quote appear to be making, perhaps even considering them to be state-of-the art cultural criticism. But what does this choice of image and quote appear to say?

Lewandowski was a German Jew with connections to 1920s sexologists, including Hirschfeld.[50] One of his first books, published in 1926 and titled *Das Sexualproblem in der modernen Literatur und Kunst* (The sexual problem in modern literature and art), was an attempt to understand sexuality as a driving force in culture on par with its importance for personality. Following a similar aim, in this later book Lewandowski sets out to complicate the common narrative that moral decline caused the fall of the Roman Empire by providing an account of how Roman culture fused together apparently contrasting elements of culture – heathen cults and Christian worship, or sublime art and political, social decline – to then present this history as a mirror to his own times.

Lewandowski prints this image of a hermaphroditic statue in a chapter on the "Vita sexualis Romanorum," following a discussion of amulets of erect phalluses as cultural objects to which heathens ascribed magic powers, which Lewandowski uses to rebut modern charges that showing such ancient erotic representations might be considered obscene. This discussion of phallic amulets is followed by a discussion of hermaphrodites as a phenomenon that seems to have completely disappeared from "our world" but can be found, if "suppressed," in the history of art. Lewandowski first cites modern sexology (Hirschfeld) and research into hormones as proof of a fundamental "bisexuality" of the human being – a term that in his usage seems to refer, without any disambiguation, both to sex and to sexual preference. This discussion of "hermaphrodites" then quickly becomes a discussion of male homosexuality, specifically of the emperor Hadrian, followed by a discussion of "marriage in antique Rome." The upshot of this sequence is an argument that charges of sexual deviancy in this Roman history must be read primarily as political smears, and in a contrast to the strict moral expectations of chastity placed on Roman women before and after marriage.

The placement and function of this statue in Lewandowski's book thus has very little to do with understanding or depicting hermaphroditism as a phenomenon on its own terms. Rather, it is used to illustrate an argument that turns to hermaphrodites in order to explain heteronormative political and social structures, and to distinguish heathen depictions of sexuality from mere obscenity. The discourse of art that Lewandowski employs to represent hermaphrodites serves a similar function. It is marked, on the one hand, as "aesthetic speculation" reflecting modern fascination with such sexual phenomena and with erotic representations as themselves strange and exotic, if not threatening. This is underscored by Lewandowski's decision to append as the image's caption a quote from the first novel published by the Italian decadent writer, Gabriele D'Annunzio, referenced however by its German title, "Lust" or "desire."[51] Lewandowski nevertheless also points to this art as reflections of a truth that he considers modern sexology and medicine to have now more fully revealed – if only we could see past its exoticizing, othering, aesthetic fantasy. The implicit point is that what we should see instead is the social and political function of this fantasy – and specifically, of fantasy that springs of desire to produce an "astounding" yet amazing "monster" – in defining heterosexual norms of marriage and male political power.

Benjamin's decision to use this image and caption without any critical commentary can be taken as evidence that Lewandowski's norms and assumptions also structured Benjamin's thinking about gender and sexuality, or art and science. At the same time, however, what Benjamin does make of this reference only intensifies a reading of the image as a fantasy at odds with "normal" or "healthy" social reality. For one thing, Benjamin's gloss completely inverts the literary caption that Lewandowski took from D'Anunzio: "Lust." The German word can mean lust, desire, or pleasure. Taken by itself as a caption to this statue, the German word "Lust" asks

us to read the meaning of the work on multiple levels: physically, in the erection; in the figure's gaze at its own body and its erection; and in the desire or pleasure that the sculpture might arouse in us as an erotic object and a work of art. But in viewing the sculpture as a depiction of a "typical male transsexual" rather than a work of art, Benjamin gives the impression that he is seeing through this aesthetic-erotic pleasure to find a facial expression of "disgust" – an emotion, he writes, that many male transsexuals felt toward their genitals.

It is significant that this is the only erection we find in Benjamin's book, since showing an actual erection might have brought charges of obscenity. What we have here is a displacement of *Lust* – including eroticism and naked sexuality – onto a work of art, to distinguish it from the "transsexual phenomenon" Benjamin is trying to demystify and treat as a natural medical condition. Even his choice to leave the German word "Lust" untranslated contributes to this aim: *Lust* is not lust, which in English carries a much narrower meaning and is how English speakers would undoubtedly read this word. Benjamin was a native speaker of German; he knew what he was doing. What Benjamin sees in the *Lust* of this figure's nonbinary body and sexuality is a pathological lust reflecting underlying disgust.

The statue must also be read together with the triptych that Benjamin published on the facing page. There are photographs in Benjamin's papers that show various attempts to re-create the exact pose of this statue. We do not know if this was at Benjamin's direction or if it was the idea of the person it depicts. But it was obviously staged to make a point. In her discussion of photography and shame, Kathrin Peters refers to a medical tradition of photography in which women copy neoclassical sculptures.[52] I have no doubt that Benjamin must have at least been aware of this tradition. Peters argues that the intention of this practice is paradoxical: copying a work of art is intended to overcome the "conventional" shame taught by culture, allowing a presentation of the body in its naturalness and lifelikeness. Peters situates this practice in the context of how medicine, prompted in part by the photographic documentation of nonbinary bodies, developed visual strategies for constructing the beautiful body, and specifically the female body, as "normal."[53]

Benjamin's photographs echo this practice; they are likely meant to ennoble the body they present, showing it as a "natural" occurrence while also aligning it with the ideals of beauty the statue represents and the evidence it is taken to give that transsexuality is a naturally occurring, historical phenomenon. The posing might also have been intended to help the patient overcome the shame of exhibiting her entirely naked body, with its male genitals and enlarged breasts. But as a prelude to the statue of *Lust*, the photos say more. They stage a moment of exposure expressly meant to be sexual – yet not shameful, not disgusting. Benjamin means to present a modern diagnosis of this "phenomenon" of transsexualism in contrast to the false, mythical understanding of hermaphroditism that he also sees in this statue. Yet his

interpretation of the statue as *Lust* reminds us of the central premise of his new category: "transsexualism" is not about clothing, but about the body itself. Just as the statue pulls up its dress to reveal its shocking, exciting sexual secret, we as readers of the book might wonder what psychological secrets are left hiding beneath the neoclassical beauty that adorns this naked body like a gown. The arrangement of all four images practically invites us to become psychosexual voyeurs.

Cross-dressing here becomes undressing – a laying bare of the body that makes it visible as transsexual and available for treatment. This is a sense of sex that clothing might hide, and which clothing cannot treat, and Benjamin undresses it to show it. But he then paradoxically re-dresses it, in the cloak of art, in order to strip it of supposedly mistaken social conventions and reveal what he takes to be its natural history. Art functions here as a norm laid upon the body, to which the nonbinary body must conform to regain its natural beauty, rather than as means of self-expression or self-fashioning. Or, as with Benjamin's actor/actress, successful treatment makes it possible to turn oneself into a work of art, apart from the threat of gender performance as masquerade. Yet hiding beneath this surface, as Benjamin's analysis of this statue shows, there is always the danger of arousal, desire, and disgust, of pathological "wish-fulfillment."

Hirschfeld's depictions of cross-dressing as transvestitism tell a slightly different story. The truth they aim to depict can be seen only through the arrangement of multiple photographs, but this truth still remains elusive, defined as a hidden desire. Conversely, single images often hide or fail to show the act of crossing over, or they invest it with the threat of deception or with outright ridicule. Here, too, we find works of art that reflect a power to perform rather than to picture gender, and it is these images that most strikingly fail to fit within the photographic medical framing Hirschfeld and Benjamin both employ.

In the final essay of this book, we now turn to our exhibition – to how we ourselves came to look beyond the gaze of medical diagnosis inherent to so many of these images and focus instead on the practices with which they were made, the ways in which they were shared and made public, and the private stories they leave untold.

GALLERY NOTES: Photomontage of Lili Elbe

1   Niels Hoyer, ed., *Lili Elbe: Ein Mensch wechselt sein Geschlecht: Eine Lebensbeichte* (Dresden: Carl Reissner Verlag, 1932); Niels Hoyer, ed., Man into Woman: An Authentic Record of a Change of Sex, trans. H. J. Stenning (New York: E. P. Dutton & Co., Inc., 1933); Niels Hoyer, ed., *Man into Woman: The First Sex Change: A Portrait of Lili Elbe: The True and Remarkable Transformation of the Painter Einar Wegener*, trans. James Stenning (London: Blue Boat Books, 2004).

2   For a history of Dorchen, named at birth as Rudolf Richter, see Herrn and Taylor, "Transvestites/Transsexuals," esp. 181–2. 3 Sabine Meyer, *"Wie Lili zu einem richtigen Mädchen wurde": Lili Elbe: Zur Konstruktion von Geschlecht und Identität zwischen Medialisierung, Regulierung und Subjektivierung* (Bielefeld: transcript, 2015). For a briefer summary, see Rainer Herrn and Annette F. Timm, "Elbe, Lili (1882–1931)," in *Global Encyclopedia of Lesbian, Gay, Bisexual and Transgender LGBTQ History*, vol. 3 (Farmington Hills, MI: Charles Scribner & Sons, 2019), 500–502.

NOTES TO CHAPTER 5

1   Magnus Hirschfeld and Max Tilke, *Der erotische Verkleidungstrieb (Die Transvestiten)*, illustrated volume (Berlin: Alfred Pulvermacher & Co., 1912), 100–15. In the account that Hirscheld relates, J. notes that she was teased as a child with names like "'Mädli,' 'Mädchengesicht' oder 'Johanna'" ("'little girl,' 'sissy-face,' or 'Johanna'." *Die Transvestiten*, 105; and *The Transvestites*, 87, translation modified), and J. tells of a scene in San Fransisco where she is called Jenny, at least in private: "Wer war froher als ich, wenn die Frau sagte: 'Jenny – die weibliche Anrede war mir, wenn wir allein waren, lieber – Rich. und ich wollen ausgehen oder gar verreisen" ("Who was happier than I when the woman said, 'Jenny – I liked to be called by my feminine name when we were alone – Rich. and I want to go out or go on a trip." *Die Transvestiten*, 110; and *The Transvestites*, 90).

2   Susan Stryker, *Transgender History* (Berkeley, CA: Seal Press, 2008), 42–43.

3   The original German reads: "der heftige Drang … in der Kleidung desjenigen Geschlechts zu leben, dem die Betreffenden ihrem Körperbau nach *nicht* angehören. Der Kürze halber wollen wir diesen Trieb als *transvestititischen* (von trans = entgegengesetzt und vestis = Kleid) bezeichnen. Dabei sei vornherein betont … dass das Kleid uns hier nicht … '*als totes Ding*' entgegentritt, dass die Art des Kostüms nicht die beliebige Auesserlichkeit einer willkürlichen Laune ist, sondern als *Ausdrucksform der inneren Persönlichkeit*, als *Zeichen* ihrer Sinnesart zu gelten hat." Emphasis in the original. Magnus Hirschfeld, *Die Transvestiten: Eine Untersuchung über den erotischen Verkleidungstrieb* (Berlin: Alfred Pulvermacher & Co., 1910), 159.

4   See chapter 3, "Gesten der Scham," in Kathrin Peters, *Rätselbilder des Geschlechts: Körperwissen und Medialität um 1900* (Zurich: Diaphenes, 2018), 85–108. See also Katharina Sykora, "Umkleidekabinen des Geschlechts: Sexualmedizinische Fotografie im frühen 20. Jahrhundert," *Fotogeschichte: Beiträge zur Geschichte und Ästhetik der Fotografie* 24, no. 92 (2004): 15–30, who emphasizes how the images were staged or constructed in ways to avoid voyeurism and guide the gaze toward a scientific perspective. See also the various discussions of Fredericke Schmidt in Michael Thomas Taylor, Annette F. Timm, and Rainer Herrn, eds, *Not Straight from Germany: Sexual Publics and Sexual Citizenship Since Magnus Hirschfeld* (Ann Arbor: University of Michigan Press, 2017), and especially the essay by Sabine Kriebel, "Sexology's Beholders: The Exhibition *PopSex!* in Calgary," 80–2.

5   In other words, my sense of this collage of John O. is that it resists this medicalizing impulse, and that as the only image of nudity in *Die Transvestiten*, it must be read separately from Hirschfeld's *Geschlechts-Übergänge* (1905). In this regard, I also slightly disagree with Katie Sutton's perspective on these photos. Sutton lists this arrangement as an example of how some photos of transvestites used by Hirschfeld are to be read primarily in a medicalized context, "their aesthetics governed less by the photographed subject than by the scientific

priorities of the researcher and targeted more obviously toward Hirschfeld's medical readers"; Katie Sutton, "Sexology's Photographic Turn: Visualizing Trans Identity in Interwar Germany," *Journal of the History of Sexuality* 27, no. 3 (2018): 442–79, here 464.

6   Hirschfeld uses the same technique of combining images to portray tranvestites in the second volume of *Sexualpatholgie*, but this time as a triptych of the person dressed in female clothing, naked, and then in men's clothing. See Magnus Hirschfeld, *Sexualpathologie: Ein Lehrbuch für Ärzte und Studierende*, vol. 2 (Bonn: A. Marcus & E. Webers Verlag, 1918), 144.

7   Jordan Bear and Kate Palmer Albers, *Before-and-After Photography: Histories and Contexts* (New York: Bloomsbury Academic, 2017), 2.

8   Ibid.

9   Allan Sekula, "The Body and the Archive," *October* 39 (Winter 1986): 3–64.

10   On the use of photography in medical contexts, see especially (in addition to Peters), Molly Rogers, *Delia's Tears: Race, Science, and Photography in Nineteenth-Century America* (New Haven, CT: Yale University Press, 2010); Gunnar Schmidt, *Anamorphotische Körper: Medizinische Bilder vom Menschen im 19. Jahrhundert* (Cologne: Böhlau, 2001); Anne Maxwell, *Picture Imperfect: Photography and Eugenics, 1879–1940* (Eastbourne: Sussex Academic Press, 2008); Jennifer Tucker, *Nature Exposed: Photography as Eyewitness in Victorian Science* (Baltimore, MD: Johns Hopkins University Press, 2005); and Ludmilla Jordanova, *Sexual Visions: Images of Gender in Science and Medicine between the Eighteenth and Twentieth Centuries* (Madison, WI: University of Wisconsin Press, 1989). For a perspective attentive to queer histories of sexuality, see Dana Seitler, "Queer Physiognomies; Or, How Many Ways Can We Do the History of Sexuality?," *Criticism* 46, no. 1 (2004): 71–102. For the context of German sexology specifically, see also David James Prickett, "Magnus Hirschfeld and the Photographic (Re)Invention of the 'Third Sex,'" in *Visual Culture in Twentieth-Century Germany: Text as Spectacle*, edited by Gail Finney (Bloomington: Indiana University Press,

2006), 103–19. For a broader consideration of photography and the claims it makes to provide historical evidence, see John Tagg, *The Disciplinary Frame: Photographic Truths and the Capture of Meaning* (Minneapolis: University of Minnesota Press, 2009), as well as Tagg, *The Burden of Representation: Essays on Photographies and Histories* (London: Macmillan, 1988). For the context of criminal archives, see Susanne Regener, *Fotografische Erfassung: Zur Geschichte medialer Konstruktionen des Kriminellen* (Munich: Fink, 1999).

11 See Shawn Michelle Smith, *American Archives: Gender, Race, and Class in Visual Culture* (Princeton: Princeton University Press, 1999); Shawn Michelle Smith, *Photography on the Color Line: W .E. B. Du Bois, Race, and Visual Culture* (Durham and London: Duke University Press, 2004); and Maurice O. Wallace and Shawn Michelle Smith, *Pictures and Progress: Early Photography and the Making of African American Identity* (Durham and London: Duke University Press, 2012). See also Lisa Bloom, *With Other Eyes: Looking at Race and Gender in Visual Culture* (Minneapolis: University of Minnesota Press, 1999).

12 Donna West Brett, *Photography and Ontology: Unsettling Images* (New York: Routledge, Taylor & Francis Group, 2019), 5.

13 Elizabeth Edwards, *Raw Histories: Photographs, Anthropology, and Museums* (Oxford: Berg, 2001), here 13 and 18. See also Elizabeth Edwards, *Uncertain Images: Museums and the Work of Photographs* (London: Routledge, 2014).

14 Following Susan Stryker, Persson Perry Baumgartinger has emphasized this genealogical method for transgender studies; see *Trans Studies: Historische, begriffliche und aktivistische Aspekte* (Vienna: Zaglossus, 2017), especially 39–44.

15 See Roland Barthes, *Camera Lucida: Reflections on Photography* (New York: Hill and Wang, 1980); and Susan Sontag, *Regarding the Pain of Others* (New York: Picador/Farrar, Straus and Giroux, 2003).

16 Elspeth Brown and Thy Phu, *Feeling Photography* (Durham and London: Duke

University Press, 2014), especially their introduction, 1–28.

17 Ibid., 3.

18 Brown has further developed this perspective in Elspeth H. Brown, *Work! A Queer History of Modeling* (Durham: Duke University Press, 2019).

19 See Sabine Kriebel and Andrés Mario Zervigón, "Introduction," in *Photography and Doubt* (London: Routledge, 2016), 2. For a concise summary of how various theorists have written about photography, as a medium "dependent on technological change" and characterized by "multiplicity and malleability," see Sabine Kriebel, "Theories of Photography: A Short History," in *Photography Theory*, ed. James Elkins, 3–49, here 4 (New York: Routledge, 2007).

20 Peters, *Rätselbilder des Geschlechts*, 20; all quotes in this paragraph are from this page.

21 "In Sachen Geschlecht dingfest zu machen, was nicht dingfest war, sichtbar zu machen, was nicht sichtbar war, zu vereindeutigen, was nicht eindeutig war. Aber gerade dann, wenn immer genauer hingesehen werden konnte, öffneten sich zugleich immer größere Bereiche des Nicht- oder Noch-Nicht-Wissens, der Nicht-Sichtbarkeit; Bereiche, die wiederum mit neuen Visualisierungstechniken geschlossen werden sollten. In diesem Prozess stellten geschlechtliche Uneindeutigkeiten gewissermaßen Präzedenzfälle dar, von denen ausgehend sich Aussagen über das 'Wesen' des Geschlechts ganz allgemein treffen lassen sollten." Peters, *Rätselbilder des Geschlechts*, 20.

22 See chapter 3, "Gesten der Scham," in *Rätselbilder des Gechlechts*, 85–108; the remaining quotes in this paragraph are from page 86.

23 For such a view emphasizing visual violence, see especially Susanne Regener, *Visuelle Gewalt: Menschenbilder aus der Psychiatrie des 20. Jahrhunderts* (Bielefeld: transcript, 2010).

24 "Wer sich schämt, weiß sehr genau, dass er oder sie gesehen wird, anders als der Voyeur, der davon ausgeht, dass sein Blick nicht erwidert wird, dass er selbst nicht sichtbar ist (oder vielleicht doch?)" Peters, *Rätselbilder des Gechlechts*, 86.

25 For three recent books documenting and reflecting on this ongoing practice, see Mark Seliger, *On Christopher Street: Transgender Stories* (New York: Rizzoli, 2016); Dave Naz, *Genderqueer: And Other Gender Identities* (Los Angeles: A Barnacle Book/Rare Bird Books, 2014); and Jess T. Dugan, *To Survive on This Shore: Photographs and Interviews with Transgender and Gender Nonconforming Older Adults* (Heidelberg: Kehrer, 2018).

26 Jay Prosser, *Second Skins: The Body Narratives of Transsexuality* (New York: Columbia University Press, 1998).

27 Jay Prosser, *Second Skins*, especially 230. This fact also means, Prosser argues, that one imperative of work in transgender history is to sustain a truth of individual experience in the face of how that experience is expressed, reflected, and often displaced or otherwise refracted through representations. Or similarly, as contributors to *TSQ: Transgender Studies Quarterly* have noted, we need to be attentive to the specific consequences that archives and historical practices of archiving have for transgender histories. For instance, K. J. Rawson glosses the term "archive" like this: "In its radical recontextualization of historical materials, the archive emerges as a discrete object of selection and representation that always involves silences and exclusions. This cycle of inclusion and exclusion, of representation and misrepresentation, is the permanent shadow of any trans archival project, even digital ones; while transgender archives fight historical neglect, silences, and misrepresentations, the selection and discrimination involved in archiving creates a residual silencing of others. And what of the history that is hoped to be forgotten? Transgender people who transition their gender presentation may feel betrayed by the archive's stubborn and insistent refusal to forget. Thus, while archiving transgender materials is important for community and personal identity formation, political advocacy, and historical memory, it should be treated as a powerful mechanism of memory and identity with far-reaching impacts." *TSQ: Transgender Studies Quarterly* 1, nos 1–2 (2014): 25. See also the special issue on "Archives and Archiving," *TSQ: Transgender Studies Quarterly* 2, no. 4 (November 2015).

28 Jennifer Blessing, *A Rrose is a rrose is a rrose: Gender Performance in Photography* (New York: Guggenheim Museum, 1997), 8.

29 Benjamin, *The Transsexual Phenomenon: A Scientific Report on Transsexualism and Sex Conversion in the Human Male and Female* (New York: The Julian Press, 1966), 11–12.

30 For a brief overview of these categories from a medical and popular perspective, see Rainer Herrn and Michael Thomas Taylor, "Transvestites/Transsexuals," ed. Howard H. Chiang, *Global Encyclopedia of Lesbian, Gay, Bisexual and Transgender (LGBTQ) History*, vol. 3 (Farmington Hills, MI: Charles Scribner & Sons, 2019)

31 In the 1980s, Benjamin developed the standards of care for medical gender transition that carried his name until 2011 and are still being used today in a modified form as the *Standards of Care for the Health of Transsexual, Transgender, and Gender-Nonconforming People* published by the World Professional Association for Transgender Health (7th version, 2012). See also Herrn and Taylor, "Transvestites/Transsexuals," 1643. These standards reflected clinical practices that developed in the Netherlands in connection with many of Benjamin's patients, as Alex's essay retraces. In contrast to Benjamin's approach, the current standards do not require that individuals gain medical approval or live for a period of time in the other sex before beginning treatment, emphasizing instead that medical professionals should obtain informed consent before beginning treatment; and in contrast to Benjamin's approach of "identifying appropriate candidates for sex-reassignment," the standards also emphasize that "while many individuals need both hormone therapy and surgery to alleviate their gender dysphoria, others need only one of these treatment options and some need neither" (8). The guidelines point to a diversity in how individuals understand their own gender identity as the basis for treatment of gender dysphoria.

32 Hirschfeld and Tilke, *Der erotische Verkleidungstrieb*.

33 See Samuel Clowes Huneke, "Death Wish: Suicide and Stereotype in the Gay Discourses of Imperial and Weimar Germany," *New German Critique* 46, no. 1 (2019): 127–66.

34 Michael Pettit, "Becoming Glandular: Endocrinology, Mass Culture, and Experimental Lives in the Interwar Age," *American Historical Review* 118, no. 4 (2013): 1052–76.

35 Ibid., 1055.

36 Benjamin, *The Transsexual Phenomenon*, 12.

37 Indeed, bourgeois theatre in the eighteenth century – with its anti-theatrical ideals of natural or genuine representation, i.e., of representation that negated or denied its address to the audience and its very nature as artificial, and with its focus on tragic plots revolving around the exposure and elimination of female characters – developed precisely together with this gendered double-bind of theatrical representation. See Christopher Wild, *Theater der Keuschheit – Keuschheit des Theaters: Zu einer Geschichte der (Anti) Theatralität von Gryphius bis Kleist* (Freiburg: Rombach, 2003). More broadly, as Paul Friedland has argued, the prejudice against "actors" as threats to a democratically conceived public sphere based in authenticity, transparency, and reason has a long historical tradition, reflecting the fact that theatre has often appeared to be an evil twin of politics. For emerging ideals of democracy in the eighteenth century, calling politics "theatrical" often meant insinuating that it was driven by behind-the-scenes machinations, that is was all rhetoric, manipulation, or disingenuous, and that it was incapable of truly representing the body politic; similarly, people who could act for a living were not trusted to act honestly in public and politics. See Paul Friedland, *Political Actors: Representative Bodies and Theatricality in the Age of the French Revolution* (Ithaca: Cornell University Press, 2002).

38 These have been published in English as Karl Heinrich Ulrichs, "Four Letters to His Kinsfolk," in *Sodomites and Urnings: Homosexual Representations in Classic German Journals* (Binghamton, NY: Harrington Park Press, 2006), 1–20. Ulrichs was quickly claimed by the emerging homosexual movement, and he thought of himself as a different kind of sex, an "Urning," characterized by having a female soul in a male body. Of course, however, this description might also fit within a genealogy of transgender identities.

39 Benjamin, *The Transsexual Phenomenon*, 177–8.

40 See Sekula, "The Body and the Archive," 27. See also Peter Doyle, "Hard Looks: Faces, Bodies, Lives in Early Sydney Police Portrait Photography," in *Photography and Ontology: Unsettling Images*, edited by Donna West Brett, 56–71, who shows that "tricksters" were vastly overrepresented in one Sydney photographic archive, reflecting worries about "confidence trickery" as a "particularly modern, urban type of crime" (59) arising in the context of a new "dispensation of mobility and fluid identity" (60).

41 For a brief discussion of this point, see Rainer Herrn and Michael Thomas Taylor, "Magnus Hirschfeld's Interpretation of the Japanese Onnagata as Transvestites," *Journal of the History of Sexuality* 27, no. 1 (2018): 63–100, esp. 80–1.

42 Katie Sutton's analysis of the images in this illustrated volume to *Die Transvestiten* offers an excellent discussion of the photographic practices that informed their production and the interplay of subjectivity and medicalization they represent. She also situates the images in the context of queer history and studies of photography and the distinctive modes of analysis they claim. Sutton, "Sexology's Photographic Turn."

43 Charles Darwin, *The Descent of Man, and Selection in Relation to Sex* (New York: Penguin, 2004; 2nd ed. originally 1879), see Part III, "Sexual Selection in Relation to Man, and Conclusion," 621 ff.; here 675.

44 Herrn, *Schnittmuster des Geschlechts*, 55.

45 For one discussion of how Hirschfeld was publicly perceived, see Rainer Herrn, Michael Thomas Taylor, and Annette F. Timm, "Magnus Hirschfeld's Institute for Sexual Science: A Visual Sourcebook," in *Not Straight from Germany: Sexual Publics and Sexual Citizenship since Magnus Hirschfeld*, eds., Michael Thomas Taylor, Annette F. Timm, and Rainer Herrn (Ann Arbor, MI: Michigan University Press, 2017), 37–9.

46 Sabine Kriebel, *Revolutionary Beauty: The Radical Photomontages of John Heartfield* (Berkeley: University of California Press, 2014), 1–6. On Heartfield, see also Andrés Mario Zervigón, *John Heartfield and the Agitated*

Image: Photography, Persuasion, and the Rise of Avant-Garde Photomontage (Chicago: University of Chicago Press, 2012).

47   Benjamin, *The Transsexual Phenomenon*, 184–5.

48   For Renaissance views of hermaphroditism, see Thomas Laqueur, *Making Sex: Body and Gender from the Greeks to Freud* (Cambridge, MA and London: Harvard University Press, 1990), 135–42.

49   Herbert Lewandowski, *Römische Sittengeschichte* (Stuttgart: Hans E. Günther Verlag, 1964).

50   See "Lewandowski, Herbert," in *Lexikon deutsch-jüdischer Autoren*, vol. 15 Kurw–Lewa, ed. Archiv Bibliographica Judaica and Renate Heuer (Munich: K. G. Saur, 2007), 411–24, here 411–12. Lewandowski was a prolific German writer (he wrote at least seventy books) who emigrated to Holland in 1923 and then France in 1937, where he was interned as a German citizen when the war broke out. He escaped, however, to Switzerland where he remained until he died, nearly 100 years old, in 1996. Lewandowski attended the 1932 congress of

the World League of Sexual Reform in Brno, Czechoslovakia. See also Donald A. Prater, "Der Haltlose: Zum Tod des Schriftstellers Herbert Lewandowski," *Neue Züricher Zeitung*, 21 Mar 1996. Lewandowski himself provides an account of his escape from France to Switzerland in "Herbert Lewandowski: Lyon und Flucht in die Schweiz," in *Herbert Lewandowski – Lee van Dovski: Festschrift zum 92. Geburtstag*, ed. Peter Adamski, 101–14 (Kassel: Geschichtswerkstatt am Friedrichsgymnasium, 1988).

51   *Il Piacere* was published in 1889 and translated into German in 1898.

52   Peters, *Rätselbilder des Geschlechts*, 105–8.

53   On this aesthetic construction of gender, see also Kathrin Peters, "Sichtbarkeit und Körper: Wilhelm von Gloeden, eine Revision," in *Zeigen und/oder Beweisen? Die Fotografie als Kulturtechnik und Medium des Wissens*, ed. Herta Wolf, 283–305 (Berlin: de Gruyter, 2016), as well as Kathrin Peters, "Anatomy Is Sublime: The Photographic Activity of Wilhelm von Gloeden and Magnus Hirschfeld," in Taylor, Timm, and Herrn, eds, *Not Straight from Germany*, 170–90.

TransTrans: Exhibiting Trans Histories

Michael Thomas Taylor

For us as curators, *TransTrans*, the name we chose for our exhibition in Calgary in 2016, means many things. It refers, of course, to the transgender transatlantic histories that give this book its title. It also points to transvestite and transsexual, the two medical terms and identities structuring these histories. The doubling of trans further signifies our intention to avoid telling any single history of trans identities but to instead explore moments of transfer, transformation, translation, transposition, transgression, and transparency. Instead of presenting a heroic story of influence and progress, our intention has been to emphasize processes of rupture, renewal, and re-appropriation. We have aimed to make visible the uneven ways that knowledge about sexuality moves across time and geographical boundaries through imagery and terminology.

Like this book, restaging *TransTrans* in Berlin after our first exhibition in Calgary continued the back-and-forth movement across the Atlantic that we trace in our research, following how these transgender stories returned to Holland and Morocco after traveling from Europe to the United States. The previous chapters of this book have emphasized

Our intention was to make visible the networks that the images reflect and the future histories that they made possible.

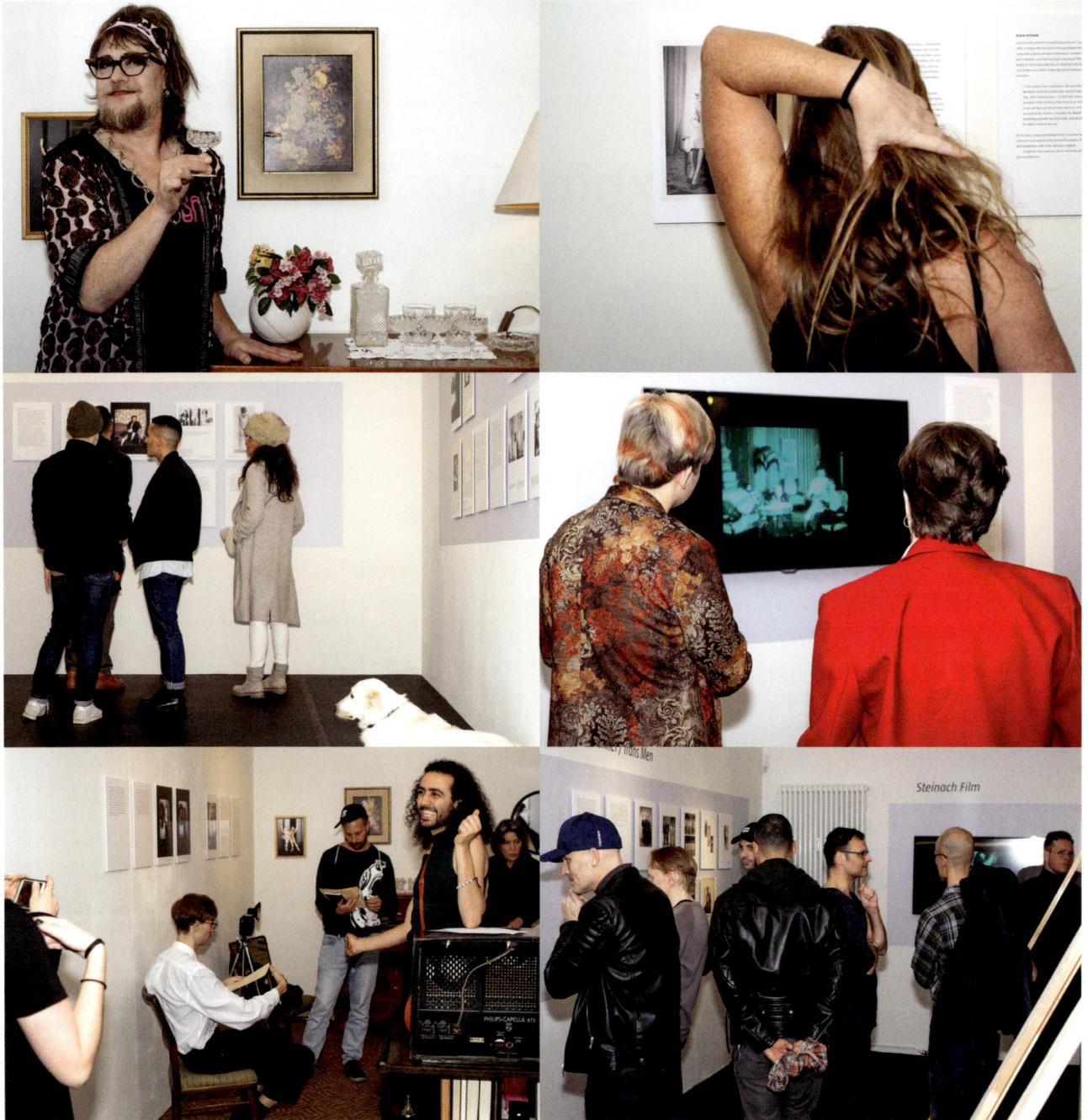

Figure 6.1: Photographs from opening of *TransTrans* in Berlin, 7 November 2019. Photos: Paul Sleev.

that deep layers of interpersonal and cross-national relationships lie behind the images we are exhibiting. As we saw it, making visible these connections and the stories they tell posed several challenges. One was to represent the networks of individuals and institutions that produced the images. Another was to show how images had migrated between contexts and sources, reflecting a range of interests and intentions. We hoped that bringing out these two dimensions would clearly document the medicalized forms of looking and normative framings reflected in many of the images and how they were used, while also highlighting how the origins of the images in other practices and discourses situate them at odds to these framings.

Our network wall, which we discussed in the introduction to this book, was one first solution to these dilemmas. Another solution was to divide both exhibitions into two sections or areas. One area of the exhibition was devoted to the public circulation of images in print sources, including excerpts from the *Steinach Film* (discussed in a gallery in this book), and another was devoted to private networks of trans individuals sharing images and stories. In both exhibitions, this more privately focused area of the exhibition centered on a reimagination of the living room where Carla Erskine took pictures of her friends. In both exhibitions, we also created or commissioned a film in

Floorplan

FIGURE 6.2: Exhibition Layout of *TransTrans* in Calgary

FIGURE 6.3: "Trans Histories in Print," north wall. Photo credit: Dave Brown, LCR Photo Services, University of Calgary.

which people today respond to the historical material in the show. I will discuss all of these elements below.

In Berlin, the dual exhibition structure was realized by placing the public images from these transgender histories along the outside walls of the gallery, with the living room and the commissioned film occupying the centre of the space. In Calgary, we made use of two separate spaces in the gallery, which we called "Trans Histories in Print" and "Trans Circles of Knowledge."

As the layout diagram in figure 6.2 shows, the exhibition in Calgary also had two points of entry, corresponding to these two rooms. This was an accidental

FIGURE 6.4: "Trans Histories in Print," view of south wall towards entrance. Photo credit: Dave Brown, LCR Photo Services, University of Calgary.

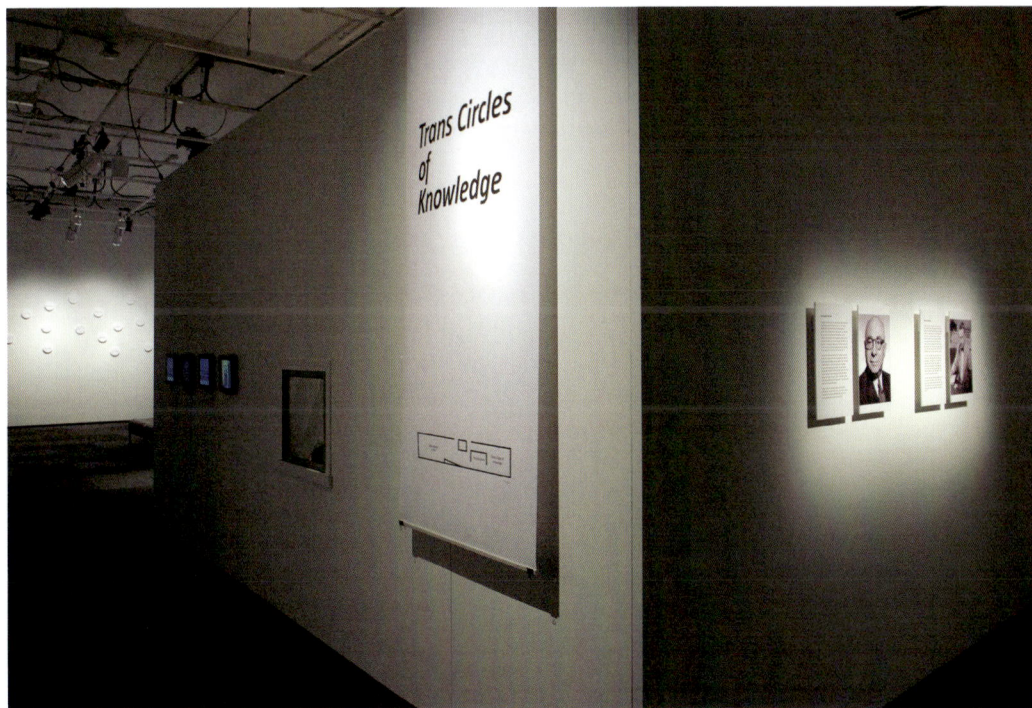

FIGURE 6.5: Entrance to "Trans Circles of Knowledge." Photo credit: Dave Brown, LCR Photo Services, University of Calgary.

FIGURE 6.6: Network Wall in Berlin. Photo credit: Paul Sleev.

FIGURE 6.7: Entrance to "Four Trans Stories" in Calgary. Photo credit: Dave Brown, LCR Photo Services, University of Calgary.

FIGURE 6.8: Rows of "Medical Publications" and "Popular Magazines" in Calgary. Photo credit: Dave Brown, LCR Photo Services, University of Calgary.

constraint of the space, dictated by the location of an elevator shaft. However, we took this constraint as an occasion to underscore how the stories we meant to tell are not linear but exist in layers and networks. And in both exhibitions, the network wall was the most prominent element encountered by visitors upon entering the space. In Berlin, it was the first thing visitors saw, visible through the entryway into the room. And in Calgary, it was located directly across the wall from the entrance to "Trans Histories in Print." It offered an immediate visual contrast and anchor point for our decision to depict four trans stories around the elevator shaft – Otto Spengler, J., Carla Erskine, and Katharina T. – while also highlighting how the images we showed moved between contexts and archives.

(The images of Otto Spengler are discussed in this book in the image gallery on pages 13–17.) The wall traced these networks by means of threads between its subjects, and it emphasized the place of trans individuals in these histories with red lines emanating from their nodes.

To present the images that circulated in print, we designed thematic clusters with the images in two rows. These clusters focused on topics in this history, such as "Gender Play," "Passing," or "Artists," or on key moments and stories, such as the Benjamin-Hirschfeld-Kinsey connection, how Benjamin used Carla's images in his book, or the stories of the trans women who had surgery in Amsterdam between 1954 and 1955. The structure of two rows also allowed us to make visible the different contexts in which images circulated. On the top row, we showed images from medical and scientific sources and the archive of the Kinsey Institute. On the bottom row, we showed images from popular sources, mainly consisting of the magazines published by Friedrich Radszuweit in the 1920s and early 1930s. These magazines included *Das 3. Geschlecht* (The 3rd sex), as well as *Die Insel* (The island), which was aimed at gay men, and *Die Freundin* (The girlfriend), which was aimed at lesbians.

Three key points from Rainer's essay should be emphasized here. First, both these medical and popular publications used images from a range of sources that included historical depictions, fashion photographs, publicity materials for performing artists, and personal photographs provided by patients or readers. Second, the same or very similar photographs were often published in both medical and popular contexts, framed accordingly in very different ways. In Radszuweit's publications, for instance, the same photographs were often published in different magazines aimed at very different audiences, which entirely changed the identity being ascribed to the person in the image. The same image may appear to depict a gay man in one context and a "female transvestite" in another. Finally, these reframings almost always reflected the normative judgements of editors and/or authors. For Hirschfeld and Benjamin, this normative framing concerned the scientific explication of a natural phenomenon,

arguments for popular understanding and acceptance intended to spur social reform, and possibilities of medical treatment. For the popular magazines, two main concerns were issues of passing – rooted primarily in norms about bourgeois respectability – and sensationalist or erotic appeals to readers.

But it is equally important to note that how these images were used generally diverged from the intentions with which they were made. Both Hirschfeld and these popular magazines published explicit calls to readers to send in photographs. The images that readers sent in reflect a range of practices and intentions; but as we have documented in this book, most of these were not medical or scientific. Here, however, images of trans men are an exception. As we discuss in our image gallery, depictions of trans men are relatively rare in published and archival sources from this time – in part because it was much more acceptable for female-bodied individuals to dress and act in masculine ways, and in part because the categories of identity ascribed to them were often more fluid and less visible than those ascribed to homosexuals, effeminate men, or trans women. Thus not only are many of the images we have of trans women explicitly medicalized and pathological, but they are also not balanced by other representations.

The way in which many of the images were collected, however, does indicate that some form of implicit or explicit consent for them to be published was given by those who sent them in. For the images in Benjamin's book, for instance, we have signed consent forms archived in his files.

Yet the intentions of the editors in asking for these images varied. When Hirschfeld asked for images for his illustrated volume, he framed his request in a universalizing way: "For this work does indeed follow the good and worthy purpose of creating understanding and just judgement for so many of our fellow humans who have been misrecognized in their own, unique way of being."[1] This perspective is reflective of Hirschfeld's general strategy to couch his claims for minority sexual rights in terms of human rights, though as Katie Sutton surmises, he likely also had commercial motives.[2] This universalizing rhetoric, in any case, is completely missing in the popular publications aimed specifically at transvestites. Rainer shows this, for instance, in looking at the appeals for photographs that were made in *Das 3. Geschlecht*, which make no pretense of speaking to any audience other than the transvestites who will be able to send in the photos the editors want. Whether the photos collected in this way were then mainly aimed at and spoke to these same transvestites when they were published is another question entirely.

What we see in many of the images is a need to make visible and explain forms of gender fluidity or transformation – whether labeled as cross-dressing, transvestitism, or transsexualism – that aspired to norms of passing. This is an intention shared both by the individuals who made the photographs and by those who published and edited them. At times this revelation could appear emancipatory and playful, and at other times it is very clearly associated with a threat of gender trouble or dissimulation.

Moreover, this threat is evident both when this fluid or incongruous gender presentation is overt and also when it fades into the background, though continuing to lurk beneath the surface of what appears to be normal gender presentation. Another striking feature of the images that circulated in public is that the images published in medical or scientific contexts often give us considerable insight into individual stories or personalities. Even though these medical images are framed by clinical, often pathologizing discourse, they are often accompanied with case studies or individual biographies. By contrast, many of the images used in popular magazines were taken from contexts dominated by clichéd motifs or personas created for publicity (such as the theatre), or they are reduced to judgements about how well the individuals pass or fit certain gendered norms of style or comportment. Yet as we have also demonstrated, even the medical publications had a popular reading audience, and published images and life stories inspired many transgender readers to appropriate this medical knowledge in refashioning their own identities and seeking out recognition and treatment.

The cluster we devoted to "Artists" in each of our exhibitions illustrates these dynamics particularly well. In the cluster depicted in figure 6.9, for instance, we see vividly how similar images – in this case, of the performer Voo-Doo – circulated in both medical and popular contexts but with very different intentions and effects. Voo-Doo can be seen here in the first three panels of the top row, and in the first panel of the bottom row. A more detailed discussion of

Artists

FIGURE 6.9: Cluster of "Artists" in "Trans Histories in Print" in Calgary, with medical images on the top row and images from popular magazines on the bottom row.

Voo-Doo's images can be found in this book in the gallery devoted to Voo-Doo, and the other two images of artists on the top row are discussed in Michael's essay. But it is worth noting that the images of Voo-Doo in the top row are immediately striking especially because they do not conform to categories of binary gender difference or to a difference between lived and performed identity. The juxtaposition of a photograph with a self-drawn expressive drawing also aligns this depiction of Voo-Doo with other artistic images that Hirschfeld used to shed light on the inner psychological reality of his subjects. By contrast, all the images in the bottom row – including the photo of Voo-Doo – largely perpetuate gender norms and conventions of theatrical performance, and they give us no insight beyond the stage persona they depict. The photograph of Voo-Doo as a "dance phenomenon who has, as a woman, achieved world success in his snake-dances" circulated in *Das 3. Geschlecht* in a semiotic space in which it is functionally similar to the other images of performers we exhibited in this cluster: "Henriette," a "New York transvestite" on tour in Germany, and a "Male artist who enjoys world fame as an oriental dancer."

FIGURE 6.10: "Big Head/Small Neck" performed by kloetzel&co at the opening of *TransTrans* in Calgary. Photo credit: Dave Brown, LCR Photo Services, University of Calgary.

To reflect on the tensions between modes of self-fashioning and conventions of theatrical performance that we find within these histories, we also invited Melanie Kloetzel, associate professor in the School of Creative and Performing Arts at the University of Calgary, to create a dance performance for the space with her company, kloetzel&co. Choreographed by Kloetzel with a spoken-word script by Kloetzel and the Scottish playwright/performer Rose Ruane, "Big Head/Small Neck" used a projection of historical images to examine the medicalization and modification of trans and all gendered bodies through wit, satire, and precision. The dancers' movements and their provocative questions and provocations skewered social expectations of behaviour in relation to gender and sexuality.

Such public image histories and performances, however, were only the most visible part of the stories we told. The private, personal networks we uncovered formed the emotional centre of the exhibition, which we presented in spaces designed to prompt visitors to go beyond merely looking in order to find and experience deeper emotional connections. Our recreation of Carla's living room

Figure 6.11: View through the window into the living room in *TransTrans*, Berlin, 2019. Photo credit: Paul Sleev.

focal point around which the rest of the exhibition was organized on the gallery walls. But in order to establish the living room as a personal space that was welcoming but also somewhat protected, the entryway was located only on one side, directly opposite a wall telling the stories of the medical and scientific authorities who publicly shaped these histories. (The wall contained the Steinach Film, a cluster on the Hirschfeld-Benjamin-Kinsey connection, and a cluster contrasting the story of how Benjamin used Carla's images in his book with Annette's reconstruction of Carla's life history.) The space was nevertheless clearly marked as a construction of our own making. The wall with the curtain and window consisted only of a plywood frame – the film set used to produce the video *Carlas Wohnzimmer* to be discussed below.

In Calgary, too, we designed the space so that visitors would enter the living room only indirectly. Visitors came to the entrance through a corridor, along which we mounted digital frames displaying slideshows of many of the slides that we had found in Benjamin's archive. Many of these were the photos that Carla made of her friends in Louise Lawrence's living room. Visitors then came upon the window in the wall that allowed them to look into Carla's living room.

Annette was inspired to create this window by a slide of a woman reading a book (figure 6.15), which gives some sense of the location of Lawrence's apartment in the inadvertent capturing of a San Francisco street, likely Pine Street.[3] We found the images in figures 6.15, 6.16, and 6.17 in a box of slides upon which Benjamin

in both exhibitions (first designed and envisioned by Annette) and the exhibition elements we used to tell these personal stories were intended as invitations for visitors to imagine themselves stepping into these histories and to reflect on their own positions today – specifically, to reflect on today's norms about gender and sexuality and how public discussion about transgender identity is rapidly shifting.

In Berlin, this living room was the spatial centre of the exhibition – the

FIGURE 6.12: View of the wall creating the living room in *TransTrans*, Berlin, 2019. Photo credit: Paul Sleev.

FIGURE 6.13: Rotating images on five digital screens at the entrance to "Trans Circles of Knowledge" in Calgary. Image from KILSC-HB 17. Copyright © 2017, The Trustees of Indiana University on behalf of the Kinsey Institute. All rights reserved. Photo credit: Dave Brown, LCR Photo Services, University of Calgary.

FIGURE 6.14: View through the window into "The Living Room," *TransTrans*, Calgary, 2016. Photo credit: Dave Brown, LCR Photo Services, University of Calgary.

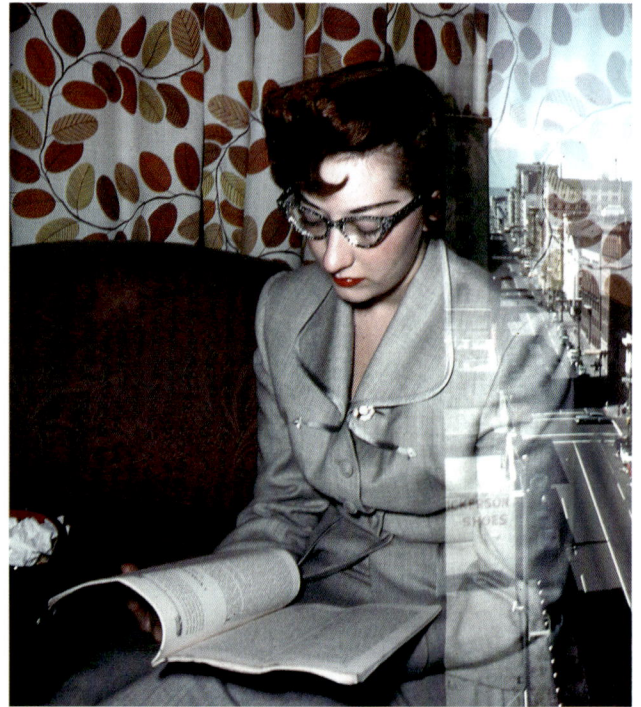

FIGURE 6.15: A slide in Benjamin's personal effects, 1954. Likely a picture of Carla's friend Karen (pseudonym), KILSC-HB 17. Copyright © 2017, The Trustees of Indiana University on behalf of the Kinsey Institute. All rights reserved.

had scrawled only the name "Terry" and the dates 1954, 1955, and 1956. They were taken in 1954 and we believe that they are of Carla's friend Karen (a pseudonym). (In a 1954 letter to Benjamin, Carla mentioned that Karen was an excellent seamstress: "She makes herself beautiful clothes.")[4] Two years later, Benjamin received more images of the same woman. Here we place the two poses side by side – though they could not originally have been viewed this way, since they were created as two separate stereoscopic slides (figures 6.16 and 6.17).

The photos are strikingly beautiful. Their beauty lies in the symmetry of the images and the figure they depict; in the ideals of feminine perfection that she

embodies; and in her success – in these images – in passing. The fact that she had been arrested for "masquerading" as a woman just two months before this photo was taken is nonetheless a sharp reminder that the beauty of these images also rests in their power to capture a fleeting moment presenting its subject as she would have liked to be seen.[5] As witnesses to this scene, we can honour and appreciate this self-presentation, which also means understanding its complexity. Although the images depict a personal moment, staged no doubt in a private and protected space, the photographs explicitly point beyond these limits. For us, the most poignant aspect of the image on the right is the

FIGURES 6.16 and 6.17: Images of Karen likely taken by Carla in 1956, KILSC-HB 17. Copyright © 2017, The Trustees of Indiana University on behalf of the Kinsey Institute. All rights reserved.

acknowledgement of its beholders: Karen gazes into the mirror, looking past herself to smile directly at the camera.

Our exhibitions and this book also aim to look back, as it were, and to also look beyond: to see the stories and images we encounter as reflections of much more, and to create the context we need to see this depth. The mirror in the photograph also marks a layer of distance – a decision of its subject to look at us by first looking away – that we must also note and respect. One can only feel sadness when one realizes that such an image could hardly find a place in Benjamin's book (with its clinical framing and need to illustrate his theories

of "transsexualism"), or that it was nearly lost in his archive, boxed up together with vacation slides. The beauty of the images also lies in unexpectedly discovering some of the personal story they do not show and in recognizing the historical forgetting and invisibility of which they are an emblem.

As we expanded *TransTrans* to include the histories that Alex tells about the Netherlands in the 1950s, we found many moments that similarly document these two opposing sides of transgender history. On the one hand, as Alex argues, the images in his chapter demonstrate the emerging visual openness about trans lives within the popular culture of the boulevard press and in the context of new forms of night life in Amsterdam and other European cities. We see the self-awareness and fearless attitudes of trans pioneers who did not hide themselves, even if their images were perhaps being exploited by others for commercial gain. Pictures of Christine Jorgensen, Tamara Rees, Aaïcha Bergamin, and Bambi show women who carried the public image of what it meant to be trans. They were portrayed both as examples of the extravagant lifestyles of the jet set and as inhabitants of the seedier corners of urban culture. Both kinds of images stereotyped trans women and trans experiences for generations to come.

Yet, much like the stories revealed in the other chapters of this book and in our *TransTrans* exhibitions, there was another, far more secret side to the histories we are telling in both the United States and Europe. Alex, too, found pictures of people who wanted to remain anonymous and invisible. These pictures were taken in private, either as self-creations or with the help of a trusted trans friend. Catherine J., for example, images of whom are reproduced in Alex's chapter (figures 4.19 and 4.20), likely took self-portraits to show her doctor how she looked in female attire. Using the same visual rhetorics deployed by Hirschfeld and Benjamin, the double images show her in virtually the same posture, in both masculine and feminine presentation, in a hotel room. (It could be Hotel Hegra, but we cannot be sure.) The nervous, but excited, look on the face of Dauphine P. – who dared to be photographed outside, but still on the safe steps of Hotel Hegra – is touching, because

it similarly reveals the private hopes and fears of these individuals.

For these reasons, among others, we felt strongly that in staging *TransTrans* we needed strategies to respectfully open up these private spaces and moments. We wanted to make them accessible and to invite visitors to come into Carla's living room, as it were, but we wanted to do this in a way that would avoid or at least resist the voyeuristic, exhibitionist, and sensationalist tendencies that are embedded in these histories. For us, this meant emphasizing the context in which the images were produced, making their materiality clear, and explaining the history of how they were shared, preserved, and came to us. It also meant asking questions about what these images might mean today in our very different gender landscapes.

One strategy we chose to achieve these aims began with our publicity. In Berlin, the poster for the Berlin exhibition used the image of Karen looking into the mirror. In Calgary, we chose to use three images to create three different exhibition posters.

The decision to use the image of Carla showing her tattoos (figure 3.5), in particular, was difficult and carefully considered. In Calgary, we made many decisions about the exhibition in consultation with an advisory committee that Annette assembled from local Calgary members of the trans, LGBTQ, and queer artist communities.[6] Like all of our choices about what images to display, however, the decision remained that of the co-curators. With the knowledge of context behind the image of Carla showing her tattoos, we tend to read it is a playful tease and a

FIGURES 6.18, 6.19 and 6.20: *TransTrans* posters, designed by Andreas Puskeiler.

delicate moment in which Carla reveals this very beautiful, feminine ornamentation. Without more context, though, the image risks being depersonalizing and titillating and threatens to invite a leering curiosity about the genitals hidden from view. Such (sensational) curiosity is explicitly part of the histories we tell, as is apparent in the second image we chose for our posters in Calgary, which was used as a cover to *Das 3. Geschlecht* and printed again inside the issue with the question, "woman or man?" The carefully placed mirror, for instance, is placed on the floor where it might reflect the figure's genital area, teasing us to imagine looking up the skirt at what we cannot see. And as Michael discusses in his essay, the image in the third poster was published as a self-confession offering insight into the

artist's own personality. We hoped that the series of all three posters would introduce the range of historical periods and kinds of documents shown in the exhibition, while also emphasizing dimensions of gender-play and self-fashioning that are so utterly different from the medicalized frame of so much of our material.

Another strategy for exhibiting these images was the video project we developed, called *Carla's Couch* in Calgary and – in a substantially revised format – *Carlas Wohnzimmer* (Carla's living room) in Berlin, where it was produced by two filmmakers, Brian Andrew Hose and Sabrina Rücker. (In the next chapter, Nora Eckert provides an account of the making of the Berlin version of the film from the perspective of the interviewees.) For the

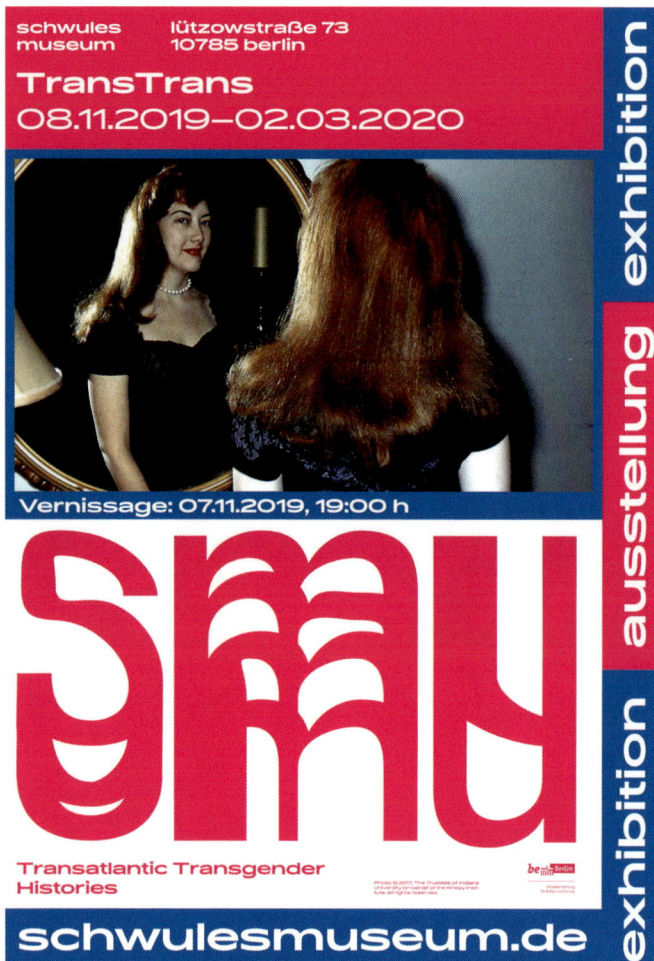

FIGURE 6.21: Poster for *TransTrans* at the Schwules Museum, Berlin; Credit: Schwules Museum

first version in Calgary, Annette began by sending out a call we wrote together inviting individuals to come and sit on a couch similar to the one we found in these slides. (Amelia Marie Newbert helped organize the generous loan of this and other furniture from Theatre Calgary, and she helped Annette design the film set.) We initially planned to ask those who entered the Living Room where the film was shot the following questions: What is your gender? Why does it matter? Where, and to whom? How do you show it? Live it? How do others see your gender? Do you have just one?

In practice, Annette and her assistants, Amy Herr and Shawn Brackett, found that the conversations evolved more naturally, with the interviewees making their own decisions about what, if anything, they wanted to say. These interviews were then edited together into a video presentation spread across four screens, with storyboarding by Annette and editing by Veronica Reeves. The four screens were placed directly opposite from a reproduction of Hirschfeld's Wall of Sexual Transitions, and historical images from the slides we found in the Benjamin archival collection were interspersed between the interviews. The goal was to highlight the historical construction of sexual categories (symbolized by the frames on Hirschfeld's wall and the separate video screens on ours) and to reveal something about real people who have accepted or struggled with those categories. Amelia Marie Newbert's reaction to completing her interview perfectly expressed the joy of self-fulfillment that this video sought to capture (figure 6.23).

In Calgary, interviewees also wrote single words to describe their gender identity onto pieces of paper, which Annette (with the help of curator Michele Hardy) turned into bubbles (figure 6.24) to be arranged on the large end wall of the "Trans Circles of Knowledge" space – a metaphor both for the disruption of the taxonomical grid of Hirschfeld's Wall of Sexual Transitions and for the "circles" of intimate relationships that help form these identities.

In the Berlin exhibition, the film created by Brian Hose and Sabrina Rücker similarly

Figure 6.22: "Carla's Couch" video project. Photo credit: Dave Brown, LCR Photo Services, University of Calgary.

Figure 6.23: Amelia Marie Newbert in "Carla's Couch."

FIGURE 6.24: Gender circles. Photo credit: Dave Brown, LCR Photo Services, University of Calgary.

asked how our view of gender has changed since the early twentieth century. In this film, however, the focus was more explicitly on an engagement with the historical material presented in the exhibition. Hose and Rücker explored these contemporary perspectives through interviews with trans and nonbinary people living in Berlin today, and they asked protagonists to reflect on the past and connect to their lived experiences. The protagonists in the film read out and react to excerpts from Magnus Hirschfeld's "Psycho-biological Questionnaire" from 1925 (its sixth edition), as well as to excerpts from letters that Carla Erskine sent to Harry Benjamin in the early 1950s. As in Calgary, this representation of present-day trans and gendered realities played directly opposite a

reproduction of Hirschfeld's "Wall of Sexual Transitions."

Both films recreated a scene reminiscent of the room we find in many of Benjamin's slides. In Calgary, Amelia Marie Newbert used skills critical to her job as production manager at Theatre Calgary to help Annette produce this space; and in Berlin, this set design was the work of Christina Chelaru. Both designers reproduced the curtain from Louise Lawrence's living room that had first allowed us to connect a pile of randomly sorted slides from Benjamin's personal effects. Yet this replication of the curtain and the creation of a living room was meant only as a gesture – a historical reference to create material reality and invite visitors to physically inhabit a memory and a moment

FIGURE 6.25: Visitors on opening night *TransTrans*, Berlin, 2019. They are watching the video *Carlas Wohnzimmer*. Hirschfeld's Wall of Sexual Transitions is visible to the right.

captured in the slides and reimagined in the films.

In the living rooms in both versions of the exhibition, a camera was placed to point directly at the couch. This piece of furniture represented the place where Carla and her friends had posed for the pictures in the slides in San Francisco; and it was the same couch used in the film. In Berlin, the coffee table in front of the couch also displayed printed copies of the excerpts from Carla's letters to Benjamin. Visitors to the gallery could thus contemplate these historical documents in relative quiet and seclusion. In Calgary, the camera was interactive, turning the living room into a photobooth operated from a visitor-activated iPad on the table in front of the couch. Visitors could pose (as the three co-curators do in

figure 6.28), click on the iPad, and then print out a classic photobooth sticker that they could either keep or paste on the interactive wall outside the living room.

In both living rooms, we also displayed several of the stereoscopic slides themselves on a lightbox. In Calgary, this box was directly positioned beneath a short biography of Carla and a print of a photo where she poses so confidently in her elegant dress, with her handbag; in Berlin, it was on a side table across from the images of Karen in front of a mirror and the photo of Carla with three of her girlfriends (see figure 3.18 in chapter 3). As material artefacts of this history, the slides are also reminders of the imaginative leap that viewing them entails. Created to be seen in a personal viewfinder, they are themselves

FIGURE 6.26: View of the living room in *TransTrans*, Berlin 2019.

FIGURE 6.27: Sabrina Rücker, co-director of *Carlas Wohnzimmer*, in the living room of *TransTrans*, Berlin, 2019.

windows into a private world. As slides, however, they are also transparencies able to be projected onto a larger screen, which can serve as a metaphor for what we have done in blowing them up and printing them as elements in our exhibition or this book.

The slides we chose for this lightbox included the images of Carla used by Benjamin in his book, as well as the beautiful images of Karen looking into a mirror. One reason we displayed these sensitive slides of Carla only in their original form, in this very small format, was to emphasize their private nature. Yet this presentation was also meant to shift our gaze away from the images as projections and back to the fragility and delicacy of the slides themselves. The lightbox was meant to shine light *through* but also to help us see *what* we are looking at – to witness the life stories of these men and women, transposed and transformed on(to) images they made to be shared, though not necessarily for us. In highlighting this dual dynamic as we retraced and retold these stories in *TransTrans*, our intention was to make visible the networks that the images reflect and the future histories that they made possible.

FIGURE 6.28: Michael Thomas Taylor, Annette Timm, and Rainer Herrn in the *TransTrans* photobooth.

Figure 6.29: Photoboxes showing slides in Berlin and Calgary. Photo credit: Paul Sleev and Andreas Puskeiler.

*Trans*Trans

Transgender Histories Between
Germany and the United States, 1882–1966

Nickle Galleries, University of Calgary
27 May to 10 June 2016

Exhibition Production
Annette F. Timm

Curated by
Rainer Herrn, Michael Thomas Taylor & Annette F. Timm

Exhibition Design for Trans Histories in Print
Andreas Puskeiler
Exhibition Design for Trans Circles of Knowledge
Annette F. Timm

Loans & Images
**Kinsey Institute for Research in Sex, Gender, and Reproduction,
Magnus Hirschfeld-Gesellschaft Berlin, Murnau-Stiftung/Bundesfilmarchiv,
Rainer Herrn, Theatre Calgary**

Set, Film Editing & Filming Assistance
Amelia Marie Newbert, Veronica Reeves, Amy Herr & Shawn Brackett

Advisory Committee
**James Demers, Tonya Callaghan, Mason Jenkins, Amelia Marie Newbert,
Anne Drew Potter, Zac Slams**

Funding
**Social Sciences and Humanities Research Council of Canada
Federation for the Humanities and Social Sciences
Faculty of Arts, University of Calgary
Reed College**

In Cooperation with
**Nickle Galleries, University of Calgary
Magnus-Hirschfeld-Gesellschaft in Berlin
Institute for History and Ethics in Medicine of the Charité Clinic, Berlin
Kinsey Institute for Research in Sex, Gender, and Reproduction in Bloomington, Indiana**

Kinsey Institute — INDIANA UNIVERSITY   CHARITÉ — UNIVERSITÄTSMEDIZIN BERLIN   UNIVERSITY OF CALGARY — Nickle Galleries

TransTrans

Transatlantic Transgender Histories
Transatlantische Transgendergeschichten

Schwules Museum, Berlin
7 November 2019 to 2 March 2020

Kuratiert von/Curated by
Alex Bakker, Rainer Herrn, Michael Thomas Taylor & Annette F. Timm

Ausstellungsgestaltung/Exhibition Design
Andreas Puskeiler

Leihgeber und Bildquellen/Loans & Images
Kinsey Institute for Research in Sex, Gender, and Reproduction
Magnus-Hirschfeld-Gesellschaft Berlin
Murnau-Stiftung/Bundesfilmarchiv
Rainer Herrn
Cor Jaring/Amsterdam City Archives
The Danish Royal Library

Film *Carlas Wohnzimmer*
Filmemacher, Interviews und Produktion/Filming, Interviews & Production
Brian Hose & Sabrina Rücker
Szenenbild/Set Design
Christina Cheleru
Konzeption/Original Concept
Annette F. Timm
Historische Beratung/Historical Consultation
Annette F. Timm, Rainer Herrn, Michael Thomas Taylor & Alex Bakker

Finanzierung/Funding
Senatsverwaltung für Kultur   **Schwules Museum**
und Europa, Berlin

NOTES TO CHAPTER 6

1   The original German reads: "Gilt diese Arbeit doch dem guten, würdigen Zweck, zahlreichen in ihrer Eigenart verkannten Mitmenschen Verständnis und gerechte Beurteilung zu verschaffen." Magnus Hirschfeld and Max Tilke, *Der erotische Verkleidungstrieb (Die Transvestiten),* vol. 2: *Illustrierter Teil* (Berlin: Alfred Pulvermacher & Co., 1912), 2.

2   Katie Sutton, "Sexology's Photographic Turn: Visualizing Trans Identity in Interwar Germany," *Journal of the History of Sexuality* 27, no. 3 (2018): 442–79, here 455.

3   We have been unable to confirm the precise address of Lawrence's apartment, but Don Lucas told Susan Stryker that he remembered it was on Pine Street. See Susan Stryker, Don Lucas Interview: Recorded at Lucas's home in San Francisco, Transcript, 13 June 1997, GLBT Historical Society, http://www.glbthistory.org.

4   Erskine to Benjamin, 22 Jan 1954, KILSC-HB, Box 4, Ser. II C.

5   Carla had introduced this woman to Benjamin with the line: "Our new transvestite, [Karen], of whom Louise will probably tell you, if not already – was arrested and held 4 days for drag and given 6 months probation." Letter dated 24 Nov 1953, KILSC-HB, Box 4, Ser. II C.

6   Some members of this committee also spoke with Michael via Skype. Advisory board members included James Demers, Tonya Callaghan, Mason Jenkins, Amelia Marie Newbert, Anne Drew Potter, and Zac Slams.

7

Trans Transatlantic

Nora Eckert

Translated by Michael Thomas Taylor and Annette F. Timm

The day of my interview was one of the very hot days of the summer of 2019, and it was a Sunday. The interview took place in a recording studio. Was it in Tempelhof or was this already Neukölln? It isn't actually important where exactly the border between these two Berlin districts runs; it was far more important to me that the bus dropped me off right in front of the entrance to the studio grounds. And yet the realization that the interview took place somewhere in this in-between space still seems to me, in retrospect, delightful. After all, we trans* people are born border crossers, and we are at home in the in-between.[1] We know only too well what border crossings feel like within ourselves and in society, in everyday life and wherever our trans and nonbinary bodies make us conspicuous.

And so today the interview for a video that would accompany an exhibition at the Gay Museum in Berlin. Some people unknown to me had discovered a piece of previously unknown trans* history – doubtless something like that famous suitcase in the attic, bulging with a true treasure trove of knowledge. There was talk about a collection of letters documenting an early transatlantic network of trans women. It is actually strange that we today celebrate something like this as a discovery. We do this, I would argue, because we trans*

We said to the world: hey you all, your model is too limited; there are more than two genders and there's nothing new about that.

people essentially have no history, and we therefore worship every discovery as proof of our existence. This also distinguishes us from other humans – who, after all, have their own history of humanity in which one finds many men and fewer women, but rarely us. In the meantime we certainly have one or two historical studies on the subject of trans* histories, but they are all primarily about how we have been viewed by science and society – we the mysterious beings who despite countless sexological, psychological, and medical theories about us remain mysterious beings. Where do we come from and where do we get the knowledge about being what we are? Most people probably think that we come straight out of a freakshow. But I mean something else: I see myself and my kind as one possibility in nature. We simply belong to it, and we fit exactly between man and woman; we are men in female bodies and women in male bodies – bodies that we change individually. This is the way I see it, and this is the way I live it.

My favourite biologist explained it to us with only three words: nature loves variety. For me, this is the key: like all humans we are part of natural history. For me this means that we have existed at all times and everywhere. Questions of livability and the resulting visibility are an entirely different matter. And this is where culture draws a line through the accounting, at least our binary, heteronormative culture, because Milton Diamond's sentence has a second half, and it goes like this: unfortunately society hates it. And there's the rub. Our trans* history could be told as a history of humankind since it was always and remains

a part of this history, but so rarely has it been written down. This would also be a history with long stretches of absence, and for the most part it would be a sad history, because often enough we paid for our nature with our lives, violently snatched away from too many of us in the past and still today; transphobia and transmisogyny remain our dogged shadows.

But back to that hot Sunday. The studio was easy to find on the expansive grounds, because Sabrina – one of the two directors of the film, who had invited me for the interview – had provided perfect directions. The difference between indoors and outdoors could not have been more extreme. Barely having stepped out from under the glaring and brooding sun I was now standing in this dark and cool room, completely cut off from the outside world. Like a black hole, the studio seemed to have swallowed everything that was of the outside world – there was no ray of light, no sound penetrated the walls. Inside I saw just one small illuminated island. Only as I came closer did I recognize a furnished corner room, set up with great attention to detail as a piece of scenery. Sabrina's friendly welcome was that of a familial hostess. She asked me to take my place on the sofa. And then there was also a cameraman, and suddenly I felt incredibly important, as if I were sitting in the middle of a film set and it was really all about me, about my life story. After all, I was intimately acquainted with this '50s ambiance; it brought back memories. This was my childhood. I remembered living rooms that looked like this or something like this. Sabrina explained that this was

Carla's room and that Carla was one of the main characters in a recently discovered trans* history. The exhibition would show many photos of Carla's friends taken in a living room like the one reconstructed here. So I started telling how it was for us trans* women in the '70s, and I got to meet some trans* women who had still been living in the intolerant and stuffy '60s. That's why for me it wasn't mainly this film set or even the particular history told in the exhibition, which was the occasion for our encounter, that made me realize how much I myself have become a piece of trans* history. I have been living as a trans* woman for forty-three years, and for Carla I would have been something like the next generation. She could have been my aunt. The scene from the 1950s was like a connecting flight into my own past, taking me to the history that was a prelude to my trans* biography.

During our conversation on the sofa in Carla's room, the term "pioneer" came up. We wouldn't have called ourselves that, but in the end that's what we were, because through the lives we lived as trans* we conquered a convivial and social space in which we had not previously existed. We literally took possession of reality, from where we could no longer be driven away. We did not yet have a voice in the sociopolitical realm, but we had stopped being invisible. We did pioneering work, approaching the binary world with growing self-awareness and self-confidence. We said to the world: hey you all, your model is too limited; there are more than two genders and there's nothing new about that. We gradually gained a presence in the media, which often merely served as a vehicle for

cis voyeurism. Nevertheless, the discussion shifted and it was no longer possible to deny our legal existence. What was more important for us was that we, too, like Carla and her friends, built and maintained private networks. There was still a very long way to go to before trans* folk came together to found their own organizations. In a big city like Berlin, where I've lived since 1973, a lot of things were easier than in the countryside, where you were left to think you were the only trans* person in the world. As I look at this previously unknown transatlantic bridge, built by trans* women, I also see unexpected continuity in our still unwritten history. For me, the crucial factor in such a history is that it needs to be told from our very specific life perspective: how did we experience and understand it, how did we live and experience being trans*? What do our forms of self-discovery looks like? What hindered them, what encouraged them? Claiming the power to interpret ourselves – this will be our project for the future.

The simple and tidy world in which Carla lived suggests normality, which is something we obviously often long for as border crossers and gender troublemakers. What always mattered then and still matters now is the ability to live our lives, social acceptance, the feeling of belonging. And however natural it might seem, we cannot misunderstand this to mean conforming or fitting in. The passing that is so important to us is in fact basically a euphemism for conforming, and yet it is also a tool that makes our lives easier by allowing us to be perceived and accepted by others in the role that is ours. For Carla and her friends,

experiencing acceptance and understanding was probably itself a sense of achievement. Today, we should tackle our long-overdue emancipation – this "I am what I am."
This is one of my aims as an activist. I felt comfortable in Carla's room; I would have liked to speak with her, as an eye-witness to history – what I have also become in the meantime. Carla has strengthened my conviction in the importance of another project, in addition to our emancipation: our unwritten trans* history, which I hope will help establish our identity. Having been accepted by society, we will only be truly emancipated when our self-determination and equal rights have been achieved, when we can be who we are, everywhere in the world, without any question. It's about belonging. Reading the work of the psychologist Brené Brown, an expert in questions about human vulnerability and our protection mechanisms, I came across an interesting observation. Young people were asked to think about the difference between conforming and belonging, and they came up with some amazing answers:

> *Belonging* means being where you want to be and where others want you to be. *Conforming* means being where you want to be, without it mattering to others at all. *Belonging* means being accepted as you are. *Conforming* means being accepted because you are like others. I am me when I *belong*. I have to be like you when I *conform*.

NOTE TO CHAPTER 7

1   Note from the co-authors: Nora Eckert's contribution should be viewed as that of an eyewitness, and we have therefore not enforced our usage on her. We chose not to use the asterisk after trans in this book, because for the most part we are writing only about people who wished to remain within a binary gender system. Here, however, Eckert is explicitly including nonbinary people by using the asterisk, reflecting a present-day Berlin setting.

8

Historicizing Transgender Terminology

Annette F. Timm with Michael Thomas Taylor

The stories this book tells span from the late nineteenth century to the early 1960s. Within these seven decades, terminology referencing individuals who disagreed with the gender they were assigned at birth or who wished to play with or challenge norms of gender comportment went through several dramatic transformations. While recognizing that these linguistic transformations are still underway and that we cannot hope to represent a true consensus on current usage, we have been very self-conscious about choosing terms and phrases and about formulating our historical descriptions in ways that at least contain and contextualize the painful effects of terms that are today often used to denigrate rather than to empower trans individuals. Although we have raised this issue at key points in this book, we would like to also provide a general discussion of the terminological landscape and our efforts to navigate it.

Our decisions about terminology were grounded in a resolutely historical perspective. While recognizing that we are writing to and must therefore respect the sensibilities of present-day readers, we insist upon *also* respecting the identities, experiences, and self-understandings of our

Our decisions about terminology were grounded in a resolutely historical perspective.

historical actors. We therefore reject the argument that being sensitive entails linguistic sanitation of historical realities that cannot be fully understood without appreciating how and why people used the words they did to describe themselves during the period under investigation. Particularly in the first half of the period we analyze in this book, trans individuals had *no* words to describe themselves. In the book *Trans*: A Quick and Quirky Account of Gender Variability*, Jack Halberstam introduces a discussion of how alienating it can be to lack identification with a very personal reflection: "If I had known the term 'transgender' when I was a teenager in the 1970s, I'm sure I would have grabbed hold of it like a life jacket on rough seas, but there were no such words in my world."[1] Socially marginalized or living in self-imposed silence about their deepest fears and longings, transgender people were often relieved to be provided with terminology – any terminology – that might validate their experiences as something shared with others. The passive construction – "to be provided with" – is intentional. Explaining how we arrived at our present-day usage requires us to acknowledge that, aside from localized slang, trans people were not initially in control of the terms that they eventually adopted to achieve a sense of belonging and self-understanding. That this is no longer true today – that there is a vibrant academic field of transgender studies and an international proliferation of trans activist groups, whose members are adamantly asserting their rights to self-definition – does not obliterate the

historical reality that linguistic shifts from terms like "transvestite" to "transsexual" and, to a lesser extent, to "transgender" were often orchestrated not by trans people themselves but by physicians, sexologists, and psychiatrists – self-declared experts seeking to categorize and treat conditions that they viewed as primarily pathological.[2] One of our key aims in this book, however, has been to explain how previous histories have placed too much emphasis on the agency of medical experts and not enough on the influence and actions of trans people themselves. As George Chauncey has argued for the word "homosexuality" in the late nineteenth century, it "would be wrong to assume … that people uncritically internalized the new medical models."[3] Even the taxonomical shifts occurred primarily because trans people themselves actively sought out medical expertise and because they often (if not always) viewed the new terminology as empowering.

To understand precisely how this could be true, we must become etymologists, meaning that we must appreciate the meanings of words as they were originally used in different national contexts. Rather than providing a glossary, which, as Julia Serano argues, "gives the impression that all of these transgender-related words and phrases are somehow written in stone, indelibly passed down from generation to generation,"[4] we have chosen to contextualize our terminology and to add this note to explain our general philosophy of word choice in more detail.

A key problem has always been *whose* words are being used. The overarching word that we rely on – "transgender" – is a case in point. Although the precise person to have originally coined it remains disputed, Susan Stryker and Paisley Currah emphasize that it came into common use in the 1960s and that some of the first to employ it were members of "self-organized communities of predominantly white, middle-class, male-bodied individuals who persistently expressed feminine comportment, identities, and dress."[5] Even though medical experts such as Harry Benjamin claimed ownership through their publications, the essential point, Stryker and Carrah emphasize, is that the goal in adopting the term was to resist medical, psychiatric, or sexological labelling either as "transvestites," which connoted episodic cross-dressing primarily for reasons of erotic gratification, or as "transsexuals," which implied medicalized bodily transformations of sex-signifying physical attributes through which a permanent legal change of social gender could be accomplished. "Transgender," on the other hand, was meant to convey a nonpathological sense that one could live in a social gender not typically associated with one's biological sex or that a single individual should be able to combine elements of different gender styles and presentations. Thus, from the beginning, the category "transgender" represented a resistance to medicalization, to pathologization, and to the many mechanisms whereby the administrative state and its associated medico-legal-psychiatric institutions sought to contain and delimit the socially disruptive potentials of sex/gender atypicality, incongruence, and nonnormativity.[6]

For precisely these reasons, we chose to use the words "transgender" or "trans" (fairly interchangeably) whenever we are discussing the experiences of transgender people from a point of historical remove. These are *our* words to describe *their* experience, though we believe that they are respectful and appropriate. However, we also use words like "transvestite" and "transsexual" in cases where we are paraphrasing our historical actors, because these words were also used by trans people themselves and thus helped to form their sense of self. The fact that this book tracks a transatlantic and multilingual history complicates (or enriches) the etymological project, since usage varies geographically *and* over time in the three primary sites we explore: Germany, the United States, and the Netherlands. To demonstrate the dilemmas, let us take the example of the word "transvestite."

The German physician and sexologist Magnus Hirschfeld coined the word "transvestite" in his 1910 book *Die Transvestiten: Eine Untersuchung über den erotischen Verkleidungstrieb* (The transvestites: an investigation of the erotic drive to cross-dress).[7] Note first of all that the German word *Verkleidungstrieb* cannot be easily translated and literally means something closer to "instinct," "drive," or "desire" to clothe – or even, as Michael has argued, to disguise oneself. Along with "transvestite," it is a Hirschfeldian neologism – an attempt to corner the market on terminology by replacing psychiatrist Carl Westphal's 1870 term "konträre Sexualempfinden" ("contrary sexual feeling") with a term that deemphasized the pathological while distinguishing cross-dressers from homosexuals. This was a new perspective on Hirschfeld's part, and his growing conviction that cross-dressing was not the same thing as homosexuality had slowly formed after years of angry exchanges with the cross-dressers themselves.[8] Although these people then adopted the term "transvestite," most of them also insisted that their drive to cross-dress had nothing to do with erotic desire but was rather motivated by the need to adequately present themselves in the clothing that matched their own sense of gender. Nonetheless, Hirschfeld's word caught on (despite the fact that his book was not translated into English until 1991), and by the 1920s it had won out over alternative suggestions from cross-dressers themselves, and from other sexologists, such as Havelock Ellis's "eonism" (after the eighteenth-century French diplomat known as the Chevalier d'Éon, who is profiled in a gallery and in Michael's essay in this volume).[9] For instance, the popular magazine about which Rainer Herrn writes in this book, which was published in Germany between 1930 and 1932, was explicitly aimed at and for *Transvestiten*. Hirschfeld overcame his initial surprise in discovering that cross-dressers were not necessarily homosexuals, and he described one particular variant as belonging more or less to the domain of what he termed *sexuelle Zwischenstufen* (sexual intermediaries – this could also be translated as "variations," "interstages," or "in-betweens").[10] He later elaborated on how these people fit into the wide spectrum of gender identities in various works, including

Geschlechts-Übergänge (a variation of the term "sexual intermediaries" that translates into something like "gender transitions") and *Geschlechtskunde* (the study of gender, or sexual knowledge), which included many images of transvestites in one of its five thick volumes. Hirschfeld viewed those who wished to live out their lives in a different sex from the one assigned to them at birth as extreme variants within a broader transvestite scene, which also included those who lived fundamentally heterosexual lives but enjoyed cross-dressing in private or as a public performance. The emphasis on erotic gratification created by the book's title was thus a bit misplaced; Hirschfeld's own awkward writing style contributed to misreadings that continue to haunt his legacy.

Finally, it should be noted in passing that there is no German equivalent for the term "cross-dresser," which has garnered more acceptance as a less derogatory term in historical literature about the phenomenon in English-speaking contexts. One could argue that we could simply translate the German word *Transvestit* into "cross-dresser," but this would deny our historical actors' possession of a word that they adopted as their own.

English readings of Hirschfeld's terminology are also complicated by the fact that there really is also no direct equivalent for the word "gender" in German, which is why the English term has been used in discussions of gender theory and social analysis since the explosion of scholarly interest in gender theory at the end of the twentieth century.[11] While the word "gender" now implies the social construction of a gender identity (as opposed to biological/anatomical sex) in both German and English usage, the German word "Geschlecht" cannot be so easily separated from biology. The most basic translation might be "genus," and the history of the word marks intersections between biology and social reproduction: the word "Geschlecht" is used to denote groups of ethnically homogenous people, aristocratic dynasties, or even the human race (*das menschliche Geschlecht*).[12] *Geschlecht* as Hirschfeld used it must also be understood as related to anatomy (it is not a translation for "gender"), as is clear in the German word for genitals: *Geschlechtsorgane*. These fine distinctions are often missed in translation, since the lines between what is biological and what is socially/psychologically perceived is much more blurred in German usage than it is in present-day English. In the post-First World War years, Hirschfeld and his followers came to speak of the "true transvestite," a concept that was gradually replaced by the word "transsexual" ("seelischer Transsexualismus," "psychological transsexualism"), which Hirschfeld first used in a 1923 lecture titled "Die intersexuelle Konstitution" (The intersexual constitution).[13]

This last point raises another problem of terminology: Hirschfeld also used the word "intersexuality" in a very different way than we would today. What he meant can most easily be demonstrated in a graphic produced for his article on the intersexual constitution:

With this schema, Hirschfeld was seeking to depathologize conditions of

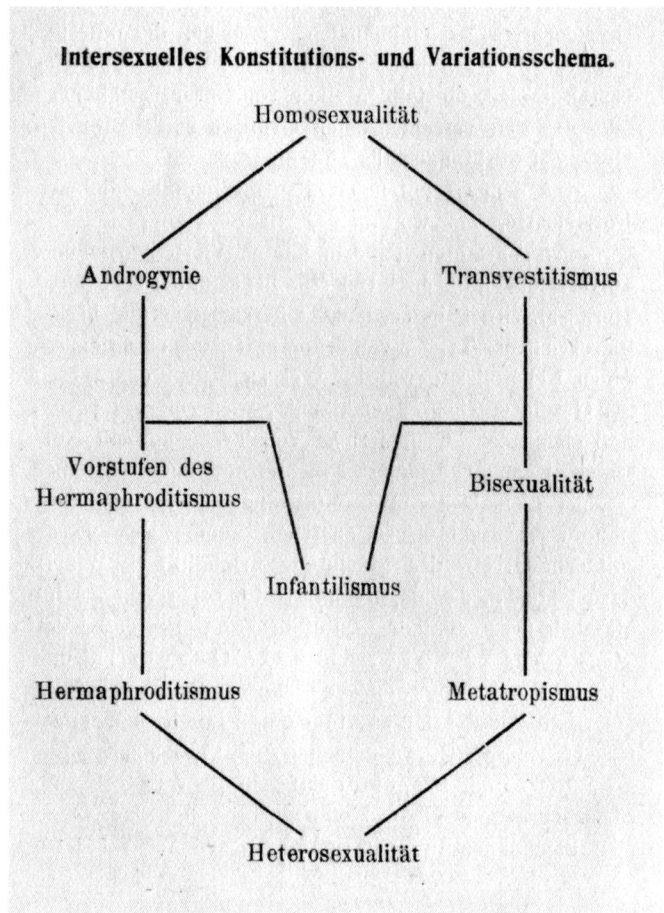

FIGURE 8.1: Intersexual and Constitution and Variation Schema. Originally printed in Magnus Hirschfeld, "Die intersexuelle Konstitution," *Jahrbuch für sexuelle Zwischenstufen* 23 (1923): 3–27. Clockwise from the top: homosexuality, transvestism, bisexuality, metatropism (the reversal of active and passive gendered qualities), heterosexuality, hermaphroditism, early stages of hermaphroditism, androgyny.

sexual anatomy and behaviour that did not conform to heteronormative standards, and he used the term "intersexuality" to describe the entire spectrum of naturally occurring sexual variation. "For a biologist trained in Darwin's theories," he wrote in 1910, it was an "untenable position" to pathologize sexually intermediary stages. He argued that "all of these intermediary sexes" should be recognized as "sexual varieties" similar to the diversity of species. Hirschfeld was thus breaking with the majority of sexologists of the era and with public opinion in refusing to distinguish more clearly between "pathological" and "healthy" sexual characteristics. He uses the word "intersexual" in a much broader way than we would today to describe all of this naturally occurring variation. This does not mean, however, that Hirschfeld was entirely consistent in his attitude toward depathologization or that he always accepted individual self-assessments of gender. When he helped people whom he called pseudo-hermaphrodites and whom we would call intersex, he insisted that it was his anatomical findings (the presence or absence of sperm, for example), rather than the individual's self-perception, that should determine the legal gender.[14] Hirschfeld's taxonomical practices were peculiar, and not all of his neologisms gained the acceptance of "transvestite." His use of "intersexuality" is a case in point.[15] We have therefore not adopted this definition of "intersex" in this volume, and, for other reasons, we have also chosen to not use the word "hermaphrodite" uncritically, even though it was commonly used in the period under investigation in this book by individuals with genitalia that did not conform to expectations of a clear line between male and female bodies. Our justification for this exception to the practice of respecting historical individuals' own word choices is that "hermaphrodite" has a long history of

allusion to monsters and freaks, and it is anatomically misleading.[16] As the story of Carla Erskine in Annette's chapter demonstrates, terminology surrounding intersex conditions was both disputed and obscure to those diagnosed throughout the first seven decades of the twentieth century.

It would seem that problems of translation and Hirschfeld's tendencies towards constantly coining new terms and defining them in convoluted German has defeated American readers, who are less familiar with the fact that he was involved in the world's first cases of gender affirming surgery, such as that of Lili Elbe, whose story we describe in a gallery in chapter 4. That Hirschfeld was also quite keen to sell books (with which he funded his Institute for Sexual Science in Berlin) and thus often chose titillating titles, did not help. All of this explains why English-speakers have misread Hirschfeld's use of the word "transvestite" and why they have generally missed that he did indeed also coin the word "transsexual" to refer to those people who were seeking to change both the anatomy with which they were born and their social presentation/recognition.[17] Most English-speaking authors attribute its first use either to Harry Benjamin or to a 1949 article by David Oliver Cauldwell, editor of the American *Sexology* magazine and author of many popular books about sexual health and education.[18] Although we would grant Hirschfeld the credit for first using the term, the fact that Hirschfeld died in 1935, two years after the Nazis had attempted to obliterate his legacy by destroying his institute, makes it unsurprising that the later American introductions of the term "transsexuality" received more attention in the post-Second World War period.[19] The term is still in use today (perhaps most notably in the title of Julie Serano's pathbreaking book *Whipping Girl: A Transsexual Woman on Sexism and the Scapegoating of Femininity*),[20] although it now more often takes a back seat to the umbrella term "transgender." How Serano uses the term actually conforms to a short-lived usage coined by the Dutch psychiatrist Coen van Emde Boas, who used "transsexist" as a replacement for "transvestite" instead of "transsexual." Van Emde Boas wanted to emphasize that what was being described was not primarily a matter of clothing or biological sex but the individual's sexuality. Benjamin agreed but found "transsexist" awkward in English. He briefly used the term "transexualist," which also failed to catch on.[21]

The word "transsexuality" remained the most frequently used term for almost fifty years after its re-popularization by Benjamin and Cauldwell, and it was meant to identify people who wished to undergo sex-affirming hormonal treatment and/or surgery. Within the broad spectrum of trans identities, transsexuals were those who could not avoid seeking the help of others – they required medical help to live the lives they wanted to lead. Yet, for much of the period under investigation in this book, very few doctors were willing to prescribe hormone treatment or to perform transgender surgery of any kind. Those who were willing quickly became central to the lives and well-being of trans people. Today the word "transsexual" can offend, primarily because it presumes that all trans people have or want to undergo surgical modification or that medical treatment defines what it means to be transgender.[22]

But just as we must be sensitive to the violence that words can do today, we are equally sensitive to the self-definition and need for self-validation of our historical actors. As Gillian Frank and Lauren Guttermann put it in a recent episode of their *Sexing History* podcast, we need to pay attention to "how trans folks calibrated their personal arguments for sex change in response to the shifting medical criteria of doctors and psychiatrists." Even in our use of terminology, we must not paint trans people as "simply the victims of an oppressive medical gaze" but point out how "they also helped to shape medical opinion."[23] In other words, the fact that trans people themselves have used the term "transsexual" as a form of empowerment cannot be easily erased from the historical record without denying these people their own linguistic agency. There are discomforts involved in this recognition. For example, the Texas-born recording artist, Canary Conn, who transitioned in the early 1970s after having been married and fathering a child, insisted that she was a "true" transsexual, "comparing herself to others whom she perceived as less authentically trans and therefore undeserving of medical treatment."[24] Even these judgemental self-categorizations are part of trans history.

They are also, it must be stated, part of the trans present. Not all trans people accept that "transgender" should replace "transsexual" (though most are happy to see the death of "transvestite"). As the poet, essayist and actor Max Wolf Valerio has put it in describing his transition,

> I did not change my core gender identity, I changed my biological sex ... I dislike the use of the word transgender because it increasingly lumps me in with any number of other people who might be transgressing gender boundaries, people who might actually have very little in common with me. While I'm not against these people expressing their gender, I do have a real fear: The word transgender has the potential to entirely erase who I am. ... Finally, transgender doesn't connect me decisively to my spiritual ancestors, the other transsexuals of the latter half of the twentieth century, who have endured ostracism, loneliness and intensive struggle to transform their bodies and lives. Transgender ignores the medical aspects of my transition that have enabled me to create my life. I have made use of the medical tools available to me, against all the odds and the voices that told me I couldn't do it – and that I shouldn't want to.[25]

The lesson here is that it is essential to name people *as they wish to be named* and to use categories that respect *their* sense of self rather than our socio-political sensibilities, whether they live in the present or lived in the past. That "transgender" has gained wide acceptance does not make it the most appropriate term in all cases.

"Transgender" is of relatively recent (if somewhat disputed) origin, but the term had achieved acceptance within trans communities by the 1990s. As K. J. Rawson has argued, it is now commonly accepted as "a broad category encompassing many gender identities and expressions, including transsexual, genderqueer and cross-dresser, among many other."[26] We would argue that the word "transgender" can be deployed without the implication of prejudice as an umbrella term to describe all individuals who wish to live within a gender that does not conform to the one they were involuntarily assigned at birth, whether or not they are seeking physical transition or acceptance on either side of a male/female binary. However, as Viviane Namaste has noted (echoing Valerio's fears), such umbrella terminology can also go too far, risking what she calls "queer theory's erasure of transgender subjectivity."[27]

In sum, there simply is no perfect solution to the debates about terminology, and, as in other books on the subject, the decisions we have made here represent a snapshot in time rather than the final word on how historians should deal with such issues. Whenever possible, we use the terms that the individuals we describe have used themselves. And we must admit that, historical accuracy aside, we do need to find present-day language with which we are comfortable – with which we can describe a past from the perspective of our own values. When we are speaking in more general, descriptive ways in this book, we therefore very often use the term "trans," mostly because it implies the least (about the specifics of identity and/or surgery) while still conforming to present-day usage.

We have also chosen to stick primarily to North American English usage. For example, the term "transgenders," as a noun, is accepted in some countries, including India and the Netherlands.[28] But we here stick with "trans individuals" and "trans persons," or – when we are referencing an individual as a historical actor in our narrative, "trans subjects" – in order to avoid any connotations of a slur. We are aware of the bind described by Julia Serano in writing of the "Activist Language Merry-Go Round," which dictates constantly shifting terminology; "because trans people are highly stigmatized and face undue scrutiny in our culture, all of the language associated with us will also eventually face similar stigma and scrutiny."[29]

And again, as we noted earlier, the meanings of all the terms we are using, and of "transvestite" in particular, can easily get lost in translation. Highlighting these moments of cultural difference and asking about how terms and ideas are translated between languages and between historical and cultural contexts is crucial to our project. And, of course, what is most interesting about this history is precisely the shifts and differences in what this word, "transvestite," meant to different people. The term "transvestite" marked contested terrain – precisely because it was so widely used. We would argue adamantly that explaining these distinctions rather than erasing them is our responsibility as historians. This does not deny but only contextualizes the obvious fact that it is no longer appropriate to use the word "transvestite" as a general term to describe people who would themselves never use the word.

Our choices were more difficult when it came to other terms. Should it be "trans women" and "trans men" or "transwomen" and "transmen." Experts on the subject differ. Julia Serano follows the former practice, while Jack Halberstam prefers the compound-noun version. We have somewhat arbitrarily chosen the former. Some scholars reject terms like "female-to-male" (FTM) or "male-to-female" (MTF) transition. Given that the author of an important new textbook, Ardel Haefele-Thomas, has argued that these terms should be avoided (because "it is crucial not to assume that the person has necessarily had any hormones or surgery"), we suspect that these terms will increasingly be rejected by a new generation.[30] Once again, our decisions have been based on the historical context. The individuals whose lives we will describe lived in the late nineteenth and the early twentieth centuries, a period during which the social and legal consequences of attempting to thwart heterosexist and cissexist norms were significantly more dire than they are in the democracies of our present. Laws against "masquerading" in the clothing of the other gender or against creating a public nuisance could be, and often were, used to repress and punish trans people, who literally lived under the threat of being asked to display their genitals to police. In this context, the distinction between gender comportment and anatomical configuration could be existential. To point this out by discussing whether these individuals had been successful in their quest for surgery is not, in other words, simply a matter of sensitive labelling; it is an essential part of the story of their marginalized and threatened existence.

Moreover, elders such as Kate Bornstein point out that the empowerment of trans women to claim a fully female identity without surgery is a recent development. Even in the early 1980s, Bornstein writes, "I knew for a fact that I could never be a woman so long as I had a penis. So I transitioned from male to female by means of gender confirmation surgery – it was the only way I could possibly live as the woman I believed myself to be. In Denmark some fifty years earlier, Lili Elbe knew for a fact that she could never be a woman so long as she had no uterus."[32] Bornstein follows this statement with a convincing justification for replacing many terms that she used in the original 1994 edition of her book with more current usage. The two perspectives are not, we think, self-contradictory. They simply require nuanced and thoughtful wording. As historians it is our responsibility to find terminology that is respectful of our readers while still avoiding any exaggeration of social choices available to our historical actors.

Having said this, we follow Eric Plemons and Chris Straayer in being aware that any discussion of surgery can play into "lurid and voyeuristic concerns with dissected body parts" and can thus overshadow "extraclinical and never-clinical trans ways of being."[33] For this reason, it seems self-evident to us that older terms such as "sex change operation" or even "sex reassignment surgery" are unnecessarily disrespectful of the lifelong self-understandings of trans people and should be avoided. We therefore chose to use "gender-affirming surgeries" whenever we are not directly quoting historical sources. Since this book has discussed the quest for surgery in many different contexts, it is important to acknowledge, as Plemons and Straayer point out, that surgical outcomes varied enormously in both physical and psychological terms, "resulting in self-actualizing triumph" in some cases and "crushing disappointment and lifelong chronic health problems" in others.[34] Although our cast of characters in this book almost all sought hormonal or surgical transformation, however, we do not consider medical treatment or its successes and failures as a criterion to define or describe them. Instead, whenever possible, we have used the words that they would have used to describe themselves.

In some cases, unfortunately, calling our historical subjects by the names they would have chosen is impossible, because we have no record of those names. Given the dangers of being discovered as trans in societies with legal sanctions against changing one's gender, trans lives were shrouded in secrecy and often left few archival traces. The only way that we could avoid deadnaming these people – using the gendered names that they actually did or would have rejected if they had had the choice – would be to not name them at all, a solution we found even more problematic. It is also does not help the cause of tolerance to fail to acknowledge that in certain historical circumstances it has in fact been impossible for individuals to safely socially transition. In sum, both naming and labels matter for transgender histories because they determine what is historically visible or recognizable at all. This is a point that the editors of a special issue of *TSQ: Transgender Studies Quarterly* on "Archives and Archiving," K. J. Rawson and Aaron Devor, underline by choosing articles that highlight challenges of researching a field full of silences, taxonomical debates, and ethical challenges.[35] We have, however, replaced deadnames with those chosen by our historical subjects wherever possible, placing the new name in square brackets when it appears in quotations or archival citations.

As historians, we are sensitive to the legal and social contexts in which our specific historical subjects lived, and we are cognizant of the fact that their bodily integrity and their own self-understandings depended on their abilities to pass. We therefore use the pronouns that we believe they would have chosen themselves, as far as we have been able to determine. In cases where we know that it was never possible for the person to live in their true gender in any social setting outside of the home (and particularly where we know only their birth names), we have chosen to use the only pronouns that they were able to expect in public – the ones they were assigned at birth. To do otherwise would be to make implicit and false claims about the degree of social acceptance they were able to achieve. For similar reasons, we have generally eschewed the use of more modern gender-neutral variants, such as "they" or the various neologisms with which trans individuals are today raising awareness and pushing the boundaries of tolerance in our societies. We certainly have used "they" as a gender-neutral singular designation of

individuals about whom our knowledge of gender self-identification is completely uncertain, such as interwar transvestites for whom we have photographs but no biographies. But with all due respect to the linguistic practices of contemporary trans individuals who justifiably seek to be described as they see themselves, we feel that directly imposing modern terminology onto historical subjects – putting words in their mouths that they would never themselves have used – would be disrespectful to their self-understandings and their existential struggles and would constitute a distortion of the historical record.

To reiterate then, our guiding principle throughout has been to make the voices of trans subjects of the past heard, while also acknowledging the difficult balance between the desires that some of them had for privacy and what we feel is a need to tell these histories. We wanted to represent them literally as subjects: as agents in their own stories whose self-definitions must be respected and whose actions are at the core of our narrative. This will certainly create dissonance for readers unaccustomed to reading about trans people in the past and who are understandably uncomfortable with words that have become slurs. But we expect this dissonance to be productive rather than offensive, and we are convinced that a sustained engagement with the historical creation of "transgender" will provide hope for further transformations in the future.

NOTES TO CHAPTER 8

1   Jack Halberstam, *Trans*: A Quick and Quirky Account of Gender Variability* (Oakland, CA: University of California Press, 2018), 1.

2   For a summary of the origins of the field of transgender studies, see Susan Stryker and Paisley Currah, "Introduction," in "Post-posttranssexual: Key Concepts for a Twenty-First-Century Transgender Studies," ed. Susan Stryker and Paisely Currah, special issue, *TSQ: Transgender Studies Quarterly* 5, no. 1 (2018): 1–18. Stryker and Paisely are not alone in dating the beginning of transgender studies as an academic field to the publication of Sandy Stone's "The Empire Strikes Back: A Posttranssexual Manifesto," *Camera Obscura: Feminism, Culture, and Media Studies* 10, no. 2 (1 May 1992): 150–76.

3   George Chauncey, "From Sexual Inversion to Homosexuality: Medicine and the Changing Conceptualization of Female Deviance," *Salmagundi*, no. 58/59 (1982): 114–46.

4   Julia Serano, *Whipping Girl: A Transsexual Woman on Sexism and the Scapegoating of Femininity*, 2nd ed. (Berkeley, CA: Seal Press, 2016), 23. Evidence of how rapidly contemporary usage for terms in gender and sexuality is shifting, requiring contemporary arbiters of meaning and style to react, can be found (to give one example) in the new style guide made available on the Associated Press website in honour of the fiftieth anniversary of the Stonewall riots in New York City. "Stonewall 50th Anniversary Topical Guide," *Associated Press Stylebook*, accessed 28 Jan 2020, https://www.apstylebook.com/topicals/topicals-stonewall-50th-anniversary-topical-guide-stonewall-50th-anniversary-topical-guide.

5   Stryker and Currah, "Introduction," 5.

6   Ibid.

7   Note that there is a (much later) English translation of this book, but it does not contain the subtitle. This is therefore our translation of the original German title. The English edition is: Magnus Hirschfeld, *Transvestites*, trans. Michael A. Lombardi-Nash (Buffalo, N.Y: Prometheus Books, 1991).

8   For an early example of Hirschfeld's contact with cross-dressers, see the autobiographical essay he published in his journal: "Mitgeteilt von Lehrer J. G. F., 'Ein Fall von Effemination mit Fetischismus,'" *Jahrbuch für Sexuelle Zwischenstufen* 2 (1900): 324–44.

9   For more detailed description of these developments and the discussions between sexologists and cross-dressers about terminolgy, see Rainer Herrn, *Schnittmuster des Geschlechts: Transvestitismus und Transsexualität in der frühen Sexualwissenschaft* (Giessen: Psychosozial-Verlag, 2005), esp. 36.

10 Magnus Hirschfeld, *Die Transvestiten: Eine Untersuchung über den erotischen Verkleidungstrieb* (Berlin: Alfred Pulvermacher & Co., 1910), 4–5. He defined sexual intermediaries like this: "All of these sexual varieties form a complete circle, in which a given type of intermediary simply represents one notable point, between which, however, there are unbroken lines of connection." Magnus Hirschfeld, *Geschlechtskunde*, vol. II. Bilderteil. Folgen und Folgerungen (Stuttgart: Julius Püttmann, 1930), 599.

11 The seminal scholarly article in the field of gender history, which explains the deployment of "gender" as being distinct from "sex" while still related to sexuality is Joan W. Scott, "Gender: A Useful Category of Historical Analysis," *American Historical Review* 91, no. 5 (1986): 1053–75.

12 The historical *Zedlers Unviersallexicon*, for instance, defines it as "genus, famille, maison; die Abkunft, das Abstammen und das Herkommen eines Menschen von dem andern" ("genus, famille, maison: the descent, origination, and coming from of a person from another"); Johann Heinrich Zedler, *Grosses vollständiges Universal-Lexicon aller Wissenschafften und Künste*, vol. 10 G-Gl, "Geschlecht," column 1222 (Halle and Leipzig, 1735).

13 Magnus Hirschfeld, "Die intersexuelle Konstitution," *Jahrbuch für sexuelle Zwischenstufen* 23 (1923): 3–27.

14 In some cases, of course, the anatomical findings matched the self-perception. This

was the case for Karl M. Baer, who had lived his childhood as a girl and his early life as a mannish woman, before finding Hirschfeld, having surgery, and being able to legally become a man and marry his female lover. See N. O. Body, *Memoirs of a Man's Maiden Years*, trans. Deborah Simon (Philadelphia: University of Pennsylvania Press, 2009), and Sander L. Gilman's helpful preface: "Whose Body Is It, Anyway? Hermaphrodites, Gays, and Jews in N. O. Body's Germany," vii–xxiv. In other cases, such as for the intersex woman Friederike Schmidt, Hirschfeld's advice met resistance. Schmidt continued to live as a woman, even though Hirschfeld's examination uncovered functioning testes. For longer discussions of the case of Friederike Schmidt see the following sections of Michael Thomas Taylor, Annette F. Timm, and Rainer Herrn, eds, *Not Straight from Germany: Sexual Publics and Sexual Citizenship since Magnus Hirschfeld* (Ann Arbor, MI: Michigan University Press, 2017): Michael Thomas Taylor, "Magnus Hirschfeld's Institute for Sexual Science as Archive, Museum, and Exhibition," 25–9; Rainer Herrn, Michael Thomas Taylor, and Annette F. Timm, "Magnus Hirschfeld's Institute for Sexual Science: A Visual Sourcebook," 42; and Sabine Kriebel, "Sexology's Beholders: The Exhibition PopSex! In Calgary," 80–2.

15   As Geertje Mak has demonstrated, European doctors specializing in intersex conditions slowly began to relinquish their insistence that sex could be diagnosed – seen – in the body and started seeing themselves as surgeons who could help individuals transform their bodies to match the "inner truth" of their self-perceptions. The internationally recognized expert on what was called pseudo-hermaphroditism was not Hirschfeld but Franz Ludwig von Neugebauer (born in Poland as Franciszek Ludwik Neugebauer, who published a survey of 1,100 cases from all over the world in 1908, and who developed surgical procedures to change appearance and improve function). See Geertje Mak, *Doubting Sex: Inscriptions, Bodies and Selves in Nineteenth-Century Hermaphrodite Case Histories* (Manchester and New York: Manchester University Press, 2013), 232; and Geertje Mak, "Conflicting Heterosexualities. Hermaphroditism and the

Emergence of Surgery around 1900," *Journal of the History of Sexuality* 24, no. 3 (2015): 402–27.

16   As the Intersex Society of North America puts it on their web site, "the terms fail to reflect modern scientific understandings of intersex conditions, confuse clinicians, harm patients, and panic parents." See: "Is a Person Who Is Intersex a Hermaphrodite?," Intersex Society of North America, accessed 27 June 2019, http://www.isna.org/faq/hermaphrodite. For a discussion of the history of these debates see Elizabeth Reis, "Divergence or Disorder?: The Politics of Naming Intersex," *Perspectives in Biology and Medicine* 50, no. 4 (2007): 535–43.

17   Hirschfeld was involved in several cases of individuals seeking surgery, including Lili Elbe, about whom we have included a gallery in this book.

18   David Oliver Cauldwell, "Psychopathia Transexualis," *Sexology*, Dec 1949. Even the English Wikipedia entry for Cauldwell asserts that he "coined the term transsexual as used in its current definition." The entry does cite Hirschfeld's 1923 article but implies that he did not use it to suggest the desire to change one's sex ("David Oliver Cauldwell," *Wikipedia*, accessed 26 June 2019, https://en.wikipedia.org/wiki/David_Oliver_Cauldwell), contradicting the following German-language Wikipedia entry on transsexuality: "Transsexualität," *Wikipedia*, accessed 26 June 2019, https://de.wikipedia.org/wiki/Transsexualit%C3%A4t. This fact makes Joanne Meyerowitz's simultaneous assertion that Hirschfeld used the word transsexualism, but that the "word did not enter the medical parlance or connote a desire for sex-change surgery until 1949," rather self-contradictory. Joanne J. Meyerowitz, "Sex Research at the Borders of Gender: Transvestites, Transsexuals, and Alfred C. Kinsey," *Bulletin of the History of Medicine* 75, no. 1 (2001): 72–90. For another discussion of the disputed origins of the word "transsexual" see: Michael Thomas Taylor, "Review of *Schnittmuster des Geschlechts: Transvestitismus und Transsexualität in der frühen Sexualwissenschaft* by Rainer Herrn," *Journal of Homosexuality* 55, no. 2 (2008): 312–15. More evidence that the word originated in Germany is provided by the fact that Alfred

Kinsey cited it in 1948 (so before Cauldwell) in a context that makes it seem clear he was inspired by Hirschfeld's work. (He uses terms still uncommon in American English, such as "third sex.") See Alfred C. Kinsey, Wardell R. Pomeroy, and Clyde E. Martin, *Sexual Behavior in the Human Male* (Philadelphia and London: W. B. Saunders Company, 1948), 612; and my longer discussion of Kinsey in this book.

19 As Friedemann Pfaefflin notes, German speakers are far less likely to make this mistake, and credit Hirschfeld with first using the word. See Friedemann Pfaefflin, "Sex Reassignment, Harry Benjamin, and Some European Roots" *The International Journal of Transgenderism* 1, no. 2 (1997). https://cdn.atria.nl/ezines/web/IJT/97-03/numbers/symposion/ijtc0202.htm.

20 Serano, *Whipping Girl*. Serano discusses her terminological choices in a reflective preface to the second edition of her book.

21 Harry Benjamin, *The Transsexual Phenomenon: A Scientific Report on Transsexualism and Sex Conversion in the Human Male and Female* (New York: The Julian Press, 1966), 30.

22 Julian Gill-Peterson has argued that the word "explicitly mark[s] a *medical* discourse and biopolitical apparatus, a colonial form of knowledge with racializing and disenfranchising effects … transsexuality arrogantly pretends to know and seize trans life as an object, making it a difficult concept to write with and against … [It] is an artifact of a dominant knowledge system to be constantly questioned and undermined from the inside." Without wishing to deny the power of medical authority or the influence of biopolitical thinking on the gender norms that governed treatment for trans people, we find this formulation overstated. It fails to capture how the trans people whose memoirs we cite and whose history we are exploring used the term, including, for example, those whom Alex Bakker has interviewed. Julian Gill-Peterson, *Histories of the Transgender Child* (Minneapolis: University of Minnesota Press, 2018), 9.

23 Gillian Frank and Lauren Gutterman, "Canary," *Sexing History*, accessed 1 July 2019, https://www.sexinghistory.com/episode-24.

24 Frank and Gutterman, "Canary."

25 Max Wolf Valerio, "'Why I'm Not Transgender' by Max Wolf Valerio," *Making Our Lives Easier LLC* (blog), 9 Feb 2014, http://makingourliveseasier.org/why-im-not-transgender-by-max-wolf-valerio/. See also his memoir: *The Testosterone Files: My Hormonal and Social Transformation from Female to Male* (Emeryville, CA: Seal Press, 2006).

26 For a concise discussion of etymological origins, see K. J. Rawson, "Debunking the Origin behind the Word 'Transgender,'" *News Minute*, 27 May 2015, accessed 28 June 2019, https://www.thenewsminute.com/article/debunking-origin-behind-word-transgender. Rawson credits the American psychiatrist John F. Olivan with first using the word in 1965 to denote the "urge for gender ('sex') change." The trans activist Virginia Prince, however, insisted that she first used the word (though in the form "transgenderal") to distinguish herself from transsexuals, because she considered herself female but had no wish to alter her body with hormones or surgery.

27 Viviane Namaste, "'Tragic Misreadings': Queer Theory's Erasure of Transgender Subjectivity," in *Sex Change, Social Change: Reflections on Identity, Institutions & Imperialism*, (Toronto: Women's Press, 2011), 205–38.

28 Stryker and Currah, "Introduction," 7. An example that might well foretell the future of this usage can be found in India, where the word "transgenders" is frequently being used to describe how the 2018 decriminalization of homosexuality will affect trans citizens. For example: Express News Service, "Section 377 Verdict: For Transgenders, Battle for Respect, Dignity, Acceptance in Society Bigger, Far from Over," *Indian Express*, 7 Sept 2018, https://indianexpress.com/article/india/section-377-verdict-for-transgenders-supreme-court-5343983/.

29 Julia Serano, "A Personal History of the 'T-Word' (and Some More General Reflections on Language and Activism)," *Whipping Girl* (blog), 28 Apr 2014, accessed 26 June 2019, http://juliaserano.blogspot.com/2014/04/a-personal-history-of-t-word-and-some.html.

30 Ardel Haefele-Thomas, *Introduction to Transgender Studies* (New York: Harrington Park Press, LLC, 2019), 20. This argument is

certainly not universal. Several prominent transgender studies scholars, such as Genny Beemyn, Susan Rank, and Aaron Devor continue to use FTM and MTF. See Genny Beemyn and Susan Rankin, *The Lives of Transgender People* (New York: Columbia University Press, 2011); and Aaron Devor, *FTM: Female-to-Male Transsexuals in Society* (Bloomington: Indiana University Press, 2016).

31 We also decided against the practice of using an asterisk to write "trans.*" Halberstam notes, for instance: "I have selected the term 'trans*' for this book precisely to open the term up to unfolding categories of being organized around but not confined to forms of gender variance. As we will see, the asterisk modifies the meaning of transitivity by refusing to situate transitions in relation to a destination, a final form, a specific shape, or an established configuration of desire and identity. The asterisk holds off the certainty of diagnosis; it keeps at bay any sense of knowing in advance what the meaning of this or that gender variant form may be, and perhaps most importantly, it makes trans* people the authors of their own categorizations … This terminology, trans*, stands at odds with the history of gender variance, which has been collapsed into concise definitions, sure medical pronouncements, and fierce exclusions" (*Trans*: A Quick and Quirky Account of Gender Variability*, 4–5). In Germany, the asterisk (borrowed from English) has even entered general usage – it is known as the *Gendersternchen*, or "little gender star" – as a means of breaking away from the binary implications of grammatical/social gender. (The word was chosen as "Anglicism of the year in 2018" by the Leibniz Institut für deutsche Sprache.) It does not denote trans identity but is used in combinations such as "Kolleg*innen" to replace the usual masculine or feminine forms ("Kollegen/Kolleginnen") or the existing option of denoting male and female (KollegInnen) with a form that is meant to be less gender specific. However, we felt using an asterisk was in fact too contemporary – tied to usages and meanings that are too anchored in our present moment – for our historical perspective.

32 Kate Bornstein, *Gender Outlaw: On Men, Women, and the Rest of Us* (New York: Vintage, 2016), xii. On Lili Elbe, see Sabine Meyer, *"Wie Lili zu einem richtigen Mädchen wurde": Lili*

Elbe: Zur Konstruktion von Geschlecht und Identität zwischen Medialisierung, Regulierung und Subjektivierung (Bielefeld: transcript, 2015); and Rainer Herrn and Annette F. Timm, "Elbe, Lili (1882–1931)," in *Global Encyclopedia of Lesbian, Gay, Bisexual and Transgender (LGBTQ) History*, vol. 3 (Farmington Hills, MI: Charles Scribner & Sons, 2019), 500–502..

33 Eric Plemons and Chris Straayer, "Introduction: Reframing the Surgical," *TSQ: Transgender Studies Quarterly* 5, no. 2 (1 May 2018): 165.

34 Plemons and Straayer, "Introduction," 166.

35 As the general editors of the journal, Susan Stryker and Paisley Currah, put it: "the editors [of this special issue] call our attention not only to pragmatic problems encountered by archival practitioners when they try to collect, preserve, describe, and render accessible the material traces of transgender actions in the world but also to equally vexing taxonomic, evidentiary, and semiotic questions about what counts as 'trans,' what counts as evidence, and how we make sense and meaning of what we encounter through transgender archiving and archives. They grapple with the fragmentary nature of surviving documentation, the conscious and unconscious biases and selection criteria that determine what records are saved, and the unequal accessibility of those records that are available for study and inspiration." Susan Stryker and Paisley Currah, "General Editors' Introduction," in "Archives and Archiving," *TSQ: Transgender Studies Quarterly* 2, no. 4 (2015): 541.

Press and hold the red button.

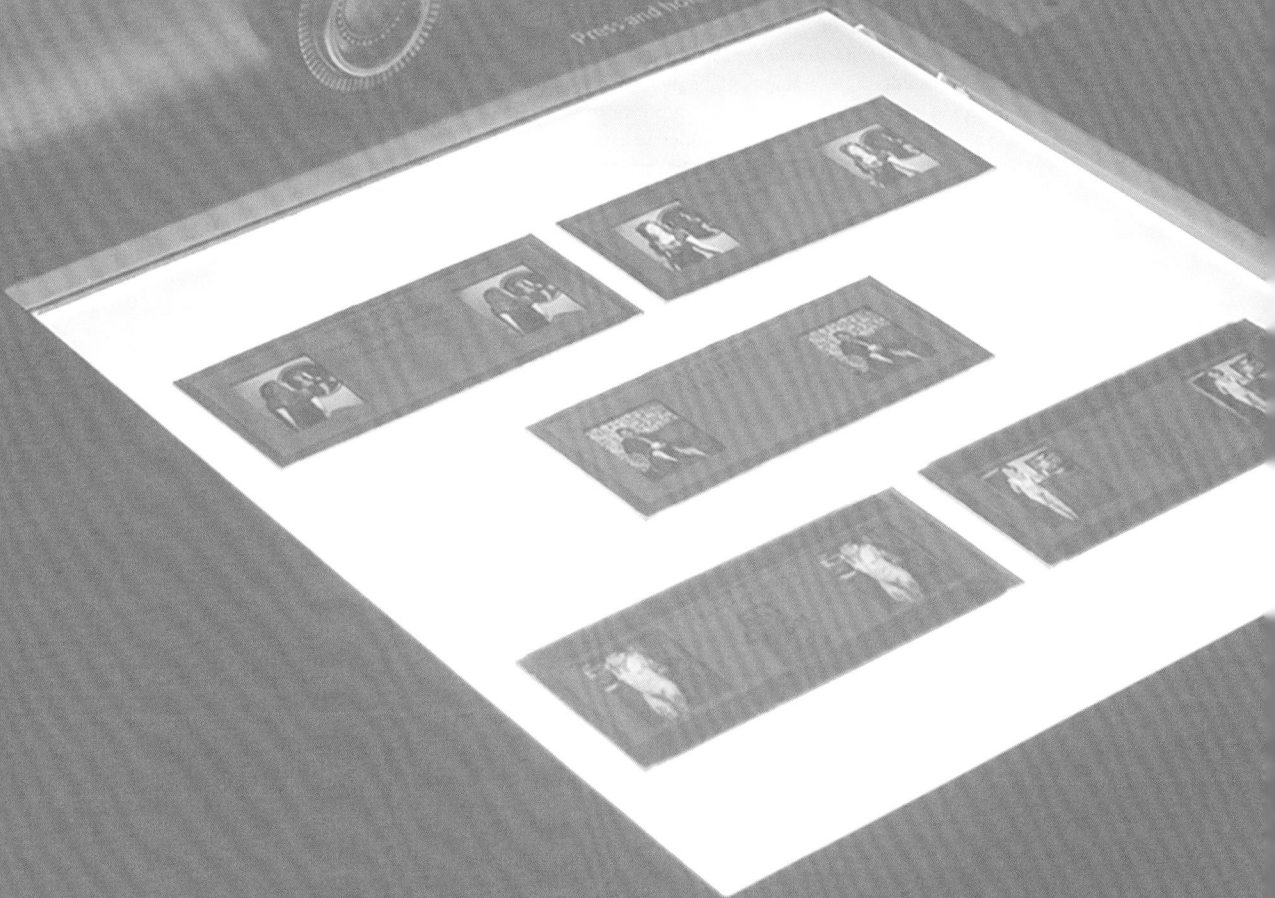

Bibliography

ARCHIVAL FILES

Archives Foundation Netherlands Gender Centrum (NGC), Historisch
    Documentatiecentrum Voor Het Nederlands Protestantisme, Vrije Universiteit.
    Amsterdam, n.d.
Christine Jorgensen Collection, Archives Royal Danish Library. Copenhagen, n.d.
Personal Archives of Van Emde Boas, Family Archive. Amsterdam, n.d.

KINSEY INSTITUTE LIBRARY AND SPECIAL COLLECTIONS, BLOOMINGTON, INDIANA

Correspondence., Benjamin, Folder 1. May 1944–December 1950.
Harry Benjamin Collection, Box 4, Series II C, 1953.
Harry Benjamin Collection, Box 25-1, Permissions, 1964.
Harry Benjamin Collection, Box 28, Series VI E. to Series VI. G., n.d.

ORAL INTERVIEWS

Bakker, Alex. Interview with Aaïcha Bergamin, 2013.
———. Interview with anonymous trans man, 2015.
———. Interview with Colette Berends, 2010.
———. Interview with Joris Hage, 2017.
———. Interview with Henk Asscheman, 2016.
———. Interview with Jill Pattiradjawane, 2017.
———. Interview with Margreet Groot, July 2017.
———. Interview with Ms. B., 2010.
Stryker, Susan. Aleshia Brevard Crenshaw Interviews. Transcript, 2 Aug 1997. GLBT
    Historical Society. http://www.glbthistory.org.
———. Don Lucas Interview: Recorded at Lucas's home in San Francisco. Transcript, 13 June
    1997. GLBT Historical Society. http://www.glbthistory.org.
———. Eliot Blackstone Interview. Transcript, 6 Nov 1996. GLBT Historical Society. http://
    www.glbthistory.org.

PUBLISHED SOURCES

Abraham, Hans. *Der weibliche Transvestitismus.* Berlin: Ebering, 1921.

Aizura, Aren Z. *Mobile Subjects: Transnational Imaginaries of Gender Reassignment.* Durham and London: Duke University Press, 2018.

Allen, Erin. "World War I: A Wartime Clipping Service." Webpage. Library of Congress Blog, 27 July 2016. https://blogs.loc.gov/loc/2016/07/world-war-i-a-wartime-clipping-service/.

Anonymous. "Harry Benjamin: Part 2 Rejuvenation." *A Gender Variance Who's Who* (blog), 5 Oct 2012. https://zagria.blogspot.com/2012/10/harry-benjamin-part-2-rejuvenation_5.html.

Apel, Dora. *Imagery of Lynching: Black Men, White Women, and the Mob.* New Brunswick, NJ: Rutgers University Press, 2004.

Apel, Dora, and Shawn Michelle Smith. *Lynching Photographs.* Berkeley: University of California Press, 2007.

Bakker, Alex. *Mijn valse verleden.* Amsterdam: Nieuw Amsterdam, 2014.

———. *My Untrue Past: The Coming of Age of a Trans Man.* Victoria, BC: Castle Carrington Publishing, 2019.

———. *Transgender in Nederland: Een buitengewone geschiedenis.* Amsterdam: Boom Uitgevers, 2018.

Baronin Rotenburg, Hilde. "Die Not der Transvestiten." *Die Welt der Transvestiten.* Sonderteil der Zeitschrift *Die Freundin,* 1929.

Barthes, Roland. *Camera Lucida: Reflections on Photography.* New York: Hill and Wang, 1980.

Bauer, Heike. "Sexology Backward: Hirschfeld, Kinsey and the Reshaping of Sex Research in the 1950s." In *Queer 1950s: Rethinking Sexuality in the Postwar Years,* edited by Heike Bauer and Matt Cook, 133–49. New York: Palgrave MacMillan, 2012.

———. *The Hirschfeld Archives: Violence, Death, and Modern Queer Culture.* Philadelphia: Temple University Press, 2017.

Baumgartinger, Persson Perry. *Trans Studies: Historische, begriffliche und aktivistische Aspekte.* Vienna: Zaglossus, 2017.

Bax, H. R. "Letter to the Editor." *Nederlands Tijdschrift Voor Geneeskunde,* 6 Feb 1960, 303.

Bear, Jordan, and Kate Palmer Albers. *Before-and-After Photography: Histories and Contexts.* New York: Bloomsbury Academic, 2017.

Beekhuis, W. H. "Letter to the Editor." *Nederlands Tijdschrift Voor Geneeskunde,* 12 Mar 1960, 536.

Beemyn, Genny. "Transgender History in the United States: A Special Unabridged Version of a Book Chapter from *Trans Bodies, Trans Selves,* edited by Laura Erickson-Schroth." In *Trans Bodies, Trans Selves: A Resource for the Transgender Community,* edited by Laura Erickson-Schroth, 1-51. Oxford and New York: Oxford University Press, 2014. https://www.umass.edu/stonewall/sites/default/files/Infoforandabout/transpeople/genny_beemyn_transgender_history_in_the_united_states.pdf.

———. "US History." In *Trans Bodies, Trans Selves: A Resource for the Transgender Community,* edited by Laura Erickson-Schroth, 501–36. Oxford University Press, 2014.

Beemyn, Genny, and Susan Rankin. *The Lives of Transgender People.* New York: Columbia University Press, 2011.

Benjamin, Harry. "Eugen Steinach, 1861–1944: A Life of Research." *Scientific Monthly* 61, no. 6 (1945): 427–42.

———. "Introduction." In *Transsexualism and Sex Reassignment,* edited by Richard Green and John Money, 1–10. Baltimore: Johns Hopkins University Press, 1969.

———. "Reminiscences." *Journal of Sex Research* 6, no. 1 (1970): 3–9.

———. *The Transsexual Phenomenon: A Scientific Report on Transsexualism and Sex Conversion in the Human Male and Female.* New York: The Julian Press, 1966.

———. "Transsexualism and Transvestism as Psycho-Somatic and Somato-Psychic Syndromes." *American Journal of Psychotherapy* 8, no. 2 (1954): 219–30.

———. "Transvestism and Transsexualism." *International Journal of Sexology* 7, no. 1 (1953): 12–14.

Benjamin, Harry, Emil Arthur Gutheil, Danica Deutsch, and Robert V. Sherwin. "Transsexualism and Transvestism – A Symposium." *American Journal of Psychotherapy* 8, no. 2 (1954): 219–44.

Biess, Frank. "History of Emotions." *German History* 28, no. 1 (1 Mar 2010): 67–80.

Blessing, Jennifer. *A Rose Is a Rose Is a Rrose: Gender Performance in Photography.* New York: Guggenheim Museum, 1997.

Bloom, Lisa. *With Other Eyes: Looking at Race and Gender in Visual Culture.* Minneapolis: University of Minnesota Press, 1999.

Boag, Peter. *Re-Dressing America's Frontier Past.* Berkeley: University of California Press, 2011.

Body, N. O. *Memoirs of a Man's Maiden Years.* Translated by Deborah Simon. Philadelphia: University of Pennsylvania Press, 2009.

Bornstein, Kate. *Gender Outlaw: On Men, Women, and the Rest of Us.* New York: Vintage, 2016.

"Boston Traveler," 8 Nov 1954, 15 and "Omaha World Herald," 8 Nov 1954.

Brett, Donna West, ed. *Photography and Ontology: Unsettling Images.* New York: Taylor & Francis Group, 2019.

Brown, Elspeth. *Feeling Photography.* Durham: Duke University Press, 2014.

Brown, Elspeth H. *Work! A Queer History of Modeling.* Durham: Duke University Press, 2019.

Bullough, Vern L., and Bonnie Bullough. *Cross Dressing, Sex, and Gender.* Philadelphia: University of Pennsylvania Press, 1993.

Bullough, Vern L., and Magnus Hirschfeld. "Introduction." In *The Transvestites: The Erotic Drive to Cross-Dress,* 9–14. Buffalo, NY: Prometheus Books, 1991.

Caen, Herb. "Baghdad-by-the-Bay." *San Francisco Chronicle,* n.d., clipping in KI-HB25.

———. "San Francisco: Herb Caen." *Honolulu Advertiser.* 18 Nov 1972.

Cagle, Dewey. "What's New … on the Avenue?" *Theatre Organ Bombarde: Journal of the American Theatre Organ Enthusiasts,* Apr 1968.

Califia, Pat. *Sex Changes: The Politics of Transgenderism.* San Francisco, CA: Cleis Press, 1997.

Carp, E. A. D. E. "Over het psychisme van de waan van de verandering van geslacht." In *Psycho-pathologische opsporingen,* 1951.

———. *Psychopathologische opsporingen.* Amsterdam: Strengholt, 1951.

———. "Transvestitisme." *Nederlands Tijdschrift voor Geneeskunde,* 29 May 1954, 1474–7.

"Casa Susanna: On Photography and the Play of Gender." Art Gallery of Ontario. Accessed 12 June 2019. https://ago.ca/events/casa-susanna-photography-and-play-gender.

Cauldwell, David O. *Transvestists' Unexpurgated Letters: Intimate Letters Written to a Doctor with the Request That They Be Published as Written by Cross-Dressers.* Big Blue Book (Girard, Kan.); B-882. Girard, Kan.: Haldeman-Julius Publications, 1950.

Cauldwell, David Oliver. "Psychopathia Transexualis." *Sexology,* Dec 1949.

———. "Psychopathia Transexualis." *International Journal of Transgenderism* 5, no. 2 (2001): 274–80.

———. *What Is a Hermaphrodite? A Study of Persons of Either Sex Whose Genital Organs, Mental Integration and Chemical (Hormonal) Characteristics Embrace the Characters or Characteristics of Both Sexes.* Haldeman-Julius Publications, 1947.

Chauncey, George. "From Sexual Inversion to Homosexuality: Medicine and the Changing Conceptualization of Female Deviance." *Salmagundi,* nos 58–59 (1982): 114–46.

———. *Gay New York: Gender, Urban Culture, and the Making of the Gay Male World, 1890–1940.* New York: Basic Books, 1994.

Chiang, Howard. *After Eunuchs: Science, Medicine, and the Transformation of Sex in Modern China.* New York: Columbia University Press, 2018.

Chiang, Howard H. "Liberating Sex, Knowing Desire: Scientia Sexualis and Epistemic Turning Points in the History of Sexuality." *History of the Human Sciences* 23, no. 5 (2010): 42–69.

"The Chip Collection – Artwork Series 11-100400 – Smithsonian Institution." National Museum of American History, accessed 12 May 2020. http://smithsonianchips.si.edu/ice/s11-100400.htm.

Clark, Anna. *Desire: A History of European Sexuality.* New York: Routledge, 2008.

"Commissie zegt 'neen' tegen geslachtstransformatie." *Het Vrije Volk,* 1 Oct 1966.

Conn, Canary. *Canary: The Story of a Transsexual.* Los Angeles: Nash Pub, 1974.

Corners, George F., and A. S. Blumgarten. *Rejuvenation: How Steinach Makes People Young.* New York: Seltzer, 1923.

Cowell, Roberta. *Roberta Cowell's Story*. New York: British Book Centre, 1954.

Cryle, Peter, and Elizabeth Stephens. *Normality: A Critical Genealogy*. Chicago: University of Chicago Press, 2017.

Currah, Paisley, and Susan Stryker. *Making Transgender Count*. Duke University Press Books, 2015.

Darwin, Charles. *Descent of Man, and Selection in Relation to Sex*. New York: Penguin, 2004.

"David Oliver Cauldwell." In *Wikipedia*, 19 Mar 2016. https://en.wikipedia.org/w/index.php?title=David_Oliver_Cauldwell&oldid=710810323.

Davis, Bob. "Using Archives to Identify the Trans* Women of Casa Susanna." *TSQ: Transgender Studies Quarterly* 2, no. 4 (1 Nov 2015): 621–34.

Davis, Georgiann. *Contesting Intersex: The Dubious Diagnosis*. New York: New York University Press, 2015. http://nyupress.org/books/9781479887040/.

Davis, Heath Fogg. *Beyond Trans: Does Gender Matter?* New York: New York University Press, 2017.

"Deaths." *San Francisco Examiner*, 1 Dec 1976.

"De Gynaecoloog Die Vrouwen Maakt." *Nieuwsblad van het Noorden*, 15 June 1974.

DeMello, Margo. *Bodies of Inscription: A Cultural History of the Modern Tattoo Community*. Durham: Duke University Press, 2000.

Deutsch, Albert. "What Dr. Kinsey Is up to Now!, Part I." *Look*, 8 May 1951.

———. "What Dr. Kinsey Is up to Now!, Part II." *Look*, 22 May 1951.

Devor, Aaron. *FTM: Female-to-Male Transsexuals in Society*. Bloomington: Indiana University Press, 2016.

Devor, Aaron H., and Nicholas Matte. "One Inc. and Reed Erickson: The Uneasy Collaboration of Gay and Trans Activism, 1964–2003." *GLQ: A Journal of Lesbian and Gay Studies* 10, no. 2 (2004): 179–209.

Devor, Aaron, and Nicholas Matte. "Building a Better World for Transpeople: Reed Erickson and the Erickson Educational Foundation." *International Journal of Transgenderism* 10, no. 1 (2007): 47–68.

Dickinson, Edward Ross, and Richard F. Wetzell. "The Historiography of Sexuality in Modern Germany." *German History* 23, no. 3 (2005): 291–305.

Dobler, Jens. "Der Travestiekünstler Willi Pape alias Voo-Doo." *Invertio – Jahrbuch für die Geschichte der Homosexualitäten* 6 (2004): 110–21.

———. "Nachwort." In *Männer zu verkaufen: Ein Wirklichkeitsroman aus der Welt der männlichen Erpresser und Prostituierten*, 159–78. Hamburg: Männerschwarm Verlag, 2012.

———. *Vom anderen Ufer: Geschichte der Berliner Lesben und Schwulen in Kreuzberg und Friedrichshain*. Berlin: Bruno Gmünder Verlag GmbH, 2003.

———. *Zwischen Duldungspolitik und Verbrechensbekämpfung: Homosexuellenverfolgung durch die Berliner Polizei von 1848 bis 1933*. Frankfurt a.M.: Verlag für Polizeiwissenschaft, 2008.

Dobler, Jens, and Kristine Schmidt. "Die Bewegung der Weimarer Republik beginnt in Pankow." In *Verzaubert in Nord-Ost: Die Geschichte der Berliner Lesben und Schwulen in Prenzlauer Berg, Pankow und Weißensee*, edited by Jens Dobler, 43–51. Berlin: Gmünder, 2006.

Docter, Richard F. *Becoming a Woman: A Biography of Christine Jorgensen*. New York: Routledge, 2007.

Domeier, Norman. *Der Eulenburg-Skandal: Eine politische Kulturgeschichte des Kaiserreichs*. Frankfurt am Main: Campus Verlag, 2010.

Dose, Ralf. *Magnus Hirschfeld: The Origins of the Gay Liberation Movement*. Translated by Edward H. Willis. New York: Monthly Review Press, 2014.

Doyle, Peter. "Hard Looks: Faces, Bodies, Lives in Early Sydney Police Portrait Photography." In *Photography and Ontology: Unsettling Images*, edited by Donna West Brett, 56–71. New York: Taylor & Francis Group, 2019.

Dreger, Alice Domurat, ed. *Intersex in the Age of Ethics*. Hagerstown, MD: University Publishing Group, 1999.

Drucker, Donna J. *The Classification of Sex: Alfred Kinsey and the Organization of Knowledge*. Pittsburgh: University of Pittsburgh Press, 2014.

Dugan, Jess T., and Vanessa Fabbre. *To Survive on This Shore: Photographs and Interviews with Transgender and Gender Nonconforming Older Adults*. Heidelberg: Kehrer Verlag, 2018.

Eakins, Richard. *The Transgender Phenomenon.* London: SAGE, 2006.

Eder, Franz X. *Kultur der Begierde: Eine Geschichte der Sexualität.* CITY: Verlag C. H. Beck, 2002.

Eder, Sandra. "The Volatility of Sex: Intersexuality, Gender and Clinical Practice in the 1950s." In *Historicising Gender and Sexuality,* edited by Kevin P. Murphy and Jennifer M. Spear, 166–81. Malden, MA: Wiley-Blackwell, 2011. http://site.ebrary.com. ezproxy.lib.ucalgary.ca/lib/ucalgary/reader. action?docID=10501311.

Edwards, Elizabeth. "Der Geschichte ins Antlitz blicken: Fotografie und die Herausforderung der Präsenz." In *Zeigen und/oder Beweisen?: Die Fotografie als Kulturtechnik und Medium des Wissens,* edited by Herta Wolf, 305–26. Berlin: de Gruyter, 2016.

———. *Raw Histories: Photographs, Anthropology, and Museums.* Oxford: Berg, 2001.

———. *Uncertain Images: Museums and the Work of Photographs.* London: Routledge, 2014.

Ein Transvestit aus der Provinz. "Stimmen aus dem Leserkreis über Das 3. Geschlecht." *Die Freundin,* 1930.

Ekins, Richard. "Science, Politics and Clinical Intervention: Harry Benjamin, Transsexualism and the Problem of Heteronormativity." *Sexualities* 8, no. 3 (2005): 306–28.

Ellis, Havelock. "Sexo-Aesthetic Inversion." *Alienist and Neurologist* 34, no. 2 (1 May 1913): 156–67.

———. "Sexo-ästhethische Inversion." *Zeitschrift für Psychotherapie und medizinische Psychologie* 5 (1914): 134–62.

Ellison, Treva, Kai M. Green, Matt Richardson, and C. Riley Snorton. "We Got Issues: Toward a Black Trans*/Studies." *TSQ: Transgender Studies Quarterly* 4, no. 2 (1 May 2017): 162–9.

Emde Boas, C. Van. "De behandeling van transseksisten in Nederland 1953–1973. Een les van 20 jaar attitudeschommelingen." *Medisch Contact* 29 (1974): 475–8.

———. "Transseksisme: wat is dat eigenlijk?" *Medisch Contact,* 5 Apr 1974, 443–5.

"Ex-GI Becomes Blond Beauty." *New York Daily News,* 1 Dec 1952.

Express News Service. "Section 377 Verdict: For Transgenders, Battle for Respect, Dignity, Acceptance in Society Bigger, Far from Over." *Indian Express,* 7 Sept 2018. https:// indianexpress.com/article/india/section-377-verdict-for-transgenders-supreme-court-5343983/.

Feinberg, Leslie. *Transgender Warriors: Making History from Joan of Arc to Rupaul.* Boston: Beacon Press, 1996.

Foucault, Michel. *Herculine Barbin.* Translated by Richard McDougall. New York, NY: Vintage, 1980.

———. *History of Sexuality.* Vol. 1: An Introduction. New York: Pantheon Books, 1978.

Frank, Gillian, and Lauren Gutterman. "Canary." Sexing History. Accessed 1 July 2019. https://www.sexinghistory.com/episode-24.

Frayser, Suzanne G., and Thomas J. Whitby. *Studies in Human Sexuality: A Selected Guide.* 2nd ed. Englewood, Colorado: Libraries Unlimited, 1995.

Frevert, Ute. "Does Trust Have a History?" In *Max Weber Programme: Lectures Series.* San Domenico di Fiesole: European University Institute, 2009. http://cadmus.eui.eu// handle/1814/11258.

Friedland, Paul. *Political Actors: Representative Bodies and Theatricality in the Age of the French Revolution.* Ithaca: Cornell University Press, 2002.

Fuechtner, Veronika, Douglas E. Haynes, and Ryan M. Jones, eds. *A Global History of Sexual Science, 1880–1960.* Oakland, CA: University of California Press, 2018.

Gathorne-Hardy, Jonathan. *Sex the Measure of All Things: A Life of Alfred C. Kinsey.* Bloomington and Indianapolis: Indiana University Press, 1998.

Gathorne-Hardy, Jonathan, Linda Wolfe, and Bill Condon. *Kinsey: Public and Private.* New York: Newmarket Press, 2004.

Germon, Jennifer E. "Kinsey and the Politics of Bisexual Authenticity." *Journal of Bisexuality* 8, nos 3–4 (2008): 243–58.

Gezondheidsraad. "Rapport betreffende plastisch-chirurgische geslachtstransformatie: Verslagen en Mededelingen betreffende de Volksgezondheid." January 1966.

Gillies, Harold, and D. Ralph Millard Jr. *The Principles and Art of Plastic Surgery.* Vol. 2. London: Butterworth & Co., 1957.

Gill-Peterson, Julian. *Histories of the Transgender Child.* Minneapolis: University of Minnesota Press, 2018.

Goldmann, Lothar. "Über das Wesen des Umkleidungstriebes." *Geschlecht und Gesellschaft* 12 (1924): 281–96 and 334–78.

Grete M. "Transvestiten über sich selbst, Gedanken zum Transvestitismus." *Das 3. Geschlecht*, 1932.

Griffith, R. M. "The Religious Encounters of Alfred C. Kinsey." *Journal of American History* 95, no. 2 (2008): 349–77.

H. E., Anna Maria. "Etwas zum 'Sammeln.'" *Die Welt der Transvestiten*. Sonderteil der Zeitschrift *Die Freundin*, 1931.

Hayes, Elinor. "Old Films, Organ Revived." *Oakland Tribune*, 6 July 1969.

Haefele-Thomas, Ardel. *Introduction to Transgender Studies*. New York: Harrington Park Press, LLC, 2019.

Haeseker, B., and J-P. A. Nicolai. "De eerste geslachtsveranderende operatie van vrouw naar man in Nederland, 1959/'60." *Nederlands Tijdschrift voor Geneeskunde*, 3 Mar 2007, 548–52.

Hage, J. Joris, Refaat B. Karim, and Donald R. Laub. "On the Origin of Pedicled Skin Inversion Vaginoplasty: Life and Work of Dr. Georges Burou of Casablanca." *Annals of Plastic Surgery* 59, no. 6 (2007): 723–9.

Halberstam, Jack. *Trans*: A Quick and Quirky Account of Gender Variability*. Oakland, CA: University of California Press, 2018.

Hamburger, Christian. "The Desire for Change of Sex as Shown by Personal Letters from 465 Men and Women." *Acta Endrologica* 14 (1953): 361–72.

Haritaworn, Jin. *Queer Lovers and Hateful Others: Regenerating Violent Times and Places*. London: Pluto Press, 2015.

Henry, George W. "Rudolf von H." In *Sex Variants: A Study of Homosexual Patterns*, 487–98. New York and London: P. B. Hoeber, 1948.

———. *Sex Variants: A Study of Homosexual Patterns*. New York and London: P. B. Hoeber, 1948.

Herrn, Rainer. "Bildergeschichte(n): Metamorphotische Inszenierungen der sexualwissenschaftlichen Fotografie." *Mitteilungen der Magnus-Hirschfeld-Gesellschaft*, 104–8, 37/38 (2007).

———. *Das 3. Geschlecht: Reprint der 1930–1932 erschienen Zeitschrift für Transvestiten*. Hamburg: Männerschwarm Verlag, 2016.

———. "Die operative Geschlechtsumwandlung als Experiment am Menschen." In *Sexualität als Experiment? Identität, Lust und Reproduktion zwischen Science und Fiction*, edited by Nicolas Pethes and Silke Schicktanz, 45–70. Frankfurt am Main and New York: Campus Verlag, 2008.

———. "Ge- und erlebte Vielfalt – Sexuelle Zwischenstufen im Institut für Sexualwissenschaft." *Sexuologie: Zeitschrift für Sexualmedizin, Sexualtherapie und Sexualwissenschaft* 20, nos 1–2 (2013): 6–14.

———. "Magnus Hirschfelds Geschlechterkosmogonie: Die Zwischenstufentheorie im Kontext hegemonialer." In *Hegemoniale Männlichkeiten und Moderne: Geschlecht in den Wissenskulturen um 1900*, edited by Ulrike Brunotte and Rainer Herrn, 173–96. Bielefeld: Transcript Verlag, 2007.

———. *Schnittmuster des Geschlechts: Transvestitismus und Transsexualität in der frühen Sexualwissenschaft*. Giessen: Psychosozial-Verlag, 2005.

———. "Transvestismus in der NS-Zeit." *Zeitschrift für Sexualforschung* 26, no. 4 (2013): 330–71.

Herrn, Rainer, and Christine N. Brinckmann. "Of Rats and Men: The Steinach Film." In *Not Straight from Germany: Sexual Publics and Sexual Citizenship since Magnus Hirschfeld*, edited by Michael Thomas Taylor, Annette F. Timm, and Rainer Herrn, 212–34. Ann Arbor: University of Michigan Press, 2017.

Herrn, Rainer, and Michael Thomas Taylor. "Magnus Hirschfeld's Interpretation of the Japanese Onnagata as Transvestites." *Journal of the History of Sexuality* 27, no. 1 (2018): 63–100.

———. "Transvestites/Transsexuals." In *Global Encyclopedia of Lesbian, Gay, Bisexual and Transgender (LGBTQ) History*, 3:1640–44. Farmington Hills, MI: Charles Scribner & Sons, 2019.

Herrn, Rainer, Michael Thomas Taylor, and Annette F. Timm. "Magnus Hirschfeld's Institute for Sexual Science: A Visual Sourcebook." In *Not Straight from Germany: Sexual Publics and Sexual Citizenship since Magnus Hirschfeld*, edited by Michael Thomas Taylor, Annette F. Timm, and Rainer Herrn, 37–79. Ann Arbor, MI: Michigan University Press, 2017.

Herrn, Rainer, and Annette F. Timm. "Lili Elbe." In *Global Encyclopedia of Lesbian, Gay, Bisexual and Transgender (LGBTQ) History*, 3:500–502. Farmington Hills, MI: Charles Scribner & Sons, 2019.

Hill, Darryl B. "Sexuality and Gender in Hirschfeld's *Die Transvestiten*: A Case of the 'Elusive Evidence of the Ordinary.'" *Journal of the History of Sexuality* 14, no. 3 (2005): 316–32.

Hirschfeld, Magnus. *Berlins drittes Geschlecht: Mit einem Anhang: Paul Näcke, Ein Besuch bei den Homosexuellen in Berlin.* Edited by Manfred Herzer. Bibliothek rosa Winkel; Bd. 1 Schriftenreihe der Magnus-Hirschfeld-Gesellschaft; Bd. 5. Berlin: Verlag rosa Winkel, 1991.

———. "Das Ergebnis der statistischen Untersuchungen über den Prozentsatz der Homosexuellen." *Jahrbuch für sexuelle Zwischenstufen* 6 (1904): 109–78.

———. *Die Homosexualität des Mannes und des Weibes.* Handbuch der Gesamten Sexualwissenschaft in Einzeldarstellungen 3. Berlin: Louis Marcus Verlagsbuchhandlung, 1914.

———. "Die intersexuelle Konstitution." *Jahrbuch für sexuelle Zwischenstufen* 23 (1923): 3–27.

———. *Die Transvestiten: Eine Untersuchung über den erotischen Verkleidungstrieb.* Berlin: Alfred Pulvermacher & Co., 1910.

———. *Geschlechtskunde.* Vol. 1: *Die körperseelischen Grundlagen.* Stuttgart: Julius Püttmann, 1926.

———. *Geschlechtskunde.* Vol. 2. *Folgen und Folgerungen.* Stuttgart: Julius Püttmann, 1928.

———. *Geschlechtskunde.* Vol. 4: *Bilderteil.* Stuttgart: Julius Püttmann, 1930.

———. *Geschlechts-Übergänge: Mischungen männlicher und weiblicher Geschlechtscharaktere (sexuelle Zwischenstufen).* Leipzig: Verlag der Monatsschrift für Harnkrankheiten und sexuelle Hygiene, W. Malende, 1905.

———. *Geschlechts-Übergänge: Mischungen männlicher und weiblicher Geschlechtscharaktere (sexuelle Zwischenstufen).* 2nd ed. Leipzig: Max Spohr, 1913.

———. "Geschlechtsverkleidung auf der Bühne." *Die Freundin,* 1924.

———. *Sexualität und Kriminalität.* Vienna: Interterritorialer Verl. "Renaissance," 1924.

———. *Sexualpathologie: Ein Lehrbuch für Ärzte und Studierende.* Bonn: A. Marcus & E. Webers Verlag, 1918.

———. *Transvestites.* Translated by Michael A. Lombardi-Nash. Buffalo, N.Y: Prometheus Books, 1991.

Hirschfeld, Magnus, and Max Tilke. *Der erotische Verkleidungstrieb (Die Transvestiten).* Vol. 2: *Illustrierter Teil.* Berlin: Alfred Pulvermacher & Co., 1912.

Hooper, Tom. *The Danish Girl.* 2015.

Hoyer, Niels, ed. *Man into Woman: An Authentic Record of a Change of Sex.* Translated by H. J. Stenning. New York: E. P. Dutton & Co., Inc., 1933.

Huneke, Samuel Clowes. "Death Wish: Suicide and Stereotype in the Gay Discourses of Imperial and Weimar Germany." *New German Critique* 46, no. 1 (2019): 127–66. https://doi.org/10.1215/0094033X-7214709.

Hurst, Michael, and Robert Swope. *Casa Susanna.* New York: PowerHouse Books, 2005.

Irvine, Janice M. *Disorders of Desire: Sexuality and Gender in Modern American Sexology.* Temple University Press, 2005.

Irving, Dan, and Rupert Raj, eds. *Trans Activism in Canada: A Reader.* Toronto: Brown Bear Press, 2014.

"Is a Person Who Is Intersex a Hermaphrodite?" Intersex Society of North America. Accessed 27 June 2019. http://www.isna.org/faq/hermaphrodite.

Jagose, Annamarie. *Orgasmology.* Durham and London: Duke University Press, 2013.

Johnson, Niel M. "George Sylvester Viereck: Poet and Propagandist." *Books at Iowa* 9 (November 1968): 22–4, 28–36.

Jones, James H. *Alfred C. Kinsey: A Public/Private Life.* New York: W. W. Norton & Company, 1997.

Jordanova, Ludmilla. *Sexual Visions: Images of Gender in Science and Medicine between the Eighteenth and Twentieth Centuries.* Madison, WI: University of Wisconsin Press, 1989.

Jorgensen, Christine. *Christine Jorgensen: Personal Autobiography. With an Introd. by Harry Benjamin.* New York: P. S. Eriksson, 1967.

Katero, Ema. "Stimmen aus dem Leserkreis über Das 3. Geschlecht." *Die Freundin,* 1930.

Katz, Jonathan Ned. "Earl Lind: The Cercle Hermaphroditos, c. 1895." OutHistory.org. Accessed 4 July 2019. http://outhistory.org/exhibits/show/earl-lind/related/cercle-hermaphroditos.

———. *Gay American History: Lesbians and Gay Men in the U.S.A.* New York: Plume, 1992.

Keller, Phyllis. "George Sylvester Viereck: The Psychology of a German-American Militant." *Journal of Interdisciplinary History* 2, no. 1 (1971): 59–108.

Kennedy, Pagan. "20th Century Boy." *Bitch Media*, 20 Nov 2018. https://www.bitchmedia.org/article/laura-dillon-transgender-man.

Kinsey, Alfred C., Wardell B. Pomeroy, Paul H. Gebhard, Clyde Martin, and John Bancroft. *Sexual Behavior in the Human Female.* Philadelphia and London: W. B. Saunders Company, 1953.

Kinsey, Alfred C., Wardell B. Pomeroy, Clyde E. Martin, and Paul H. Gebhard. "Concepts of Normality and Abnormality in Sexual Behavior." In *Psychosexual Development in Health and Disease*, edited by Paul H. Hoch and Joseph Zubin. New York: Grune & Stratton, 1949.

Kinsey, Alfred C., Wardell R. Pomeroy, and Clyde E. Martin. *Sexual Behavior in the Human Male.* Philadelphia and London: W. B. Saunders Company, 1948.

Krafft-Ebing, Richard von. "Neue Studien auf dem Gebiete der Homosexualität." *Jahrbuch fur sexuelle Zwischenstufen* 3 (1901): 1–36.

———. *Psychopathia Sexualis, with Especial Reference to Contrary Sexual Instinct: A Medico-Legal Study.* Translated by Charles Gilbert Chaddock. London: F. J. Rebman, 1894.

Kriebel, Sabine. *Revolutionary Beauty: The Radical Photomontages of John Heartfield.* Berkeley, CA: University of California Press, 2014.

———. "Sexology's Beholders: The Exhibition PopSex! in Calgary." In *Not Straight from Germany: Sexual Publics and Sexual Citizenship since Magnus Hirschfeld*, edited by Michael Thomas Taylor, Annette F. Timm, and Rainer Herrn, 80–102. Ann Arbor: University of Michigan Press, 2017.

———. "Theories of Photography: A Short History." In *Photography Theory*, edited by James Elkin, 3–49. New York: Routledge, 2007.

Kriebel, Sabine, and Andrés Mario Zervigón, eds. *Photography and Doubt* (London: Routledge, 2016).

Laqueur, Thomas. *Making Sex: Body and Gender from the Greeks to Freud.* Cambridge, MA and London: Harvard University Press, 1990.

Laub, Donald. Many People, Many Passports (blog), 11 Apr 2011. https://dlaub.wordpress.com/2011/04/11/.

Laub, Donald R., and Patrick Gandy. *Proceedings of the Second Interdisciplinary Symposium on Gender Dysphoria Syndrome.* Stanford, CA: Stanford University Medical Center, 1973. https://catalog.hathitrust.org/Record/003521724 and http://ai.eecs.umich.edu/people/conway/TS/Burou/Burou.html.

Lewandowski, Herbert. "Herbert Lewandowski: Lyon und Flucht in die Schweiz," in *Herbert Lewandowski – Lee van Dovski: Festschrift zum 92. Geburtstag*, edited by Peter Adamski, 101–14. Kassel: Geschichtswerkstatt am Friedrichsgymnasium, 1988.

———. *Römische Sittengeschichte.* Stuttgart: Hans E. Günther Verlag, 1964.

Lewis, Abram J. "'I Am 64 and Paul McCartney Doesn't Care': The Haunting of the Transgender Archive and the Challenges of Queer History." *Radical History Review* 2014, no. 120 (2014): 13–34.

Lewis, Sophie. "How British Feminism Became Anti-Trans." *New York Times*, 8 Feb 2019, sec. Opinion. https://www.nytimes.com/2019/02/07/opinion/terf-trans-women-britain.html.

"Liberating Sex, Knowing Desire: Scientia Sexualis and Epistemic Turning Points in the History of Sexuality – Howard H. Chiang, 2010." Accessed 4 July 2019. https://journals-sagepub-com.ezproxy.lib.ucalgary.ca/doi/abs/10.1177/0952695110378947.

Lindinger, Michaela. *Sonderlinge, Aussenseiter, Femmes fatales: Das "andere" Wien um 1900.* Vienna: Amalthea Signum, 2015.

Linfield, Susie. *The Cruel Radiance: Photography and Political Violence.* Chicago: University of Chicago Press, 2010.

Lockhorn, Elisabeh. *Andreas Burnier, metselaar van de wereld.* Amsterdam: Atlas Contact, 2015.

Logan, Cheryl A. *Hormones, Heredity, and Race: Spectacular Failure in Interwar Vienna.* New Brunswick, NJ: Rutgers University Press, 2013.

Magnus-Hirschfeld-Gesellschaft. "Magnus Hirschfeld – Brief an Sylvester Viereck." Magnus-Hirschfeld-Gesellschaft. Accessed 4 Aug 2018. http://www.hirschfeld.in-berlin.de/frame.html?http://www.hirschfeld.in-berlin.de/hirschfeld/brief_an_viereck.html.

Mak, Geertje. "Conflicting Heterosexualities. Hermaphroditism and the Emergence of Surgery around 1900." *Journal of the History of Sexuality* 24, no. 3 (2015): 402–27.

———. *Doubting Sex: Inscriptions, Bodies and Selves in Nineteenth-Century Hermaphrodite Case Histories.* Manchester and New York: Manchester University Press, 2013.

———. "Hirschfeld und die Transvestiten: Warum es nie was geworden ist zwischen Frauen in Männerkleidern und der Sexualwissenschaft." In *Dokumentation einer Vortragsreihe in der Akademie der Künste:100 Jahre Schwulenbewegung*, edited by Manfred Herzer, 157–69. Berlin: Rosa Winkel, 1998.

———. "'Passing Women' in the Consulting Room of Magnus Hirschfeld: On Why the Term 'Transvestite' Was Not Employed for Cross-Dressing Women." *Österreichische Zeitschrift für Geschichtswissenschaften* 9, no. 3 (1998): 384–99.

Malatino, Hilary. *Queer Embodiment: Monstrosity, Medical Violence, and Intersex Experience.* Lincoln: University of Nebraska Press, 2019.

Manning, Martin J. "Viereck, George Sylvester." In *Encyclopedia of Media and Propaganda in Wartime America*, edited by Martin J. Manning and Clarence R. Wyatt, 1:483. Santa Barbara, Denver, and Oxford: ABC-CLIO, 2011.

Marhoefer, Laurie. *Sex and the Weimar Republic: German Homosexual Emancipation and the Rise of the Nazis.* Toronto: University of Toronto Press, 2015.

Maxwell, Anne. *Picture Imperfect: Photography and Eugenics, 1879–1940.* Eastbourne: Sussex Academic Press, 2008.

McLaren, Angus. *Reproduction by Design: Sex, Robots, Trees, and Test-Tube Babies in Interwar Britain.* Chicago: University of Chicago Press, 2012.

McNabb, Charlie. *Nonbinary Gender Identities: History, Culture, Resources.* Lanham: Rowman & Littlefield Publishers, 2018.

Melnick, Ralph. *The Life and Work of Ludwig Lewisohn: A Touch of Wildness.* Detroit: Wayne State University Press, 1998.

Merlin, V. "L'homme qui change le sex." *Paris Match*, 1974.

Meyer, Sabine. *"Wie Lili zu einem richtigen Mädchen wurde": Lili Elbe: Zur Konstruktion von Geschlecht und Identität zwischen Medialisierung, Regulierung und Subjektivierung.* Bielefeld: transcript, 2015.

Meyerowitz, Joanne. *How Sex Changed: A History of Transsexuality in the United States.* Cambridge and London: Harvard University Press, 2002.

———. "Sex Change and the Popular Press: Historical Notes on Transsexuality in the United States, 1930–1955." *GLQ: A Journal of Lesbian and Gay Studies* 4, no. 2 (1 April 1998): 159–87.

Meyerowitz, Joanne J. "Sex Research at the Borders of Gender: Transvestites, Transsexuals, and Alfred C. Kinsey." *Bulletin of the History of Medicine* 75, no. 1 (2001): 72–90.

Mitgeteilt von Lehrer J. G. F. "Ein Fall von Effemination mit Fetischismus." *Jahrbuch für sexuelle Zwischenstufen* 2 (1900): 324–44.

Mottier, Veronique. *Sexuality: A Very Short Introduction.* Oxford and New York: Oxford University Press, 2008.

"Moving Trans History Forward 2018 – University of Victoria." University of Victoria, Chair in Transgender Studies. Accessed 12 June 2019. https://www.uvic.ca/research/transchair/what-we-do/conferences/MTHF16/index.php.

Mühsam, Richard. "Chirurgische Eingriffe bei Anomalien des Sexuallebens." *Therapie der Gegenwart* 67 (1926): 451–5.

Namaste, Viviane. *Sex Change, Social Change: Reflections on Identity, Institutions and Imperialism.* Toronto: Women's Press, 2011.

———. "'Tragic Misreadings': Queer Theory's Erasure of Transgender Subjectivity." In *Sex Change, Social Change: Reflections on Identity, Institutions & Imperialism*, 205–38. Toronto: Women's Press, 2011.

Namaste, Viviane K. "Review of *Schnittmuster des Geschlechts. Transvestitismus und Transsexualität in der frühen Sexualwissenschaft* by Rainer Herrn." *Journal of the History of Sexuality* 16, no. 2 (19 Nov 2007): 326–8.

Naz, Dave, Jiz Lee, Jenny Factor, Sarah B. Burghauser, Ignacio Rivera, and Morty Diamond. *Genderqueer: And Other Gender Identities.* Los Angeles: A Barnacle Book/Rare Bird Books, 2014.

Nordholt, A. E. "Letter to the Editor." *Nederlands Tijdschrift Voor Geneeskunde*, 9 Apr 1960, 742.

"Nuttige notities No. 9. Verslag van een bespreking op een stafvergadering van het Gemeente-Ziekenhuis te Arnhem." *Nederlands Tijdschrift voor Geneeskunde* 103 (26 Dec 1959): 2647–9.

Nye, Robert A., ed. *Sexuality*. Oxford: Oxford University Press, 1999.

"Obituary: John 'Bunny' Breckinridge." SFGate, 9 Nov 1996. https://www.sfgate.com/news/article/OBITUARY-John-Bunny-Breckinridge-2959951.php.

Oosterhuis, Harry. "Sexual Modernity in the Works of Richard von Krafft-Ebing and Albert Moll." *Medical History* 56, no. 2 (Apr 2012): 133–55.

———. *Stepchildren of Nature: Krafft-Ebing, Psychiatry and the Making of Sexual Identity*. Chicago: University of Chicago Press, 2000.

"Otto Spengler (1876? – 194?) Businessperson." *A Gender Variance Who's Who* (blog), 18 Nov 2016. https://zagria.blogspot.com/2016/11/otto-spengler-1876-194-businessperson.html.

Peters, Kathrin. "Anatomy Is Sublime: The Photographic Activity of Wilhelm von Gloeden and Magnus Hirschfeld." In *Not Straight from Germany: Sexual Publics and Sexual Citizenship since Magnus Hirschfeld*, edited by Michael Thomas Taylor, Annette F. Timm, and Rainer Herrn, 170–90. Ann Arbor, MI: Michigan University Press, 2017.

———. *Rätselbilder des Geschlechts: Körperwissen und Medialität um 1900*. Zürich: Diaphenes Verlag, 2010.

———. "Sichtbarkeit und Körper: Wilhelm von Gloeden, eine Revision." In *Zeigen und/oder Beweisen?: Die Fotografie als Kulturtechnik und Medium des Wissens*, edited by Herta Wolf, 283–305. Berlin: de Gruyter, 2016.

Pettit, Michael. "Becoming Glandular: Endocrinology, Mass Culture, and Experimental Lives in the Interwar Age." *American Historical Review* 118, no. 4 (2013): 1052–76.

Pfaefflin, Friedemann. "Sex Reassignment, Harry Benjamin, and Some European Roots" *The International Journal of Transgenderism* 1, no. 2 (1997). https://cdn.atria.nl/ezines/web/IJT/97-03/numbers/symposion/ijtc0202.htm.

Phillips, Sandra S. *Exposed: Voyeurism, Surveillance, and the Camera Since 1870*. New Haven: Yale University Press, 2010.

Pierrat, Jérôme, and Éric Guillon. *Marins tatoués: portraits de marins 1890–1940; Portraits of Sailors, A Portrait Gallery*. Paris: La manufacture de livres, 2018.

Plate, W. P. "Het verlangen om van geslacht te veranderen." *Nederlands Tijdschrift voor Geneeskunde*, 13 Mar 1954, 726–7.

Plemons, Eric, and Chris Straayer. "Introduction: Reframing the Surgical." *TSQ: Transgender Studies Quarterly* 5, no. 2 (1 May 2018): 164–73.

Pomeroy, Wardell Baxter. *Dr. Kinsey and the Institute for Sex Research*. New York: Harper, 1972.

Prater, Donald A. "Der Haltlose: Zum Tod des Schriftstellers Herbert Lewandowski." *Neue Züricher Zeitung*, 21 Mar 1996.

"Preisfrage, homo- oder heterosexuell?" *Die Insel*, 1926.

Prickett, David James. "Magnus Hirschfeld and the Photographic (Re)Invention of the 'Third Sex.'" In *Visual Culture in Twentieth-Century Germany: Text as Spectacle*, edited by Gail Finney, 103–19. Bloomington: Indiana University Press, 2006.

Prosser, Jay. *Second Skins: The Body Narratives of Transsexuality*. New York: Columbia University Press, 1998.

Rawson, K. J. "Archive." *TSQ: Transgender Studies Quarterly* 1, nos 1–2 (2014): 24–6.

———. "Debunking the Origin behind the Word 'Transgender.'" *News Minute*, 27 May 2015. https://www.thenewsminute.com/article/debunking-origin-behind-word-transgender.

Rawson, K. J., and Aaron Devor, eds. "Archives and Archiving," Special issue, *TSQ: Transgender Studies Quarterly* 2, no. 4 (2015).

Raymond, Janice G. *The Transsexual Empire: The Making of the She-Male*. Boston: Beacon Press, 1979.

Rees, Tamara. *Reborn: A Factual Life Story of a Transition from Male to Female*. n.p., 1955.

Regener, Susanne. *Fotografische Erfassung: zur Geschichte medialer Konstruktionen des Kriminellen*. Munich: Fink, 1999.

———. *Visuelle Gewalt: Menschenbilder aus der Psychiatrie des 20. Jahrhunderts*. Bielefeld: Transcript Verlag, 2010.

Regener, Susanne, and Katrin Köppert. "Medienamateure in der homosexuellen Kultur." In *privat/öffentlich: Mediale Selbstentwürfe von Homosexualität*, edited by Susanne Regener and Katrin Köppert, 7–17. Vienna: Turia & Kant, 2013.

Reijt, Frans van der. "De bejegening van transsexuele mensen in Nederland in de jaren 1960 tot 1990," 1993. Nederlands Gender Centrum, 259. Historisch Documentatiecentrum voor het Nederlands Protestantisme (1800-heden) VU Amsterdam.

Reis, Elizabeth. *Bodies in Doubt: An American History of Intersex*. New Haven: Johns Hopkins University Press, 2010.

———. "Divergence or Disorder?: The Politics of Naming Intersex." *Perspectives in Biology and Medicine* 50, no. 4 (2007): 535–43.

Reiss, Tom. *The Orientalist: Solving the Mystery of a Strange and Dangerous Life*. New York: Random House Publishing Group, 2005.

Roberts, Monica. "TransGriot: Who Was the First African-American Transwoman?" *TransGriot* (blog), 26 May 2009. https://transgriot.blogspot.com/2009/05/who-was-first-african-american.html.

Robinson, Paul A. *The Modernization of Sex: Havelock Ellis, Alfred Kinsey, William Masters and Virginia Johnson*. Ithaca, NY: Cornell University Press, 1989.

Rodriguez, Sarah B. *Female Circumcision and Clitoridectomy in the United States*. Rochester, NY: University of Rochester Press, 2014.

Rogers, Molly, and David W. Blight. *Delia's Tears: Race, Science, and Photography in Nineteenth-Century America*. New Haven, CT: Yale University Press, 2010.

Roman, Vera von. "Sehr geehrte Redaktion!" *Die Welt der Transvestiten*. Sonderteil der Zeitschrift *Die Freundin*, 1930.

Roots of Equality, Teresa Wang, Melissa Lopez, Diem Tran, Andy Sacher, Kersu Dalal, and Justin Emerick. *Lavender Los Angeles*. Charleston, SC: Arcadia Publishing, 2011.

Rosenbaum, Jack. "Our Man on the Town." *San Francisco Examiner*, 21 Mar 1972.

———. "Our Man on the Town." *San Francisco Examiner*, 30 Mar 1972.

Rudacille, Deborah. *The Riddle of Gender: Science, Activism, and Transgender Rights*. New York: Pantheon Books, 2005.

Schader, Heike. *Virile, Vamps und wilde Veilchen: Sexualität, Begehren und Erotik in den Zeitschriften homosexueller Frauen im Berlin der 1920er Jahre*. Königstein: Helmer, 2004.

Schaefer, Leah Cahan, and Connie Christine Wheeler. "Harry Benjamin's First Ten Cases (1938–1953): A Clinical Historical Note." *Archives of Sexual Behavior* 24, no. 1 (1995): 73–93.

Scheer, Monique. "Are Emotions a Kind of Practice (and Is That What Makes Them Have a History)? A Bourdieuian Approach to Understanding Emotion." *History and Theory* 51, no. 2 (2012): 193–220.

Schmidt, Gunnar. *Anamorphotische Körper: medizinische Bilder vom Menschen im 19. Jahrhundert*. Cologne: Böhlau, 2001.

Schoppmann, Claudia. *Nationalsozialistische Sexualpolitik und weibliche Homosexualität*. Pfaffenweiler: Centaurus, 1997.

Scott, Joan W. "Gender: A Useful Category of Historical Analysis." *American Historical Review* 91, no. 5 (1986): 1053–75.

Sears, Clare. *Arresting Dress: Cross-Dressing, Law, and Fascination in Nineteenth-Century San Francisco*. Durham: Duke University Press, 2014.

Seitler, Dana. "Queer Physiognomies; Or, How Many Ways Can We Do the History of Sexuality?" *Criticism* 46, no. 1 (2004): 71–102.

Sekula, Allan. "The Body and the Archive." *October* 39 (Winter 1986): 3–64.

Seliger, Mark. *On Christopher Street: Transgender Stories*. New York: Rizzoli, 2016.

Sengoopta, Chandak. "The Modern Ovary: Constructions, Meanings, Uses." *History of Science* 38, no. 4 (2000): 425–88.

———. *The Most Secret Quintessence of Life: Sex, Glands, and Hormones, 1850–1950*. Chicago: University of Chicago Press, 2006.

Serano, Julia. "A Personal History of the 'T-Word' (and Some More General Reflections on Language and Activism)." *Whipping Girl* (blog), 28 Apr 2014. http://juliaserano.blogspot.com/2014/04/a-personal-history-of-t-word-and-some.html.

———. *Whipping Girl: A Transsexual Woman on Sexism and the Scapegoating of Femininity*. Emeryville, CA: Seal Press, 2007.

"Sex Operation on Self Fails." *San Francisco Examiner*, 19 Aug 1953.

Simon, William. "Review of Judith A. Reisman and Edward W. Eichel's *Kinsey, Sex and Fraud: The Indoctrination of a People. An Investigation into the Human Sexuality Research of Alfred C. Kinsey, Wardell B. Pomeroy, Clyde E. Martin, and Paul H.*

Gebhard." *Archives of Sexual Behavior* 21, no. 1 (1992): 91–3.

Skidmore, Emily. "Constructing the 'Good Transsexual': Christine Jorgensen, Whiteness, and Heteronormativity in the Mid-twentieth-century Press." *Feminist Studies* 37, no. 2 (2011): 270–300.

———. *True Sex: The Lives of Trans Men at the Turn of the Twentieth Century.* New York: New York University Press, 2017.

Smith, Jill Suzanne. *Berlin Coquette: Prostitution and the New German Woman, 1890–1933.* Ithaca: Cornell University Press, 2014.

Smith, Shawn Michelle. *American Archives: Gender, Race, and Class in Visual Culture.* Princeton, NJ: Princeton University Press, 1999.

———. *Photography on the Color Line: W. E. B. Du Bois, Race, and Visual Culture.* Durham and London: Duke University Press, 2004.

Snorton, C. Riley. *Black on Both Sides: A Racial History of Trans Identity.* Minneapolis: University of Minnesota Press, 2017.

Soloway, Jill. "Transparent." 2014–18.

Sontag, Susan. *Regarding the Pain of Others.* New York: Picador/Farrar, Straus and Giroux, 2003.

Spengler, Otto, ed. *Das deutsche Element der Stadt New York: Biographisches Jahrbuch der Deutsch-Amerikaner New Yorks und Umgebung.* New York: Spengler, 1913.

Stein, Arlene. *Unbound: Transgender Men and the Remaking of Identity.* New York: Pantheon Books, 2018.

Stoff, Heiko. *Ewige Jugend: Konzepte der Verjüngung vom späten 19. Jahrhundert bis ins Dritte Reich.* Cologne: Böhlau, 2004.

Stone, Amy L., and Jaime Cantrell, eds. *Out of the Closet, into the Archives: Researching Sexual Histories.* Albany, NY: SUNY Press, 2015.

Stone, Sandy. "The Empire Strikes Back: A Posttranssexual Manifesto." *Camera Obscura: Feminism, Culture, and Media Studies* 10, no. 2 (1 May 1992): 150–76.

———. "The Empire Strikes Back: A Posttranssexual Manifesto." In *The Transgender Studies Reader,* edited by Susan Stryker and Stephen Whittle, 221–35. New York & London: Routledge, 2006.

"Stonewall 50th Anniversary Topical Guide." Associated Press Stylebook. Accessed 26 June 2019. https://www.apstylebook.com/topical_most_recent.

Stryker, Susan. "Biopolitics." *TSQ: Transgender Studies Quarterly* 1, nos 1–2 (2014): 38–42.

———. *Transgender History.* Berkeley, CA: Seal Press, 2008.

———. *Transgender History.* Berkeley, CA: Seal Press, 2017.

Stryker, Susan, and Paisley Currah. "Introduction." In "Post-Posttranssexual: Key Concepts for a Twenty-First-Century Transgender Studies." *TSQ: Transgender Studies Quarterly* 5, no. 1 (1 Feb 2018): 1–18.

Stryker, Susan, and Stephen Whittle, eds. *The Transgender Studies Reader.* New York and London: Routledge, 2006.

Suresha, Ron. *Bisexual Perspectives on the Life and Work of Alfred C. Kinsey.* Abingdon, Oxfordshire: Routledge, 2014.

Suresha, Ron Jackson. "'Properly Placed before the Public': Publication and Translation of the Kinsey Reports." *Journal of Bisexuality* 8, nos 3–4 (4 Dec 2008): 203–28.

Sutton, Katie. *Sex between Body and Mind: Psychoanalysis and Sexology in the German-Speaking World, 1890s-1930s.* Ann Arbor: University of Michigan Press, 2019.

———. "Sexology's Photographic Turn: Visualizing Trans Identity in Interwar Germany." *Journal of the History of Sexuality* 27, no. 3 (2018): 442–79.

———. "'We Too Deserve a Place in the Sun': The Politics of Transvestite Identity in Weimar Germany." *German Studies Review* 35, no. 2 (2012): 335–54.

Swaab, Dick. *Wij zijn ons brein: Van baarmoeder tot Alzheimer.* Amsterdam: Olympus, 2010.

Sykora, Katharina. "Umkleidekabinen des Geschlechts: Sexualmedizinische Fotografie im frühen 20. Jahrhundert." *Fotogeschichte* 24, no. 92 (2004): 15–30.

Tagawa, Beth. "When Cross-Dressing Was Criminal: Book Documents History of Longtime San Francisco Law." *SF State News.* San Francisco State University, Feb 2015. https://news.sfsu.edu/when-cross-dressing-was-criminal-book-documents-history-longtime-san-francisco-law.

Tagg, John. *Burden of Representation: Essays on Photographies and Histories.* Minneapolis: University of Minnesota Press, 1988.

———. *The Disciplinary Frame: Photographic Truths and the Capture of Meaning.* Minneapolis: University of Minnesota Press, 2009.

Talmey, B. S. "Transvestism: A Contribution to the Study of the Psychology of Sex." *New York Medical Journal* 99 (Jan–June 1914): 362–8.

Talmey, Bernard S. *Love: A Treatise on the Science of Sex-Attraction. For the Use of Physicians and Students of Medical Jurisprudence.* New York: Eugenics Publishing Company, 1919.

———. *Woman: A Treatise on the Normal and Pathological Emotions of Feminine Love.* New York: Practitioners' Publishing Company, 1908.

Taylor, Michael Thomas. "Magnus Hirschfeld's Institute for Sexual Science as Archive, Museum, and Exhibition." In *Not Straight from Germany: Sexual Publics and Sexual Citizenship since Magnus Hirschfeld*, edited by Michael Thomas Taylor, Annette F. Timm, and Rainer Herrn, 12–36. Ann Arbor: University of Michigan Press, 2017.

———. "Review of Schnittmuster des Geschlechts: Transvestitismus und Transsexualität in der frühen Sexualwissenschaft by Rainer Herrn." *Journal of Homosexuality* 55, no. 2 (2008): 312–5.

Taylor, Michael Thomas, Annette F. Timm, and Rainer Herrn, eds. *Not Straight from Germany: Sexual Publics and Sexual Citizenship since Magnus Hirschfeld.* Ann Arbor: University of Michigan Press, 2017.

Teich, Nicholas M. *Transgender 101: A Simple Guide to a Complex Issue.* New York: Columbia University Press, 2012.

Terry, Jennifer. *An American Obsession: Science, Medicine, and Homosexuality in Modern Society.* Chicago: University of Chicago Press, 1999.

———. "Anxious Slippages between 'Us' and 'Them': A Brief History of the Scientific Search for Homosexual Bodies." In *Deviant Bodies: Critical Perspectives on Difference in Science and Popular Culture*, edited by Jennifer Terry and Jacqueline L. Urla, 129–69. Bloomington: Indiana University Press, 1995.

"The Louise Lawrence Transgender Archive." *Louise Lawrence Transgender Archive* (blog). Accessed 19 June 2019. https:// lltransarchive.org/.

Timm, Annette F. "Queering Friendship: What Hirschfeld Could Teach Hegel and Arendt." Paper presented at Rethinking Amity: Workshop in Honour of Michael Geyer, University of Chicago, April 2013.

"Transsexualität." In *Wikipedia*, 17 July 2018. https://de.wikipedia.org/w/index.php?title= Transsexualit%C3%A4t&oldid=179219207.

Tucker, Jennifer. *Nature Exposed: Photography as Eyewitness in Victorian Science.* Baltimore, MD: Johns Hopkins University Press, 2005.

Ulrichs, Karl Heinrich. "Four Letters to His Kinsfolk." In *Sodomites and Urnings: Homosexual Representations in Classic German Journals*, 1–20. Binghamton, NY: Harrington Park Press, 2006.

Vaal, Otto de. *Man of Vrouw? Dilemma van de Transseksuele Mens.* Amsterdam: Wetenschappelijke Uitgeverij, 1971.

Valentine, David. *Imagining Transgender: An Ethnography of a Category.* Durham: Duke University Press, 2007.

Valerio, Max Wolf. *The Testosterone Files: My Hormonal and Social Transformation from Female to Male.* Emeryville, CA: Seal Press, 2006.

———. "'Why I'm Not Transgender' by Max Wolf Valerio." *Making Our Lives Easier LLC* (blog), 9 Feb 2014. http:// makingourliveseasier.org/why-im-not- transgender-by-max-wolf-valerio/.

Verlag und Redaktion. "'*Das 3. Geschlecht*,' Heft II erscheint demnächst!" *Die Freundin*, 1930.

"Viereck Called Chief Nazi Propagandist in the U.S. Helmut von Gerlach Asserts Pro-German Agent of War Days Is Enacting Same Role for Hitler." *Jewish Daily Bulletin*, 17 Dec 1933.

Viereck, George Sylvester. *Glimpses of the Great.* London: Duckworth, 1930.

———. "Hitler the German Explosive." *American Monthly*, Oct 1923.

———. "'No Room for the Alien, No Use for the Wastrel.'" *Guardian*, 17 Sept 2007. https:// www.theguardian.com/theguardian/2007/ sep/17/greatinterviews1.

Viereck, George Sylvester Viereck, and Paul Eldridge. *My First Two Thousand Years – The Autobiography of the Wandering Jew.* Gold Label Books, 1945.

Walch, Sonja: *Triebe, Reize und Signale: Eugen Steinachs Physiologie der Sexualhormone. Vom biologischen Konzept zum Pharmapräparat, 1894–1938.* Vienna: Böhlau Verlag, 2016.

Wallace, Maurice O., and Shawn Michelle Smith, eds. *Pictures and Progress: Early Photography and the Making of African American*

Identity. Durham and London: Duke
    University Press, 2012.
Wegner, Dr. "Männer als Frauen – Frauen als
    Männer." *Das 3. Geschlecht*, 1930.
Weiß, Volker. "*... mit ärztlicher Hilfe zum richtigen
    Geschlecht?*": *Zur Kritik der medizinischen
    Konstruktion der Transsexualität*.
    Hamburg: Männerschwarm Verlag, 2009.
Wild, Christopher J. *Theater der Keuschheit,
    Keuschheit des Theaters: zu einer Geschichte
    der (Anti-)Theatralität von Gryphius bis
    Kleist*. Freiburg: Rombach, 2003.
Woo, Elaine. "Peter R. Viereck, 89; Pulitzer-Winning
    Poet Spurned by Fellow Conservatives."
    Los Angeles Times, 20 May 2006. http://
    articles.latimes.com/2006/may/20/local/
    me-viereck20.
Worden, Frederic G., and James T. Marsh.
    "Psychological Factors in Men Seeking Sex

Transformation: A Preliminary Report."
    Journal of the American Medical Association
    157, no. 15 (9 Apr 1955): 1292–8.
World Professional Association for Transgender
    Health. "Standards of Care for the Health
    of Transsexual, Transgender, and Gender-
    Nonconforming People." 7th Version,
    2012. https://www.wpath.org/media/cms/
    Documents/SOC%20v7/Standards%20
    of%20Care_V7%20Full%20Book_English.
    pdf.
Zedler, Johann Heinrich. *Grosses vollständiges
    Universal-Lexicon aller Wissenschafften und
    Künste*. Vol. 10. Halle and Leipzig: Zedler,
    1735.
Zervigón, Andrés Mario. *John Heartfield and the
    Agitated Image: Photography, Persuasion,
    and the Rise of Avant-Garde Photomontage*.
    Chicago: University of Chicago Press, 2012.

Index

retouching, 55, 64. See also *Das 3. Geschlecht* (periodical)

Progynon. *See* hormone therapy

psychiatry and psychoanalysis, 20, 27, 60, 65, 72–73, 75, 79–81, 95–96, 102–104, 106, 118, 134, 148–150, 154–157, 160–163, 247; mental health, 52, 91, 110–111, 190; pre-operative evaluation, 161–162, 164, 166, 167, 170; "real life test," 155; view of trans people as disordered, 80, 87–91, 148, 161, 165–171

Psychopathia Sexualis, 81

R

Radszuweit, Friedrich, 12, 37–39, 41, 58, 66, 83, 144, 226. See also *Das 3. Geschlecht* (periodical); *Die Freundin* (periodical); *Die Insel: Magazin der Einsamen* (periodical)

Rees, Tamara, 154, 234

Richter, Rudolf (Dora or Dorchen), 18, 189

S

San Francisco, 6, 12, 19, 71, 95, 106–108, 103, 113, 115, 148, 177, 179, 230, 239

Scientific Humanitarian Committee (Wissenschaftlich-Humanitäres Komitee), 78, 83, 196

Serano, Julia, 11, 252, 257, 259

Sex Variants: A Study of Homosexual Patterns, 14, 88

Sex without Guilt, 95

sexology (field), 3–4, 10, 12, 23, 25, 27, 78, 92, 95–98, 102, 108, 113, 151, 161, 166, 179, 199, 209–210, 247, 252, 256

Sexual Behavior in the Human Female, 79, 93–94, 96–98, 102, 112. *See also* Kinsey, Alfred

Sexual Behavior in the Human Male, 79, 93–94, 96, 98, 112. *See also* Kinsey, Alfred

sexuality: desire, 38–39, 78, 87, 91, 94, 112-113, 118, 184, 194–195, 198–199, 201, 211, 254; history of, 2–3, 77–78, 80; identity, 1, 13, 20, 39, 80-82, 87, 91, 96–98, 105–108, 112, 184; medical study, 80-82; orientalism in, 53. *See also* sexology (field);

trans people; transvestites and transvestitism

Spengler, Otto, 6, 12–16, 19, 21, 86–91, 93–94, 140, 181, 225; and Harry Benjamin, 14–16, 89–90, 118

Steinach, Eugen, 12, 89–90, 92–93, 102, 139–140, 221

Stone, Sandy, 11

Sturm, Hansi, 61–62

T

T., Katharina, 99, 225

Talmey, Bernard, 12–14, 86–88, 91, 94, 181

tattoos, 73–76, 117, 202 234,

terminology and language, 2, 5, 21, 77, 80, 86, 88, 94–95, 105, 108, 179–180, 227, 251–261; of Harry Benjamin 139, 162, 185, 253, 256–257; of Magnus Hirschfeld, 27, 36–39, 64–65, 96–97, 99–100, 136–139, 185, 190, 195–200, 253–256

The Danish Girl, 18, 189

The Transsexual Phenomenon, 26, 73–75, 77, 100, 168, 185, 187, 191–194, 207–208

Tilke, Max, 202–203

trans people: and class, 47–49, 58, 66, 91, 141, 191, 194–196, 199–203, 226; and race, 22–24, 165, 202–203; as performers, 39–40, 52–54, 104, 110–111, 134–135, 141–142, 164–165, 169, 190–191, 225–228 (*see also* Travesty Art); as sex workers, 134–135, 141–142, 165, 169, 191, 201; history of, 2–3, 10–11, 35, 96–98, 105, 110, 179, 182, 184–185, 202, 207, 247–250; in media and the arts, 19, 27, 72, 143–148, 155, 208–211, 225, 228; interactions with homosexual advocacy, 36–37, 44, 58, 66, 91, 253–254; marginalization, 51, 80, 91, 110, 134, 141, 169, 178–179, 190, 249; rights and advocacy, 185, 190, 227, 252; trans men, 22, 40–44, 93, 97–100, 133–139, 163, 165–166, 171, 198, 226; urbanity, 51–56, 249. *See also* terminology and language; transphobia and persecution; transvestites and transvestism

transphobia and persecution, 21, 25, 50, 88, 94, 106, 111, 142, 155, 190, 248, 259; bans on medical procedures, 26, 72, 153, 167–169; legal protection and tolerance, 50, 80–85, 99, 190; stereotypes, 141, 191, 234

transsexual. *See* terminology and language; trans people; transvestites and transvestitism

TransTrans exhibit, 2, 12, 26, 77–78, 113, 144, 177, 179, 182, 185, 197, 202, 204, 219–241

transvestites and transvestitism, 36–37, 39–55, 211, 227; anachronistic term for trans people, 27, 86–88, 91, 94–97, 99–100, 105, 112, 136–140, 179–181, 185, 195, 219, 253–255; as deception or disguise, 59, 88, 201–202, 253; as sexual gratification, 112, 195, 252–254. *See also* clothing; *Das 3. Geschlecht* (periodical); terminology and language; trans people; Voo-Doo

Travesty Art, 39–40, 142

V

Van Emde Boas, Coen, 134–135, 151, 153, 155–163, 166, 169–171, 257

Viereck, George Sylvester, 92–93

Viereck, Louis, 91–92

von Gloeden, Wilhelm, 59–60

von Krafft-Ebing, Richard, 81

von Teschenberg, Hermann, 196

Voo-Doo, 39, 52–55, 205, 227–228

W

Walker, Mary, 87

Weimar Republic. *See* Germany

Westphal, Carl, 253

Weston, Mark (*formerly* Mary), 93

Woudstra, Siebren, 166–168